Owning Development

As pillars of the post-1945 international economic system, the International Monetary Fund (IMF) and the World Bank are central to global economic policy debates. This book examines policy change at the IMF and the World Bank, providing a constructivist account of how and why they take up ideas and translate them into policy, creating what we call 'policy norms'. The authors compare processes of policy emergence and change and, using archival and interview data, analyse nine policy areas including gender, debt relief, and tax and pension reform. Each chapter traces the policy norm process in order to shed light on the main sources and mechanisms for norm change within international organizations. *Owning Development* details the strength of these policy norms which emerge, then either stabilize or decline. The book establishes valuable insights into the strength of current development policies propounded by international organizations and the possibility for change.

SUSAN PARK is a Senior Lecturer at the University of Sydney in Australia.

ANTJE VETTERLEIN is Assistant Professor in the International Center for Business and Politics at the Copenhagen Business School in Denmark.

Owning Development

Creating Policy Norms in the IMF and the World Bank

Edited by

Susan Park

and

Antje Vetterlein

CAMBRIDGE UNIVERSITY PRESS
Cambridge, New York, Melbourne, Madrid, Cape Town,
Singapore, São Paulo, Delhi, Mexico City

Cambridge University Press
The Edinburgh Building, Cambridge CB2 8RU, UK

Published in the United States of America by Cambridge University Press, New York

www.cambridge.org
Information on this title: www.cambridge.org/9781107407046

First published 2010
First paperback edition 2012

A catalogue record for this publication is available from the British Library

Library of Congress Cataloguing in Publication Data
Owning development : creating policy norms in the IMF and the World
Bank / editors, Susan Park, Antje Vetterlein.
    p. cm.
Summary: "As pillars of the post-1945 international economic system, the
International Monetary Fund (IMF) and the World Bank are central to global
economic policy debates. This book examines policy change at the IMF and the
World Bank, providing a constructivist account of how and why they take up ideas
and translate them into policy, creating what we call 'policy norms'. The authors
compare processes of policy emergence and change and, using archival and
interview data, analyse nine policy areas including gender, debt relief, and tax and
pension reform. Each chapter traces the policy norm process in order to shed light
on the main sources and mechanisms for norm change within international
organisations. Owning Development details the strength of these policy norms
which emerge, then either stabilise or decline. The book establishes valuable
insights into the strength of current development policies propounded by
international organisations and the possibility for change" – Provided by
publisher. Includes bibliographical references and index.
ISBN 978-0-521-19895-0
1. Economic policy. 2. Economic development. 3. International Monetary
Fund. 4. World Bank. I. Park, Susan, 1976– II. Vetterlein, Antje.
HD87.O935 2010
332.1´0532–dc22
                                                                    2010033847

ISBN 978-0-521-19895-0 Hardback
ISBN 978-1-107-40704-6 Paperback

Contents

Figures

Tables

Contributors

ANDRÉ BROOME is Lecturer in the Department of Political Science and International Studies at the University of Birmingham.

MARTIN KOCH is Lecturer in the Department of Sociology at the University of Bielefeld.

MARTIN LARDONE is Dean of the Faculty of Political Science and International Relations at the Catholic University of Cordoba (Argentina) and Ph.D. candidate at the Institut d'Etudes Politiques de Paris Sciences Po.

RALF J. LEITERITZ is Assistant Professor in the Department of Political Science at the Universidad de los Andes in Bogotá.

BESSMA MOMANI is Associate Professor in the Departments of Political Science and History at the University of Waterloo and Senior Fellow at the Centre for International Governance and Innovation.

MANUELA MOSCHELLA is Post-Doctoral Fellow in the Faculty of Sociology at the University of Trento.

SUSAN PARK is Senior Lecturer in the Department of Government and International Relations at the University of Sydney.

LEONARD SEABROOKE is Director of the Centre for the Study of Globalisation and Regionalisation and Professor of International Political Economy in the Department of Politics and International Studies at the University of Warwick.

ANTJE VETTERLEIN is Assistant Professor in the International Center for Business and Politics at Copenhagen Business School.

CATHERINE WEAVER is Associate Professor in the Lyndon B. Johnson School of Public Affairs at the University of Texas, Austin.

VERONIKA WODSAK works as a professional officer for the ILO Social Security Department.

Preface and acknowledgements

Economics. Politics. Society. How do these three work together and in what order? Questioning the order in which societies organize is fundamental to understanding economic development and international political economy. International organizations such as the International Monetary Fund (IMF) and the World Bank are integral to how developing societies determine that ordering, by proffering development norms and sanctioning appropriate economic behaviour. This book takes a step back to look at how the Fund and the Bank take up the ideas they do and translate them into policies that are then propagated throughout the developing world. We did not know that we shared these concerns until we met in 2005. We both had the pleasure of attending a World Bank workshop organized by Diane Stone in Budapest. We didn't know each other then, but the workshop brought us together with a number of like-minded people who have contributed to this volume, people we now call friends.

The workshop was important for identifying researchers who had taken up the constructivist challenge identified by Michael Barnett and Martha Finnemore in 1999: to open the proverbial black box of international organizations (IOs) to see how and why they make the decisions they do. We view this edited collection as representative of a new generation of IO scholars who do just that. All of the people in this book examine how and why the IMF and the World Bank operate the way they do by tracing how ideas enter into these institutions and become policies that the Fund and the Bank promote to developing countries, which is a process that creates what we call 'policy norms'. We therefore owe an intellectual debt to Barnett and Finnemore, and a personal debt to Diane Stone. Not only did she arrange the first meeting in Budapest, but we would meet more contributors to this volume when Diane organized a third World Bank workshop that we both attended in Bled in 2007.

In the time between these World Bank workshops the idea for a volume capturing the constructivist work being undertaken on ideas within these two IOs grew. Antje was then persuaded to come to Australia over

Christmas and it was in Adelaide that we set to work to determine what such a volume might look like. We organized a panel at the International Studies Association (ISA) in Chicago in 2007 with Jeff Chwieroth and others, which despite being last on the programme for the conference that year was very well attended. It provided impetus for us to continue. We then brought all of our participants and discussants together at an ISA workshop in San Francisco in 2008, followed by a panel in New York in 2009. By that stage, we had our manuscript and were hoping to find a home for it. We found that with Cambridge University Press. Later in 2009 we polished the work in Copenhagen, which shows just how many miles have been covered in putting this book together!

In terms of the IMF and the World Bank, their practices also show the distance these institutions have covered in areas like gender, social development, debt, sustainability, and in taking up new public management. But they also demonstrate how some ideas that are picked up wane in importance. The volume is unique therefore in showing not only how positive 'good' ideas are consumed by IOs, but also how ideas are filtered through the policy-making process, and how norms may decline in importance in these institutions. In this regard we see the value-added of this collection as not only in bringing the constructivist norms literature into our analysis of these IOs, but in showing that examining ideas should not be, and is not, solely focused on tracing successful stories of the diffusion of 'liberal' ideas.

In tracing how these institutions take up ideas and turn them into policy we hope that the volume will appeal to development scholars as well. Our nine cases of policy norms cover vital issue areas that are fundamental to development – not just debt and gender as mentioned earlier, but also current and capital account liberalization, and pension and tax reform. How policies are decided, and on what normative basis, is critical for the Fund and the Bank in terms of their relationship with societies in their attempts to develop. It is also central to perceptions of the IMF's and the World Bank's importance and power in the international political economy. The 2008 global recession has reinvigorated the IMF and boosted World Bank lending after their decline in importance stemming from criticism of their actions during the Asian financial crisis and as a result of the abundance of private capital flowing to developing countries from the 1990s. Yet the book also points out how external shocks like financial crises and the end of the Cold War are just one of the triggers for new thinking and new policy norms to enter into these institutions. The book also recognizes that IOs tend to have staying power in light of uncertain political, economic and social conditions. We hope this book helps in making sense of the waxing and waning of Fund and Bank influence, through tracing how their ideas emerge and how their policies are formulated both as reflexive responses to their member states and non-state actors, and from pushes for change by staff inside these organizations.

Work on this book began in December 2006 in a library in Adelaide, Australia. This was the first of many intense sessions to come, some of which took place in cafés around the world, but most of which occurred through email and phone conversations. All of the authors were brought together at the workshop in San Francisco in 2008 when the main ideas of this book had already begun to take shape. We asked our contributors to present their specialized knowledge on IMF and World Bank policies and to fit it within our conceptual framework of emerging, stabilizing and declining 'policy norms'. An intensive period of revisions followed before submission to the publisher. Our thanks go to the contributors to this volume, for their patience and excellent collaboration. Chapters arrived on time, they came with lots of good humour and great ideas – you have made this such a straightforward process that we cannot thank you enough.

We have so many more colleagues and scholars to thank for helping to bring the ideas in this book to fruition. We would like to thank Diane Stone for arranging a series of World Bank workshops, especially the first one in Hungary where many of us met for the first time, and the third workshop in Slovenia where we were introduced to other scholars who would then join this volume. The workshops were part of the Research Bank on the World Bank project initiated by Diane Stone and first hosted by the Central European University (co-sponsored by the World Bank and the Economic and Social Research Council). The workshops would also establish the Research Alliance for Development to promote a sharing of ideas and research between scholars and the World Bank. We would like to thank everyone who commented on the various papers and acted as discussants to panels for this collection: Steven Bernstein, Jacqueline Best, Toby Carroll, Ralf Leiteritz, Leonard Seabrooke, Ole Jacob Sending, Jason Sharman, Diane Stone, Mike Tierney and Antje Wiener. We would like to thank the International Studies Association for the Catalytic Research Workshop grant that funded the 2008 workshop in San Francisco where we were able to have all of the contributors in one place and to take apart and put back together the ideas in each of the chapters. ISA also hosted our panels before the workshop and after. Knowing that ISA was arriving every February was a good boost for getting drafts finished! We would also like to thank Tom O'Brien for doing the hard slog of putting together our bibliography: we really appreciate it.

Susan would like to thank her interviewees, especially Robert Goodland for sharing his wealth of knowledge of and experience in the Bank. Funding was also provided by Deakin University for some of the research undertaken in Washington, DC. I would also like to thank the Centennial for Political Science and Public Affairs for hosting me in Washington, DC, and Jack Ireland for putting me up – again! Thanks also go to my partner, Matt, for not minding the hours spent hunched over email and Skype late at night to discuss the book with Antje and the hours spent at my desk rather than being there.

Antje thanks her interviewees in the Bank and the Fund, in particular Michael Cernea and Jitendra G. Borpujari. Funding was provided by the British Academy. The first draft manuscript was largely completed while a visiting scholar at the International Center for Business and Politics at Copenhagen Business School funded by the GARNET mobility fund. I would like to thank my colleagues at the Center for being such fantastic fellows and making work much more fun. Thanks go also to Stine Haakonsson, Christiane Mossin, Ove Kaj Pedersen and Grahame Thompson for offering their thoughts and comments on earlier drafts, and to Lars Bo Kaspersen for his incredible support – he has helped make research projects like this book much easier to undertake.

Finally we would both like to thank John Haslam and Cambridge University Press and two anonymous reviewers for their comments. The book has been made stronger as a result of the process.

SUSAN PARK
AND
ANTJE VETTERLEIN

St Petersburg

Acronyms and abbreviations

ADB	Asian Development Bank
BIS	Bank for International Settlements
BP	Bank Procedures
BWI	Bretton Woods institutions
CAC	current account convertibility
CAL	capital account liberalization
CAS	Country Assistance Strategy
CODE	Committee on Development Effectiveness
CoE	Council of Europe
CSA	Country Systems Approach
DfID	Department for International Development, UK
DIPRES	Budget Office, Ministry of Finances, Chile
EA	Environmental Assessment
EB	Executive Board
EBM	Executive Board Minutes
EBS	Executive Board Specials
ED	Environmental Department
EIA	environmental impact assessment
ESAF	Enhanced Structural Adjustment Facility
ESD	environmentally sustainable development
ESSD	Environmentally and Socially Sustainable Development Network
ESW	Economic and Sector Work
EU	European Union
FAD	Fiscal Affairs Department
FDI	foreign direct investment
FI	financial intermediary
FPSI	Finance Private Sector and Infrastructure
G7	Group of Seven
GAD	gender and development
GAP	Gender Analysis and Policy
GP	good practices

GTZ	Gesellschaft für Technische Zusammenarbeit
HD	human development
HIPC	heavily indebted poor country
IADB	Inter-American Development Bank
IBRD	International Bank for Reconstruction and Development
IDA	International Development Agency
IEO	Independent Evaluation Office
IIF	Institute of International Finance
ILO	International Labour Organization
IMF	International Monetary Fund
IMFC	Interim Committee of the Board of Governors on the International Monetary System
IOs	international organizations
IR	international relations
ISA	International Studies Association
IUCN	International Union for Conservation of Nature
MDBs	multilateral development banks
MDF	Multilateral Debt Facility
MDGs	Millennium Development Goals
MDPP	Pilot Project of Municipal Development
MICs	middle-income countries
MOP	Ministry of Public Works
NATO	North Atlantic Treaty Organization
NDC	non-financial defined contribution
NEPA	National Environmental Policy Act
NGOs	non-governmental organizations
NPM	new public management
NUPI	Norwegian Institute of International Affairs
OD	operational directive
OECD	Organization for Economic Co-operation and Development
OED	Operations Evaluation Department
OMS	Operational Manual Statements
OP	Operational Policy
OPCS	Operations Policy and Country Services
OPCSN	Operations Policy and Country Service Network
OPN	Operational Policy Note
OSCE	Organization for Security and Co-operation in Europe
PA	principal–agent
PAYG	pay-as-you-go
PER	Public Expenditure Review

PREM	Poverty Reduction and Economic Management
PRGF	Poverty Reduction and Growth Facility
PRSP	Poverty Reduction Strategy Paper
PSIA	Poverty and Social Impact Analysis
SAF	Structural Adjustment Facility
SAL	Structural Adjustment Lending
SBA	Stand-By Arrangement
SDN	Sustainable Development Network
SDRM	Sovereign Debt Restructuring Mechanism
SM	Seminar Memorandum
TFAP	Tropical Forest Action Plan
UN	United Nations
UNDP	United Nations Development Programme
UNEP	United Nations Environment Programme
UNESCO	United Nations Educational, Scientific and Cultural Organization
UNICEF	United Nations Children's Fund
USAID	United States Agency for International Development
VAT	Value Added Tax
WCD	World Commission on Dams
WDR	World Development Report
WID	women in development
WTO	World Trade Organization

Part One

Introduction

1 Owning development: creating policy norms in the IMF and the World Bank

Susan Park and Antje Vetterlein

Introduction

How are policies devised by the International Monetary Fund (IMF or the Fund) and the World Bank? Considering the central role played by these two international organizations (IOs) in the post-1945 international economic system, it is not surprising that there is considerable disagreement over what motivates these institutions. For example, critics of the Fund and the Bank argue that they merely do the bidding of their most powerful member, the United States (Babb and Buria 2005: 73; Woods 2006: 379). Indeed this fits current theoretical models that focus on the primacy of (powerful) member states over their IO agents (Hawkins *et al.* 2006). Others argue that the IMF and the World Bank are purveyors of globalization, and act to further the interests of hegemonic capitalist elites through upholding and extending the capitalist system (Bøås and McNeill 2004; Goldman 2005; Moore 2007; Wade and Veneroso 1998). Still others argue that these organizations have power precisely because they are relatively autonomous in their decision-making, which gives them leeway to determine how to implement their mandates (Barnett and Finnemore 2004; Weaver 2008).

This book takes a different tack. It examines the sources, triggers and mechanisms of change in the IMF's and the World Bank's ideas and policies. It undertakes detailed, fine-grained empirical research into the policy-making processes of the Bretton Woods institutions. Analysing the Fund and the Bank in this way allows us to ascertain whether power-based explanations, such as the rationalist principal–agent (PA) model, neo-Gramscian accounts of hegemonic elites or IO autonomy, fit with empirical accounts tracing how and why these international organizations take up certain ideas and turn them into policies that shape the economic development of a majority of states. This book, therefore, investigates the processes by which certain ideas were picked up by these IOs and how they were turned into the policies currently advocated by the Bretton Woods institutions. The volume is constructivist in asking 'how' the

3

IMF and the World Bank came to own their existing suite of policies and the ideas that underpin them. It seeks to assess the capacity for normative change within the Fund and the Bank while evaluating the strength of their current policies.

In investigating the ability of these international organizations to take up new ideas and turn them into policies, the book makes three arguments. First, that all policies are grounded in ideas, which when traced, come not just from the member states of the Fund and the Bank, but from a variety of actors both inside and outside these institutions. The book therefore investigates where these norms come from and how and why they were taken up by these international financial institutions and turned into globally applicable approaches to economic growth and development. We argue that this process creates 'policy norms' to highlight the importance of understanding how ideas originate and how they shape decision-making in these two IOs. Policy norms are defined as *shared expectations for all relevant actors within a community about what constitutes appropriate behaviour, which is encapsulated in (Fund or Bank) policy.*[1] Norms shape how policies are devised in certain ways and not others. Examining the norms underlying economic growth and development in this way is to unpack how particular issues are considered problems to be solved and how this led to specific IMF and World Bank policy solutions. Bringing these components together through the concept of a policy norm is to analyse how certain ways of understanding and operationalizing economic growth and development became appropriate for the Fund and the Bank.

In this respect, all the chapters in this volume empirically examine where the policy norms of the IMF and the World Bank came from, and identify the triggers and mechanisms that enabled these policy norms to come to fruition. Some of the policy norms came from inside the Fund and the Bank, others from outside. Some came from member states, many did not. Some support the globalization agenda, others do not. Some extend the reach and therefore power of these IOs, others do not. By examining nine policy norms, including capital account liberalization, current account liberalization, debt relief, tax reform and poverty alleviation in the IMF, and environmental safeguards, gender equity, pension reform and new public management in the World Bank, we obtain a more accurate picture of what forces are able to propel change within these international organizations and under what conditions. We systematically analyse our findings in the book's conclusion.

---

[1] The term 'policy norm' has been used, for example, in Simmons *et al.* (2008), but they do not define the concept and used it interchangeably with policy.

Second, the book challenges us to think more about the power of norms. The book demonstrates how norms come to be seen as socially appropriate for the IMF and the World Bank, to the point where they then devise or revise policies on specific economic growth and development issues that may have previously been outside their domain or way of thinking. In tracing this process, we can point to the power of norms as the norm is translated into a policy, which is then promoted throughout the international political economy. To date, constructivists have examined how international norms emerge and shape states' interests and behaviour (Finnemore 1996). If states adopt new policies and change how they behave, then a norm has causal power. While this is an important insight and one we readily affirm throughout the contents of this book, we want to show that there is more to norms than this. A key constructivist insight is that international norms exert influence on actors' behaviour but actors' behaviour in turn reconstitutes norms. Norms are not immutable structures; they change through collective action. As such, we make the case that policy norms are not uniform in their power; they may gain or lose strength according to the degree to which they are accepted and adhered to.

We identify three stages of policy norm change. First, a policy norm emerges where it is increasingly seen to be the right thing to do by relevant actors to the point where it solidifies as a policy norm. Tracing this process follows much of the constructivist literature on norms and applies it to change in the IMF and the World Bank. Second, a policy norm may then stabilize such that it becomes taken for granted. This is the height of the policy norm's power, and relevant actors accord with the policy norm without much in the way of deviant behaviour or outright opposition. The third stage is a policy norm's decline. We demonstrate that policy norms can wane, where alternative approaches to specific issues emerge to challenge certain ways of behaving. We account for policy norms that weaken either before they have been diffused from the institutions to their borrowers or after they have become entrenched. The policy norm declines, even, in some cases, irrespective of the interests of powerful member states.

This book is not, therefore, an outright celebration of the positive power of norms. We show that not all 'norms' scholarship demonstrates success stories. We examine the strength of the policy norm to ascertain whether it is emergent, has stabilized or is in decline. The volume highlights the relatively under-examined area of norm decline where ways of thinking and acting, in this case in international political economy, are no longer socially accepted. While much of the constructivist literature assumes some norms decline in order to make way for new norms to ascend and reach a tipping point (Finnemore and Sikkink 1998), we explicitly demonstrate how this might occur. We point to policy norms that were powerful in their ascendance but now seem to be declining (chapters by Leiteritz and Moschella, Park, and Lardone) compared with policy norms that are in their initial emergence phase (chapters by Momani, Wodsak and Koch, and Weaver), or policy norms that seem to be stabilizing or at the height of their 'taken for grantedness' (chapters by Vetterlein, Broome, and Seabrooke).

We therefore assess each policy norm's strength, which is based on three constitutive components. First is its formal validity where it has become an international agreement, or been made part of the IO's constitution or Articles of Agreement, its operational strategy, and/or is included in Fund and Bank loan contracts. This indicates a high degree of institutionalization where states agree to make a policy norm binding. Second, a policy norm's strength is based on social recognition, where it is understood as socially appropriate by those inside and outside the IO such that all agree that it is the right thing to do. This is the informal power of the policy norm such that it is readily recognized as accepted behaviour. The third component is the cultural validity of the policy norm where it is culturally adapted to local contexts in the case of IMF and Bank borrowers (Wiener 2007b: 62). Examining the strength of the policy norm in different situations sheds light on how it might be considered robust in various realms. Analysing the different ways actors engage with policy norms gives us a greater insight into how they are understood as strong enough to be taken as given.

Determining a policy norm's strength in this way is not to split the concept of a policy norm to make it more easily measurable. All three aspects are important and all three are ultimately based on the policy norms' intersubjectivity. Yet each facet may lead actors to engage with the policy norm according to different processes even though the actions and responses to the policy norm all stem from the same impulse. For example, promoting the formal validity of a policy norm is an attempt to institutionalize it to make it binding based on the fact that the policy norm has social recognition, while examining the disconnect between an already formally valid policy norm and its social recognition is to examine how a policy norm is losing or gaining informal strength (which in turn may or may not affect its formal validity). Lastly, assessing whether a policy norm that is socially recognized within the Fund or Bank is perceived as culturally valid indicates the policy norm's strength in terms of how a majority of actors involved respond to and accord with the policy norm in domestic contexts (i.e. outside the realm of policy norm formation within the IO). To reiterate, each of these constituent components of the policy norm stems from the intersubjective understandings of the relevant actors over what is appropriate behaviour for the Fund and the Bank, although one or more of the constituent factors may be subject to contestation leading to policy norm change. Which of these three constitutive components is subject to change is detailed in each of the chapters.

Finally, the book aims to locate the policy norms advocated by the IMF and the World Bank within a broader normative framework. While this may be considered unusual for a book tracing the policy-making process within the Fund and the Bank, we think it necessary to recognize that there are broader developments at work. The IMF has shifted over time, sometimes radically, in terms of the policies it promotes (as chapters by Vetterlein, and Leiteritz and Moschella demonstrate), while the World Bank could be accused of development fad-ism – forever taking up new ideas and insights. We show how policy norms emerge, stabilize and weaken. In showing the varying strength of policy norms in this way, we go beyond merely identifying when an idea reaches a tipping point to become an international norm (Finnemore and Sikkink 1998). In fact we take issue with current explanations of norms that suggest a path of norm progression. While we agree that there is more to norms than their emergence and stabilization, we do not subscribe to the idea that norm change and evolution follows a pattern of liberal progressivism as identified by Risse and Sikkink (1999) in their conception of a 'norm spiral'. A norm spiral denotes the evolution of international norms in the international system. For Risse and Sikkink, norms such as human rights emerge and are adopted by a number of actors such as human rights violating states. The norm may have setbacks but over time the norm progresses towards some ideal liberal end-point where all actors globally will recognize the importance of human rights.

We do not incorporate liberal ideals in our understanding of norm change. Instead, we recognize that norms, politically and economically liberal or not, can emerge if enough actors view them as socially appropriate. While we recognize how controversial many of the policy norms in this volume are, we do not advocate on their behalf. Policy norms will decline when enough relevant actors think that they are no longer socially appropriate and this will be indicated through a loss of formal validity, social recognition and cultural validity. Documenting the nine cases herein is not to favour one economic theory over another, nor to subscribe to one ideology over another. Rather the volume seeks to identify the sources, triggers and mechanisms for change that make these nine policy norms possible. Precisely because we reject the progressivism of the norm spiral, we situate our policy norms within the context of a norm *circle*. This is a heuristic device for examining how and why the strength of policy norms changes over time, while recognizing that ideas never fully disappear. In other words, the book promotes the concept of the norm circle as a framework for understanding the status of the separate policy norms, as emergent, stabilizing or declining. While norms can fade away, they may later re-emerge in a new form. This recognizes that ideas never die, they just change form.

In short, the book explicitly makes clear that norms are not merely structures that determine how states behave, rather that norms themselves evolve over time (Sandholtz 2008; Wiener 2008). Although we do not agree with the progressive approach currently outlined by Risse and Sikkink (1999), we recognize that the combination of policy norm change can help constitute a broader shift in understandings of international economic growth and development. This volume locates the strength of the nine policy norms within the norm circle as a means of better understanding the relationship between ideas and the policy formation process. Empirically, the book documents changes to how we understand international economic growth and development.

The remainder of this chapter is structured as follows: the next section identifies a gap in explanations of Fund and Bank behaviour, particularly in relation to (policy norm) change. We identify sources of change within the IMF and the World Bank as norm advocates that operate within material and ideational structures both inside and outside these IOs. The following section highlights the triggers and mechanisms through which policy norm change becomes possible and proposes that we analyse policy norms as existing within the context of a norm circle or as circular, dynamic, social processes that emerge, stabilize, transform and subside. We argue that this is an ongoing process which cumulatively may influence the direction of overall understandings of economic growth and development. The final section briefly introduces the nine cases examined in the volume.

Theorizing the Bretton Woods institutions in the world economy

Why examine the 'policy norms' of the IMF and the World Bank? Despite increasingly volatile international capital markets and recurrent and devastating financial crises, the IMF and the World Bank still play an important role in the global economy. Not only do their policies inform many developing country economic development agendas, but they underpin the international economic order by way of meeting the needs of the Group of Eight (G8) and the Group of Twenty (G20). While much ink has been spilled on these two powerful international organizations, one could argue that we are no closer to understanding how and why they create the policies they do. Scholarly attention towards the IMF and the World Bank is often focused on the institutions' operational effectiveness and demands for reform (Buira 2003b; Paloni and Zanardi 2006; Pincus and Winters 2002; Ritzen 2005; Woods 2006). Much of the literature demonstrates the combined challenges facing these institutions and their inability to change, or details proposals for their improvement (Birdsall 2006; Vines and Gilbert 2004). Few analyses actually investigate how ideas are generated and change within either organization (recent exceptions include Chwieroth 2010; Park 2010; Weaver 2008).

The book deviates from the current literature on these two IOs by demonstrating *how* the IMF and the World Bank arrived at their current position on specific development issues. We provide empirical data by 'opening up' the IMF and the World Bank. Both institutions remain under-studied in terms of how they take up ideas and produce policy. The collection documents how the IMF and the World Bank come to *own* the policy prescriptions they provide for developing countries while some chapters detail their implementation in borrower states. The focus is not therefore on whether borrowers own the policies the Fund and the Bank think they should, but on how the Fund and the Bank thought these ideas and policies were worth owning themselves. In examining this process, the book demonstrates how each policy norm fits within the various stages of the norm circle, thus linking theoretical and empirical research on IOs (Best 2005; Chwieroth 2007b; Park 2005b, 2006; Vetterlein 2006, 2007; Weaver 2007) to the study of norms in IR (Bernstein 2001; Guzzini 2000; Wiener 2007a). This is done by tracing the circular norm dynamic whereby norms emerge, strengthen, weaken and regenerate over time.

The IMF's and the World Bank's policies continue to have great sway in how international economic growth and development is understood. Since the early 1980s efforts by the IMF and the World Bank have focused on devising macroeconomic policy for developing countries using a neo-liberal economic model. Often identified with the 'Washington Consensus', policy prescriptions included fiscal discipline, reordering public expenditure priorities, tax reform, liberalizing interest rates, establishing a competitive exchange rate, trade liberalization, liberalization of inward foreign direct investment, privatization, deregulation, and establishing and securing property rights (see Kuczynski and Williamson 2003; Williamson 1999, 2003). When the scope of the Fund's and Bank's activities dramatically increased with the rise of structural adjustment and conditionality in the 1980s and the collapse of communism in the 1990s, critics' voices reached a crescendo at the turn of the twenty-first century, challenging the effectiveness, legitimacy and reach of these institutions.[2] Additions to the neoliberal agenda were made throughout the 1990s as concerns by various interest groups came to the fore, including poverty alleviation, debt relief, gender equality and environmental safeguards amongst others.[3] How and why some of these ideas were taken up by the IMF and the World Bank to become policy norms, and how and why some entrenched policy norms substantially changed requires detailed investigation.

Tracing the strength of policy norms like capital account liberalization and gender equality within the IMF and the World Bank is therefore central to debates over what influences IO action and change. We argue that there is more to these institutions than the power of their member states. The dominance of neorealism and neoliberalism throughout the 1980s and 1990s overshadowed the autonomy and independence of IOs in international policy-making (see Baldwin 1993; Keohane 1988; Mearsheimer 1994/5). Current approaches all now recognize that IOs like the Fund and the Bank have some autonomy in determining their actions. In examining the activities of relatively autonomous IOs, competing research agendas have emerged: the rationalist research agenda focuses (along with neo-Gramscian approaches) on material power and interests in contrast with ideational explanations of IO behaviour and change.

Power- and material-based accounts of IO behaviour and change

Rationalist scholars have established a research agenda using the PA model to examine how to eliminate the gap between member state directives and IO actions (Hawkins *et al.* 2006; Pollack 2003). This establishes a puzzle of how, why and when the Bretton Woods institutions fail to meet (powerful) members' interests (Gutner 2005a; Nielson and Tierney 2003, 2005; Nielson *et al.* 2006). While this is an important question generating a new research agenda, we argue that how financial and development problems and their solutions are socially constructed and historically situated gives greater insight into the specific set of policy norms advocated by the Fund and the Bank today.

---

[2] See for instance the 'Fifty Years is Enough' campaign (Danahar 1994). In addition, mass protests were also held outside the IMF and World Bank annual and spring meetings in 2000 and 2001.

[3] A debate then ensued as to whether this constituted a Post-Washington Consensus (Stiglitz 1998a, 1998b), moving away from neoliberal tenets, or a 'Washington Consensus Plus' (Williamson 2000: 260), where new concerns were merely added to the neoliberal model. Since the end of the 1990s there has been a shift in development practice (such as the inclusion of gender analysis; Elson 2002: 88–9). This is discussed fully in the Conclusion.

Recognizably, member states are important for setting IO constitutions, agendas, budgets and staffing. However, decisions over how to practise economic development are not solely determined by states when delegating authority to IOs. While IOs such as the Fund and the Bank are relatively autonomous in determining how they will meet their mandates within the constraints states place on them, not enough has been done to understand how and why they make the decisions they do. The argument proposed here is that the Fund and the Bank are permeable IOs that take up and internalize norms from various sources. The role of developed and developing states, other multilateral institutions, and non-state actors such as NGOs helps determine what economic development is and how it ought to be achieved. As we demonstrate throughout the volume, policy norms do not emerge in a singular fashion. We document that the Fund and the Bank incorporate norms that are both internally generated and externally advocated. As a result, Fund and Bank staff may propel specific policies that become policy norms such as capital account liberalization, or they may absorb norms such as gender equality that are manifested by external actors.[4] New policy norms can be initiated by the Executive Board or the management of both organizations, by other norm entrepreneurs in the development community, or from the field of operations.

This demonstrates that policy norm emergence is much more complex than the PA model relationship allows with its narrow focus on member states' instrumental relationship to their IOs. Moreover, rationalist approaches underplay the importance of competing economic ideas propagated within international economic development, such as debt relief and poverty alleviation, that feed into the policy-making process and frame the interests of the various actors involved in policy deliberations (Blyth 2002; Hobson and Seabrooke 2007; Widmaier et al. 2007). The contributors here point to the importance of ideas and often non-materially powerful norm advocates in transforming IMF and World Bank policy norms, which may in turn shape international economic development.

In contrast to rationalist PA model explanations of IO behaviour, alternative material explanations view IOs as important for maintaining unequal power relations for state and non-state actors. Neo-Gramscian approaches, for example, argue that a hegemonic bloc of global elites in powerful industrialized states and IOs such as the IMF and the World

---

[4] The recent shift towards donor harmonization contributes pressure for all bi- and multilateral lenders to follow the same policies, thus reinforcing the power of Fund and Bank policy norms.

Bank construct dominant ideas to reinforce their material interests (Bøås and McNeill 2004; Goldman 2005; Lee 1995). While neo-Gramscian analyses could be used to examine how ideas become policy norms that shape IO practice, the absence of industrialist or financier interest in the formulation of many of the policy norms discussed here undermines the use of such an approach. Even if policy norms like debt relief and gender equality help maintain the global economic system in such a way as to favour the long-term interests of a hegemonic global elite, there is little evidence in the volume to suggest that private interests were at the forefront of either norm advocacy or the actual policy negotiations within the Fund or the Bank. Moreover, critics of neo-Gramscian approaches identify difficulties with using this approach for explaining the emergence of global policy because structuralist accounts 'run the risk of reducing international policy processes and outcomes to manifestations of immovable structures of business power at the cost of political agency. Despite theoretical advances in structuralist approaches that seek to overcome the deterministic tendency of historical materialism, structuralist accounts still struggle to deal with the observable variation in policy outcomes' (Falkner 2008: 13).

In short, there is much more at stake in the formulation of Fund and Bank policies than combined elite interests (which may be shifting and non-aligned in any case). Empirical research is required to ascertain the extent to which privileged or materially powerful actors are able to shape international policies in ways that suit their own interests (an excellent example is Gould 2003). Thus far, critical scholars have not turned their attention to how economic ideas are formulated within IOs, tending to focus on broad economic analysis rather than specific finance and development problems.[5] A recent neo-Gramscian analysis of the World Bank, for example, continues to ignore the very real policy variations evident within the Bank's engagement with issues like the environment. In making the case that NGO challenges to World Bank hegemony have reinforced rather than undermined Bank power, Goldman (2005) assumes a degree of uniformity in non-state actor engagement with these presumed monolithic IOs that ignores research to the contrary (Keck and Sikkink 1998; Park 2005b). Although these IOs do wield material power, and they do have relationships with their member states and private interests, the book demonstrates that explanations of IMF and World Bank behaviour must account for the role of ideas and non-materially powerful actors.

---

[5] On critical approaches to global governance generally see Hurrell (2005); Laffey and Weldes (2005). For an exception see Weber (2002) for an account of microcredit.

Constructivist and ideas-based accounts of IO behaviour and change

In contrast to power-based material approaches are various strands of thought that emphasize the role of ideas in shaping actors' behaviour. Constructivism analyses the emergence of international norms, including a substantial literature on how IOs diffuse norms to states (Checkel, 1999, 2001; Finnemore 1996; Flockhart 2006; *IO* 2005; Johnston 2001; Linden 2002; Schimmelfennig 2006). Distinct from this literature is our use of 'policy norms' where we examine how norms emerge, stabilize and decline within IOs. We do this by tracing the internal IO processes through which policy norms are formulated and change. This is a constructivist approach to explaining IO behaviour which includes analysing an IO's internal culture, routines and identity (Barnett and Finnemore 2004; Chwieroth 2010; Park 2010; Weaver 2008). The contributions in this book assess the extent to which the internal normative environment influences the policy-making process. This goes beyond examining IOs in terms of how they are shaped by external material or ideational forces, although these do obviously play a role. We locate norm change with the role of norm advocates, which may operate within the IO or externally to it. The specifics of each idea and the emergence of Fund and Bank policy norms are outlined throughout the chapters.

We undertake process tracing to analyse how norms become influential enough to form policy norms. Our contributors all recognize the inherently social process of formulating or implementing IMF and World Bank policy through discussion, negotiation and contestation between state and non-state actors, both within and outside IOs. All the contributors thus share an adherence to the importance of norms for how we understand international economic development problems and why the IMF and World Bank propose the solutions they do. Ontologically the contributions to this volume share a focus on 'collective understandings and systems of meanings', while epistemologically engaging in 'truth-seeking' and a belief that 'causal generalization in the form of middle range theorizing ... is possible' (Risse and Wiener 1999: 776). The chapters employ a range of constructivist approaches that cover a 'terrain that is not limited by an exclusive pole mentality' by speaking to both reflectivists and rationalists (Risse and Wiener 1999: 776; Katzenstein *et al.* 1999).

The book therefore focuses on how social interaction constitutes policy norms. A broadly held definition of norms in international relations (IR) is that norms are 'shared expectations about appropriate behaviour held by a collectivity of actors' (Checkel 1999: 83).[6] Norms are intersubjectively shared, collectively legitimated and/or institutionalized, and in this volume are encapsulated in IMF and World Bank policy to become policy norms (Bernstein 2001: 8; Finnemore 1996: 22). This means that norms establish certain expectations that, on the one hand, regulate and constrain action and, on the other hand, make action predictable and structured. They may be codified in legal rules and regulations such as international conventions and/or made actionable in the policies of IOs and states. Norms may lead to informal or formal sanctioning procedures in the case of non-compliance (for example, ideational practices such as shaming and shunning or material economic or military sanctions).[7] The sanctioning mechanisms attached to a norm are often not acknowledged in definitions of norms in the IR literature (see Finnemore and Sikkink 1998: 891; Jepperson *et al.* 1996: 54).[8] For sociologists, however, norms are expectations held against people in certain positions and 'a pattern of sanctions' (Scott 1971: 65). Whether a norm is strong depends on the compliance and enforcement of the norm by a majority of the members of a group or the relevant members of a group.[9]

In taking a constructivist perspective, we do not reject material power (Abbot and Snidal 1998; Nielsen *et al.* 2006). Both the Fund and the Bank draw significant attention precisely because of the material inequities between member states within them. For some, the IMF's and World Bank's unequal voting structures and their decision-making processes are evidence that the Fund and the Bank are merely conduits for United States and Western foreign policy interests (Buira 2003b). For others, the argument that developing countries often do not or cannot heed IMF and World Bank advice, combined with the rise of 'middle income countries' like China and India, demonstrates there is more than US and

---

[6] Similarly, norms are defined as 'collective expectations about proper behaviour for a given identity' (Jepperson *et al.* 1996: 54; Finnemore and Sikkink 1998: 891). According to Khagram *et al.* (2002: 14), international norms are 'shared expectations or standards of appropriate behavior accepted by states and intergovernmental organizations that can be applied to states, intergovernmental organizations, and/or non-state actors of various kinds'. While this definition reflects our position it is unnecessarily prescriptive.

[7] Formal sanctions may not necessarily entail material sanctions, such as blacklisting tax havens as a means of casting them as deviant (Sharman 2007). Similarly, informal sanctions may be based on the threat of coercion (material) or shaming (ideas).

[8] The role of sanctioning in upholding norms is well developed in relation to European IOs; see Kelley 2004 and Schimmelfennig 2005.

[9] We do not examine the role of ideas in policy-making through the neoliberal institutionalist approach used by Goldstein and Keohane (1993), where ideas are defined as individually held beliefs. Rather we examine how collectively shared ideas on appropriate behaviour emerge, strengthen and decline.

Western power at play.[10] Arguably, material resources may facilitate or prevent the dissemination of policy norms from the Fund and the Bank but, as demonstrated throughout the chapters, this alone cannot explain their formation and change.

The volume explicitly focuses on the policy-making process within the IMF and the World Bank. Current constructivist research traces how ideas influence economic policy formation (Blyth 2002: 17; Campbell 1998: 384–5; McNamara 1999). Blyth, for example, has argued that competing economic ideas come to the fore during times of uncertainty such as financial crisis, thus modifying existing institutions (Blyth 2002). Moreover, Widmaier (2007) articulates how different understandings of monetary trends can reshape how policy-makers view their economic interests in starkly divergent ways despite similarities in economic crises propelling action. Internationally, Best (2005) demonstrates how changing ideas led to a reinterpretation of IMF policies over time which was possible because of ambiguity in the international financial architecture. Further, both Sharman (2007) and Hobson and Seabrooke (2007) demonstrate how weak players in the world economy may, through their rejection of dominant ideas, change the everyday international political economy and regulations on tax havens respectively, outside traditional subaltern protest movements.

Like constructivism, other theoretical strands examine the diffusion of ideas and policies, such as the Stanford School (Boli and Thomas 1999; Drori et al. 2006a, 2006b; Meyer et al. 1997) and the policy diffusion literature (Sharman 2008; Simmons and Elkins 2004; Simmons et al. 2008; Weyland 2006). The Stanford School examines whether a world culture (Boli and Thomas 1999; Meyer et al. 1997), based on Western norms and Weberian organizational forms (Drori et al. 2006b), is spreading globally. The Stanford School's central argument is that socially generated organizations such as the nation-state are increasingly moving towards homogeneity. They further argue that this process is occurring at the global level and that this is derived from an expanding world society (Drori et al. 2006b; Simmons et al. 2008: 32; Wotipka and Ramirez 2008: 304). Although there is a common concern amongst the Stanford School and constructivists about what constitutes socially appropriate behaviour and how it emerges, our focus here is not on a world culture, and we do not examine how norms are diffused globally, although this work is premised on the view that the IMF and the World Bank do diffuse policy norms to their borrowers (and donors in the case of Leiteritz and Moschella's

---

[10] On rational action: both Schimmelfennig (2006) and Kelley (2004) demonstrate how IOs have greater normative leverage with material power in the case of European IOs.

chapter on capital account liberalization in the IMF). Further, we do not use quantitative methods and longitudinal studies as employed by the Stanford School (and much of the policy diffusion literature) to show the global uptake of policies across a range of policy areas (see Drori *et al.* 2006a, 2006b; Simmons *et al.* 2008). While these could be used to ascertain the extent to which policy norms are taken up by Fund and Bank borrowers, this is not the aim of our research.

In contrast, the policy diffusion literature tends to focus on the mechanistic processes that account for the spread of policies amongst states. Simmons *et al.* (2008: 9), for example, identify coercion, competition, learning and emulation (Simmons and Elkins 2004: 172, n. 2 lump these mechanisms together). Most of these mechanisms do not fit explanations of IO change and IMF and World Bank policy norm formation and revision. For example, coercion 'can be used by a range of actors … through the threat or use of physical force, the manipulation of economic costs and benefits, and even through the monopolization of information or expertise'. According to Simmons *et al.* (2008), coercion involves 'power asymmetries that strong actors exploit to impose their preferences on the weak' (2008: 10). For IOs coercion could only come from member states. Yet, as will be shown throughout this volume, member state coercion is not, in most cases, the dominant reason for the Fund and the Bank to create new policy norms. Indeed, this is one of our principal findings as seen throughout the volume and discussed in the Conclusion.

Another diffusion mechanism is competition. Yet there is limited evidence that these IOs explicitly compete against each other (or other IOs) in determining how borrower states should implement economic policies, despite there being some overlap on macroeconomic guidance. While the IMF and the World Bank often collaborate *and* compete with each other and other IOs like the United Nations (see chapters 2 and 5 by Momani and Vetterlein, this volume), there is no evidence to suggest that this was the motivating factor for the emergence of the policy norms analysed in this volume. Competition could refer to norm advocates championing their own ideas, but this is not how Simmons *et al.* understand the term (2008: 17–24), which is based on the actor choosing to take up the policy in order to compete more effectively against like units, but where pressures promoting the policy are decentralized (see also Sharman 2008: 649–51).

The third form of policy diffusion is learning. For Simmons *et al.* the process of learning may be through a rational Bayesian learning model or through 'cognitive shortcuts which channel attention to highly successful countries or to highly successful outcomes' (2008: 29). This is similar to

Weyland (2006) who argues that policy diffusion results from states' proximity to policy models where cognitive heuristics and bounded rationality determine policy diffusion. Learning may be simple and tactical or may be a more complex revision of both the means and ends of actor behaviour. Processes of learning may come from peer groups or from expert networks (such as epistemic communities; see Haas 1992). Fundamental to the emergence and change of policy norms within the Fund and the Bank are considerations of how ideas are transmitted and how and why they are taken up by these IOs. The processes documented here are not dissimilar to complex learning, although this language is not used owing to its 'positive evaluative connotations' (Nye 1987: 379). In some cases professional networks were fundamental to these IOs taking up ideas and formulating them as policy norms (see chapter 8 by Leiteritz and Moschella, this volume, on capital account liberalization); in other cases norm advocacy came from a composite of actors sharing similar ideas (for example, Momani's chapter on multilateral debt relief). As a result professional networks are an important component for policy norm formation and change in some circumstances but not others.

This leads to the final policy diffusion mechanism: emulation. Simmons *et al.* point to this as a distinct process separate from learning (2008: 31), although in practice this is not so clear-cut. They argue that emulation is a process of social construction and point to sociologists such as the Stanford School (Boli and Thomas 1999; Meyer *et al.* 1997), English School theorists such as Hedley Bull (1977) and constructivists (Finnemore 1996; Katzenstein 1996) for promoting the power of ideas in shaping international practices. For Simmons *et al.* emulation comes down to a common benchmark (for example, in the policy diffusion literature on liberal policies, this is based on the policies of advanced liberal economies). This clearly is not transferable to IOs where there is no single template to observe. In short, if the IMF and the World Bank are emulating someone or something, it is unclear who or what this could be.

Finally, other scholars (Sharman 2008) have examined policy diffusion through mimicry as a separate mechanism where actors copy organizational leaders in their field to gain legitimacy, not because they believe there are material gains from doing so. To enact this approach we would need to assume that there may be an organizational leader that the IMF and World Bank may seek to copy. It could then be used to explain why the IMF and the World Bank took up policy norms such as gender equality and environmental sustainability. Yet this does not really explain the extent to which policy norms were taken up and how they shaped the operations of the organization. In other words, the ideas became institutionalized in ways perhaps unanticipated either from a purely strategic calculation on behalf of IO management or as a means to further their legitimacy. Irrespective, the social acceptance of doing so came not from peers such as other IOs (although this is evident in some chapters such as that by Vetterlein) but through a heterogeneous group of both state and non-state actors, both with and without material power.

Rather than starting out with these predetermined mechanisms of policy diffusion, we examine a variety of triggers and mechanisms at play within the constructivist framework of norm emergence and institutionalization. Each chapter traces the formation and development of one policy norm in order to identify its sources and triggers. Reviewing and comparing all nine policy norms across the Fund and the Bank, the volume identifies three triggers for policy norm formation or change: policy failure; moments of uncertainty due to external shocks such as financial crises; and changing public sentiment as expressed through mass campaigns. These triggers may operate separately or in combination. Recognizably, these triggers are not purely ideational: changing strategic or material conditions are important in so far as actors may radically revise their understanding of the need for, and appropriateness of, a policy norm.

For example, policy norms such as gender are dominant across many policy fields and were taken up by the World Bank. The gender norm is used as a 'truth claim' in policy discourse without being questioned.[11] As a result of changing public sentiment it was picked up by the World Bank to become a policy norm in the international political economy.[12] Gender equality was taken up by World Bank staff and was developed from the bottom up inside the organization to become a Bank policy norm. Debt relief is diametrically opposite in that it was a case of outside external pressure by a range of actors but was pushed from the top down by a few member states on to IMF management. The conclusion to this volume analyses the sources and triggers of change in detail. In sum, while we share with the Stanford School and the policy diffusion literature many of the same concerns regarding the power and ability of ideas to spread, we do not focus on the mechanisms for diffusion that they do. Rather, we examine how and why the IMF and the World Bank take up ideas that become policy norms while explicitly engaging with rationalists and constructivists on the ability of IOs to change. The mechanisms for policy norm formation and change within IOs are detailed next.

---

[11] This is not to say that gender discrimination does not exist any longer. The existence of a norm is distinct from its outcome and consequences.

[12] The chapters establish which policy norms are advocated by either the Fund or the Bank.

Policy norm formation and the norm circle

The contributors analyse how a particular policy norm became the benchmark for how to understand and therefore address economic and development issues.[13] In this way, the book demonstrates how policy norms are formulated: from the definition of the policy problem, to the germination of a norm with widespread organizational acceptance to become an IO policy, thereby becoming a policy norm. The contributors demonstrate that norms with global reach do not necessarily begin within the institutions themselves, or if they do so, may have originally been constituted very differently from the final policy norm. The emergence and evolution of these policy norms are analysed through the circular conception of a norm's existence (emerging, stabilizing or declining) within the norm circle. Each chapter maps the policy norm's formation and change by tracing its strength through interactions between the IMF or the World Bank, norm advocates, critics, state and non-state actors. Here we discuss mechanisms we see operating within the norm circle.

Examining policy norm formation and change within the IMF and the World Bank follows research on the capacity of non-state actors to embody (and diffuse) international norms. Yet there is surprisingly little written on whether and how norms change in actors' engagement with them. Apart from Risse and Sikkink's 'norm spiral' (1999) discussed above, only Finnemore and Sikkink (1998) are notable in their account of the 'life cycle' of norms. They distinguish three different stages of a norm's life cycle: norm emergence, norm cascade and norm internalization (1998: 898). Building on this perspective we argue that ideational change is a circular process.[14] A norm emerges not from thin air but always out of a specific context of an already existing norm which may be contested or inflexible in a changing context. There are many potential norms, yet only one will resonate with relevant actors, become accepted and stabilize. This norm can eventually be referred to as a 'normative claim' without any further explanation. Nevertheless, while this norm then exists as stable, accepted and legitimate, it may over time be subject to contestation. At any given time, one can assume that a norm will be

---

[13] This is not to suggest that dominant Fund and Bank policies are never contested, even during the height of their use, but to argue that they constitute norms when they are seen to be appropriate by most development actors.

[14] Risse and Sikkink (1999) identify the norm process as a spiral, although we close this circular motion. Risse and Sikkink assume that the evolution of norms through a spiral motion is an evolution towards positive practices based on non-specified but recognizably liberal tenets.

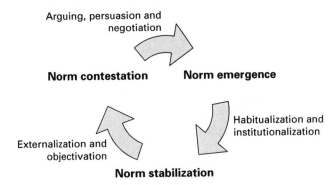

Figure 1.1 Stages and mechanisms in the norm circle

challenged either by specific actors or a group of actors or as a result of events that undermine the norm's appropriateness.[15]

The circular perspective goes further than the partial trajectory identified by Finnemore and Sikkink (1998). It adds a historical/temporal element such that a norm is not just 'born' and at some point 'dies'. Rather, a norm emerges at a specific point in time and is based on its own historical antecedents. That the process is circular also frees us from merely examining a norm in the emergence to stabilization phase: norms can be examined at every stage of the norm circle (from emerging to stabilizing, stabilizing to declining, declining to re-emerging). There is no beginning and end as such; norm change is ongoing. This therefore allows us to assess the norm's strength within the norm circle. As mentioned above, we identify three different phases of a norm's development: first, norm emergence, second, norm stabilization, and finally norm contestation and change. Figure 1.1 demonstrates the norm circle and explicates the different mechanisms enacted in each of the stages, that is, arguing, persuasion and negotiation; habitualization and institutionalization; and externalization and objectivation. We detail the mechanisms at play in each of the three norm development phases by using the example of the normative shift away from the Washington Consensus approach to a broader, more 'holistic' understanding of international economic growth and development. While the chapters in this book focus on a specific policy norm's formation and development, we argue that these changes cumulatively may imply a broader shift away from a narrow

[15] See the special issue of *Comparative European Politics* (2007).

understanding of economic growth and development to one that incorporates the social, the cultural and the political. We discuss the connections between the individual policy norms and the overall normative order in the volume's conclusion.

Norm emergence

The first stage in the norm circle is norm emergence. This occurs after a period of norm contestation (there is no beginning or end in the norm circle). Norms are not merely regulative in guiding actors' behaviour by establishing social rules, but help constitute actors' identity and therefore dispositions. Yet, at any given time, actors (re)construct the world by projecting their understanding of reality through their actions, or in other words by externalizing their interests through action. Although there may be deviance from a particular norm at any given time, such as borrower state inaction in relation to structural adjustment conditions, not all of these instances of non-compliance will be known and therefore sanctioned. However, some of them enter the realm of shared, or objective, knowledge. In other words, there have always been actors who have different interests and ideas (or dispositions) about development and depart from the dominant norm (such as the developmental state model of north-east Asia compared with neoliberalism). Not all of these 'deviant behaviours' turn into a new norm or will change an existing norm. It needs a particular constellation of structural conditions which enable norm entrepreneurs or advocates actively to foster the spread of particular ideas (Finnemore and Sikkink 1998; Florini 1996).

Any actor can be a norm advocate. What is of interest here is the conditions under which some are more successful than others. NGOs, for instance, opposed structural adjustment loans of the IMF and the World Bank but their critique only reached a 'tipping point' in the 1990s (Finnemore and Sikkink 1998). Often, criticism is supported by other crucial events that undermine the formal validity, social recognition or cultural validity of entrenched understandings of international economic development and open up policy space for new norms to settle into the void. Following challenges from NGOs, intellectuals and the UN, the World Bank began to foster a 'human development approach', while the Fund loosened its neoliberal grip (see Sen 2001; Toye and Toye 2005). Norm advocates used argument, persuasion and negotiation to influence the Fund and the Bank to adopt a much broader approach to development. Slowly both organizations established social policies such as the poverty alleviation policy norm.

Norm stabilization

The second stage of the norm circle is norm stabilization. This is characterized by the growing legitimacy of the emergent norm. Through repeated habitualized action certain behaviour turns into patterns that can be reproduced (such as policy creation and monitoring). If these patterns are reciprocally reproduced through interaction they become institutionalized whereby policies are acted upon by other development actors. Once policy norms have been institutionalized they guide and constrain action. Norms are re-projected into actors' consciousness during this process, leading to socialization and internalization. We do not focus on the last two steps of socialization and internalization in terms of the IMF and the World Bank although this is a logical progression (see, for example, Park 2010). The majority of chapters focus on the practices of the various actors within and outside the Fund and the Bank to assess the degree of habitualization and institutionalization, although some chapters question whether IMF and Bank staff have internalized a particular policy norm (see the chapters by Weaver and Vetterlein). If the process of institutionalization is successful the norm will be taken for granted and is no longer subject to debate, rather standing for the dominant standard of appropriateness.

The shift from the Washington to the Post-Washington Consensus illustrates this stage of the norm circle. Today, acknowledging differences in positions, no one would reject the claim that development is more than just economic growth. That has not always been the case. Challenges to the narrow focus of the Washington Consensus began to emerge in the beginning of the 1990s in the form of the United Nations Development Programme's (UNDP) call for a human development approach. Change did not happen quickly. Over time, the Fund and the Bank adopted new policy norms such as gender, debt relief, poverty reduction and sustainability which eventually led to changes at the institutional level such as organization-wide strategy papers, shifts in budgeting, resources and organizational restructuring (which in most cases furthered formal validity and social recognition of new socially oriented policy norms). This in turn fed into the overall normative shift towards a broader understanding of economic growth and development that could be called 'holistic' for its inclusion of the social, cultural and political.

However, the process of institutionalization is not just limited to the IO. For a policy norm to stabilize it must resonate and gain acceptance among relevant actors. In other words, policy norms must have broad legitimacy to be accepted as standards for appropriate behaviour. Legitimation produces new meanings that serve to integrate already existing meanings and practices and justifies them through cognitive and normative elements. Therefore, if a specific policy norm emerges and begins to stabilize we can expect struggles of interpretation over meanings. The conflict between John Williamson and Joseph Stiglitz (1998a, 1998b) over the terms 'Washington Consensus' and 'Post-Washington Consensus' at the end of the 1990s epitomizes this. Williamson's attempt to embrace the newly arising consensus by offering a softer version called 'Washington Consensus *Plus*' documents the struggle in shifting to a new normative order (Kuczynski and Williamson 2003; Williamson 2000, 2003). However, not every potential policy norm will lead to the reconstitution of the normative discourse. The different case studies in this book offer insights into conditions under which individual policy norms emerge. Different triggers, such as external shocks like the Asian financial crisis in 1997/8, may lower the threshold and provide the opportunity for quicker although not necessarily lasting change.

Norm contestation

Once a norm is accepted and used to make legitimate normative claims in order to justify policies, it may then become a subject of contestation. As described in stage one, at any given time actors externalize actions that can be objectivated. Norms are not independent of actors and their interests. On the contrary, if relevant actors are not convinced that a norm is (still) appropriate, it will change. To explain, norms change if relevant actors give new *meaning* to the situation in which the norm usually applies. As a result, something quite powerful must happen for a norm to change since according to our definition norms are not external to actors (and therefore only a constraint on actions) but are constitutive of actors' identity, which determines their dispositions. Conformity to a norm and the appropriateness of attendant policies are not likely to be questioned. Normative change requires powerful driving forces such as external shocks, mass condemnation or the acknowledgement that certain policies do not work according to expectations. These are crucial factors because one can expect significant resistance to change. Usually change is costly since habits and traditions have to be reinvented. As we will see in some of the chapters, the organizational cultures of the IMF and the World Bank are a significant factor slowing change. The Fund is an economic institution, staffed almost exclusively by economists; the Bank is a large development agency that is often considered unwieldy. Different levels of resistance may be evident. The organizational differences are returned to in the volume's conclusion.

In sum, the norm circle allows for a much broader analysis of norm change that emphasizes its context and historical conditions while recognizing that norms may emerge, strengthen, decline and regenerate. Based on this conceptual framework the chapters trace how ideas become policy norms through documenting their sources (inside or outside the IO and whether the idea comes from the bottom up or the top down in the organization). Each chapter details the triggers and mechanisms for change. Our conclusion not only analyses the results of the individual policy norms, but examines the connections between the policy norms cumulatively and the (re)constitution of a normative order. We reflect on whether policy norms such as poverty alleviation, debt relief, gender equity and sustainability provide evidence of a shift from the Washington Consensus to a more holistic approach to economic growth and development.

Organization of the book

Each chapter examines how the Fund and the Bank take up norms and devise their policies. The contributors question the perception of these IOs as operating as instruments of powerful states such as the USA, or purely in the material interests of hegemonic elites, or conversely, as institutions that operate irrespective of external critics. In this way, the tensions and nuances between the IMF and the World Bank as relatively autonomous organizations and their principal member states become clear, as do their relations with civil society and the private sector. In demonstrating the means through which policy norms are established, the various contributors weigh the role of the external environment in determining the organization's actions with the dominant organizational cultures and routines that shape institutional responses. The volume thus documents when and where various factors shape IMF and World Bank policy formation while attempting to evaluate the strength of the policy norm. The norm circle framework allows us to detail how strong the various policy norms here are (as emergent, stable or declining), and we have arranged the chapters of the book according to their position in the norm circle.

Chapters 2 to 4 examine emerging policy norms. In chapter 2, Bessma Momani traces how multilateral debt relief increasingly became recognized as an important means of redressing the unsustainable debt burdens of (newly categorized) heavily indebted poor countries (HIPCs). She demonstrates how the external normative environment shaped IMF staff and then management thinking on devising the HIPC initiative. However, the resultant policy norm was based on the IMF staff's internal strategic relationship with its Executive Board such that the content of the HIPC policy norm reflected the Fund's technocratic, economistic, conservative and interventionist organizational culture. Veronika Wodsak and Martin Koch's contribution (chapter 3) traces the evolution of the World Bank's approach to pension systems over more than a decade. It demonstrates the main mechanisms of how policy norms emerge in the Bank. As opposed to the gender and development policy norm outlined by Catherine Weaver (chapter 4), the main trigger in pension reforms was pressure from Bank management combined with the predicament of transition countries. The World Bank independently occupied a particular policy field but its position was immediately contested, leading it to revise its policy to accord better with the norms of pension reform advocates. Catherine Weaver's chapter undertakes an agent-centred analysis of the role of internal norm advocates in attempting to institutionalize the gender and development (GAD) policy norm within the Bank. She documents how a small group of committed internal advocates reformulated the ideas on gender into the GAD policy norm for the World Bank.

Chapters 5 to 7 depict norms that have stabilized. In chapter 5 Antje Vetterlein traces the evolution of a social development policy norm in the IMF from the 1980s to today. Poverty reduction is now one of the priority objectives of the Fund, which was not the case twenty-five years ago. The IMF accommodated this policy norm which came from outside the organization and was introduced by member states. However, by engaging with the norm the Fund significantly shaped its content to bring it into line with its organizational mandate and beliefs. Chapter 6 by André Broome traces the development of the current account convertibility policy norm from its emergence in the IMF's Articles of Agreement in 1946 until today. Over time, this policy norm lost social recognition by member states. Yet the Fund never stopped promoting it. Today, states are not considered to be politically credible if they do not accept the policy norm. This story is a case of the IMF's persistence in furthering a policy norm that it has fully internalized while demonstrating the waning and waxing power of the Fund in relation to its members. Leonard Seabrooke in chapter 7 also examines the disjuncture between the IMF's stated policy goal to reform tax policies (IMF friendly tax policies) and borrower states' willingness to formally validate and socially recognize the policy but refusal to culturally validate it. The chapter provides a compelling account of how a policy norm shifted to being dominant inside the Fund and among borrowers in terms of formal validity and social recognition, but where a lack of cultural validation has also become entrenched.

Chapters 8 to 10 provide cases of policy norms that are in decline. Chapter 8 by Ralf Leiteritz and Manuela Moschella examines how IMF staff actively pushed for the formal validity of the capital account liberalization policy norm. This policy norm emerged from the staff. Eventually, outside pressure and the decision of the Executive Board curbed the Fund staff's attempt to include the capital account liberalization norm in the IMF's Articles of Agreement. Although significant social recognition existed inside the Fund, the lack of consensus in the external economics and development community, reinforced by the events in East Asia at the end of the 1990s, meant that the policy norm failed to become part of the Fund's Articles of Agreement. Susan Park's contribution (chapter 9) traces the emergence of the World Bank's environmental and social safeguard policy norm. The safeguard policy norm was formed from three processes in the 1980s: the internal innovation of World Bank staff, increasing interactions between IOs discussing the need for assessment procedures, and crucially, the role of environmental NGOs with key member states, pushing for comprehensive Bank-wide policies and procedures. Yet the policy norm was challenged, and may be declining in the 2000s, as a result of changing understandings of the needs of borrowers, and failures in donor provision of official development assistance. Chapter 10 by Martin Lardone examines the emergence of new public management within the World Bank. The chapter demonstrates how the new public management policy norm was taken up by the Bank and introduced into its borrower agreements. New public management conditions vary across borrower agreements with the Bank based on two factors: the Bank's internal political bargaining and interdepartmental cultural differences; and negotiations between the Bank and its borrowers. Lardone, however, demonstrates that despite formal validity and social recognition, the new public management policy norm has not been culturally validated within borrower states and remains dependent on the strategic needs of the state. The Conclusion discusses the main findings arising from the empirical research.

Part Two

Norm emergence

2 Internal or external norm champions: the IMF and multilateral debt relief

Bessma Momani

Introduction

The views of a small number of industrialized states, along with non-governmental organizations (NGOs), and eventually the World Bank converged in favour of the appropriateness of multilateral debt relief for poor countries. They attempted to persuade powerful member states and the International Monetary Fund (IMF) to endorse an emerging policy norm on multilateral debt relief. Yet, the IMF staff, trained as neoclassical economists and socialized within a technocratic organizational culture that had been hesitant to adopt the multilateral debt relief norm, was unable to translate debt relief into policy without serious modifications, leading to an IMF-devised policy norm. This chapter traces how IMF staff and management interactions with the Fund's board and other external actors enabled the emergence of the heavily indebted poor countries (HIPC) policy norm. The HIPC policy norm was more compatible with the Fund's belief system and organizational culture (compared with the social development norm, for example; see Vetterlein, chapter 5 this volume).

Key states, acting as norm advocates, first raised the idea of giving debt relief to poor countries in the early 1980s. These states attempted to negotiate and persuade other states, IO leaders and staff that debt relief was necessary to ensure the economic viability of what would become known as 'heavily indebted poor countries'. The HIPC had per capita income below US$785 and could only borrow under the terms of both the World Bank's International Development Agency (IDA) and the IMF's Poverty Reduction and Growth Facility (PRGF) (Teunissen and Akkerman 2004: xxiii). Major Western creditors, the private sector and multilaterals, however, resisted the idea and rejected calls to turn debt relief into actionable policy. Despite a number of states acting as norm advocates for debt relief, particularly the United Kingdom, Canada, the Netherlands and the Nordic states, a number of the IMF's largest shareholders remained hesitant to endorse and champion a debt relief norm owing to fears of moral hazard, contagion and free-riding behaviour.

The external normative environment, however, eventually triggered the norm's emergence as other actors continued to converge in favour of the idea. Social influence from NGOs, the World Bank and key Group of Seven (G7) states began to mount as they advocated the idea in the late 1980s. Prior to this, the idea of debt relief was rejected categorically: the notion that the IMF would become involved in relieving clients of their obligation to repay sovereign debt would have been viewed with suspicion, if not receiving an a priori rejection. Gradually, multilateral debt relief has changed and evolved to reflect a wider normative shift in social and political perceptions about how best to achieve economic growth and development. As this chapter will show, multilateral debt relief is an *emerging* policy norm that has originated and gained traction owing to the social advocacy of select state actors and NGOs, but was only adopted by the IMF (as well as other states) under certain conditions.

While there was some progress in advancing norms of bilateral and commercial debt relief, the norm of multilateral debt relief was slower to become legitimized and institutionalized by the IMF. Upon prompting from the G7 meeting in Halifax in the summer of 1995, the Interim Committee of the Board of Governors on the International Monetary System (known as the Interim Committee or IMFC) asked the IMF and World Bank Executive Boards to suggest ways to meet the challenges of poor countries' multilateral debt. The G7 turned to the IMF and the World Bank to suggest specific ways of achieving debt relief for the poorest countries. The G7 needed the expertise of the Bretton Woods staff to devise a debt relief proposal that had a strong analytical and theoretical basis (Gstöhl 2007). The IMF staff, prompted in large part by the United Kingdom, conducted a number of studies and proposed policy recommendations to the IMF Executive Board.

By the autumn of 1996, the heavily indebted poor countries (HIPC) initiative was presented to the Interim Committee and accepted by the IMF's Board of Governors. This policy surprised many, including the Chairman of the Interim Committee, Belgian Finance Minister Philippe Maystadt, who noted:

When, in October 1995 – less than a year ago – the Interim Committee encouraged the Fund and the World Bank to continue their work on ways to address the problem of the burden of multilateral debt, few observers would have thought that a credible strategy could have been devised and endorsed by the international financial community as early as today. Even fewer observers would have found it likely that *the IMF could be a key partner in this strategy*. Today, I am delighted that we have reached an agreement on a set of proposals to help the poorest countries to achieve an exit from unsustainable debt. (IMF 1996c, emphasis added)

What role did the IMF staff play in shaping a policy for the emerging multilateral debt relief norm? After all, this would be the first time that the G7 had entrusted the IMF with devising a policy to meet the challenges of low-income country multilateral debt. Previously, the G7 worked in the confines of the Paris Club to determine ways of transferring debt relief to debtors (Gstöhl 2007). Moreover, the IMF staff's technocratic organizational culture had generally been resistant to a version of debt relief that did not involve their continued monitoring and measuring of countries' policies (conditionality). As a consequence of its selective recruitment of conservative macroeconomists and its rigid hierarchical organizational structure (see Momani 2004, 2005), the IMF's belief system and resultant organizational culture tended to resist unconditional and widespread debt relief. Fund staff had been trained to believe that the solution to poor countries' debt problems lay in fixing debtors' underlying policy failures while injecting liquidity into the economy to help countries' short-term balance of payment deficit. Moreover, the Fund's organizational mandate requires staff to 'safeguard resources' by devising programmes that 'ensure timely repayment' of Fund financing. Bearing these organizational features in mind, coupled with continued contestation among key IMF shareholders, how would the IMF staff renegotiate and frame debt relief to management and, more importantly, to the IMF Executive Board when debt relief did not resonate with its organizational culture and organizational mandate?

Using internal IMF documents including Executive Board meeting minutes and IMF staff reports, this chapter traces how the IMF staff played a key role in determining the policy norm on multilateral debt relief. By opening up the 'black box' of the IMF, this chapter aims to show how the Fund staff's analysis of the low-income countries played an important and yet under-theorized role in shaping the emergence of the HIPC initiative. Without opening this black box, the story of how the HIPC initiative emerged would be half told. Moreover, focusing on strategic interests and external material power cannot explain how this policy norm emerged. Instead, this chapter is inspired by non-material explanations of IO behaviour (see Checkel 1999; St Clair 2006). By 'going micro', as Johnston (2001) has challenged IO scholars to do, this chapter looks at the 'pathways and mechanisms' of policy-making in IOs. Asking scholars to search for the origins of norms (see Park 2006), norm internalization within IOs (Park 2005b) and the consequences of IO diffusing norms on power relations (Bøås and McNeill 2004) are all important to our understanding of IOs' role in world politics.

While the multilateral debt relief policy norm continues to evolve and be contested throughout the norm circle, this chapter focuses on its emergence in the mid-1990s and examines how the IMF staff, through a process of social recognition, eventually became its advocate. In the first phase of the norm circle, there is arguing, negotiation and persuasion regarding the multilateral debt relief policy norm. It would only be taken up by the IMF after it had been reconciled with the Fund staff's particular belief system and organizational culture. To that end, IMF staff would view multilateral debt relief as appropriate only after translating the norm of debt relief into the HIPC initiative that adhered to the Fund's organizational culture and operational procedures. Here the second stage of the policy norm circle kicks in: norm stabilization, whereby the HIPC initiative is habitualized and institutionalized. In policy terms, this meant that the HIPC initiative would have conditionality and back-loaded graduation of debt relief at its core, thereby fixing what the staff believed were the underlying policy failures of debtors. The proposed multilateral debt relief policy norm therefore resonated with the Fund's economistic belief system. The idea of multilateral debt relief was accepted and given analytical grounding within the existing institutional framework of the Fund. It was, in other words, adopted in a way that was socially and implicitly congruent with common practice, rather than being imposed externally as if by sanction or regulation. Moreover, the HIPC initiative would fit with the Fund's technocratic organizational culture and organizational mandate that has always valued timely debt repayment through graduated monitoring of debtors. This would then be easily operationalized through conditionality procedures already used by the IMF in implementing programme loans. In the final stage of the norm circle, the policy norm is challenged, contested and further modified into HIPC II. Ultimately the HIPC initiative helped push the realization of a more holistic approach to development, whereby poor countries were able to reduce their debt commitments to allow them to focus more on social welfare and poverty reduction. The HIPC initiative therefore supports the move towards holistic development by facilitating and co-ordinating donor strategies and promoting policy coherence among creditors.

Still, IMF executive directors did not fully endorse the norm of multilateral debt relief underpinning the HIPC initiative proposed by the IMF staff. The UK, Nordic countries, Canada and eventually the United States wanted a more aggressive form of HIPC, one that would be more far reaching than the policy norm advocated by the Fund. Germany, Japan, France and Italy, by contrast, wanted little to do with debt relief at the IMF. Staff and management, who both viewed the idea of multilateral debt relief with trepidation from the very beginning, would endorse a policy norm that could resonate with their organizational culture. Taking advantage of continued divisions in the Board, the IMF staff and management were able to get their way in endorsing an HIPC initiative which was heavy-handed and interventionist. The IMF staff would be at the core of the initiative, monitoring and graduating debtors towards debt relief. Only then would the Fund's staff begin to recognize the policy norm socially and, with World Bank and NGO pressure, push for its institutionalization. Thus, despite considerable intellectual and institutional resistance, multilateral debt relief began to gain social acceptance within the Fund.

Norm building: external support for debt relief

In the early 1980s, the debt incurred by many of the world's poorest countries was rapidly increasing. As former UK Executive Director to the IMF Huw Evans noted, the international community had believed that these debtors were hurting but could pay back in time. Markets, however, were more pessimistic than state governments, marking down the face value of many of these states' commercial debts by significant margins. The UK and Sweden were sympathetic to the issue of debt relief, and the two norm advocates took the idea forward to the Paris Club in an effort to share the burden of the initiative with other official creditors (Evans 1999). By the mid-1980s, the Paris Club considered rescheduling debt by extending the terms of payment and adjusting interest rates, but a policy for multilateral debt relief was often rejected as it was believed that giving debt relief to countries with poor policies would promote free-riding and moral hazards; debt relief would not provide a long-term fix to the underlying policy issue and debt could be repaid over time (Evans 1999). In other words, Western creditors believed that the debtors had a liquidity problem but were not actually insolvent. Moreover, economic research had not concluded that cutting debt could result in either reduced poverty or improved economic growth (Evans 1999). Up until the late 1980s, the consensus in the economic profession was not conducive to the idea of multilateral debt relief.

However, by the late 1980s bilateral debt relief was being endorsed and championed by the US administration but only for select countries deemed to be of geostrategic importance, namely middle-income countries in the backyard of the USA. The 1989 Brady plan, for example, was envisioned to help key Latin American countries overcome their immense debt owed to commercial banks through the use of 'Brady Bonds'. The United States also orchestrated a large debt relief through the Paris Club for Egypt in 1991, in exchange for Egypt's contribution of military forces to the US-led coalition in the first Gulf War (Momani 2004). As Evans describes, by the early 1990s, support for official and bilateral debt relief increasingly coalesced and the external normative environment showed signs of being ripe for change. The United States, for example, started to revise its views on debt relief with support from the Clinton administration, the sympathy of Treasury Secretaries Lawrence Summers and Robert Rubin, the pressure of NGOs on the US Congress, and the precedent of the generous debt forgiveness given to Latin America, Egypt and Poland (Evans 1999). The United States began to internalize the idea that high levels of official and bilateral debt were harmful to US geopolitical interests.

In addition, at the fiftieth anniversary of the Bretton Woods organizations, the UK's Chancellor of the Exchequer, Kenneth Clarke (with the Dutch and Nordic states), took a debt relief proposal to the 1994 spring meetings of the IMF and the World Bank (Evans 1999). Soon after, a number of European NGOs, led by Eurodad, Oxfam and Novib, met to develop a common position on how best to spread ideas on debt relief by raising the question of whether the multilateral creditors should keep their preferred creditor status. Writing a common letter to the Group of Seven meeting in Naples in early July, the NGOs agreed that the IMF and World Bank should have a preferred creditor status, but should not be exempt from debt relief efforts (Bokkerink and Van Hees 1998). Bowing to the external pressure of advocates for debt relief, the G7 responded with the Naples Terms of up to 67 per cent debt relief on bilateral debt through the Paris Club. The G7 would now pressure the Bretton Woods organizations also to formulate a policy position.

The IMF and World Bank began studying the question of extending official and bilateral debt relief to the multilateral debt held by these institutions. As bilateral debt relief and restructuring started taking form, the debt stock of heavily indebted poor countries changed. As bilateral aid started to be delivered to HIPCs in the form of grants instead of loans, the share of debt owed to multilaterals increased (Birdsall and Williamson 2002). By 1996, those later identified as heavily indebted poor countries were paying nearly half of their debt payments to multilateral creditors (see Figure 2.1); moreover, 30 per cent of the long-term debt stock of these countries was owed to multilateral creditors (Bokkerink and Van Hees 1998). The issue of multilateral debt relief could no longer be ignored nor be discounted as a small portion of the HIPCs' overall debt stock.

Both the IMF and the World Bank management had issued studies that would help them to continue to defend their 'preferred creditor status', which in effect meant that the IMF's loans and interest would be paid before outstanding loans to commercial banks (many of which were represented by the London Club) and to official creditors (many of the

a Total external debt

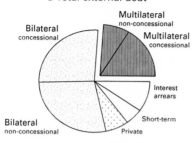

Total external debt: US$230.2 billion

b Multilateral debt

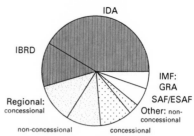

Total multilateral debt: US$55.5 billion

c Present value of total external debt

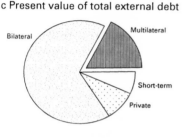

Total present value: US$192 billion

d Present value of multilateral debt

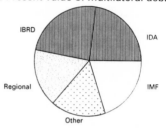

Total present value: US$34 billion

Figure 2.1 HIPC debt, 1993

Source: IMF 1995f: *Multilateral Debt of the Heavily Indebted Poor Countries* (Washington, DC: IMF Archives) (9 February) SM/95/30:5.

Western countries that were represented in the Paris Club).[1] The IMF and World Bank issued a joint paper on 7 February 1995 noting that 'there is no evidence of an unmanageable hump of debt servicing to the multi-laterals for the vast majority of heavily indebted poor countries, and multilateral institutions as a group can continue to provide positive net transfers without adverse implications for debt service profiles for the foreseeable future' (IMF 1995b: 2). The IMF and World Bank resisted the multilateral debt relief norm. In response, the NGO community highlighted the errors in using optimistic growth projections used by the IMF/World Bank staff in their analysis. It appeared that as preferred creditors, the IMF and World Bank management had strategic interests

---

[1] While the Bretton Woods institutions' preferred creditor status is not enshrined in interna-tional law, it has been understood and implicitly accepted by Fund members. Both commercial and official creditors accepted that the IMF loans and interest would be repaid before theirs in case of a sovereign debt crisis. Had the Sovereign Debt Restructuring Mechanism been enacted at the Fund, the legal basis of the Fund's preferred creditor status would have been enshrined.

in underplaying the overhang of multilateral debt. On these grounds NGOs began to engage the Bretton Woods institutions on their own terms, allowing multilateral debt repayment to be questioned on empirical grounds, showing that debt relief was more than a social cause.

At the IMF Executive Board meeting on 24 February, the reaction to the IMF/World Bank joint paper remained mixed. The UK, the Dutch and the Nordic-Baltic countries pressured others to consider more active engagement on multilateral debt relief. At the board meeting, the UK Executive Director, Huw Evans, stated: 'My conclusion is that the problem is more serious than the Fund staff paper admits. And that the Fund has a role in resolving this problem' (IMF 1995d: 8). Those who were mild supporters of the idea and yet remained worried about the implications of debt relief for the Fund's mandate included the United States, Canada, China, Switzerland and Australia. Canada's Executive Director, Ian Clark, responded to the study, saying: 'the analysis loads most of the responsibility for alleviating the debt burden onto bilateral creditors through the Paris club stock-of-debt reduction programme and onto multilateral lenders other than the IMF ... the IMF and World Bank cannot be grant agencies. Nevertheless, these multilateral credit organizations cannot ignore the fact that their interest charges, regardless of how concessionary, divert some productive resources away from the debtor country' (IMF 1995d: 14). The Germans, French, Italians and Japanese remained hesitant in supporting multilateral debt relief at the meeting. As France's Executive Director had stated, 'I draw the following conclusion from this excellent set of papers: our strategy remains valid' (IMF 1995d: 15). The Germans took the hardest stance against the idea of debt relief. The German Alternate Executive Director, von Kleist, stated: 'We are ... quite uncomfortable with the fact that in the papers the Fund, which is a monetary institution, is not distinguished clearly enough from the various multilateral development institutions ... [and] we agree with the staff's conclusion that there is no evidence of a widespread problem of multilateral debt among the heavily indebted poor countries' (IMF 1995d: 54–5).

The mixed reaction to the staff paper at the IMF Board started to prompt debate outside the meeting. Eventually the second, hesitant board group were persuaded by fellow board members and their respective NGOs of the merits of a multilateral debt relief policy norm; however, the third group of resisters – including the Germans, French, Italians and Japanese – continued to fight forcefully against the idea (Callaghy 2002). The mixed reaction to the first joint set of IMF/World Bank studies prompted the Executive Directors to ask for further IMF and World Bank staff analysis of the issues.

The subsequent 31 March joint report revised some of the optimistic assumptions used in the growth projections of the February report and qualified the assumptions made in estimating the size of the multilateral debt burden, but the basic conclusion of the February report remained unchanged: multilateral debt was still sustainable and therefore not a problem (IMF 1995c). The IMF Managing Director, Michel Camdessus, proposed expanding the purview of the Enhanced Structural Adjustment Facility (ESAF) to give more loans on better concessional terms through the use of the Fund's own gold resources. This did not appease some of the forceful proponents of multilateral debt relief. Huw Evans made the most vigorous argument for change: 'These [HIPC] countries should not have to rely on repeated Fund lending solely to cover their debts to this institution. And the Managing Director's approach ignores the very real problems that stem from debt overhang' (IMF 1995e: 10). The Americans supported the British, as Karin Lissakers noted:

I have to say that I think we have a problem. It is not a big problem for the institution, it is not a big problem for the world economy, but it is a big problem for a small number of member countries in this institution and the multilateral development banks. I think it is time we acknowledge that. The staff paper dances around that issue a little bit. But the facts speak for themselves, as Mr Evans has argued very effectively ... He lays out the case very strongly and I endorse his statements. (IMF 1995e: 26–7)

On the other extreme, the Germans continued to argue vehemently against IMF involvement in 'development issues' and rejected the idea of using IMF gold sales to finance ESAF. The Board remained deadlocked, but the United States was indeed becoming increasingly persuaded by the UK's arguments and the case for a more aggressive debt relief policy. With the United States holding a veto at the IMF Executive Board and the need for management to encapsulate the essence of the meeting and put forward ideas that would produce consensus at the board, the IMF's voting rules and procedures would present an important opportunity to carve a space for the creation of the multilateral debt relief policy norm.

In the critical months after the second joint report, tension between the IMF and the World Bank grew on the issue of debt relief. Here we see the external normative environment slowly changing in favour of multilateral debt relief. The World Bank was being increasingly persuaded by NGO analysis, while IMF management and hardline members of the IMF Board continued to stick to the long-held position of downplaying the multilateral debt problem (Bokkerink and Van Hees 1998). The World

Bank was becoming increasingly sympathetic to the idea of debt relief as President James Wolfensohn, who took the helm on 1 June 1995, was trying to find his own *raison d'être* (Mallaby 2004). Wolfensohn, in many ways a norm entrepreneur in favour of progressive change at the Bank, had authorized a small World Bank working group to study quietly the issue of debt sustainability and multilateral debt. The working group fought to challenge the idea that debtors were illiquid but not insolvent, producing a critical report in June that called for a more comprehensive approach to debt relief (Callaghy 2002).

The World Bank working group, led by the Chief of the International Finance Division, Nawal Kamel, had recommended the creation of a Multilateral Debt Facility (MDF), to be used by twenty indebted countries, which would be funded by bilateral and multilateral donors (including the World Bank's and IMF's own revenue). This would not be a direct write-off of bad debts, but rather a drawing down of a special trust fund used to pay the principal of HIPC debt. The proposal, however, would not require countries to have IMF/World Bank programmes in place; in other words, the IMF would not be using their performance benchmarks to determine continued debt relief (Hertz 2004). The MDF proposal was leaked to the media in September 1995 and the IMF's response was highly critical. Stanley Fischer, Deputy Managing Director at the IMF, was reportedly 'furious at the prospect of debt relief going to these countries at all' (Hertz 2004: 114). An IMF official told the *Financial Times* that 'the Fund would not get involved ... This would undermine the Fund's position and credibility. Writing off debt is not our business', while describing the report as 'ideologically unsound' (Holman 1995: 6). Clearly, the idea of unconditional debt relief was incompatible with the staff's belief system and organizational culture. External World Bank pressure to develop a debt relief policy was rejected by Fund management and staff. Meanwhile, IMF staff had circulated their own study to the IMF Executive Board which reiterated the point that most low-income country debt stock was sustainable. To be sure, the IMF remained reluctant to alter its performance criteria – as outsiders were urging – in a way that would make debt relief compatible with the staff's mandate. It did caution, however, that for a few low-income countries the status quo would be insufficient to have countries exit their debt situation (IMF 1995h: iv).

Without the IMF, the MDF proposal would have little value, particularly because IMF loans have significantly shorter repayment terms than those of the World Bank (Evans 1999). After very public squabbling between the IMF and the World Bank on the matter (Callaghy 2002; Graham and Flanders 1995), the two organizations were asked by the Interim Development Committee to have joint studies on the issue of debt relief ready for the 1996 spring meetings. This may have been further prompted by US Treasury Secretary Lawrence Summers who reportedly told both Camdessus and Wolfensohn that the IMF/World Bank squabbling in the media needed to be stopped (Hertz 2004). Despite support among a few of the IMF shareholders and the World Bank for the adoption of debt relief as a policy norm – a policy that would accept the empirical evidence in favour of the multilateral debt relief norm – the idea was widely criticized on principle within the Fund management and generally among the IMF staff for its incompatibility with the organization's mandate and culture. The analytical approach preferred by Fund staff did not reveal a fundamental need for multilateral debt relief. Nevertheless, the Development Committee asked for detailed and country-specific analysis of the HIPCs' debt situation. Top-down political pressure was building on the IMF staff.

Opposing debt relief to devising the HIPC policy norm

Based on a detailed and comprehensive document-analysis of IMF papers, acquired through the IMF archives, this chapter now moves to open the black box of the IMF's internal decision-making process in the lead up to the HIPC proposal. To recap briefly, the IMF staff and key IMF shareholders had resisted the multilateral debt relief norm for a number of years despite changes in the external normative environment and endorsement among prominent IMF shareholders. At an impasse, the IMF and World Bank staff were asked again jointly to study and report on the subject in the autumn of 1995 and to report jointly to their respective Executive Boards in January 1996. In particular, the staff were asked to use country-specific factors and move beyond 'illustrative scenarios' and 'stylized assumptions' (IMF 1996b: 4).

Two joint studies were prepared and were to be discussed at the IMF Executive Board on 20 February 1996. The first report, *Debt Sustainability Analysis for the HIPC*, studied the debt situation of forty-one countries on an individual basis.[2] The staff argued that eight countries had unsustainable debt, twelve were deemed to be 'possibly stressed' and fourteen were classified as having 'sustainable debt' (IMF 1996b: 9). In the second report, *Analytical Aspects of the Debt Problems of HIPC*, the staff raised a series of theoretical issues and considerations regarding the debt situation of the HIPC. The report tried to answer the question of whether HIPC debt was sustainable without repeated rescheduling. Simply, would

---

[2] Although there were detailed analyses for only twenty-three of the forty-one countries, the remainder being preliminary suggestions.

HIPCs be able to pay back their multilateral debt? The staff raised some doubts as to the certainty of an answer by stating that 'a good deal of judgment is required in arriving at such an assessment' (IMF 1996a: iii). This was a departure from findings in previous reports which affirmed the ability of HIPCs to repay. This report also raised the question of whether moral hazards would arise as a result of debt relief. In keeping with the technocratic IMF organizational culture and the conservative economistic belief system, the staff responded by proposing an increased oversight role in dealing with the HIPCs:

A potential advantage of refinancing/rescheduling (accompanied by conditionality) relative to explicit up front debt reduction may be that by allowing the Fund and the Bank to constantly monitor policy performance in the indebted country, it leads to better policies and less moral hazard problems. With [*sic*] a strategy of granting debt reduction after a good track record is established, on the other hand, multilateral creditors may lose their ability to influence policy after the initial period. (IMF 1996a: 14)

The staff therefore suggested that conditionality and policy monitoring could help allay the potentially negative effects of moral hazards. They cautioned, however, that this 'short-leash approach' could compromise policy ownership among the HIPCs. Nevertheless, the IMF staff would endorse a debt relief policy norm if they could effectively devise and monitor the HIPC initiative. Based on the findings of the first report, one could infer that the IMF staff found that at least eight countries could be helped with some measure of debt relief combined with conditionality. The staff had emphasized that a case-by-case approach would be needed in determining country circumstances and they had not recommended a wide-reaching mechanism that would provide debt relief to all HIPCs. Again, in keeping with their technocratic organizational culture, the Fund staff wanted absolute control in determining country eligibility for debt relief. From reading the documents, it may be inferred that the staff refrained from making too many policy recommendations; instead, they waited for the Board to deliberate and discuss the staff findings.

Prior to the scheduled IMF Executive Board meeting to discuss the findings of the staff reports, the Managing Director, UK Director Huw Evans and World Bank representatives attended a meeting in London an 12 February on the problem of multilateral debt. The meeting was hosted by the Catholic Church in England, led by the Archbishop of Westminster, Cardinal George Basil Hume. Michel Camdessus was reported to have been deeply affected by the meeting as he came 'face to face with the hostility of world Catholic leaders toward the institution he led and its economic policies' (Pettifor 2006; also see Boughton

2001: 11). When Camdessus returned to report to the Board a few days later, he noted that during the London meeting he was 'arguing against the need for a special facility' (IMF 1996d: 3). Evans countered, however, that 'the seminar participants had concluded that there was a need for further action by both the Fund and the Bank, beyond present instruments' (IMF 1996d: 3). External normative pressure on the Fund intensified.

The Board met on 20 February 1996 to discuss the two papers. The UK's Huw Evans opened the meeting by reiterating the need for the Fund to develop a policy for the emerging multilateral debt relief norm. Evans noted that the IMF staff papers were too optimistic, a view shared by the Canadians and the Americans. The US Director Karin Lissakers made the strongest attempt to persuade other Board members on debt relief, noting that '[w]e do not want these countries to be perpetual welfare cases, but that is really what we are talking about here' (IMF 1996e: 29). The French, Germans and Japanese, however, took opposite stances by noting that the staff refrained from calling the situation an all-out debt crisis. Using selected staff findings to support their position, the three states opposed the idea of a special mechanism that would provide universal debt relief to the HIPCs. Perhaps the strongest consensus among the protagonists was around the belief that the IMF needed to apply conditionality to future financing and that a 'short-leash' approach of continuous staff monitoring would be needed in devising an initiative. As France's Director put it, 'good economic policy matters more than debt' and 'there is no serious alternative to conditionality' (IMF 1996e: 11–12). These were among the strongest points of consensus in the otherwise divided Board. Taking advantage of a divided Board that also requires management, by rules and regulations of the IMF, to bring forth decisions made on a 'consensual basis', the staff would autonomously devise a policy for the strengthening of multilateral debt relief.

Building on the framework of the Paris Club mechanism of rescheduling debt, the IMF and World Bank staff proposed the HIPC policy framework that would involve debt reduction in two graduated steps, spanning six years. Debt relief would be 'back-loaded' and this could result in up to 90 per cent debt relief at the Paris Club, and this would be matched by other bilateral and commercial creditors, provided that the countries remained under the purview of the IMF and World Bank to the very end of their 'graduation'. Once the debtors received debt relief from their other creditors, then the IMF would help them achieve debt levels deemed sustainable (based on net present value of debt to exports). The IMF and World Bank would also convene a group of countries to provide 'a financing plan' that would help the HIPCs achieve debt sustainability targets set by the IMF and World Bank staff by contributing into the ESAF facility. The staff noted, moreover, 'the options considered for easing the burden of multilateral debt all involve the original claims being repaid in one way or another – there is no proposal to write off (or down) multilateral debt' (IMF 1996h: 4).

The IMF and World Bank staff's HIPC plan met the Board's key concerns about preserving the IMF's preferred creditor status while proposing a policy that would correspond to the emerging multilateral debt relief norm. The staff's suggestions for a graduated programme whereby the staff would continuously monitor and approve HIPC eligible members' progress on meeting set targets had also addressed concerns over moral hazards and free-riding behaviour. Canada, the UK and the USA tried to persuade other Board members that the proposed HIPC policy was still deemed to be 'institutionally too conservative' and that 'the sequential timing is too long. It is neither economically effective and efficient nor politically sustainable' (IMF 1996f: 7, 18). The USA noted that governments that implemented hard reforms would not be rewarded with debt relief because governments would not see debt relief during their tenure. But Camdessus countered that 'leaders could be reappointed or re-elected' (IMF 1996f: 19). The US Executive Director and the Managing Director continued to go back and forth in disagreement on the sequencing of debt relief and the ability of the HIPC polities to sustain the graduated process of debt relief. Germany, France and Japan continued to reject the underlying norm of the HIPC policy. Without a Board consensus on the HIPC policy, the Managing Director asked the staff to move forward and propose actionable policies. The staff, in collaboration with the World Bank staff, held firm on their existing policy and a few weeks later would propose to the Board a nearly identical course of action: graduated, two-step, back-loaded debt relief over six years from the ESAF. This time, however, the staff proposed more action items for the Paris Club and less discussion of the Fund's involvement in HIPCs.

When the Executive Board met again on 8 April 1996, to discuss the revised, yet essentially unchanged, staff recommendations for a HIPC policy, the US Director spoke first and forcefully criticized the staff. Lissakers noted that she was 'disappointed in the staff paper currently under consideration' (IMF 1996g: 3) and she continued to highlight the fact that the staff did not take into consideration concerns raised in previous meetings; instead the staff 'seemed to retreat' from 'ambitious' ideas in previous reports. Directors continued to disagree on the staff report, some believing the report was too conservative and others believing that it was too risky.

A number of directors, with agreement from the Managing Director, suggested that the staff's HIPC policy be presented to the Interim Committee as a proposal endorsed by management while not mentioning the Executive Board (IMF 1996g: 3). Camdessus noted that '[a]lthough the management of the World Bank and the Fund were willing to take full responsibility for the proposed report to the Interim Committee, every effort had been made to reflect the views expressed by executive directors in that report' (IMF 1996g: 5). The deadlock in the Board resulted in the staff and management getting their way. Fund staff and management were able to take advantage of the Board's divisions and move their preferred policy norm forward for its institutionalization. The top-down pressure from the IMFC to have the Fund devise a policy plan in less than a year and the external normative environment in favour of multilateral debt relief were important points of pressure on management and the Board to bring forth actionable policy. The criticisms most forcefully raised by the United States and the United Kingdom were not addressed; namely, the prolonged and back-loaded nature of debt relief under the HIPC initiative. The HIPC proposal was presented to the Interim Committee meeting a few weeks later as a proposal from management for a 'framework of action'. The same proposal was submitted and approved at the September 1996 annual meetings of the IMF and World Bank. IMF management and staff, despite the disagreement of the Executive Board, had the approval of the Interim Committee to proceed with the HIPC initiative. This way, the staff were able to adapt to the normative environment, which seemed to pull in the direction of multilateral debt relief, without compromising their own organizational culture and mandate.

IMF staff push for a limited version of the HIPC initiative

Eventually, the HIPC initiative was endorsed by the IMF Board of Governors in September 1996. The IMF staff could not draft a proposal that would meet the interests and needs of its strongest shareholders. The United States and the United Kingdom wanted a broader and more ambitious policy that would have seen greater debt relief. This was a position generally endorsed by many of the developing country members and by Canada and the Nordic states. The USA also wanted the IMF to use its own resources to pay for the ESAF contribution. Germany, France and Japan wanted to curtail the initiative as much as possible and did not want to see the use of Fund resources to finance the ESAF. They were also the most resistant to the multilateral debt relief norm. This can be partly explained by the fact that HIPCs owed a significant portion of their

Table 2.1 *G7 debt holdings, 1998–9*

	Canada	France	Germany	Italy	Japan	UK	USA
Bilateral claim – 40 countries (US$ millions)	711	13,033	6,586	4,311	11,200	3,092	6,210
As % of GDP	0.1	0.9	0.3	0.4	0.3	0.2	0.08
As % of G7 claims	1.57	28.9	14.6	9.5	24.8	6.8	13.8

Source: Busby (2007: 260).

bilateral debt to these three states (see Table 2.1). The strategic concerns of these three countries were unmoved despite the normative suasion of others at the Board.

The case of how the HIPC policy norm was eventually institutionalized cannot be explained, however, by examining external material power and strategic interests. Had this been the case, the HIPC initiative would have been forced on the Fund, as an exogenous policy imposition. Instead, the case of multilateral debt relief gained ascendance through consensus-building efforts and normative suasion. In the end, it would have to be accepted by the IMF staff, reflecting the growing social recognition of multilateral debt relief as a policy norm that can contribute to economic growth. Moreover, there is no shortage of studies that have shown how IMF policies and decisions have been determined by US geostrategic interests (Momani 2004; Stone 2002). Despite their global and IMF voting power, the United States and the United Kingdom were unable to shape the HIPC policy norm into the form that they had envisioned. Again, the institutionalized HIPC policy norm was one that resonated with the IMF's cultural constraints, despite American and British attempts to persuade other Executive Directors to accept a more comprehensive debt relief proposal. On numerous occasions, the US and the UK Directors tried also to persuade the staff to find more countries in need of debt relief by questioning the assumptions used in their studies and by prompting more in-depth country-level studies. This widened the net regarding what staff deemed to be countries with unsustainable debt.

One external factor that did have an impact on the IMF staff and their studies was the social influence of the World Bank staff. Indeed, in the critical year when the IMF staff worked with the World Bank to devise a set of policy proposals to present to the Interim Committee, there is evidence of a shift in IMF staff views on debt relief. The IMF staff moved away from arguing that there was no debt problem to a position where they agreed that, indeed, there was a real inescapable multilateral debt problem for some countries. While there is little evidence that the

IMF staff ever internalized the need for comprehensive debt relief per se, there is evidence that they did recognize multilateral debt as a problem for selected countries, which signals a substantial step in this direction. Giving the staff an opportunity to study the issue in depth seemed to be an important turning point in its social recognition of multilateral debt relief. This process has also had to fit with the Fund's technocratic organizational culture that emphasizes problem-solving through technical and macroeconomic analysis. Bluntly put, moral suasion alone would not have worked to persuade the staff of the merits of a multilateral debt relief norm, but – in a similar way to the case of the social development norm (Vetterlein, chapter 5, this volume) – the opportunity to come to a 'scientific' and technical analysis of the problem was a key means of helping the staff socially recognize the multilateral debt relief policy norm and allowed them to propose the HIPC initiative, albeit in a limited form. In this context, multilateral debt relief is best understood as an emerging norm that takes shape gradually, rather than wholly subsuming pre-existing practices.

It is also argued that having the IMF staff work with the World Bank staff helped shape the outcome of the policy proposals. Others have noted how World Bank President Wolfensohn helped to champion debt relief within his organization (Mallaby 2004). Co-operation between the IMF and World Bank staff in devising studies for the Executive Boards had helped persuade the IMF staff towards a more sympathetic position on multilateral debt relief. The IMF staff did prove to be somewhat permeable to new ideas, but based on inferences from the staff and Board documents, the staff and management also managed to limit powerful members' pressure for a more comprehensive debt relief proposal by dominating the middle position in Board meetings. This is indicative of a broader process of normative adaptation, whereby norm advocates, including powerful actors like the USA, as well as NGOs, had to persuade the sceptical IMF staff of the technical merits of multilateral debt relief.

The HIPC initiative would require a strong involvement of IMF staff in monitoring and graduating debt relief recipients; this was a departure from the World Bank's MDF proposal of June 2005 which did not require HIPC debt relief recipients to have an IMF programme in place. Clearly, it was important to the IMF staff to have control over graduating borrowers that used the HIPC initiative. Despite powerful members' concerns over conditionality and a loss of country ownership, the IMF staff reiterated the need to monitor sound economic policies. They continued to point out that the HIPCs' need for sound economic policies outweighed the rationale for debt relief. Here the IMF staff played an important role in persuading shareholders that heavily indebted poor countries would not free-ride if kept under an IMF programme. This in part supports a constructivist argument for the need better to appreciate the internal workings and culture of the IMF. Opening the 'black box' of the IMF helped to reveal how ideas generated in a strategic and normative environment are then filtered throughout an organization with a distinct culture and unique governance structure to allow for the emergence of the multilateral debt relief policy norm through an endogenously adopted HIPC initiative.

The IMF staff's noted expertise and position of 'authority' did play a key role in determining the final shape of the HIPC initiative (Barnett and Finnemore 2004). As also seen in other chapters in this volume, the IMF staff have intellectual dominance within the organization, and despite the normative suasion used by powerful Board members, they were able to capitalize further on Board divisions to push through a policy that resonated with their organizational culture. The Executive Board's reliance on the IMF staff as the gatekeepers of information and data in the organization is a crucial part of explaining how the IMF staff and management were able to determine the shape and form of the multilateral debt relief policy norm. Without opening the 'black box' of the IMF, the story about the emergence of the HIPC policy norm would remain half told.

Conclusion

Despite the external normative environment in favour of multilateral debt relief and the normative suasion of powerful members at the IMF Executive Board, the IMF staff and management were able to endorse the HIPC policy norm in a way that resonated with its belief system and organizational culture. This case suggests that the IMF staff indeed have intellectual dominance within the organization and, despite external pressures to shape the content of the HIPC initiative, once they undertook analysis of possible multilateral debt relief they were able to keep their vision of the initiative intact: strong, back-loaded conditionality that would be given in a graduated process and monitored by the IMF staff.

Despite its emergence in 1996, the HIPC policy norm has yet to stabilize. Member states continued to resist the policy norm, while others championed its extension and expansion. However, the multilateral debt relief norm has not been static since it has taken root and, just as it has been modified by the IMF, has continued to evolve since implementation and has become substantively transformed, in many ways. The Jubilee 2000 campaign successfully challenged the failures of the HIPC initiative, noting the lack of ownership in many countries and its failure to graduate borrowers. In 1999, the HIPC initiative was transformed into 'enhanced HIPC', or HIPC II, after successful moral suasion by the Jubilee 2000 campaign on powerful states (Busby 2007). The 1999 enhanced HIPC lowered the threshold of debt-to-export ratio from 200–250 to 150 per cent, removed the ex-ante conditionality, and required debtors to adopt a national consultation process to produce a consensual debt strategy document called the Poverty Reduction Strategy Papers. The Multilateral Debt Relief Initiative, again, continued to transform HIPC II. These post-HIPC initiatives were successful grassroots-level campaigns that tried to persuade Western governments to strengthen and extend the HIPC initiative. These subsequent initiatives showed more signs of a holistic approach to development than the HIPC policy norm institutionalized by the IMF staff in 1996. Accordingly, the multilateral debt relief norm continues to evolve today, showing more signs of transformation than of decay.

3   From three to five: the World Bank's pension reform policy norm

Veronika Wodsak and Martin Koch

Introduction

The problem of old age security and the resulting World Bank suggestions for pension system design emerged as a hot topic in the development community in the 1990s.[1] After the fast ascension of the World Bank's three-pillar pension reform model[2] as the state of the art in the early 1990s, external criticism as well as experiences on the ground led the Bank to reformulate its position and suggest a five-pillar pension reform model in 2005. This chapter traces the origins of the Bank's engagement in pension reform and the development of a three-pillar pension model, which was still rooted in the old Washington Consensus of fiscal discipline, reordering public expenditure priorities and securing property rights (see chapter 1). The chapter then traces the emergence of a global old age security policy norm that takes the steps of the norm circle into account (as outlined in chapter 1). In particular, criticism of the Bank's suggestions and the subsequent reformulation of the three-pillar model within the Bank are discussed. This process of norm contestation through arguing and negotiation over the norm's meaning and value contributes to its broader social acceptance and stabilization (Wiener 2009: 12). As demonstrated below, the policy norm of old age security is now in the stabilization phase: statutory pensions provided by, or regulated by, the state through

---

[1] This chapter is based on interviews and participatory observations conducted by one of the authors during a research stay at the World Bank's Social Development Department between February and September 2005. All quotations stem from interviews conducted with staff from the Social Protection Unit during that period unless otherwise indicated.

[2] The term 'multi-pillar' is used in the World Bank's (1994a) *Averting the Old Age Crisis: Policies to Protect the Old and Promote Growth* report, discussed throughout the chapter, rather than 'three-pillar'. However, the report suggests a three-pillar design and secondary literature discusses the model presented in the *Averting* report under the label 'three-pillar model'. In this chapter, the term 'three-pillar' refers to the approach outlined in the *Averting* report, to distinguish this from the 'five-pillar' design suggested in subsequent Bank publications (World Bank 2005h). 'Multi-pillar' is used as a generic term to refer to the general idea of diversifying risks by introducing several schemes to address the contingency of longevity without any specific number or design of pillars in mind.

multi-pillar pension systems have come to be taken for granted as a policy norm around the world regardless of a country's level of development. The Bank's shift to a less rigid five-pillar model is much more in tune with the holistic approach to development that includes pro-poor growth, equitable development and poverty alleviation. The chapter thus speaks to the three main points of this book: first, identifying the sources and mechanisms of policy change and norm creation in international organizations (IOs); second, tracing the different steps of norm strength and development through the norm circle; and third, relating the Bank's pension policy norm to a broader, more holistic approach to development.

Over the past two decades, we have witnessed a wave of pension reforms around the globe in industrialized and developing countries alike (Brooks 2005; Madrid 2005; Melo 2004; Orenstein 2005). These reforms were ushered in with lively debates on the best way to design old age security systems (see Barr 1994, 2006; Beattie and McGillivray 1995; Deacon *et al.* 1997; ILO 2000; E. James 1996, 1997a, 1997b, 1998; James *et al.* 2001; Tausch 2003), at domestic and global levels, in academia and IOs, and amongst policy-makers of low-, middle- and high-income countries. The dominant approach to pension reform until the early 1990s was to conduct parametric reforms, which kept publicly managed pay-as-you-go (PAYG) systems in place but changed the parameters of the system so as to accommodate current trends. For example, this included increasing contribution rates, decreasing benefit levels and increasing the retirement age. The debates throughout the 1990s went beyond questions of parametric reforms, addressing not just issues of how to adjust pension systems to cope with the demographic change of ageing societies but also the relative advantages and disadvantages of funded versus PAYG systems. The World Bank and its 1994 report *Averting the Old Age Crisis: Policies to Protect the Old and Promote Growth* (1994a) was highly influential in these debates.

The Bank quickly took the lead in the global discourse on pensions, developing pension projects in more than eighty countries (twenty-two of which conducted three-pillar reforms and established a funded pillar) between 1994 and 2004. Moreover, following an intensive dissemination effort, the 1994 report was referred to in conferences and quoted in almost three hundred journal articles over the same period. Many other countries, including high-income countries, conducted pension reforms in line with the Bank's recommendations independent of Bank projects.[3]

---

[3] This is not to say that these pension reforms can all be exclusively attributed to the Bank's influence. Weyland (2004, 2006) has convincingly demonstrated that 'contagion' from

The Bank's shift to conceptualize old age security as a *global* challenge for developed and developing countries alike, as well as the overall approach of diversifying risks by introducing multiple pillars, was universally embraced by policy-makers and academics throughout the development and social policy communities. However, the details of the Bank's recommendations, especially the idea of abandoning PAYG financing and the emphasis on funding and privatization of pension funds, provoked criticism from different epistemic communities as well as other IOs, especially the International Labour Organization (ILO) (e.g. Barr 1994, 2000; Beattie and McGillivray 1995; Holzmann and Stiglitz 2001; Merrien 2001; Orszag and Stiglitz 2001).[4] Recent publications adopt a slightly different tone, with the Bank seemingly apprehensive of the shortcomings of funding, paying more attention to the question of adequate benefit levels and being relatively open to a variety of possible reform and design choices overall. At the same time, its initial pro-funding message is now less contested as advocates of pay-as-you-go systems are becoming increasingly used to the idea that many countries opt for funded systems and that this may be a good choice under certain conditions (Cichon 2004; Queisser 2000). This chapter looks at these recent developments as part of the emergence of old age security as a policy norm.

For this investigation, the chapter seeks to enrich the norm circle with conceptions from organizational studies, specifically an open systems approach (Ness and Brechin 1988; Scott 1992). Theories of International Relations often characterize IOs either as *arenas* where states negotiate new agreements or as *actors* that influence states' behaviour (Rittberger and Zangl 2006). These two metaphors are insufficient to analyse the norm-setting behaviour of IOs. The state-centric focus on relations between states and IOs neglects other organizational factors and external influences that affected the norm's emergence in the form of the multi-pillar pension model, especially the impact that criticism from academics, non-governmental organizations (NGOs) and other development actors has on World Bank thinking (Barnett and Finnemore 2004; Ness and Brechin 1988). From an *open* systems perspective organizations are not closed systems separated from their environment, 'but are open to and dependent on flows of personnel, resources, and information from

---

Chile to other countries in the region rather than influence of international financial institutions played an important role in the diffusion of pension reform policies in Latin America. However, the World Bank certainly acted as a catalyst and, through its high-level publications with wide distribution circles, presented data and arguments that informed many domestic policy debates.

[4] Epistemic communities are defined as a 'network of professionals with recognized expertise and competence in a particular domain and an authoritative claim to policy-relevant knowledge within that domain or issue-area' (Haas 1992: 3).

outside' (Scott 1992: 25). The organization is shaped, supported and infiltrated by its environment. The environment is the basic source for the system's survival because it consists of the necessary resources and elements the organization needs to operate. Besides resources, the environment also consists of institutions. Enacting these institutions, that is, adjusting to the environment, is a source of legitimacy for organizations and increases their social acceptance and scope of influence (Meyer and Rowan 1977). This conceptual framework can be used to demonstrate that the World Bank's multi-pillar pension model shapes policy reforms in many states, while simultaneously the Bank has to react to external criticisms articulated by other IOs, academics and NGOs that led to a revision of the three-pillar pension model in order for the World Bank to survive as a legitimate development actor in the pension debate.

Furthermore, the organization is conceived of not as a monolithic entity but as a body composed of individuals/groups of individuals, units and departments that have 'differing interests and value various inducements. They join and leave or engage in ongoing exchanges with the organization ... Viewed from this perspective, participants cannot be assumed to hold common goals or even to routinely seek the survival of the organization' (Scott 1992: 25). In this respect organizations host a variety of systems of (more or less) independent activities; '[s]ome of these activities are tightly connected; others are loosely coupled' (Scott 1992: 25). This theoretical framework allows us to capture the complex processes within the Bank and between the Bank and other actors in their environment.

Applying an open system organizational concept means, on the one hand, to differentiate between an organization and its external environment that encompasses 'everything outside the organization' (Mintzberg 1979: 267) and, on the other hand, to acknowledge the complexities of the internal environment of organizations. Externally, not every part of the environment affects the organization; we are only interested in the relevant environment of the World Bank, that is, those aspects that the organization perceives as relevant. The relevant environment of the Bank consists not only of states but also of other IOs (such as the International Monetary Fund (IMF), ILO and World Trade Organization (WTO)), NGOs and epistemic communities (Park 2005b; Reinalda and Verbeek 2001). On the other hand, we also analyse the internal environment of the Bank. The Bank consists of different individuals and groups of individuals following their own agendas within the organization (Cox and Jacobson 1999). Taking both perspectives together in one model allows us to analyse the impact of external influences and inner-organizational decision-making processes on the emergence and stabilization of the old age security policy norm simultaneously.

Emergence of the pension reform policy norm

In pre-modern and early modern societies, the elderly were taken care of through informal arrangements, often within the extended family. In Europe, formal arrangements for the elderly and the sick are typically attributed to Bismarckian times. Although very modest, Bismarckian schemes were the first public arrangements creating entitlements for pensioners (as opposed to charity or private arrangements). The first Old Age Insurance conventions, 35 and 36 passed by the ILO, date back to 1933 and were later replaced by the Social Security Minimum Standards Convention 102, and the Invalidity, Old Age and Survivors' Benefit Convention 128 of 1952 and 1967 respectively. However, these initial international efforts towards establishing old age security systems suffered from a Eurocentric bias. The ratification rates remain low for these conventions and social policy was long considered a truly 'domestic' policy domain. Throughout most of the twentieth century, it was assumed that developing countries were too poor to afford to introduce social security schemes and that such redistributive measures would have to wait until a certain level of development had been achieved (Jäger *et al.* 2001). Over the past two decades, we have witnessed a change in thinking about social policies in developing countries (Leisering 2007). The argument has been turned around: social security arrangements are now argued to represent a precondition for development. Against this background, the World Bank came to play a pioneering role in establishing old age security schemes as a *global* policy norm.

Externalization and objectivation of the World Bank's pension reform policy norm: the three-pillar pension model

Social security issues in general and old age security in particular are among the more recent additions to the World Bank's agenda. Traditionally, the internal division of labour between the different United Nations (UN) institutions meant that the ILO was the main actor in the field of social and labour policy and the Bank and the IMF in that of economic and fiscal policy. In the late 1980s and early 1990s, the Bank began to put social protection issues more prominently on to its agenda. Created in 1996, the Social Protection Unit is one of the youngest sectors in the Bank. Prior to this, activities relating to social protection issues, like the production of the *Averting* report, were cross-sectoral collaborations between staff from different units. The rise of social protection has to be seen in the context of a more general move within the Bank towards 'soft' aspects of development, preceded by the focus on health and education and followed by the creation of the Social Development Department, which concentrated on topics such as participation, empowerment, conflict prevention and social capital (see Hall 2007; Vetterlein 2007).

Historical contingencies played a role in triggering the new-found interest in social protection issues: demand from the countries of the former Soviet Union – the Bank's new client countries – for advice on restructuring their collapsed social security systems; the seemingly successful track record of a complete privatization of the pension system in Chile in 1980; and the Bank's more general interest in the potential of pension funds to increase domestic saving rates and deepen capital markets during a time of favourable developments in financial markets. A few years before, the Bank had published its 1989 World Development Report *Financial Systems and Development*, which emphasized the importance for developing countries of developing their financial markets while arguing for revised 'approaches that emphasized government intervention in the economy ... to rely more heavily on the private sector' and to 'develop effective system of prudent regulation and supervision' (World Bank 1989: iii). Funded pensions systems, in the Bank's view, could play a key role in gradually building up these markets. Many people in the Bank thought pension funds should first put almost all the money into government. As one interviewee from the World Bank observed, 'this was crucial for developing a key market because once you have the government market you can have a corporate bond market, you have mortgage bond markets because they build on the infrastructure of the government markets ... and then you develop equity markets or you allow them to invest overseas, to diversify' (interview, conducted 5 June 2005). Amongst other factors, these conditions triggered the Bank's activities in the area of old age security.

The decision to publish a Policy Research Report – one of the Bank's flagship publication series – on pension reforms and subsequent marketing efforts were crucial factors in establishing pension reform as a policy norm. According to World Bank staff involved in writing the *Averting* report, this decision was closely related to Lawrence Summers joining the Bank as chief economist in 1991. He became an 'internal champion' for research on social security issues in the Bank and identified pensions as the topic for the Bank's next Policy Research Report.

The report was produced by an author team composed exclusively of economists and financial experts. No social security expert was part of the team, which may explain why it addressed primarily questions of financial sustainability and the effects of pension reform on the economy. It recommended that countries build up a three-tiered pension system consisting of a minimized public pillar providing a social pension; a fully funded, privately managed defined contribution pillar that provides an income-smoothing function; and third, additional voluntary savings. Arguably, this three-pillar system would diversify risks and produce greater results in terms of better-targeted redistribution, more productive savings and lower social costs (see World Bank 1994a: chapter 3).

Before entering into the details of pension system design choices, the *Averting* report illustrates the *global* need to introduce new or reform existing old age security systems in light of demographic changes and the breakdown of informal support systems (World Bank 1994a: chapters 1 and 2). Subsequently, the authors evaluate the pros and cons of different design choices, arguing that funded, privately managed, defined contribution systems represent the more advantageous design. They therefore recommend that if country conditions allow, states should aim for paradigmatic reforms, switching to funded pillars and replacing PAYG financing. This position marked a radical break with the norm of setting up publicly managed, PAYG pension schemes that are adjusted to changing circumstances (e.g. demographic change) through parametric reforms. The ideas of the *Averting* report were not entirely new: the Chilean reform of a full privatization of the pension system had been debated in public for several years – and the World Bank had also contributed to spreading the news about the Chilean 'success' – but now these ideas were conceptualized as a universally adaptable model and officially backed at the highest levels of this powerful international organization that has a considerable audience and reputation. The Bank had previously been involved in pension reforms in only a few countries (e.g. Mexico) and before the *Averting* report had gone along with the ILO approach of parametric reforms.

The seed for the emergence of a pension policy norm lay in the publication of the *Averting* report. This report established old age security as a global social problem, using crisis terminology such as the 'old age crisis', the 'breakdown of informal systems' and 'failures of PAYG systems' to persuade the public of the urgency of the matter at hand (World Bank 1994a: chapters 1 and 2). The report was published as a reaction to external historical conditions, on the one hand – in particular the collapse of the Soviet Union and the transition states joining the Bank as new member states – and, on the other hand, to internal organizational factors like changes in the Bank's staff and their neoliberal conviction that pension reforms should focus on funding and privatization. The content was developed according to available expertise within the Bank and the Bank's organizational ideology, showing clear affinities with the Washington Consensus by arguing in favour of privatization and focusing on capital market development and economic growth.

The Bank's persuasion efforts for its pensions policy norm

The World Bank launched a substantial dissemination campaign following the publication of the *Averting* report to persuade the social policy and development community to follow the Bank's approach to old age security. Overall, the three-pillar policy model rapidly came to be perceived as the best design choice among many policy-makers in countries that were planning pension reforms as well as in certain academic circles. Organizations like the Organization for Economic Co-operation and Development (OECD), the Asian Development Bank (ADB) and bilateral agencies like the United States Agency for International Development (USAID) also followed the World Bank's pro-funding message and three-pillar model. This can partly be attributed to the Bank's extensive persuasion efforts through inviting the development and social policy communities to book launches, seminars, workshops, training sessions and conferences around the world to present the three-pillar model, as well as pursuing three-pillar pension reforms in its lending operations.[5] As a result, the issue of old age security was widely discussed throughout the 1990s. The World Bank's power in setting the tone for development debates has been shown across a wide array of issues (Bøås and McNeill 2004; George and Sabelli 1994). Cox and Jacobsen (1989) have related this to the difference between forum organizations like the ILO or UN, which focus on standard setting through resolutions and conventions, and service organizations like the World Bank that directly service client countries. In the case of the World Bank, which is the largest single source of development funding, its recommendations are backed by loans and credits that often make up a considerable part of the public budget of receiving states. One consultant working for the Gesellschaft für Technische Zusammenarbeit (GTZ, the German bilateral development agency) in Asian countries stated that all the countries that he worked with demanded technical assistance on implementing three-pillar reforms. A consultant for the World Bank described the process through which the message of the *Averting* report became the 'only game in town' in the following way:

Policy-makers in the countries often do not have easy access to all information and for them as well as for people in operations of international organization ... the time pressures are brutal. They don't have time to keep up with the academic literature, so ... if the word from centre is 'private pensions', then, other things being equal, they will do that. So *Averting* ... empowered those who believed in it

---

[5] Twenty-two World Bank projects focused on establishing a private pillar in the receiving countries.

anyway and it nudged those who were indifferent in that direction. (interview, conducted 4 November 2006)

Today, even countries like Sierra Leone and Kazakhstan have introduced a private pillar, countries where, as one World Bank consultant stated, conditions to introduce funded systems are 'too ridiculous for words' (interview, conducted 4 November 2006).

What were the driving forces behind this rapid and widespread diffusion of the pension reform policy norm? The historical background, that is, the aftermath of the Cold War, set the overall context by reaffirming the belief in free market and privatization policies, arguably preparing fertile ground for the Bank's pro-privatization pension norm. This was combined with a rising awareness about demographic transition, the perceived success of the Chilean pension reform and the perceived positive investment climate of financial markets, all of which made the Bank's suggestion conducive to many decision-makers.

As stated above, the success of the World Bank's pension reform policy norm can also be attributed to the large amount of resources the Bank dedicated to a large variety of persuasion activities to increase the social recognition of the report both internally and externally. Internally, the report was discussed and presented at various brown bag lunches, via intranet announcements, and during internal review processes. Externally, the report gained public attention through book launches, conferences, workshops and seminars held at national and regional levels, as well as presentations on many occasions before different audiences. According to the dissemination budget that was approved, the Bank spent US$517,000 on seven conferences (one in each of the World Bank regions and one in China). Moreover, the lead author, Estelle James, went on a book tour for two years after the report had been published. Likewise, the other members of the author team were heavily involved in its dissemination. When asked about the follow-up after the report to disseminate the findings, one of the authors stated he averaged about one presentation a month on the *Averting* report in the three years after the report was published.

Additionally, the publication of the report coincided with the reorientation of the Bank from lending operations to also stressing technical assistance and knowledge transfer, expressed in the 'Knowledge Bank' idea (Wolfensohn 1996). In this context, the World Bank designed training courses on pensions through the World Bank Institute,[6] inviting policy-makers and other practitioners around the world to be trained in

---

[6] See www.worldbank.org/wbi.

designing pension reforms. The World Bank thus acts not just as a norm entrepreneur for the policy norm on pensions but also as a 'teacher of norms' (Finnemore 1996). One author of the *Averting* report explicitly stressed this educative aspect of Bank activities: 'We often had seminars in particular countries ... oriented towards educating people about what pension issues were ... I mean, all of this is sort of an education process ... raising awareness about the underlying problems' (interview, conducted 15 July 2005). World Bank staff also report that the approach articulated in the *Averting* report became part of many of the Bank's operational activities: 'There was a decision to incorporate it [the approach of *Averting*] into operations so we tried to advise countries to do something about their systems ... And often, problems that we identified afterwards, we could relate them to the fact that countries did not really follow the main ideas of *Averting*' (interview, conducted 15 July 2005). Whereas the Bank's publications, including the *Averting* report (World Bank 1994a: xiii) usually emphasize that its engagement in pensions is demand driven, reacting to requests from its client countries, this quotation seems to indicate the World Bank was attempting to instil in countries the social recognition of the need for pension reforms by advising them to 'do something about their systems' (World Bank 1994a: xiii).

In sum, after *Averting* had been published, the World Bank engaged in a range of persuasion efforts to establish the message of the report as the new pension design paradigm. The norm was introduced internally through workshops and fora in order to establish a shared meaning throughout the organization. Externally, the Bank launched a huge initiative to disseminate and stabilize the idea of a three-pillar pension model and assisted states in carrying out related pension reforms to implement the model on the ground. The Bank thus succeeded in persuading different audiences, for example, policy-makers, other IOs (OECD, ADB, USAID) and epistemic communities, to socially recognize its approach. While the issue of old age security and the multi-pillar approach were thus widely embraced as a new policy norm, the details of arguments that the Bank presented were widely criticized by other IOs, particularly the ILO and academics, especially social security experts.

Arguing about the World Bank's three-pillar pension model

This section summarizes criticism of the Bank's three-pillar pension reform policy norm. In part, the reaction was against the Bank's presentation of the issue at conferences, book launches and workshops rather than criticizing the report itself. Overall the report took a stance in favour of funding and critical of PAYG systems while discussing some of the caveats. In contrast, the way in which the report was presented in public was one-sided in its recommendations in favour of three-pillar reforms with a dominant funded pillar. A careful reading of the *Averting* report actually shows that the report discusses many of the arguments that critics raised and that the Bank's views were more balanced and nuanced than was generally perceived by the public.

The report produced a huge number of responses both favourable to and critical of the position the Bank articulated in the *Averting* report. Almost three hundred journal articles are listed in the social science citation index as citing the *Averting* report. On top of this, citations in books and coverage by the mass media further increased the report's visibility. The wide dissemination among different audiences triggered criticism from all sides, as Wiener observes: 'the transfer between different contexts enhances the contestation of meanings, as differently socialized individuals – e.g. politicians, civil servants, parliamentarians, lawyers, lobbyists, journalists and so on ... seek to interpret them' (Wiener 2009: 9). Likewise, the economic approach articulated in the *Averting* report triggered critical responses from the development community, from social policy experts and from practitioners working in various country contexts.

Much of the criticism was raised not only in publications but during discussions at the book launches, seminars, workshops and conferences. It is extremely difficult to categorize the criticism by source. Boundaries between internal and external environment, academics and practitioners are blurred in a situation where professors shift between academic positions and positions in the Bank, such as Chief Economist (e.g. Joseph Stiglitz) or Social Protection Director (e.g. Robert Holzmann); between academic positions and secondments to the Bank as consultants or fixed-term staff (e.g. Anthony Hall, Nicholas Barr); or from one organization to another (e.g. Nancy Birdsall); and where practitioners publish in academic journals (Beattie and McGillivray 1995; Bebbington *et al.* 2004).[7] Overall, a range of different actors in and outside the Bank were involved in influencing, shaping and contesting the Bank's policy. Sustained and well-founded criticism cannot be ignored by the Bank because its perceived legitimacy is in part based on its reputation for producing sound reports. As argued above, it is insufficient to analyse only the interaction between the Bank and its member states or the formal lending operations of the Bank to understand the dynamics of norm negotiation. The Bank does not develop its ideas in an

---

[7] This interchange of staff is a characteristic of IOs. In some cases such an interchange can be an opportunity for IOs to obtain better access to other IOs or NGOs (Kopp-Malek *et al.* 2009).

ivory tower isolated from ongoing debates in related epistemic communities, academic fora, policy think tanks and the media.

In short, criticism of the Bank's three-pillar pension model can be grouped into the following categories: first, general points about the Bank's methodology and analysis in the *Averting* report; second, criticism that regards the Bank's pro-funding message as part of a strategy to attack the Keynesian approach to welfare; and third, criticism of the Bank's analysis about the effects of different pension arrangements on the economy, the state and (future) pensioners.[8]

First and most generally, the report was viewed as analytically flawed and of poor academic quality, with one evaluation finding 'analytical errors that would be well understood by a first-year graduate student in economics' (Deaton 2006: 58). Orszag and Stiglitz (2001) find three flaws in the line of argument of the *Averting* report. First, the report compares the PAYG systems as they played out *in practice* with the performance of funded systems *in theory*. Many of the difficulties that plagued PAYG systems could occur just as well when trying to install a funded system, especially questions of mismanagement, corruption and difficulties in collecting contributions. Relatedly, the report implicitly follows the line of argument that PAYG systems have often failed in developing countries; therefore, a shift to funded systems is the best solution. While the Bank's analysis of the problems with existing PAYG systems is considered accurate, critics argue that it does not follow that PAYG is inherently flawed or that funded systems would necessarily perform better. The discussion of inherent features has to be kept separate from the historic tendencies regarding implementation, but these are mixed in the *Averting* report. The report makes the distinction between inherent problems and design features only to blur the distinction again a few lines further down: overly generous benefit formulas, too much weighting on the final year salary, early retirement provisions and low ceilings on taxable earnings are all listed as design flaws. However, the report holds that these design problems are impossible to fix since 'strong political factors are at work and may lead them to endure . . . in this political sense, the design features may be inherent and not incidental' (World Bank 1994a: 236–7). The report thereby defines design flaws as inherent problems after all. Finally, some argued that the message of the report is actually not as clear-cut as often alleged but rather the report sends out contradictory messages throughout the different chapters. As one of the interviewees observed:

[8] This summary of the criticism is based on document analysis, information from the interviews conducted and subsequent presentations and discussions on pension reform as well as the role of the World Bank at various workshops, seminars and international conferences.

With Bank documents with all the comments you get . . . they get a bit muddy, so *Averting* will say different things in different places. It's a bit like the bible, . . . you can find quotes and counter quotes . . . for most things . . . and it is true when you get comments on things in the Bank it's very difficult not to respond just by moderating the language slightly. (interview, conducted 4 November 2006)

Second, apart from debating the merits of the economic arguments and the effects on savings, economic growth, benefit levels, labour markets and capital market development, the criticism turned the debate into an ideological argument between neoliberalism and Keynesian approaches to the welfare state. The Bank's three-pillar model was criticized for promoting a neoliberal blueprint for pension reforms claiming universal applicability for a model that might be suitable for different country contexts. In the eyes of these critics, pension reform constituted just one part of the battle for hegemony to (re)define the current social policy paradigm. A significant part of the reactions to the report follows these ideological arguments, stating that the World Bank 'is contributing directly to attacks on the old welfare creed and its advocates' and that it is 'a major force in the invention and implementation of the new welfare paradigm in Latin America and Eastern and Central Europe' (Merrien 2001: 541). This suggests that *Averting* was written as a contribution to this ideological battle and that the Bank is inherently biased as a result of its neoliberal organizational culture. The Bank was accused of using the existing research selectively to criticize PAYG systems and present funded systems in a better light than warranted given the overall evidence, such that the 'balance was lost in favor of advocacy' (Deaton 2006: 6, 58, 117). Research on the Bank's publication has indeed challenged the integrity of the Bank's research on the basis of its ideological bias, presenting evidence that 'internal research that was favorable to Bank positions was given great prominence, and unfavorable research ignored' (Deaton 2006: 58).

Finally, critics of the *Averting* report found many of the Bank's claims regarding the effects of funded or PAYG systems lacked evidence (Deaton 2006; ILO 2000; Merrien 2001). Many caveats are mentioned in the report itself; however, they were not stated as clearly and visibly as critics wished. Also, the policy recommendations in the report result from weighing and interpreting the arguments in a way that critics disagree with, leading them to present evidence against the arguments in *Averting* regarding advantages of privately managed funded systems including their potential for economic growth, the reduced risk of political manipulation and corruption, the ability to deal with demographic change, and the incentives for participation. For example, the track record of funded systems showed that administration costs were very high, especially for low contribution rates as are common in many developing countries, and that coverage did not increase although benefits were tightly linked to contributions. These counterfactuals and criticisms came from other units within the Bank as well as from outside, for example, the regional office in Latin America, which published the controversial report *Keeping the Promise of Social Security in Latin America* (World Bank 2005g). Other issues that critics thought the report did not pay enough attention to included the cost of the transition, the administrative capacity of a country, the risks of financial market volatility for the pension benefits, the necessity and difficulty of regulating private providers, and the lack of financial education of the general public (mentioned by interviewees and in Barr 2000, 2006; Beattie and McGillivray 1995; Merrien 2001; Orszag and Stiglitz 2001). With regard to the effects on governments, the Bank's estimation of the political failures of publicly managed systems as being inevitable was thought to be too pessimistic and it was also pointed out that privately managed systems can be corrupted just as easily in the absence of rule of law.

The Bank's recommendations on pension reform reached a large audience. To achieve this degree of visibility for its approach to a new development issue is in itself remarkable. Although many policy-makers and certain international organizations embraced the recommendations articulated in the *Averting* report, the sustained criticism outlined above as well as new evidence from country experience and certain organizational changes within the Bank led to a revision of the Bank's position on pension system design. The Bank gradually produced differentiated arguments in its publications and shifted from the rigid three-pillar model to a more flexible five-pillar model. These developments are described next.

Negotiation: the World Bank's shift from the three- to the five-pillar pension model

In 1995, just after *Averting* was published, James Wolfensohn became the new President of the Bank and initiated several reform efforts including the Strategic Compact and the Comprehensive Development Framework, the 'Knowledge Bank' concept and a reorganization of the Bank's structure, including the creation of the Social Protection Department in 1996. These reform efforts were not a direct reaction to the criticism of the *Averting* report (some may have been reactions to the criticism of the World Bank more generally), but they had repercussions for the Bank's work on pensions. New personnel were hired while others left the Bank, and the creation of the Social Protection Department institutionalized the Bank's work on pensions: a specific unit received the mandate to further develop the Bank's approach to pension reform and to address the question of old age security, in lending operations as well as in further publications and working papers.

The Bank also directly reacted to criticism of the *Averting* report and to developments on the ground. As one interviewee observed, 'the Bank was under consistent attack for its view on pensions, which really annoyed people at the Bank' (interview, conducted 15 July 2005). It was in part owing to this sustained criticism – and the Bank's impression that the criticism did not adequately present the Bank's approach – that Nick Stern, the new Chief Economist at the Bank, asked Robert Holzmann, the Director of the newly created Social Protection Department, to prepare a new publication to clarify and update the Bank's view on pensions.

These recent developments in the Bank's literature on pensions have not yet attracted much attention. To the extent that they are commented on, it is typically asked whether the Bank has changed its approach or whether it continues to work along the same lines, or even whether one can observe a convergence of positions between the Bank and its critics. While the diversity of views within the Bank is not subject to investigation in this chapter, it is important to keep in mind that not everyone in the Bank agreed with all – or even most – of the arguments presented in the *Averting* report. The Bank often speaks with one voice to its environment, presenting a coherent approach, while actually harbouring a diversity of views on the inside. This diversity is difficult to detect from the outside as hiring and promotion structures, as well as resource allocation inside the Bank, are organized to promote views that are in line with the organizational culture (Miller-Adams 1999; Bøås and McNeill 2004). In particular the internal seminars and workshops as well as external dissemination activities mentioned above illustrate the need for internal as well as external persuasion to establish a shared Bank meaning (Woods 2004). One can thus find elements of both change and continuity in recent publications – also because changes in mainstream positions within the Bank can be constructed as continuities with positions that had previously been sidelined. Certainly, many disagreements on the best pension design for developing countries continue to exist. Other findings stand out more clearly: the debate is no longer driven as strongly by ideological convictions as it was in the beginning. As a result of the ongoing discussions, both the Bank and its critics have come to acknowledge that PAYG and funded systems can succeed or fail depending on the details of the design, the implementation and other contextual factors, rather than on which financing option was chosen (Reinalda and Verbeek 2004). Interestingly, the greater openness to different design choices and the new emphasis on social pensions means the new policy norm is more in tune with a shift towards a broader, more holistic approach to development.

We identify three trends in World Bank thinking on pensions. First, recent publications are written in a more open and conciliatory language, which allows for a larger scope of choices as to what constitutes the desirable path to old age security. Second, non-financial defined contribution (NDC) schemes[9] and, third, social pensions have both recently entered the agenda, which were not prominently discussed in the *Averting* report. As a result, the three-pillar system has now been expanded to include up to five pillars.[10]

The three-pillar model clearly defined the different design options and functions of each pillar as well as their relative weight. In contrast, the five-pillar model leaves more flexibility in terms of the design and relative weight of each pillar. Being open to different design preferences and local adaptations is crucial for the cultural validation of a policy norm (see Lardone, chapter 10, this volume). A striking change in the recent publications is therefore in their language. The *Averting* report clearly conveys the message that funded systems are the most desirable. While acknowledging that many countries do not meet the conditions to introduce funded systems *yet*, it strongly recommends that countries should create the necessary background conditions so that they will be able to do so in the future. This leaves no doubt that this is the best choice that every country should aspire to. This position was voiced in strong technical language: the World Bank identified a problem and presented the solution. In contrast, recent publications are phrased much more carefully, stressing the fact that the Bank favours multi-pillar designs but that many different combinations can have satisfactory outcomes. The wording is conciliatory towards opposing views and the emphasis is more on sound implementation and management whatever the design choice (World Bank 2005h: 1–4, 9–20). The reports still argue in favour of funded systems but are more apprehensive of the limitations of funding. Overall, in recent publications the Bank presents itself as a learning organization engaged in the search for the best policy recommendations on pension reforms (Dixon 1994; Kopp-Malek *et al.* 2009). Here, the Bank claims to do more than *adjustment learning*, that is, taking into account the criticism raised against the report and responding to it by reformulating the report. Rather, the Bank presents its progress as *turnover*

---

[9] NDC schemes are essentially PAYG schemes; contributions are used to pay the pensions of the current retirees. However, the NDC scheme ties benefits closely to contributions since the worker's contributions are recorded in a virtual account and the pension is calculated on the basis of the amount accumulated (see later discussion).

[10] We have identified these trends by analysing recent World Bank publications, especially working papers published in the Bank's Pension Reform Primer Series in addition to three additional publications: World Bank 2001, 2003d, 2005h.

learning because it challenges some of its own hypotheses and assumptions and clarifies its position (Hedberg 1981): 'The extensive experience in pension reforms … since the early 1990s has motivated Bank staff to review and refine the Bank's framework' (World Bank 2005h: 3).

In contrast to the *Averting* report, the most obvious change in the 2005 report is the lack of coherence and clarity. Although the report still emphasizes that the World Bank favours advance funding, it then mentions a long list of other crucially important components. These are listed as 'additions to the Bank's perspective' (World Bank 2005h: 3). In fact, the change in language has led to a change in content where less rigorous wording now leaves the reader confused. At the same time, this vagueness also increases norm-acceptance since vaguer norms are typically less contested (Wiener 2007a). The report is replete with mixed messages and self-contradictory remarks, including statements that the Bank has been 'reassessing the continued importance but also the limitations of prefunding' and 'advance funding is still considered useful, but the limits of funding in some circumstances are also seen much more sharply' (World Bank 2005h: 3). This confusion may be interpreted as conceding to external criticisms over concern for the Bank's reputation. On the one hand, the Bank could not legitimately continue to argue in favour of funded systems in face of mounting evidence that their implementation is problematic. On the other hand, the failure to address questions of adequate benefit levels and coverage of the poor would contradict the Bank's proclaimed role as the leading actor in the global fight against poverty (e.g. the Bank's leading role through the Poverty Reduction Strategy Papers since 2000, Ayres 1983).

To add to this confusion, elements that had actually been already discussed in the *Averting* report are declared as new additions to the Bank's perspective in the 2005 report, such as the non-contributory pillar. One of the stated new additions to the World Bank's perspective is 'the need for a basic or zero (or non-contributory) pillar that is distinguished from the first pillar in its primary focus on poverty alleviation in order to extend old-age security to all of the elderly' (World Bank 2005h: 3). However, the *Averting* report made this exact argument for the first pillar in 1994:

the public pillar would have the limited objective of alleviating old-age poverty and coinsuring against a multitude of risks. Backed by the government's power of taxation, this pillar has the unique ability to pay benefits to people growing old shortly after the plan is introduced, to redistribute income to the poor, and to coinsure against long spells of low investment returns, recession, inflation and private market failures. (World Bank 1994a: 16)

The *Averting* report also discusses whether this pillar should be means tested, a universal flat benefit or a guaranteed minimum pension, and whether it should be financed through a payroll tax or general revenue. Although the idea of a social pension is not therefore new in Bank thinking, it seems to be a new focus. The explicit emphasis on the importance of a non-contributory pillar can be seen as a new development in the Bank's position compared with the emphasis on the second, funded pillar in the *Averting* report – and a potential shift towards a broader approach to development: while the funded pillar implies a focus on private management, potential for economic growth and linking benefits to contributions, the non-contributory pillar is tax funded, focusing on adequate benefits and redistribution.

Two papers in the Pension Reform Primer series are further evidence of this trend (Kakwani and Subbarao 2005; Palacios and Sluchynsky 2006). Most importantly, these papers explicitly address social pensions in the context of countries with large informal sectors and low coverage for contributory schemes, neither of which was discussed in the *Averting* report. The papers stress the important role social pensions can play to close this coverage gap if certain initial conditions like administrative capacity are met.

Truly new – and to a certain extent surprising given the Bank's criticism of PAYG systems in *Averting* – is the Bank's recent enthusiasm for non-financial defined contribution (NDC) schemes. This again underpins the argument that the Bank rethought the three-pillar model and compromised messages stated in the *Averting* report. It was also an opportunity for the new Director of the Social Protection Unit, Robert Holzmann, who became a decisive promoter of NDC financing, to sharpen his own profile within the Bank. NDC schemes are essentially PAYG schemes; contributions are used to pay the pensions of the current retirees. However, the scheme ties benefits closely to contributions since worker contributions are recorded in a virtual account and the pension is calculated on the basis of the amount accumulated. This change from defined benefit to defined contribution means that the incentive structure of the funded system remains intact. The virtual account is credited with a rate of return reflecting growth of productivity in real wages and labour force growth; the benefit is calculated according to life expectancy on entering retirement. It is necessary under NDC schemes to build up reserves or buffer funds to accommodate demographic changes, but this does not amount to the kind of financial savings effects that funded systems are expected to produce. Again, the interest in NDC schemes is also reflected in the Pension Reform Primer series and the 2005 publication (World Bank 2005h: 73–4). In addition, the proceedings of a conference on NDC schemes were published in book form (World Bank 2003d). While a paper by Disney (1999) evaluated NDC reforms as inferior to reforms enhancing funded elements, subsequent publications shed a more positive light on NDC-type reforms. Discussion of NDC schemes preceded the publication of the *Averting* report and people from the author team later felt that it was a flaw of this report that it did not include NDC schemes.

Adding another contributory pillar as well as counting informal arrangements as an additional pillar means the Bank's reformulated multi-pillar system now numbers as many as five pillars instead of the previous three. In sum, the five pillars are described as: a non-contributory or 'zero pillar' (in the form of a universal pension) that provides a minimal level of protection; a 'first-pillar' contributory system that is linked to varying degrees to earnings and seeks to replace some portion of income; a mandatory 'second pillar' that is essentially an individual savings account that may be variously constructed; voluntary 'third-pillar' arrangements that may take many forms (individual, employer-sponsored, defined benefit, defined contribution); and finally informal intra-family or intergenerational sources of both financial and non-financial support for the elderly (World Bank 2005: 1–2). The *Averting* report devoted an entire chapter to informal arrangements so that this again cannot be seen as a change or new addition to World Bank thinking. The exercise of renumbering the pillars from three to five served as an opportunity to stress the fact that the Bank is advocating a multi-pillar system and that irrespective of the overall number or the relative weight and specific design of individual pillars, it is important to diversify risks and avoid 'putting all the eggs in one basket'. The five-pillar system replaced the previous fully funded, privately managed second pillar with two contributory pillars that are not defined in much detail; only the individual savings account pillar is recommended to be mandatory.

Stabilization of the policy norm on old age security

As discussed earlier, the Bank reached a wide audience with its flagship publication on old age security. The *Averting* report is referred to by policy-makers and academics alike when discussing pension system design options. As demonstrated, many of the follow-up communications objected to the report and criticized the Bank's recommendations. According to Wiener, this contestation of norms is to be expected: 'Since norms – and their meanings – evolve through interaction in context, they are therefore contested by default' (Wiener 2009: 179). In fact, Wiener argues that processes of arguing and negotiation about norms contribute to their stabilization as 'norms are likely to acquire political significance where their meaning is disputed. At that point, they obtain political visibility' (Wiener 2009: 182). The lively debates ensuing after the publication of *Averting*, arguing about adequate pension systems design, thus contributed to establishing old age security as a new policy norm. While the question of pension system financing (PAYG or funded), and the number, relative weight and concrete design of each pillar remains contested, old age security in general and the concept of a multi-pillar pension design are socially recognized by all participants of the debate. No participant in the global discourse on pensions questions the universal validity of old age security as a policy norm. It is taken for granted that pension systems should be introduced and that reforms are needed. It could well be argued that states that are far from facing a demographic transition or states in Sub-Saharan Africa have more pressing needs than reforming or establishing pension systems, but the validity of the old age security norm is not questioned along these lines. Also, the multi-pillar design has become universally accepted. Many states have adapted multi-pillar reforms and many more have at least debated introducing such policies (Orenstein 2005; Weyland 2004, 2006). In contrast, nobody suggests that states should focus their efforts on running a single system properly rather than having to administer and regulate three or more pillars. However, the disadvantages of higher administration costs for introducing several pillars and of low contribution rates that are typical in many low-income countries may yet outweigh the benefits of risk diversification.

Conclusion

The evolution of the World Bank's thinking on pension reform has led to a reinterpretation of its policy and discursive responses to old age security. This we argue has shaped the emergence of pension reform as a global policy norm. The chapter starts with the description of the drafting of the *Averting* report. In the following step it depicts how the Bank disseminated the three-pillar pension model in its internal and external environment. The considerable persuasion efforts of the Bank are identified as a crucial factor in the institutionalization of pension reform as a policy norm (norm stabilization). Although the norm was widely accepted, the details of the Bank's recommendation for implementation triggered both internal and external criticism. The criticism of the three-pillar model as well as evidence from country experiences persuaded the Bank to re-evaluate its model. Throughout this process, the Bank adjusted its position after addressing criticism from policy-makers, epistemic communities and IOs. The Bank changed its language, becoming less prescriptive and less rigorous, revising the three-pillar model into a five-pillar model. The new model leaves more flexibility for country preferences in the design and weight of the different pillars.

The Bank's recent publications still advocate funding but less rigorously, while acknowledging the feasibility of other reform choices. The World Bank has thus become more open towards different reform designs and has made a step in the direction of a broader, more holistic approach to development. These changes have been cast in a language that depicts the Bank as a flexible, learning organization. The introduction of the 2005 report, for example, attributes developments in the Bank's position to its involvement in pension reform in more than eighty countries, which 'has significantly expanded knowledge and insights of Bank staff and stimulated an ongoing process of evaluation and refinement of the policies and priorities that guide the work in this area' (World Bank 2005h: 1). This increased flexibility was necessary for cultural validity since the norm will undergo different interpretations as it is enacted in different contexts. The strong emphasis on the privately managed plank in the three-pillar model led to norm contestation since a paradigmatic shift to a funded system was technically and politically not feasible in many countries. The policy was originally very rigid and it was impossible to adapt it to certain contexts, for example, in states that do not have developed capital markets or in those that emphasize a strong role for the state in the provision of social security. In contrast, the five-pillar model allows a flexible interpretation of risk diversification, allowing countries to pick and mix aspects according to their preferences and needs.

Throughout this chapter, the emphasis lay on illustrating how the Bank's internal and relevant external environment plays an important role at every step throughout the norm circle. We argued for taking an open system perspective on the Bank in order to display and understand the origins and evolution of World Bank policies. This model offers an analytical basis for policy- and decision-making processes within the Bank as a non-monolithic entity and interactions between the Bank and various actors within its environment. The open system approach allows us to conceptualize the complexity of the legitimating pressures and discursive field in which the Bank is situated. The different Bank units and staff, other international organizations, policy-makers, epistemic communities, NGOs and the mass media influence Bank thinking on different development issues.

As stated above, the *Averting* report was criticized for epitomizing the Washington Consensus rather than reflecting a true concern for the livelihoods of the elderly in developing countries. This chapter discussed the evolution of the Bank's approach to pension reform in light of this criticism and the resulting need for greater flexibility, which led to the emphasis on social pensions and the concession to the PAYG system through NDC schemes. This revised Bank position is more in line with a holistic approach to development than the three-pillar model that emphasized funding. As described in the introductory chapter of this volume, a holistic approach to development emphasizes social development issues, poverty alleviation and sustainability, and seems to be rooted in a new development strategy (Blackmon 2008). The Bank's initial policy norm on pension system design represented a mixture of the Washington Consensus and holistic development: the focus on old age security in itself emphasizes a social development issue, but the initial approach drew on the economistic approach and principles of the Washington Consensus. The newly developed five-pillar model is broader. This initial overlap, drawing on elements of both approaches, might be typical for transitional periods between different normative orders. Instead of being rejected outright, the Washington Consensus still serves as a point of reference and is still used to frame new (social) issues. The characteristics of transition periods between normative orders would be an interesting avenue for further research.

4   The strategic social construction of the World Bank's gender and development policy norm

Catherine Weaver

Introduction

Central to this book's constructivist study of policy norms is the question of how international financial institutions produce the ideas and practices that 'frame the world' and become the 'common sense' that governs many aspects of the world economy (Bøås and McNeill 2004; see also Finnemore 1996). These have been critical questions in scholarship on the World Bank, the largest lender in the field of international development aid and the self-identified 'Knowledge Bank' that produces and disseminates cutting-edge research and data on development. How the World Bank (henceforth the Bank) accepts or rejects development ideas, how policy norms are internalized and subsequently diffused within the organization, how (or whether) these ideas and norms are translated into the real operational practices of the Bank and what degree of validity they reach are salient issues to anyone interested in understanding how development is thought about and acted upon in the world today.

This chapter accepts the challenge posed by Park and Vetterlein to examine how ideas are 'taken up' by international institutions and transformed into policies and practices. My chosen case is the Bank and the gender and development (GAD) policy norm. Notably, this is not a case where the Bank's embrace of GAD represents the origins of or catalyst for an emerging global policy norm. Rather, this is a unique case where the Bank has responded, rather late in the game, to a policy norm that already was more or less firmly adopted by corresponding institutions. More critically, the existing gender and development policy norm clashed with the Bank's existing modus operandi and organizational culture. The Bank's foray into GAD work was neither the effect of fluid institutional isomorphism nor the imposition of new policies by powerful member states or international non-governmental organizations (NGOs). Rather, the embrace and subsequent institutionalization and diffusion of the GAD policy norm has been largely contingent upon the efforts of internal policy advocates or norm entrepreneurs (Finnemore and Sikkink 1998; Kardam 1993).

To this end, I broach the exploration of the evolution of the GAD policy norm in the Bank's broader development agenda by utilizing Anthony Bebbington et al.'s (2006) actor-oriented approach, which focuses on the strategies of staff in pushing for discursive and operational changes within the institution. In their chosen study of the debate of social capital and development ideas, Bebbington et al. brilliantly describe – often at the level of 'water cooler discussions' (Bebbington et al. 2006: 15) – the manner in which internal advocates of social development concepts engage in battles over ideas and resources inside the Bank. As key participants in the process, they describe how they strategically articulated the relevance of their favoured ideas to resonate not only with Bank donors and borrowers, but also with the Bank's powerful economists and in that way enhanced social recognition of the norm inside the organization. This enabled them to get their ideas on the table, to gain allies in key areas of Bank decision-making necessary to mobilize staff and resources, and (at least modestly) have social development integrated into Bank policies and operational practices. Much like the advocacy described elsewhere in the norms literature (see Keck and Sikkink 1998), we see in this case distinct tactics of framing, shaming, leverage and accountability politics that allowed social development activists in the Bank to make significant inroads in organizational discourse and practice. At the same time, their discussion reveals the distinct constraints on internal advocacy of new development ideas – constraints that are defined by the Bank's relationship with its external authorizing and task environment and its internal ideological and material power structures.

In my chosen case of the gender and development policy norm, I seek to discern what opportunities and constraints internal change advocates face in their efforts to gain entry and traction within the Bank, and in the process examine the tactics these agents employ to make emerging norms actionable in the form of policies and practices. Thus the driving questions here include: What tactics do internal norm advocates employ to open space for new ideas? What are the opportunities and constraints that affect the viability of advocacy tactics? How do they engage in important battles over organizational ideas and resources that make policy and operational change happen (or not)? How do the choices of tactics reflect the particular opportunities and constraints posed by the cultural and political environment in which Bank staff work? Over time, as the lessons from mainstreaming emerge, how do these internal advocates change their strategies to achieve unfulfilled or new goals?

More provocatively, what happens to a policy norm in the process of its institutionalization: the translation from ideas and policies to full operationalization? Bebbington *et al.* provide a staunch warning that resonates strongly with my own observations in this chapter:

in-group members seeking greater external influence may find themselves confronting something of a Faustian bargain, namely an imperative to change their language in order to 'speak to power,' but at the risk of undermining the galvanizing coherence of their own internal discourse ... If difficult discursive trade-offs such as these have been made, the point remains that different discourses are required for different political purposes, and that effective change agents are often judiciously, and tactically, 'multilingual' in this sense. (Bebbington *et al.* 2006: 280)

Put differently, we may ask to what extent a core norm is transformed, 'co-opted' or 'localized' in order to gain institutional space, attention or traction (Bebbington *et al.* 2006: 15; see also Acharya 2004). Within the framework of the norm circle, how does the process of norm contestation or debate change the norm itself? Is there a danger hidden in employing specific advocacy tactics that leads advocates to lose 'ownership' of their ideas?

Gender and development in the World Bank

This chapter examines these questions in the case of the internal advocacy surrounding the evolution of the GAD policy norm in the Bank, with a specific focus on the period between 1995 and 2007. The GAD policy norm rests upon the essential belief that there are distinct causes and effects of poverty and socioeconomic development that can only be understood in gender disaggregated ways. The idea, originally conceived in terms of women in development (WID), took hold in the 1970s in conjunction with the worldwide feminist movement, the UN Decade for Women and the initiation of the series of World Conferences on Women. However, the GAD policy norm has only really gained significant ground in the larger international development regime and in multilateral development banks since the 1990s. In the case of the GAD policy norm in the Bank, two major points surface for understanding norm dynamics. First, unlike in other development agendas, the Bank is widely considered the last amongst similar development banks to move towards an assertive mainstreaming plan for GAD. As such, the Bank had the opportunity to benefit from 'second mover advantages', and indeed we see the adoption of successful tactics from mainstreaming processes in other organizations. However, the distinct political and cultural character of the Bank strongly influences the choice and substance of the tactics, resulting in a distinctly 'World Bank' approach to GAD that is substantively quite different from that of other IOs. Specifically, in the past decade we can discern four distinct types of tactics employed by strategic agents in the Bank to promote GAD institutionalization, each of which will be described below: (1) leverage via high-level political and financial support; (2) accountability absent coercion; (3) persuasion via 'proof'; and (4) strategic framing.

Second, the choice and use of these tactics to enhance the policy norms' social recognition, particularly in the case of persuasion and issue-framing, may represent a double-edged sword for gender norm entrepreneurs. In particular, the paths chosen to gain entry and traction for the GAD policy norm inside the Bank and with borrower states have over time led to a particularly technocratic and increasingly narrow economics-focused approach, as opposed to the rights- or security-based policy norm framework favoured by other institutions (Mehra and Gupta 2006; O'Brien *et al.* 2000; Tzannatos 2006). This approach has facilitated mainstreaming by making GAD more receptive to internal (organizational) audiences, but threatens the loss of external constituencies and partners as well as some of the core ideas and values that GAD advocates in the Bank once prioritized. This suggests that there may be some degree of localization (adaptation to the immediate organization environment) (Acharya 2004) occurring that is dramatically shaping – and even distorting – the GAD policy norm as it 'succeeds' in gaining entry into the core policies and operations of the Bank.

I begin by briefly describing what I call the 'pre-Beijing period' of gender work in the Bank, which roughly falls into the period between 1977 and 1995.[1] This period is best characterized by a shallow adoption of gender norms into the Bank's work, through formal validation in the Bank's policies and reports (Razavi and Miller 1995; Tzannatos 2006: 21). I then turn to the post-Beijing period, roughly delineated from 1995 to today. The Fourth World Conference in Beijing in 1995 turned the tide, creating multiple opportunities for external and internal advocates to promote the GAD agenda in ways that would actually make inroads into prominent areas of the Bank's analytical and operational work. Here is where my main analysis begins, focusing on the tactics employed by GAD advocates as they took advantage of the 'political opportunity structure' resulting from the Beijing conference (Hafner-Burton and Pollack 2002) and sought to 'mainstream' gender into policy and daily operations throughout the Bank. Rather than presenting a chronological summary

---

[1] For a more thorough historical treatment, see World Bank Operations Evaluation Department (2001, 2005); Hafner-Burton and Pollack (2002); Kuiper and Barker (2006); Razavi and Miller (1995); Tzannatos (2006).

of events in the post-Beijing period, I use two focal points – the 2002 and 2006 gender mainstreaming action plans – to discern patterns and outcomes of advocacy tactics. Finally, I illuminate where I perceive such tactics to have resulted in successes tainted by the aforementioned norm localization and co-optation processes colourfully described by Bebbington *et al.* (2006) as the 'Faustian bargain' of norm entrepreneurship in the Bank.

Pre-Beijing evolution of gender and development in the World Bank

The various institutional histories of the GAD movement in the World Bank emphasize that the Bank was one of the 'first movers' in terms of initiating gender work into its development operations, but one of the 'last movers' in terms of moving beyond formally validating the norm in operational policies towards full social recognition of the GAD policy norm throughout its organizational activities.[2] This is largely a result of the early but weak start for gender work in the Bank. In 1977, in response to broader changes in the external normative environment catalysed by the first United Nations World Conference on Women in Mexico City and an internal Women in Development 'lunch group', the Bank appointed a women in development (WID) adviser.[3] However, the adviser had a support staff equivalent to only one full-time employee and a largely unfunded and badly defined mandate to raise awareness inside the Bank of gender issues in development, and played a modest role in overseeing projects at their early stages. In 1984 the Bank began formally to validate the GAD policy norm by adopting the Operational Manual Statement (OMS 2.20), which required staff to carry out sociological analyses, including consideration of gender issues, during the appraisal of investment projects. OMS 2.20, however, was merely a guideline and lacked explicit mandates, training and additional staff resources to help ensure compliance with the new policy. Moreover, the WID adviser at the time was an 'institutional outsider' (a former UN official). She sought to push an equity-based WID agenda that 'did not have an easy "organizational fit" with the Bank's

---

[2] Razavi and Miller (1995); Mehra and Gupta (2006). As Razavi and Miller define it, mainstreaming entails 'integrating gender issues into the entire spectrum of activities that are funded and/or executed by an organization (i.e. projects, programmes, policies) ... and diffusing responsibility for gender integration beyond the WID/gender units ... making it a routine concern of all bureaucratic units and all staff members' (Razavi and Miller 1995: ii).

[3] The difference between the GAD policy norm and the women in development norm is detailed later in the chapter.

mandate and ideology, especially in the climate of the early 1980s when equity issues were being increasingly placed on the "back burner" ... and spent most of her time defending the Bank's WID work to the outside world, rather than on building a position of influence inside the Bank' (Razavi and Miller 1995: 35; citing Kardam 1991: 77 and 1993; see also O'Brien *et al.* 2000). According to a 1994 report from the Operations Evaluation Department, only about 11 per cent of the Bank's lending portfolio in the early 1980s contained projects with 'gender-related action', and this mostly in the rural development, education and health sectors (World Bank 1994b: Annex A; cited in Razavi and Miller 1995: 36).

In the wake of the 1985 World Conference on Women in Nigeria, a more formal WID unit was established with a total of three staff members. The newly appointed WID adviser was this time a Bank insider – a senior economist – who immediately sought a narrower, specific mandate and more explicit support from senior management (especially the operational vice-presidencies). More importantly, the new WID adviser consciously sought traction in Bank operations by demonstrating in a language and methods conducive to the Bank's economists how increased attention to women's issues contributed to the Bank's development goals and operational effectiveness (Razavi and Miller 1995: 37; World Bank OED 2001). Resources followed (including eight staff members), often supported by extra-budgetary funds provided by key donor states (especially the Nordic countries), but still remained limited. WID co-ordinators, or focal points, were assigned to each operational region, but these duties were often added on to a pre-existing position and they were not delegated any further authority in terms of project management and oversight.

As Razavi and Miller (1995: 37–8) describe, WID mainstreaming progress slowed after the 1987 Conable reorganization of the Bank, in which the WID unit was folded into the Population and Human Resources Department. The net effect of the reorganization was to signal WID's place as firmly in the 'social sector' of the Bank's lending activities and thereby largely excluded from the key areas of infrastructure, transportation and private sector development. Despite some later staff increases in the role of 'WID resource persons' in the regional units, budgets and authority were still very limited and WID staff had little recourse to formal policies or mandates to push for operational changes (Murphy 1995; World Bank OED 2005). An Operational Policy adopted in 1990 merely *recommended* women's issues be considered when designing poverty-reduction programmes. The later reorganization under Lewis Preston in 1993 closed the WID office altogether and relocated staff to a Gender Analysis and Policy (GAP) thematic group in the Education and Social Policy Department. The new GAP team was charged with responsibility for furthering the social recognition of WID through increased staff training, preparation of 'toolkits' and demonstration of how gender issues could be incorporated into country assistance strategies (Razavi and Miller 1995: 39; World Bank OED 1994). Slowly, staff capacity was built somewhat unevenly in each regional operational sector of the Bank (depending on the commitment of regional vice-presidents), and overall it continued to lack sufficient resources through which really to push for deeper integration of gender issues in all areas of Bank operations. Operational Policy 4.20 was adopted in 1994 as a result of the strategy paper *Enhancing Women's Participation in Economic Development*. OP 4.20 required staff to 'reduce gender disparity and increase the participation of economic development', and indicated that gender issues should be incorporated into poverty assessments, public expenditure reviews, and economic and sector work.[4] However, the monitoring and enforcement of the new directive largely rested in the operational units and compliance remained uneven.

Overall, as the numerous institutional histories indicate, the primary constraints to gender mainstreaming at this point in the Bank's history lay in the intellectual and operational culture of the Bank. Early gender advocates, foreshadowing later norm entrepreneurs, sought intellectual entry by casting gender issues in terms of economic efficiency rather than the rights or security framework preferred by other IOs such as the UN Development Programme and Inter-American Development Bank (and somewhat over the opposition of important external donors who regretted the loss of the equity emphasis). This issue-framing was adopted by norm entrepreneurs not only because it was perceived as amenable to the mindsets of dominant economists, but also because it fit with the Bank's apolitical mandate. Gender mainstreaming also remained limited in so far as it remained compartmentalized, with success in the 'soft social sectors' of the Bank's work (health and education) and virtually no progress in the highly profitable 'hard economic sectors', where the strong disbursement imperative in the Bank's operational culture continued to focus staff efforts on lucrative projects. This was in part due to a lack of statistical evidence decisively demonstrating the 'investment returns' of a gendered approach in areas other than health and education. Moreover, despite efforts to integrate more gender issues and analysis into key documents, including Economic

---

[4] OP 4.20 also arose in the context of discussions regarding the impact of structural adjustment programmes on women. The resulting policy, however, indicates merely that a 'sound analysis may consider the potentially adverse effect of adjustment and resulting programs may include safety nets. However, no gender-impact analysis would be required nor would the Operational Memorandum on Adjustment Programmes require that individual programmes consider gender' (World Bank OED 2005: 18).

and Sector Work (ESW) and Country Assistance Strategy (CAS) documents, operational mainstreaming still fell far short owing to perceived resistance from reluctant borrowing governments who view gender issues as incompatible with their own societal norms and hinting at Western cultural imperialism.[5] Without even a passive acceptance on the part of borrowers, the Bank's country directors – even when they themselves internalized gender norms – were in turn reluctant to push gender issues, and support from top management remained inconsistent.

The Beijing juncture

The critical turning point for the GAD policy norm in the Bank came during the months surrounding the Beijing Fourth World Conference on Women in 1995. The conference itself provided an important focal point, and GAD advocates in the Bank took great pains to prepare numerous reports and action plans in preparation for the Bank's participation in the conference (see World Bank 1995a, 1995c, 1995e). More critically, the Beijing conference produced a major opportunity for external and internal advocates to push GAD mainstreaming for two reasons. First, for the first time, the GAD movement had the visible support of the Bank's top leadership. James Wolfensohn, the newly appointed President, travelled to Beijing for the conference. Second, a coalition of NGOs self-entitled 'Women's Eyes on the Bank' used the Beijing conference and Wolfensohn's appearance to mobilize external normative pressure for gender mainstreaming in the Bank. In a petition signed by more than 900 activists and handed directly to Wolfensohn in Beijing, the coalition demanded the Bank implement the Beijing Platform for Action and called for four specific changes in the Bank: (1) the increased participation of women in economic policy-making, (2) the institutionalization of a gendered approach in the design and implementation of Bank policies and programmes, (3) increased Bank lending for gender development projects, and (4) an increase in the number and diversity of senior women in Bank management (World Bank OED 2001).

The Beijing conference provided the needed momentum to reinvigorate gender mainstreaming. Upon return from Beijing, Wolfensohn created an External Gender Consultative Group, comprising fourteen members from national women's organizations, NGOs, academic institutions and political organizations from around the world. More importantly, during the 1997 Strategic Compact reorganization (see Weaver

[5] Interview with senior Bank officials, PRMGE, World Bank headquarters, Washington, DC, January 2007.

2008: chapter 5), he gave the GAD group a home in the newly formed Poverty Reduction and Economic Management (PREM) thematic network. The resulting Gender and Development Unit was given the responsibility for 'knowledge management, monitoring and reporting on the status of policy implementation, and building staff capacity for gender analysis' (World Bank OED 2001). In addition, the Bank sponsored an internal seminar as follow-up to the Beijing conference to give greater internal visibility to the mainstreaming agenda, and the regional offices were asked to prepare gender action plans (Murphy 1997).

Overall, subsequent evaluations dampened the apparent positive effects of these institutional changes. A 2005 report from the Operations Evaluation Department (OED) claimed that the PREM home ostensibly gave the GAD Board more authority than it had before, but limited ability to influence other networks. More importantly, it did not translate into more influence over operations, which was identified as the critical area of integration needed for desired mainstreaming. The OED report argued that the GAD Board's 'influence on operations is limited to persuading country directors, as it does not have the authority to influence project processing. The lack of authority could marginalize the Board, just as the WID unit was marginalized. Further, while the Regional representatives on the Environment Board are mostly sector directors or managers, only one of the six Regional gender co-ordinators on the GAD board is an operations manager' (World Bank OED 2005: 34).

Strategic mainstreaming, post-Beijing

The period since the Beijing conference is exemplified by the remarkable mainstreaming effort on the part of a small yet very proactive and dedicated core of gender advocates in the Bank. These GAD advocates have attempted fully to diffuse and integrate gender norms into the way the Bank pursues development, by integrating gender into issue areas of Bank operations which have traditionally been, at best, 'gender neutral' and at worst 'gender blind'. The advocates have further sought organizational resources and visibility through not only the capture of more staff in higher levels of management, but also the proactive alliance of prominent managers and executive directors. Most importantly, the post-Beijing internal advocacy efforts have focused on two major 'action plans' for gender mainstreaming, in 2002 and 2006. The action plans are in effect mobilization and accountability tools, effectively attracting attention to the GAD movement through the announcements and approval of each plan, as well as setting clear benchmarks for determining the Bank's progress towards meeting espoused GAD goals (discussed below).

More interesting in the period between the two action plans is the second order question of the potential costs of advocacy tactics. This relates to the change we can observe in the substance and choice of advocacy tactics outlined in each action plan, representing both the advocates' learning about what has worked or not, and more critically, what difficult compromises have been made in order to sustain and deepen mainstreaming progress. Noticeably, the 2006 action plan (compared with the 2002 action plan) is a much narrower agenda than originally intended or desired by GAD advocates. To organize this analysis, I identify four primary sets of tactics that characterize the efforts of GAD advocates over the past ten to fifteen years. I then turn to the question of the 'Faustian bargain' we may find in the current strategies to further institutionalize GAD into the Bank.

Tactic I: *leverage politics and resource mobilization*

GAD advocates inside the Bank have focused a great deal of their efforts on gaining financial and staff resources as well as greater voice and influence through positions of decision-making authority within the institution. These two goals often go hand in hand, considering where agenda-setting and budget allocation occurs in the Bank. In addition to the creation of the aforementioned GAD Board and the placement of the group within PREM, there has been a concerted effort to increase the number of women in the Bank, with a target set at 45 per cent of professional staff and 30 per cent of managers and senior technical staff. These goals were more or less met by 2005 (World Bank 2005f). However, even by 2007 (when interviews for this chapter were conducted) many still perceived a dearth of women in the key positions of the Bank that control the resources to help mainstream the agenda, either in the Bank's policies or in operations. Note US Executive Director Jan Piercy's comments in her foreword to the Regional Gender Workshops in July 2001:

Somewhat to my surprise, I was the first woman to represent the US on the Board, and there was only one other woman ED when I joined the Bank ... With average terms of two years, many Directors changed during my tenure. Never, however, has the Board had more than three woman directors simultaneously ... reflect[ing] the broader reality that there are still very few women 'at the table' making critical development and economic policy decisions, either at the country level or internationally.[6] (Piercy 2001)

---

[6] Notably, it matters not only if there are women in these key decision-making positions, but also whether they are supporters of the GAD agenda. Interviews with Bank senior officials in January 2007 revealed US support for the gender agenda waned when Jan Piercy was replaced by Carole Brookins (an appointee of the Bush administration).

GAD advocates have also sought to increase the number of lower line staff (male or female) delegated to work on gender issues. This has been most visible in the emphasis on 'gender focal points': staff in mission offices abroad or in regional offices inside the Bank's headquarters who are responsible for monitoring and enforcing gender policies and main-streaming gender issues. While there has been some success in increasing the number of focal points, my interviews with key participants as well as internal reviews of gender mainstreaming reveal shortcomings of this strategy. Depending upon the degree to which regional vice-presidents or country directors wish to invest in the gender agenda, these focal points may be full-time positions with real authority and resources, or they may simply be staff members whose role as a gender focal point constitutes only a small and underfunded portion of their overall job description.[7] In many cases, these gender focal points often are marginalized, tend not to be gender experts, and are often young, inexperienced, and lacking clout and influence (Mehra and Gupta 2006: 5).

Absent abundant and consistent support from the inside for this kind of resource mobilization, particularly from the Bank's mid-level manage-ment, GAD advocates have sought external leverage to build political and financial support for gender mainstreaming. Over the past ten years, such leverage has emerged in three forms. First, the agenda was naturally provided a major external boost by the UN-sponsored Millennium Development Goals (MDGs) signed in 2000. The MDGs provided sig-nificant political and moral leverage to the GAD agenda, particularly since the third goal of the MDGs focuses on women's well-being and empower-ment. The added benefit of internal attention to the progress of the MDGs has in turn provided a powerful external accountability measure (see next section).

Second, advocates sought to increase internal and external visibility and support by initiating a series of high-level conferences attended or hosted by prominent political leaders from national governments, international organizations, and international and local non-government and civil soci-ety groups.[8] In 1999–2000, the Bank hosted four regional workshops (in Manila, Nairobi, Quito and Warsaw). Importantly, these workshops were attended by several high-level officials who had potential influence over agenda-setting in the Bank, including the then United States Executive

---

[7] Interviews with Bank senior officials indicate that the Latin American and Caribbean region has been the most progressive in terms of hiring and empowering gender focal points, whereas the Middle East and North Africa, South Asia, and Sub-Saharan Africa regions have not yet fully pursued this goal.

[8] See the various reports that came out of these workshops at www.worldbank.org/oed/gender_workshops.

Director Jan Piercy. In November 2004, the GAD Board sponsored another workshop on the development implications of gender-based violence, with opening statements by Bank President James D. Wolfensohn and Mary Robinson, former United Nations High Commissioner for Human Rights. In February 2006, they convened a high-level meeting with partner agencies and governments to identify ways to accelerate progress towards the gender goals of the MDGs. Finally, in September 2006 at the annual meetings, the new gender action plan was formally announced by President Wolfowitz and championed by German Minister Heidemarie Wieczorek-Zeul, who later in 2007 hosted a high-level conference specifically on the Bank's gender action plan. The opening speech at the 2007 conference was given by German Federal Chancellor Angela Merkel, and the conference included prominent participants from various European and African development ministries, Danny Leipsiger (Vice-President of the World Bank) and Richard Manning (Chairman of the OECD's Development Assistance Committee).

Finally, the third leverage tactic used to promote the GAD agenda is the ongoing strategic targeting of donor trust funds, particularly those from countries which have already proved to be champions of the GAD policy norm (namely Norway, Germany and Britain). As will be described below, these trust funds (which are outside the regular donor contributions to the Bank's administration budget) provide the financial means necessary to pursue pilot programmes, analytical research, conferences and major reports that gender advocates claim can provide the 'demonstrable results of investment in gender programmes' necessary to persuade Bank managers to direct scarce resources towards gender work. Moreover, the Norwegian government pledged to cover more than one-third of the cost of implementing the 2006 action plan (estimated to be $10 million). Advocates view these funds as 'strategic seed financing … effective in building institutional commitment to incorporating gender into analytical and operational work' (World Bank 2006b: 2), even when they sometimes express misgivings about the specific constraints that arise from the conditions attached to the use of trust funds.[9]

Tactic II: accountability without coercion

One of the most prominent ongoing tactics used in gender mainstreaming in the Bank is accountability politics. In the past eight years, gender

[9] Interviews with senior Bank officials, conducted January 2007. Specifically, they lamented the fact that many of the trust funds have rules regarding the use of consultants, reporting procedures or particular 'pet projects' that are not always well aligned with the Bank's broader gender goals.

advocates – including those within the Bank's internal evaluation units – have made a concerted effort to meticulously track mainstreaming progress as a means of ensuring behavioural change in response to formal policy changes. Disconnects between policy and practice are quite common in the Bank, as in other large international organizations. In the case of gender policies, past mainstreaming reports have repeatedly emphasized the persistent gaps between formal rules or validity and actual implementation (social recognition within the Bank). Moreover, the results of a 2005 staff survey reveal that despite nearly unanimous awareness of gender policies (particularly OP 4.20), only 42 per cent of staff had read the policy and only 52 per cent claimed to address gender in their operational work (World Bank OED 2005: 75–6). This spurred advocates to push quite consciously for increased institutional accountability. This is largely accomplished through enhanced monitoring and reporting on Bank-wide (non-)compliance with gender operational policies, the extent to which departments are conducting country gender analyses and participating in gender training, and the degree to which various Bank departments have met expectations regarding the integration of gender issues into the procedures of Economic and Sector Work (ESW), Country Assistance Strategies (CAS), Public Expenditure Reviews (PERs) and Poverty Reduction Strategy Papers (PRSPs).

Accountability politics works best when actor behaviour can be measured against concrete, observable targets. The recent gender action reports have increasingly sought clear mainstreaming benchmarks – a lesson learned from other institutions' prior experience with gender mainstreaming. This is summed up by Carolyn Hannan, Director of the United Nations Division for the Advancement of Women, in her analysis of the Bank's 2002 action plan:

While the development of explicit policy statements on gender equality is an essential precondition for changes in policies, procedures and interventions, it is by no means sufficient in and of itself. There is a wealth of experience ... which shows very clearly that good policies can be sidelined very easily within organizations unless clear strategies and procedures, including inputs to develop the required institutional environment and accountability mechanisms, are put in place. Far too often top management in organizations have assumed that policy development will automatically lead to changes on the ground, only to find when monitoring and evaluation is undertaken that little real change results. A critical factor is bringing middle-level management on board in terms of commitment to the goals and objectives and recognition of the implications of gender perspectives in their areas of work and the need to address them explicitly. (Hannan 2002: 1)

In the past eight years, the reliance on accountability politics has been evident in the two prominent reports from the Operations Evaluation

Department (led by Gita Gopal, a long-term gender advocate in the Bank) and the annual mainstreaming update reports following the 2002 mainstreaming strategy plan, which provided a detailed list of quantifiable targets (for goals such as 'taking gender seriously' in all CAS papers) (see World Bank OED 2001, 2005; World Bank 2003b, 2005e, 2006c). Driven by a small but astoundingly dedicated and passionate group of gender advocates inside the Bank, these reports have also closely tracked the *quality* of gender integration into project design and management, as well as the quantitative amount of staff training, provision of operational toolkits, and processes for institutionalizing and enforcing new operational policies. This close attention to policy follow-through is reinforced by the reporting mechanisms put in place. In the case of the 2002 action plan, the GAD Board provided thorough progress reports each fiscal year thereafter, including lengthy statistical charts, which were provided directly to the Committee on Development Effectiveness in the Board of Executive Directors and were widely disseminated within and outside the Bank.[10]

The 2006 action plan for mainstreaming gender between 2007 and 2010 uses the same tactic of explicit targets and benchmarks. Moreover, a formal committee has been established to monitor and report on the implementation of the action plan. To attain 'buy-in' from senior Bank officials as well as ensure accountability from operational units, this committee comprises an internal Bank Group Executive Committee that draws six to eight members from the operational regions, Operational Policy and Country Services, the Legal Department, International Finance Corporation (IFC), and the PREM Network. The Committee in turn is guided by an Advisory Council of eight to ten members consisting of representatives from donor agencies, the External Gender Consultative Group, members of the GAD Board and senior Bank staff. The multi-layered nature of this set-up suggests a ratcheting up of accountability mechanisms in a way unparalleled by mainstreaming efforts I have observed in other issue areas of the Bank's work.[11]

This ultimately leads to one of the most remarkable findings regarding the accountability tactics: the conscious avoidance of formal mandates as

---

[10] The Bank's gender and development website is one of the most comprehensive of the Bank's websites, in terms of the availability of written reports, conference proceedings, and data on past and ongoing projects involving gender components. See www.world bank.org/gender/.

[11] The obvious comparison is the Bank's Anti-Corruption Strategy, also passed in 2006. There are very few clear benchmarks or accountability mechanisms in place for ensuring the implementation of the anti-corruption plan, which may ironically be because the norms of the anti-corruption agenda have enjoyed high-level support (particularly from the Bank presidents) since the mid-1990s.

a mechanism to incite behavioural change in Bank management and staff. Learning from past agenda advocacy campaigns within the Bank, notably the environment agenda, GAD advocates strategically sought a slower yet arguably more sustainable process of persuasion and socialization (a 'Type II internalization'; see Checkel 2005), wherein Bank staff internalized the goals of the GAD agenda rather than complying superficially with organizational requirements (such as environmental impact assessments in project lending and the governance and anti-corruption assessments in Country Assistance Strategy papers). This was reinforced by a December 2000 staff survey, in which managers reported that issuing gender assessment mandates, as with many environmental mandates, would incite resentment and 'lead to sterile filling-in of boxes in standard documents'.[12]

My interviews confirmed that GAD advocates are leery of the 'shallow internalization' effect of 'unfunded mandates' and aware of the necessity of inciting something deeper than instrumental rationality to produce more sustainable and self-enforcing behavioural change.[13] Progress in mainstreaming, they argue, relies much more on persuading powerful country directors and regional vice-presidencies of the value of adopting the gender and development policy norm (see also World Bank OED 2005: 35). In some cases, gender advocates claim they have been successful where country directors and regional vice-presidents were already receptive to the gender agenda or felt that it was an agenda they could engage with borrowing governments (as in the Latin America and Caribbean region). In other areas, they have met scepticism or neglect (namely the Middle East and North Africa and South Asia regions). None the less, advocates continue to prefer the choice of carrot over stick, as embodied in the 2006 action plan's 'core guiding principle' to pursue gender mainstreaming through 'incentives rather than mandates or obligations' (World Bank 2006b: 3–4).

Tactic III: persuasion via proof

The effort to promote accountability in mainstreaming without resort to more coercive policies (namely formal validity via mandates) in turn contributed to the tactic of persuasion based upon the provision of 'proof' or evidence that would facilitate the internalization of the GAD

---

[12] World Bank OED (2005, Annex D: 75–6) (citing results of a December 2000 staff survey).
[13] Interviews with senior Bank officials, conducted January 2007. See also World Bank OED (2005: 35).

goals by powerful actors within and outside the Bank. Persuasion tactics are shaped strongly by the culture of organizations. In the case of the Bank, it is the *technocratic* and *economistic* aspect of bureaucratic culture that matters.

This is a point that Bebbington *et al.* (2006) make in their discussion of advocacy efforts related to the social capital agenda in the Bank. They argue that in the Bank it is imperative to produce the kinds of evidence that will persuade operational managers to invest relatively scarce staff resources in new work, as well as expend influence in trying to persuade reluctant borrowers to address new issues in their loan and technical assistance requests. In the case of the GAD policy norm, advocates realized early on that they would need quantifiable evidence to illustrate the necessity of considering gender issues in the Bank's programmes. Increasingly, the kind of evidence deemed valuable here includes sex-disaggregated statistics, increased amounts of analytical work (in particular work that demonstrates the 'economic rates of return'), and pilot projects that could quickly and convincingly demonstrate clear measurable results.[14] There is also a discernible pressure to show successful and quick results in gender investment. This seems to have influenced the 2006 gender action plan's strategy of targeting 'focus countries' for gender projects. These are countries where political buy-in is already in place and projects could more or less be assured of success.[15]

This all ultimately relates to strategies on 'how to speak to power' within the Bank. As O'Brien *et al.* (2000) argue, the pressures to persuade reluctant managers (who in turn were responding to reluctant borrowers) led over time to the adoption of an increasingly technical approach to gender analysis that considered men's issues and stripped down seemingly feminist language. They argue that this was the result of gender advocates (who are mostly women) being in a 'counter-cultural position': 'the vast majority of the Bank's staff are economists, and they are mostly men, two facts which are not immaterial in terms of creating an organizational culture resistant to feminist concerns' (O'Brien *et al.* 2000: 56).

An OED 2000 *Precis* report similarly notes the dilemma of 'speaking to power' in a way that also reflects the pragmatic constraints of daily life within Bank operations:

---

[14] This ties into the previous discussion of leverage politics, in so far as many of these activities were funded via donor trust funds.

[15] The 2006 action plan clearly states this strategy of increasing resources to 'results-based initiatives' and policy-relevant research and statistics, with an emphasis on producing 'observable results in a reasonable time frame' (World Bank 2006b: 5).

Task managers are overworked, and gender issues must contend for limited resources with other concerns. Rather than lobby for support from the top, some Bank staff work from the bottom up, establishing credibility with task and sector managers, demonstrating the value of gender work through solid empirical research, and using the techniques of social marketing (identifying target groups and appealing to their interests) ... Economic arguments can be persuasive in convincing people of the need to do something for gender equality ... Zero in on key messages econometrically. (World Bank OED 2000: 3–5).

O'Brien *et al.* (2000) confirm this operational constraint, which they put in the context of the 1997 reorganization of the Bank. The Strategic Compact introduced a new matrix system, which created a 'demand-driven' internal market in which operational managers (usually country directors) have to contract for the services of gender specialists (but are not required to do so). They argue that 'this puts the onus on gender specialists to "sell" their services in ways which will attract project designers – and in a neoliberal economic environment this means stressing the business case for gender equity, not the social justice case, which had tended to be the stronger suit of gender advocates' (O'Brien *et al.* 2000: 44–5).

Tactic IV: strategic framing

Ultimately, the pressure to persuade via 'proof' that resonates within the organizational culture of the Bank is strongly linked to the final tactic of strategic framing. Repeated observations throughout the history of gender mainstreaming in the Bank indicate that strategic framing is the most effective tactic utilized by internal advocates to demonstrate organizational 'fit' (Bebbington *et al.* 2006: 15). It specifically involves speaking about issues in a language that resonates within the institution's dominant culture, choosing methods, concepts and theories that, as in the case above, 'speak to power' in a way that gives advocates a seat at the table.

The most obvious example of strategic framing is the 2006 action plan, strategically entitled *Gender Equality as Smart Economics*. The motivation behind the framing was the realization that the central mainstreaming gap was in the 'core' economic areas of Bank operations (finance, infrastructure, agriculture and the finance sector) and not in the 'soft social sectors' where the GAD policy norm enjoyed considerable success (see, e.g., World Bank OED 2005: 23; World Bank 2006b: 1). Gender advocates, including several members of the Bank's Board of Executive Directors and senior management, determined that a specific focus on gender mainstreaming in the economic sectors of Bank lending and technical assistance would enable gender to gain greater traction across the entire institution. In the various mainstreaming reports leading up to the 2006 action plan, a repeated punch line was the prescription to concentrate on analytical and pilot operational work related to issues such as women's access to labour markets, the share of women in non-agricultural wage employment, wage equity, and access to affordable and efficient transportation to increase women's ability to become labour market participants. Prior notions of gender equality, security and empowerment were recast almost entirely in economic terms, with emphasis on questions of how to increase women's property rights, access to credit, productivity increases, and the potential effect of these forms of economic empowerment on national economic growth.

A Faustian bargain?

Interviews with gender advocates in the Bank reveal that over time the framing tactics employed here have sometimes entailed uncomfortable compromises. In order to gain intellectual and operational entry, they consciously chose a narrowed approach that validated gender ideas through technocratic projects that could provide quick, quantifiable results and were focused on the impact on national economies (specifically, in terms of how underinvestment in women limits economic growth and slows progress in poverty reduction). The effect was more or less a 'watering down' of the policy norm's scope (Hafner-Burton and Pollack 2002: 364). Many of the deeper issues impeding women's empowerment, security and development, particularly those embedded in social relations and cultures, are neglected or overshadowed. The language of rights and security is there, but hidden in the language of 'economic empowerment of poor women'.

In fact, the recent gender action plan deviates quite significantly from the Beijing Platform, which calls for mainstreaming across interlinked 'critical areas of concern' that include poverty, human rights, the economy, violence against women and armed conflict. The Bank's conscious narrowing to the singular economic focus incites critics, who accuse the Bank of failing to uphold promises made at Beijing (Dennis and Zuckerman 2006; Hannan 2004; MacDonald 2003; Mehra and Gupta 2006; Moser and Moser 2005). Even some of the Executive Directors, who soundly supported the plan's focus on economic sectors, voiced some worry that the plan was underfunded and could potentially detract from the Bank's continuing progress in gendered dimensions of health and education.

Mehra and Gupta (2006) argue that many long-term GAD supporters within and outside the Bank understand the necessity of such a mainstreaming strategy. However, they are increasingly disillusioned with the way gender mainstreaming has worked so far and are beginning to feel that it has failed (Mehra and Gupta 2006: 1). Less sympathetic critics are visibly enraged by the framing of the 2006 action plan. They claim that the Bank's new approach neglects or obscures underlying gender power relationships or the effects of traditional Bank lending (especially through structural adjustment programmes) that actually inhibit women's economic empowerment or cause greater gender inequality. In their view, the Bank's 2006 action plan may succeed in its goal of institutional mainstreaming, but it will be the mainstreaming of a GAD policy norm that threatens to do more harm than good to women in the developing world (see, e.g., Brym *et al.* 2005; Dennis and Zuckerman 2006; Khundker 2004; Long 2006; Wichterich 2007).

The rationale for such Faustian bargains is none the less apparent. As the internal advocates I interviewed argue, the point is to get the ideas on the table, to pass the policies, and to begin to change practices in a way that will 'snowball' into the acceptance of a broader gender policy norm later on. The 'Faustian bargain' is thus intended to be short-term. The real test of the success of strategic framing as an advocacy tactic thus remains to be seen. If, in fact, the framing narrative opens doors inside the Bank previously shut tight to the gender norm, this may represent a critical 'foot in the door' that can then be used later to bring in a more broadly defined gender norm once institutional commitment is assured. None the less, a repeated concern is that this strategy may backfire if the norm is co-opted by powerful economists who may be able to exclude alternative voices from future conversation. In the end, this outcome will be largely determined by organizational leadership and the ability of gender advocates to gain more positions of authority inside the Bank.

Conclusion

Overall, this chapter described how the particular GAD policy norm has developed over time. GAD entered the organization with initially a low degree of formal validity and social recognition. Yet, over time, the policy norm gained traction and was formalized in operational policies. Nevertheless, this norm institutionalization did not lead to significant changes in organizational or operational actions since the norm was not socially recognized by staff. The empirical analysis shows how norm entrepreneurs supported by leadership have actually tried to enhance social recognition of the norm inside the organization through various tactics.

The tactics chosen by internal policy norm entrepreneurs to gain entry and traction in the Bank has long-term implications for how new concepts and goals are understood, attain validity through formal rule change, are internalized by actors, and ultimately ingrained in organizational behaviour. In this case of GAD, we can observe that advocates intentionally opted over time for a strategy of framing and marketing new issues in a language, methodology and theoretical approach that does not directly challenge or delegitimize prevailing ideologies and practices in the Bank's research and operational cultures or provoke client government resistance. This strategy enabled other organizational actors (the 'recipients'), who would otherwise experience cognitive dissonance, to relate to the concepts in a way that does not require rejection of prior mindsets. Yet the cost of such strategic advocacy may be high – the implicit danger of a Faustian bargain. Thus, while the GAD policy norm has been added on to the social dimension of World Bank policies, and therefore fits well with an emerging holistic approach to development, the signs of a Faustian bargain described in this chapter hint at the fact that holistic development is not such a great departure from the Washington Consensus.

Part Three

Norm stabilization

Lacking ownership: the IMF and its
      engagement with social development
      as a policy norm

Antje Vetterlein

Introduction

By the end of the 1990s social, instead of narrowly defined economic, development had become a global policy norm. The development order of the 1980s was marked by a consensus that fostered development policies based on classical economic theory; yet the emphasis on economic policies began to crack over the course of the 1990s. Early in that decade the United Nations (UN) was already promoting a human development approach based on Sen's idea that development is primarily about people not economics (Sen 2001). The World Bank followed these footsteps in the mid-1990s, setting up new policy initiatives and organizational reforms such as the Comprehensive Development Framework or the Strategic Compact that significantly enhanced the social development agenda inside the organization and refocused its objective towards poverty reduction. The IMF lagged behind these developments but joined the new spirit in 1999 by signing the Bank's Poverty Reduction Strategy Paper (PRSP) initiative. This was the first time in its history that the Fund officially endorsed poverty reduction as one of its priority objectives.[1] It also acknowledged the benefits of social policies for economic development. Yet to what extent has the Fund internalized this new social development policy norm?[2]

---

[1] See www.imf.org/external/np/prgf/2000/eng/key.htm, accessed 28 January 2007.

[2] The terms poverty reduction, social development and social policies are used in accordance with Fund practice in the following way. Social development as a policy norm departs from a narrow focus on economic development and aims at combining economic and social policies. Contrary to the 1980s when economic growth was the main objective of development policy, in the social development policy norm poverty reduction is seen as equally important. As a result, social policies have reached a more prominent status in IMF policies and displaced the exclusive focus on economic policies. This so-called 'social dimension' of Fund policies (see www.imf.org/external/np/exr/facts/social.htm, accessed

By tracing the evolution of the Fund's approach to social development policies from the late 1970s until today it becomes clear that the organization has not been at the forefront of promoting this policy norm and has always been reluctant to accommodate it into its operations. During the course of the 1980s the Fund struggled to acknowledge the social costs of its adjustment programmes. In the 1990s it tried to address precisely these detrimental effects of adjustment lending in the form of social safety nets and technical advice regarding social expenditure. At the turn of the century, however, it subscribed to the overall shift in favour of this policy norm. Yet internal debates have not stopped over whether or not social development aimed at poverty reduction should be on the Fund's agenda. All in all, the story is one of accommodating a policy norm which is clearly difficult to align with the organization's mandate and beliefs about how best to tackle development problems. The question therefore is *why* did the Fund as an expert in economic issues become involved in social policies in order to reduce poverty?

Theoretical approaches on norms and IOs mainly stress IOs' power to regulate and constitute specific policy areas (Barnett and Finnemore 2004). IOs are seen as embodying certain norms and 'teaching' them to states (e.g. Finnemore 1993, 1996; Risse *et al.* 1999). Yet these approaches do not shed light on where norms come from in IOs. Do IOs merely adapt to their material and normative environment or are they actively creating and setting norms? Recent studies inspired by both principal–agent (PA) models (e.g. Hawkins *et al.* 2006; Martin 2006; Nielson and Tierney 2003; Nielson, Tierney and Weaver 2006; Pollack 1997) and organizational sociology (e.g. Babb 2003; Barnett and Finnemore 1999, 2004; Park 2007a, b, 2010; Weaver 2007, 2008) inform us that IOs do not necessarily do what their principals want them to do, thus suggesting that IOs actively create norms on their own and set policy agendas. Most of these analyses study the World Bank which might be a special case of an organization with a high degree of autonomy. It remains to be seen whether this is the case for all IOs or whether there are differences among them.

By means of examining the evolution of the social dimension within the IMF I argue that in this particular example we deal with a case of norm adaptation. Three conditions of IO behaviour are derived: an organization that strongly depends on its Executive Board; a low degree of consistency of social policies with the Fund's original mandate, procedures and ideology; and its staff's professional background. In the policy case discussed here, the combination of these conditions led to a situation where a

2 June 2008) developed incrementally by adding on policy measures from dealing with income distribution (1980s), social safety nets and social funds (1990s) to the Fund's participation in the PRSP (1999).

powerful external event, the Asian financial crisis, pushed the IMF into a policy area for which it is not appropriately equipped. From the late 1980s management tried to increase staff knowledge on poverty reduction, although such efforts were discouraged by the Board. In addition, contrary to the case in other policy areas such as capital account liberalization (Leiteritz and Moschella, chapter 8 this volume), staff who consist of economists trained in conservative economic theory (Chwieroth 2007a) were not interested in pursuing social issues and therefore did not lobby for it. Like the case of debt relief (Momani, chapter 2 this volume) it was a Board decision to participate in the PRSP initiative with – given the previous resistance to social policy issues – two consequences. First, borrowing from its own language, the Fund lacks *ownership* when it comes to social policies, which in turn increases the likelihood of not taking this policy norm seriously enough. Second, the Fund lacks expertise in this area with the result that social issues will always be framed in economic terms, thus delimiting the social development policy norm.

This chapter proceeds as follows. After a brief explication of the study of norms and IOs the chapter traces the evolution of social development ideas in IMF policies based on a document analysis and interviews conducted with Fund staff. Through tracing this process the main triggers and specific mechanisms of policy norm formation become apparent. From the empirical analysis two conclusions can be drawn. First, the degree of autonomy, which is a decisive aspect of policy norm creation, varies across IOs. The Fund depicts a case of high dependency on its member states through its Board of Executive Directors. Otherwise the organization might have opted against the inclusion of poverty reduction and social issues into its policies. Second, while the policy norm has gained formal validity in the form of the Poverty Reduction and Growth Facility (PRGF), the Fund and its staff have not internalized social issues since its original mandate and professional background are antithetical to social policies. As such staff have not socially recognized the social development policy norm. The chapter concludes by embedding this single policy norm within the broader normative context of development and relates it to the norm circle described in chapter 1. The Fund has taken up the idea of poverty reduction as part and parcel of achieving economic growth, and thus, has contributed to legitimizing social development as a global policy norm despite a lack of staff social recognition.

The creation of policy norms: how do IOs 'tick'?

For some time, norms in international relations have been dealt with from a structural point of view as 'doing things' (Seabrooke and Sending 2007) or, in other words, as the independent variable. Norms *do* constrain and regulate behaviour and therefore contribute to stability, thus making the world more predictable. They also guide action by providing scripts that facilitate decision-making processes. Sociologists in particular provide numerous examples of the mechanisms of socialization and internalization through which actors learn certain norms in everyday life, such that they do not have to create everything from scratch in any given situation, for example saying 'Good morning' when meeting a colleague before 12 p.m. While there are differences when translating these concepts to collective actors, norms have been treated as generally accepted, sanctioned prescriptions. In this literature IOs play the role of 'norm diffusers or transmitters within the international realm' (Park 2006: 343). IOs teach states what to do and thus have a significant impact on domestic politics and policies. This perspective therefore privileges the structural aspect of norms at the expense of their relational impact. Norms are stabilizers, yet at the same time are also flexible and constructed. Processes of norm contestation, however, have been neglected in this approach. As Finnemore and Sikkink (1998: 896) point out: 'little theoretical work has focused on the process of "norm building"'.

Problematizing norm emergence and contestation shifts the perspective of norms as 'things to do' (Seabrooke and Sending 2007). Therefore, the norm as such becomes the *explanandum*. In the IO literature specifically, little attention has been paid to where norms come from. Park (2006) provides an excellent overview of studies that engage with the origin of norms in IOs. From a detailed discussion of various conducted case studies (UNESCO, World Bank, OSCE, NATO, the EU, the Council of Europe) she observes that '[t]he most elaborate argument posited by Finnemore is that norms emerge within IOs and the international community, or that they may come from individuals[3] before joining the IO' (Park 2006: 358). This, however, is not a sufficient answer. There are more specific questions to be asked, such as why do IOs champion certain norms but not others? Do IOs adapt to their normative environment or do they actively promote policy norms? Under what conditions do norms evolve in IOs? Park's (2006) conclusion is that the identity of an IO and the socialization processes of IOs by other collective actors in the international community (in particular NGOs) offer insights into which policy norms IOs espouse. This offers another vantage point for exploring norm diffusion within and by IOs.

Park therefore makes two points: first, the need to consider the specific context in which norms emerge or change in IOs. Yet the environment of IOs is much wider than NGOs. It might also include the situation in client countries, for example, where conflicts are possible while transmitting

---

[3] Leadership is the prominent example here (see, e.g. Finnemore 1996).

norms (see Gutner 2005a), an aspect the norm literature in IR has neglected so far. As suggested in the introduction to this volume (chapter 1), the 'life cycle' of a norm (Finnemore and Sikkink 1998) does not end with its internalization, but once norms are established they are constantly contested (Wiener 2007a). Second, social practices that constitute the meaning of norms are crucial, which in the case of IOs refer to the internal life of an organization and thus to its structure, culture and identity. What Park argues for empirically is in line with Wiener's (2007b) ontological critique of constructivists' use of norms in international relations theory. Wiener argues for appreciating the 'dual quality [of norms], that is, they are both structuring and socially constructed through interaction in context' (2007b: 5; see also Guzzini 2000). In other words, if we are interested in the emergence and transformation of norms in the IMF we have to assume that norms are being continuously contested, evolving through social practices that constitute their meaning, and are affected by the context in which they work (Barnett 1999).

How do we account for context and social practices in the analysis of norm emergence in IOs? Organizational theory conceptualizes organizations' behaviour as a balancing act between context and practice. After the foundation of an organization, the initial formal system of rules and goals, which sets out tasks, power and procedures, is given life and meaning by two organizational experiences. The first experience is its relationship with its outside world, that is, its context. Such social settings of organizational activity go beyond public relations, and thus, self-maintenance. As soon as an organization is aware of its dependency on its material and normative environment it changes its perception of itself, leading to changes in its policies, recruitment strategies and organizational structures. Second, an organization also has an internal social world which is made up of individuals that in their everyday operational life enact and transform the meaning of policy norms. The formal structure never really accounts for what staff are doing. There is an informal structure which develops through staff bringing their own interests and values to the organization that may not overlap with the organization's goals. Social relations that develop over time lead to the development of institutional values, internal interest conflicts and a fixed way of perceiving itself and the world. These developments have a unifying effect: group values are formed that determine the organization's objectives and norms, and eventually, its identity. The IO institutionalizes these responses over time into patterns through balancing and responding to organization-internal conditions and pressures from its environment.

These patterns then determine how the organization 'ticks', that is, whether it quickly picks up on ideas and pressure and translates them into policies; how it promotes new policy norms; what the main triggers are for policy norm change; and who is engaged in creating policy norms. In that sense its organizational characteristics mainly determine the way in which the organization is perceived by and handles its environment. An organization staffed with highly technical personnel might connect differently to its outside world compared with one staffed by on-the-ground development practitioners. They might also react differently to policy problems (see Bartkowski 2006). At their foundation, organizations are set up and equipped with certain features which are subject to change over time since an organization is not a stable entity but is interpreted and shaped by its environment and staff. These features are (1) its original mandate and (2) an organizational structure with a set of rules, regulations and operational procedures, specific units and departments. In addition, (3) informal regulations emerge in the daily interaction of staff. As research has shown, the professional background of staff themselves decisively shapes organizational practices (Babb 2003; Bebbington *et al.* 2006; Kanbur 2001; Miller-Adams 1999; Momani 2005). Finally, in the case of *international* organizations an important factor is (4) the organization's autonomy from its principals. These four organizational characteristics determine how the organization acts and interacts. What assumptions can be drawn from the Fund's organizational characteristics regarding mechanisms and triggers for change and how do these inform its engagement with social development as a policy norm?

1 Compared with other IOs the Fund has a clearly defined mandate: responding to balance of payments problems and providing macroeconomic stability in order to achieve economic growth.[4] This is a precise objective and leaves less leverage for redefinition as opposed to the World Bank's mandate for 'development',[5] which is a vague or at best a broad objective that can be, and has been, interpreted in many ways. What is important regarding the policy norm of social development is that the Fund's mandate is purely economic. It might therefore be difficult for the organization to accommodate social policies into its technocratic economic modelling.

2 The Fund is a highly centralized organization with clearly established hierarchies among different units as well as staff. This leads to a high level of control within the organization; it is structured and efficient, focusing on delivery. It also leads to a working atmosphere of trust and

---

[4] See www.imf.org/external/pubs/ft/aa/aa01.htm, accessed 19 February 2007.
[5] See http://web.worldbank.org/WBSITE/EXTERNAL/EXTABOUTUS/0,,contentMDK: 20049557~menuPK:63000601~pagePK:34542~piPK:36600~theSitePK:29708,00.html, accessed 19 February 2007.

security: because staff actions, their careers and promotion depend on formal procedures and hierarchy they are loyal and collegial. Additionally, staff are likely to be conformist, preferring status quo situations since other behaviour will not be rewarded. We would therefore expect, in general, high levels of compliance with management and Board decisions and less lobbying behaviour or fewer initiatives by staff.

3 The staff is homogeneous and made up of macroeconomists and financial experts. This can have two consequences. First, there might be less discussion or questioning of certain policies, in particular when it comes to social development. This is not to say that all Fund economists agree on how to achieve its goals (see Moschella 2008). However, with sociologists, civil engineers or anthropologists working together on a project the likelihood of a debate is much higher and therefore bottom-up changes initiated by staff are more likely. Second, studies have shown the impact of staff's professional background on organizational action (Barnett and Finnemore 2004; Bartkowski 2006; Bebbington *et al.* 2006; Weaver 2008). Economists recruited from conservative economics departments (Chwieroth 2007a) are more inclined to adhere to so-called neoliberal economic ideas that theorize poverty reduction as an automatic outcome of economic growth (Barnett and Finnemore 2004; Momani 2005).

4 Financially, the Fund fully depends on its member states. That leaves little or no scope for independent decisions with regard to staff hiring or shaping the organization's research agenda. In other words, the Executive Board decides upon not only the use of Fund resources and general policy initiatives but also organizational matters including future research. Combined with the hierarchical nature of the IMF and its clear structure, the Board plays a powerful role in the IMF.

All four characteristics form an organization and make it what it is, shape how it relates to its outside world and how it behaves regarding policy norm change. They are therefore related to triggers and mechanisms of norm change. An organization with a strong Executive Board and a strict hierarchical structure might be less prone to bottom-up processes of change where staff actively lobby for new policy norms. The following empirical analysis pays particular attention to these variables.

Social practices and contextualization: tracing the social development policy norm in IMF policies

In 1999 the Fund officially subscribed to the social development policy norm's objective of 'poverty reduction' by joining the Poverty Reduction

Strategy initiative. It was the first time that poverty reduction appeared on its website as a priority objective. That is not to say that poverty had not been recognized as a problem before. However, as we will see below, the Fund's position had been that poverty does not relate to its area of expertise or its scope of intervention. Yet, by the turn of the century a few social staff were hired, a Poverty and Social Impact Analysis unit was set up, and conditionality was extended to social issues. While the development order had shown signs of change almost a decade before (Emmerji *et al.* 2005), the Fund seemed reluctant to adjust to these developments. It only reacted after the East Asian financial crisis had shaken its self-understanding and image as a result of the mismatch of its predictions with the actual event. Looking more closely at how the Fund theorized the relationship between economic growth and poverty reduction and the role of social policies in fostering development, it is clear that the social dimension of development had never figured prominently in its approach. That is to say, while the policy norm has gained formal validity in the organization it has not achieved social recognition. Why is the organization now promoting the policy norm? Based on a document analysis and interviews with IMF staff, three periods can be distinguished from the late 1970s until today when social policies figured differently inside the organization: the realization of the effects of income distribution, the era of social safety nets and the discovery of poverty reduction show the strengthening of the policy norm over time.

The realization of income distribution

The Fund's first involvement with social issues dates back to the early 1980s. Yet the word *social* did not appear in papers and policies per se but entered the IMF's policies through the realization that its macroeconomic stabilization programmes have distributional effects. Confronted by critiques from the development community, the IMF at first defended its programmes with two main arguments. First, the Fund argued that inflation control benefits the poorest segments of a society by drawing on a counterfactual of a country that does not implement Fund-suggested adjustment programmes but opts for an expansion of its public sector (IMF 1986):

In general, lower-income groups tend to have the least access to assets whose values rise *pari passu* with inflation and are most likely to hold their savings in a monetary form. That these same groups are often the weakest in their ability to secure effective indexation of their wages strongly suggests that reducing inflation has egalitarian implications. (Johnson and Salop 1980: 3).

The second argument stressed the country's sovereignty and responsibility for the implementation of stabilization programmes. It is the government's remit to determine 'whose demand is reduced in the initial phase of the program' (Johnson and Salop 1980: 20) not the IMF's, which cannot intervene in domestic politics.[6]

Only in the late 1980s, when external critiques against Fund programmes mounted, did the organization start explicitly to acknowledge the social implications of its adjustment programmes. The point of departure was the basic assumption that Fund-supported programmes inevitably affect poverty groups 'because they influence not only aggregate demand, supply, and the overall price level but also the composition of demand and supply and, therefore, relative prices' (Heller *et al.* 1988: 8).

Involvement in social development was subsequently legitimized by referring to the compensation function of social policies that purportedly enhance the viability and political acceptability of stabilization programmes by buffering social costs and income distribution. In other words, '[i]mplementation of adjustment measures that are perceived to be detrimental to the poor may not only jeopardize a current adjustment programme but may also deter governments from embarking on such programmes in the future' (Heller *et al.* 1988: 1).

This was the IMF's official position on social policies in the 1980s. Looking closer at the debates and developments inside the IO sheds light on how the organization balanced economic conditions and political pressures in its organizational context, aligning it with its mandate. The world economy of the 1970s was characterized by stagflation, that is, low productivity growth, high inflation, unemployment and economic imbalances. This led to a significant increase in borrowing by developing countries. The Fund's response to the first oil crisis was to increase facilities with low conditions. After the second crisis adjustment programmes were introduced with high conditionality (Boughton 2001). However, conditionality did not seem to work. External criticisms against Fund stabilization programmes mounted, concluding that they were not achieving their objectives of balance of payments, growth and reducing inflation (Bird 1982; Helleiner 1987; Killick 1982, 1984). Furthermore, critics claimed that they had adverse social and political implications that had to be addressed (Gerster 1982).

---

[6] References to the country's sovereignty are still used today to argue for the appropriateness of Fund programmes and policy suggestions that are distorted by 'wrong' implementation. To quote one of my interviewees: 'This is not possible to control. The Fund isn't a government . . . The state remains sovereign. What they do in the end . . . is hard to monitor for the Fund. These are sovereign states' (interview conducted 19 March 2004; translation by the author).

Yet the type of knowledge required for dealing with social issues did not exist in the IMF. In 1977, then Managing Director H. Johannes Witteveen requested in-house research on the topic (Boughton 2001). In fact, Witteveen was concerned about the World Bank's development in this direction and foresaw possible conflicts between the two organizations. Thus, he suggested that the Fund do research rather than rely on the Bank for this (see Historian's files in IMF/RD, cited by Boughton 2001: 696). Two internal studies were published in 1980, one on income distribution (Johnson and Salop 1980) and the other on basic needs (Borpujari 1980). While the former became widely regarded as the Fund's response to the problem, the latter was neglected in the Fund's internal discourse. It was not cited in Fund research papers and only marginally mentioned in its history (Boughton 2001). Interestingly, Borpujari developed a framework which incorporated financial constraints into a model in which development depends on the economic ability to provide for *basic needs*. But instead of linking such an approach with its conditionality, the Fund decided to focus on *income distribution*.

A closer look at the historical accounts reveals that the search for a *basic needs approach* was externally driven by the USA (Gerster 1982). Both left and right forces in the 95th American Congress, although driven by separate motivations, pushed for a basic needs approach and threatened to reduce the IMF's funding unless it changed its programmes.[7] An agreement was achieved by amending the Bretton Woods Agreement Act and incorporating basic human needs and human rights. In the end, the basic needs approach was not proposed to the IMF Executive Board until the end of 1981. By then, presidential elections had taken place and the Carter administration was replaced by that of Reagan. The American Executive Director in the IMF was replaced and the implementation of the basic needs policy did not take place. In the IMF, the idea of a basic needs approach was dropped and replaced by a focus on income distribution to address the issue of adverse effects.

This account shows two things. First, the Fund's engagement with social issues was stimulated from the outside. The main trigger was the American threat to withdraw contributions. Second, once confronted with claims from the outside the organization developed its own approach and thus decisively shaped the policy norm. Instead of adopting the basic needs approach it opted to focus on income distribution. That might not come as a surprise given its mandate and professional culture which was

---

[7] See debates in the House of Representatives and the Senate about US participation in the so-called Witteveen Facility in 1977 and the increase of the American quota in the Fund in 1978 (Gerster 1982: 503ff.).

not geared towards social issues. The Fund lacked knowledge in this area, which took time to address. Translating *social* implications into an *economic* issue of income distribution was the consequence.

Still the income distribution approach had to be operationalized into Fund practice. In the mid-1980s, a seminar on income distributional effects of Fund-supported programmes was held in the Fund's Executive Board based on three in-house research papers that developed a methodology for operationalizing income distribution in Fund programmes (for published versions see Gupta and Nashashibi 1990; Heller *et al.* 1988; IMF 1986). An approach for how to define and measure poverty was required before designing policy measures to mitigate the adverse effects of Fund programmes. Again, all three papers point out the lack of data and knowledge as an obstacle to a comprehensive and accurate assessment of adjustment programmes' poverty impacts. But instead of establishing this expertise within the organization the Board decided that the Fund should rely on the Bank's data and research in the area of poverty. Furthermore, the Board's review of Fund conditionality concluded that social issues should not be related to conditionality (Boughton 2001). In other words, while Fund management and staff did engage with the issue, the Board was the trigger for how the Fund responded to this process. In the end, the Fund's operational solution was an emphasis on technical advice regarding subsidies and government expenditure which eventually materialized into two new lending facilities: the Structural Adjustment Facility (SAF) in 1986 followed by the Enhanced Structural Adjustment Facility (ESAF) in 1987.

The era of social safety nets

By the mid-1990s, the Fund provided a very clear framework for different kinds of safety nets that operationalized the policy norm. Social safety nets are defined as

ad hoc or permanent arrangements that mitigate possible adverse effects of economic reform measures on the poor. Different countries have different social policy instruments which provide a basis for designing social safety nets and face varying financial constraints. In many countries, a core of social safety nets would include a mix of limited subsidies on basic necessities (particularly basic foodstuffs), social security arrangements (such as pensions and unemployment benefits), and possibly public works programmes adapted for this purpose. (IMF 1993a: 23)

Furthermore, the Fund argues not only that such measures should be implemented at the time of reform but 'it is important for countries to establish cost-effective permanent social security measures to deal with "normal" contingencies' (IMF 1993a: 3). Moreover, it is acknowledged that a minimum set of such measures could be integrated into economic reform programmes (IMF 1993a: 20).

It was again through external triggers that the Fund adopted social safety nets into its set of policy tools. They were introduced to the Fund at the 39th meeting of the joint Bank–Fund Development Committee[8] and therefore from the outside, or more specifically, through discussions with the World Bank (Development Committee 1990). This is not to say that the Fund belatedly accommodated outside pressures. There were also signs of leadership from management to foster the policy norm. With the takeover of Michel Camdessus as Managing Director in 1987 there were internal developments on social policies for poverty reduction. Despite the Board's cautious position regarding the Fund's activities in social issues, Camdessus initiated seminars and workshops for Fund staff working on countries with adjustment programmes in order to sensitize them to the problem of poverty and to address conceptual and practical questions. Furthermore, management adopted a directive to include poverty in the Fund's work by preparing poverty profiles for each country, by addressing the problem in loan negotiations, and by examining whether the policy mix could be designed differently so as to decrease the negative effects of the programmes (see IMF 1990a). In addition, in 1990 Camdessus extended the Fund's goal of 'high-quality growth' to be defined as (1) sustainable growth that is resistant to external shocks, (2) growth that is accompanied by domestic and external balances as well as investment, including in human capital in order to stimulate future growth, (3) growth that takes care of the environment, and (4) growth that is accompanied by poverty reduction and equality in opportunity (Camdessus 1990). Finally, in 1991, he directed staff to include an analysis of social costs in all Fund programmes (Boughton 2001).

Compared with the Fund's standpoint a decade before, these developments signify a major change in its normative understanding. However, since the Fund's mandate is primarily economic, that is, to help countries with balance of payments problems and secure macroeconomic stability through macroeconomic and structural policies, its involvement in social

---

[8] The Development Committee, formally known as the Joint Ministerial Committee of the Boards of Governors of the World Bank and the IMF on the Transfer of Real Resources to Developing Countries, was established in 1974. It is the only joint ministerial body of both organizations and it pays special attention to the problems of developing countries and is thus an important place for the co-ordination of international economic activities. It consists of twenty-two members, usually ministers of finance, appointed for two years. It is required to report to and advise the Boards of Governors of both organizations.

issues needed to be legitimized. Two arguments were employed to justify its extended involvement in social policies. First, social policies have a positive impact on Fund programmes by ensuring political sustainability and fostering economic growth through risk reduction (IMF 1993a). Second, social policies are related to the organization's technical expertise. Since the financing of such measures is achieved through efficient public expenditure, social safety nets are an important fiscal policy issue and, thus, fall within the Fund's expertise. Therewith, the Fund's scope of action increased significantly. While the issue of social safety nets was at first only linked to the adverse effects of Fund programmes, the extended argument for social safety nets as a matter of fiscal policy legitimized the introduction of social policies as an issue of technical advice on social sector spending. At the same time it emphasized the economic value of social policies. Indeed, internally, social policies were still referred to as the strengthening of a 'broad social acceptability necessary for economic reform to succeed' or as 'a moral imperative' (Gupta and Nashashibi 1990: 14), signalling that the norm had not been internalized by the organization.[9] Again, Fund staff were not actively involved in taking on social development policy. But once engaged in debates about it the organization decisively shaped definitions of social development as a policy norm in order to align it with its original mandate.

Throughout the 1990s internal debates continued over the Fund's role in social development and sustainable growth. Two internal conferences on equity and growth took place with high-level economists in 1995 and 1998 (IMF 1995i). For the first time in official documents, the Fund uttered the following position on the relationship between economic growth and redistribution: 'an excessively unequal income distribution may be detrimental to sustainable growth by hampering the efficient use of, and investment in, physical and human capital' (IMF 1995i: 2). Controversial ideas were presented at the conferences, but in the end, conference participants adhered to the Fund's original mandate and agreed that the Fund should not become involved in social policies. Nevertheless, the issue was still on the table. The successor of the 1995 conference focused on operational aspects in addressing equity. The discussion reflects the Fund's search for a legitimate reason to engage in *social* activities. The accompanying paper, 'Should Equity Be a Goal in

---

[9] Several interviews with IMF staff confirm these accounts in the documents. The assumptions of the so-called Washington Consensus are reiterated, that is, that economic growth will lead to poverty reduction and therefore the 'right' economic policies are more important than social policies. Or social policies are seen as necessary to facilitate economic reforms. Anything that goes beyond this enters the World Bank's scope of intervention.

Economic Policy?', concludes that '[a] consensus is forming nevertheless that governments should sometimes intervene to ensure not only that the size of the pie increases, but that everybody gets a fair share' (IMF 1998f: 11). Since 'recent research suggests that inequality can hinder growth' (IMF 1998b: 18) the Fund's engagement with inequality is a technical matter. The Fund is allowed to intervene for economic growth but not for a 'normative' reason such as equality (interview, conducted 19 March 2004). According to the Fund's internal norms, economic growth is an apolitical, value-neutral goal.

The organization had to search for an appropriate means of operationalizing the growing external pressure and changing views on development with its own mandate and conviction that development equals economic growth, which it perceived as a technical matter. The overall development discourse and practice changed significantly after 1990. The UN proposed a human development approach. In 1995, the World Summit on Social Development took place in Copenhagen where heads of state adopted the Copenhagen Declaration and a programme of action stressing the objectives of poverty reduction, full employment, and just and safe societies. In addition, NGO critiques increasingly challenged the IMF (such as the Fifty Years is Enough campaign). These developments had an impact on the organization, yet no major operational or organizational changes took place from which one could conclude that the IMF took up the idea and actively engaged in translating it into a policy norm. The decisive shift in the Fund's behaviour towards an emphasis on social development that combined poverty reduction and economic growth only took place in 1999 with its participation in the PRSP programme initiated by the World Bank. This happened against the backdrop of two independent events: the external review of the ESAF and the East Asian financial crisis.

The discovery of poverty reduction

Poverty reduction, as the main objective of a *social* development policy norm, was only finally introduced into the Fund's operational reality with the Poverty Reduction Strategy Paper (PRSP) initiative in 1999. In this context it should be noted that it was not the first time that poverty had become an issue for the IMF. In 1985, Ravi Kanbur wrote an IMF research paper discussing the relationship between poverty and growth and the effects of macroeconomic adjustment (Kanbur 1987). This paper proves that most of the issues regarding poverty were already known in the mid-1980s. It delivers an argument in favour of redistributive measures.

Under the assumption that the poverty line is fixed, that the mean income of the poor is half of the poverty line, and an annual per capita growth of 3 per cent, 'it will take *more than twenty years* for the average poor person to be lifted out of poverty' (Kanbur 1987: 70). It is for this reason that '[e]xplicit redistributive strategies may well be introduced in response to slowness of "trickle down"[10] – it is simply a matter of political arithmetic' (Kanbur 1987: 70). Thus, already in 1987, the basic insights into how to reduce poverty were known inside the organization. However, this paper was ignored in subsequent studies on income distribution as well as in the Fund's historical account (Boughton 2001). In other words, the ideas and knowledge had already existed in the mid-1980s but the Fund did not pick up on them and translate them into a policy norm.

By the end of the 1990s, however, external conditions had changed. The East Asian financial crisis had shaken the IMF's self-image of being able to prevent such crises. It followed the Bank's lead and joined the PRSP initiative. In order to implement this new framework, the Fund established the Poverty Reduction and Growth Facility (PRGF), the successor of the SAF/ESAF. For the first time, social issues were incorporated into Fund conditionality. Poverty reduction is often discussed as an equal objective of the organization next to economic growth, even though it is not mentioned as an objective in its Articles of Agreement. Fund research papers address the relationship between growth and poverty, pointing out that this is not causal but that there is an association, while further noting that 'the causality could well go the other way. In such cases, poverty reduction could in fact be necessary to implement stable macroeconomic policies or to achieve higher growth' (IMF and World Bank 2001: 5). This quote signifies a major turnaround in the Fund's understanding of development, from economic to social development.

The shift took place through a combination of a major external shock and further criticisms of the IMF which opened up policy space for change. In 1996, when criticism mounted against the Fund's structural adjustment programmes and other development agencies had already started to shift their strategies significantly, the Executive Board asked for an *external* review of the ESAF. Fund programmes had never been evaluated externally before. The final review was highly critical of Fund practice and revealed three main aspects in particular. First, there was a decisive lack of programme ownership which had led to severe implementation problems in developing countries. Second, ESAF programmes had not sufficiently focused on the protection of the poor. Third, one of the findings blurred the established division of labour between the international

---

[10] This mechanism was first formalized in 1955 by Simon Kuznets.

organizations. It concludes by stating the desired objective as being to 'better focus ESAF by improving protections for the poor, by improving the co-operation with other international financial organizations and bilateral donors, and by strengthening "ownership"' (Botchwey *et al.* 1998, Part I: 4).

The report's main critique of too little country-ownership of programmes seemed plausible and was partly a more palatable explanation of why Fund programmes were not successful. More importantly, this evaluation was positively received because its convenor, Kwesi Botchwey, was a highly respected economist (and former Finance Minister of Ghana), an important factor within the IMF. From the interviews it became clear that status, hierarchy and performance play an important role in the Fund. Internally, different departments, careers and positions are attributed a certain ranking in the hierarchy.[11] These internal standards also apply to the outside world.[12] The organization is difficult to criticize if one is not an economist, and even an economist has to be highly respected for their criticism to be taken seriously.[13] Thus, Botchwey's criticisms succeeded more than any NGO protest because they resonated with the Fund's organizational culture. Furthermore, they struck at the heart of the organization's vanity by revealing its reputation as an arrogant organization that imposes its values and perceptions on developing countries (Botchwey *et al.* 1998).

The publication of the results of this review coincided with the onset of the East Asian financial crisis. This revealed in a staggering way the Fund's lack of knowledge and inability to predict and deal with every kind of financial imbalance. As a result of the detrimental effects of the crisis on people in the region, Camdessus stressed the need for a social pillar within the international financial system (see Gupta *et al.* 2000). But in general the crisis was an exogenous shock that caused a situation of uncertainty and perplexity. In this situation, the ESAF review's effect was much greater and its criticisms fell on fertile soil. Consequently the Fund

---

[11] My interviewees emphasized differences in the IMF's and the Bank's group meetings or meetings with the governments of developing countries on missions. In the Bank a much more open and egalitarian climate prevails, while in the Fund it is (informally) clear who is allowed to speak.

[12] This, combined with its technical (economic) language, is one of the reasons why the organization looks like it is being arrogant. And indeed, it is less approachable than the World Bank, for instance. Its world of highly skilled macroeconomists makes this organization seem like a clique.

[13] There are other examples. Contrary to Stiglitz, who lost his credibility after attacking the Fund in a too personal manner, Köhler was not esteemed highly by the 'hard-core economists' for reasons of performance: 'He has not published in any well-known economic journal' (interview, conducted 7 April 2004).

agreed to participate in the PRSP initiative. Using the 'back-door approach' (interview, conducted 8 April 2004), Masood Ahmed, an economist mainly responsible for the design of the PRSP in the Bank and then hired by the Fund, managed not only to persuade the Board to change the name of the lending facility from ESAF to PRGF. Following the renaming, he put a description of this new facility on the website, mentioning poverty reduction as the *first* of the PRGF's seven key features (interview, conducted 8 April 2004).[14]

Once the Fund became engaged in the PRSP, it triggered, for the first time, substantial organizational and operational changes. This was a starting point for the norm to gain validity through social recognition beyond its formal validity in policy papers and strategy documents. First, social issues were incorporated into conditionality guidelines for Fund resources (Gupta *et al.* 2000: 22). PRSPs are decisively different from the Policy Framework Papers, that is, their predecessors under the SAF and ESAF. PRSPs state precise quantitative targets and performance criteria and aim to monitor the budget allocation. These targets have been included in Fund conditionality as benchmarks. Second, such an approach also requires much more data, in particular social indicators and poverty measurements. In addition, with the introduction of the PRSP, the measure of social safety nets now requires an ex ante social impact analysis and monitoring. Therefore, in 2004, the Fund established its own Poverty and Social Impact Analysis unit (PSIA) within the Fiscal Affairs Department (FAD).[15] Finally, a few social scientists were hired in order to consult Fund economists on the social aspect of their country missions. While country teams usually only met with the respective governments, especially the Ministers of Finance, the participatory process implemented by the PRSP now requires roundtables with all the relevant stakeholders of the development strategy in the respective country. As a result, members of the IMF's country team now have to talk to NGOs and civil society which is, as one interviewee pointed out, a broadening experience for the staff (interview, conducted 29 March 2004).

While things have changed, the Fund has not fully internalized a holistic approach to development emphasizing social, political and cultural

---

[14] This happened apparently without management or Board approval (interview, conducted 8 April 2004).

[15] As in 1977, when Witteveen was concerned with Bank developments regarding a basic needs approach and thus called for a study in the Fund, one of my interviewees pointed out that the Fund did not want to rely on the Bank any longer for those kinds of data because of the sister organization's 'high inefficiency' (interview, conducted 26 March 2004). However, the same debate in 1988 did not lead to a unit on impact analysis (see above).

aspects at the same time as economic factors. Managing Director Horst Köhler (2000–4), for instance, proposed to hire more non-economists in the organization, arguing that they were needed to consult with economists on the social aspects of their work. Most likely, this would have improved the cultural validity of the policy norm inside borrowing states. Yet his proposal was defeated in the Board (interview, conducted 16 March 2004). Moreover, it is not the Fund that finances the few existing social scientists but the Department for International Development (DfID) in the UK. Furthermore, a number of Directors on the Board cautioned 'that the IMF should not allow its primary mandate to be diluted [but should rather] contribut[e] to poverty reduction mainly through its support of economic policies that provide a conducive environment for sustained growth' (Gupta *et al.* 2000: 28). This group further points out, while acknowledging the importance of social issues, that '[i]n the family of international organizations, the social components of country programmes are primarily the responsibility of the World Bank and other organizations, not the IMF' (Gupta *et al.* 2000: 1). Staff echo the Board's sentiments (several interviews with Fund staff conducted in March 2004). On the other hand, there is a group including the newly hired social scientists in the IMF that stands for policies that would clearly exceed the Fund's economic focus and thus broaden its horizon significantly.[16] It remains to be seen in which direction the Fund will go and how much influence 'soft' economists in the Fund can exert as norm entrepreneurs. In light of the IEO's 2004 report on the evaluation of the PRSP process and the Fund's role in it, there is not much room for hope. Overall the report argues not only that policy outcomes have been moderate but also that Fund engagement with the PRSP process has been weak and does not indicate major changes in the way the IMF does business (IEO 2004: 63).

Conclusion: owning development or lacking ownership?

This chapter addressed two questions. First, why did the Fund became involved in social policies and eventually subscribe to poverty reduction as a policy objective? Second, to what extent and in what way has the Fund internalized this new policy norm? As to the first question, tracing the

---

[16] See, for instance, Kende-Robb (2003) who tried to include a gender dimension in the Fund programmes. A repeated story in the organizational memory of the Fund is about a strategic move by Fund staff from the African Department who invited Horst Köhler on a mission to Senegal shortly after he was appointed Managing Director in 2000. This mission must have been a crucial experience for Köhler and apparently shaped his attitude towards development and moved the Fund's role in a more social direction (several interviews).

history of the social development policy norm in the IMF revealed the mechanisms and main triggers for norm change in the Fund as well as the way in which the Fund shaped the content of that particular policy norm. The objective was to detect conditions under which the organization engages in norm change which eventually could be used to derive some plausible statements either about norm creation in the Fund or about norm creation in IOs generally. It became clear that, in particular, two conditions are important in this specific case: the high level of dependency when it comes to policy decisions and the high degree of inconsistency of social issues with the Fund's mandate, expertise and beliefs. We could therefore assume that the IMF might behave differently when it comes to a different policy norm that is more in line with its expertise (Leiteritz and Moschella, chapter 8 this volume). Alternatively, another IO which depends less on the decisions of its Executive Board might be more active in creating policy norms (e.g. Weaver, chapter 4 this volume).

Specifically, the case study revealed that at different times various social policies have entered the Fund's discourse through top-down processes from the Executive Board. They have also come from outside the IO through a changed normative environment in combination with an external shock, when the Executive Board could not withstand external criticism and threats to the organization's legitimacy. The study showed that in a situation where the organization lacks autonomy and the Board is not in favour of a particular policy norm, the nature of the external pressure is crucial in triggering change.

While management, in particular Managing Director Michel Camdessus, tried to develop Fund expertise in social issues, the case study revealed that the Board had the final say. Contrary to the case in other IOs, there is no evidence of norm entrepreneurs among Fund staff who would proactively lobby management or the Board in this particular policy area. Such bottom-up processes are in general less likely in the IMF (see also Leiteritz and Moschella, chapter 8, and Momani, chapter 2, this volume). Internal advocates, such as the non-economic social scientists in the World Bank who have actively and strategically fostered the social agenda inside the organization by inviting guest speakers, writing research papers and the like, are difficult to imagine in the IMF (Weaver, chapter 4 this volume; see also Fox 1998; Kanbur 2001; Kardam 1993; Vetterlein 2007). This is even more the case regarding a policy area which is clearly beyond the organization's mandate and staff expertise and belief. But even if ideas match the organizational mandate and interest, originate inside the organization and management, and staff work on transforming them into policy norms as was the case with capital account liberalization (Moschella 2008) or the proposal for a Sovereign Debt Restructuring

Mechanism (SDRM), it is eventually the Board that decides. Both policies were rejected by the Board and hence all research on these topics ceased. Thus, the autonomy of an IO seems to be a very important aspect for norm creation within IOs.

Second, because it was imposed from outside the Fund, the organization did not, and does not, fully appreciate the policy norm on social development. Often, social policies are deferred to the World Bank (several interviews with IMF staff conducted in March 2004). The emerging understanding of development as a holistic process beyond economic development supports the focus on poverty reduction and thus the emphasis on social policies. Yet the Fund lacks expertise on social development issues and probably lacks the political will to engage with such policies. It does not *own* this policy norm but accommodates it, yet thereby shaping it decisively to make it consistent with its mandate. In terms of the norm circle discussed in chapter 1, the Fund has been persuaded to engage with the policy norm on social development, yet internally the norm has not been stabilized. It exists formally but as the ongoing debates in the IMF show, it has not been socially recognized by IMF staff. This has two consequences. On the one hand, if social development is not fully internalized by IMF staff it will be easy to abolish it. On the other hand, often social issues are either transformed into economic ones or the value of social polices for economic growth is emphasized. Given that the IMF is powerful in teaching policy norms to developing countries this is important. From a critical-normative point of view we might ask whether it is desirable that the IMF becomes increasingly involved in social development in light of the observation of an increased economization of the social.

6   Stabilizing global monetary norms: the IMF and current account convertibility

André Broome

Introduction: lessons from history

Policy norms do not appear out of thin air. Experiments with new policy ideas are always grounded in broader material and ideational environment changes, and are shaped by the lessons that actors draw from past experiences. The lessons policy elites draw from history serve both as a useful point of reference to help interpret their changing environment and to lend weight to their arguments for or against particular solutions to new problems in the inevitable political contests that accompany the need for policy change. The conventional wisdom in political science suggests that structural crises open up one-off windows of opportunity that can allow elite actors to achieve radical policy change at a rapid pace (Keeler 1993; Krasner 1984; cf. Broome 2009; Cortell and Peterson 1999). In this regard, windows of opportunity to drive through systemic change are seldom of a greater magnitude than those generated by global shocks such as the Great Depression and the Second World War, which set the scene for current account convertibility to emerge as a policy norm. At the same time, how actors interpret major changes in their environment is crucial for understanding how the material effects of structural crises lead to the emergence of new global policy norms that translate ideas into concrete policy changes (Widmaier *et al.* 2007).

In recent work in international political economy, scholars have concentrated a great deal of attention on assessing the move in many countries towards capital account liberalization, and the policy constraints this places on governments' room to manoeuvre in response to adverse reactions by financial markets (Chwieroth 2007a; Helleiner 1994: chapter 7; Mosley 2000; Pauly 1995; Simmons 2001; Singer 2007: chapter 5). Many of these accounts have focused on the role that the International Monetary Fund (hereafter the Fund) played in promoting capital account liberalization during the 1990s, concentrating on its attempt to formally validate an obligation for states to establish and maintain open capital accounts through an amendment to the Fund's Articles of Agreement (Leiteritz and Moschella, chapter 8 this volume; see also Abdelal 2007: chapter 6; Best 2005: chapter 6; Leiteritz 2005; Moschella 2008). Despite the high level of attention paid to the Fund's efforts to codify a commitment to capital account convertibility, a campaign the Fund abruptly abandoned in the aftermath of the Asian financial crisis (Leiteritz and Moschella, this volume), little attention has been focused on its less obtrusive efforts during the past fifteen years to push its member states to accept their existing obligations to adopt *current account* convertibility, enshrined in Article VIII of its Articles of Agreement. This chapter aims to fill this gap, as well as satisfy the criticisms that Finnemore and Toope (2001: 752) have articulated of earlier studies of the diffusion of current account convertibility. As Finnemore and Toope argue, the IMF's role in this process of normative change is either downplayed or largely absent in existing scholarship, implying that states make a unilateral calculation to adopt convertibility legally primarily to satisfy global markets (see Simmons 2000a, 2000b). This chapter illustrates that – while a changing economic environment has served to increase the material incentives for states to adopt current account convertibility – the IMF has played an important role in the process of normative change over the long term. In particular, the IMF has fostered an intellectual shift in how national decision-makers understand the importance of establishing a reputation for 'policy credibility', and which policy changes may help to achieve this.

Convertibility, which previously referred to the right to exchange a particular currency for gold at a given rate under the Gold Standard, is now commonly defined as 'the right to convert freely a national currency at the going exchange rate into any other currency' (Guitián 1996a: 22). However, the broad concept of 'convertibility' can be defined in a number of ways. Different degrees of convertibility determine who is legally permitted to exchange a country's currency, and the economic purposes for which a currency is permitted to be exchanged. Full, unrestricted currency convertibility encompasses both current account and capital account convertibility. Current account convertibility permits individuals and firms within a country to access foreign exchange in order to pay for external trade transactions, including goods, services, interest payments, share dividends and overseas travel. In contrast, capital account convertibility permits a country's residents to access foreign exchange to pay for financial assets abroad, and allows non-residents to repatriate their capital overseas (Cooper 1999: 89–90).

The goal of achieving universal current account convertibility to facilitate the worldwide liberalization of trade was enshrined in the Fund's Articles of Agreement negotiated at the Bretton Woods conference in 1944. Policy elites participating in the negotiations for a new post-war international economic order had formed new ideas about the appropriate standards of monetary conduct and the need to prioritize international monetary stability above capital mobility (H. James 1996: 38–9). Among other things, debates over international monetary ideas were informed by policy-makers' experiences of the Wall Street Crash of 1929, the Great Depression, the collapse of the interwar Gold Standard in 1931, and the 'beggar-thy-neighbour' policies that characterized trade and currency competition during the 1930s, which were widely believed to have contributed to the outbreak of the Second World War (Boughton 2004: 5–7, 13–14; Eichengreen 1996: 45–6; Helleiner 1994: 27–8; H. James 1996: 31–3).

In particular, the domestic economic and social costs that had been associated with re-establishing the Gold Standard in the interwar years, where domestic deflation in Britain led to the General Strike of 1926, had stimulated changing attitudes towards the role of the state in the economy and the need for an international monetary system that would allow governments scope for domestic policy experiments in response to changing public expectations (Seabrooke 2007a: 803, 807; cf. Ikenberry 1993). As Rawi Abdelal (2007: 44) points out, for those involved with planning for a new international economic order '[t]he failures of the interwar years were understood to be almost self-evident'. With respect to convertibility, the key difference between the interwar Gold Standard and the proposals for a post-war international monetary system was the emphasis placed on establishing universal current account convertibility as an essential prerequisite for the growth of international trade and economic recovery, but without extending convertibility to capital transactions (especially short-term speculative capital flows of 'hot money') (Eichengreen 1996: 93; Helleiner 1994: 36–8). In combination with a system of fixed but adjustable exchange rates, current account convertibility therefore formed the heart of the 'embedded liberal compromise' agreed at Bretton Woods (Ruggie 1982), in large part because 'the contemporary climate of public opinion' (Best 2005: 38) had shifted away from support for capital mobility but remained firmly in favour of open current accounts to facilitate the growth of international trade (Pauly 1997: 80–1). However, the formal validity of international policies is not sufficient for these to translate effectively into changes in behaviour: policy *norms* must also be seen as socially valid (Wiener 2007a: 5). As the following sections show, agreement at Bretton Woods on universal current account convertibility as an essential component of the post-war international economic order did not automatically receive social recognition as a global policy norm as soon as the ink had dried on the Fund's Articles of Agreement. Rather, this required a sustained campaign by the

Fund to persuade states to internalize their formal obligations to adopt current account convertibility as a *socially* valid norm that represents an appropriate standard of monetary behaviour.

The chapter proceeds as follows. In the next section, I discuss the construction of international monetary rules that were designed to create a new international economic order – based on universal current account convertibility – after the end of the Second World War. Here I focus on how the Bretton Woods negotiations led to the emergence of current account convertibility as a policy norm that states *should* adopt, which was formally validated in the Fund's Articles of Agreement. Following this, I examine how the Fund fostered a gradual shift towards the institutionalization of current account convertibility as a socially valid policy norm in Western European states during the 1950s. Here I discuss how the costly currency speculation that accompanied the early attempt at establishing sterling–dollar convertibility and subsequent currency devaluations during the late 1940s served to delay the move to convertibility in the industrialized world, and how the Fund's own limited resources proved insufficient for the new organization to exercise stronger influence over the timetable for convertibility on its own. I then explore the Fund's persuasion strategy during the 1990s to encourage developing countries to recognize current account convertibility as an appropriate policy norm. Although the majority of the Fund's member states had still not accepted their formal obligations to establish current account convertibility under Article VIII of the Fund's Articles of Agreement at the start of the 1990s, the Fund's norm advocacy had greater success during the course of the decade as a result of the changing political and economic environment that states faced with the end of the Cold War, which led governments to place greater emphasis on establishing 'policy credibility' with financial markets through enacting market-oriented liberal reforms. Finally, I conclude by reflecting on how formal policy norms acquire social recognition. In the case of current account convertibility this depended to a large extent on environmental changes in the international political and economic context states faced, which opened a window of opportunity for the Fund to promote convertibility as a global policy norm through material incentives for changes in state behaviour, intellectual arguments, and the use of informal sanctions such as public shaming and peer pressure.

Norm ambiguity and the emergence of global monetary norms

The Fund staff, senior management and the Executive Board consider that 'the working of the international monetary system is "the business of the Fund'" (IMF 1990b: 3). Prior to the establishment of the Fund, the traditional view, as expressed by the Permanent Court of International Justice in 1929, had been that 'a State is entitled to regulate its own currency' (Gold 1984: 1533). With the signing of the Fund's Articles of Agreement, however, states formally accepted the radically different principle that they should work together to prevent the currency competition and monetary disorder that had characterized the 1930s by pooling their authority to engage in permanent international monetary co-operation. As a result, the core objective of the Fund, endorsed by the twenty-nine states that were original signatories to its Articles of Agreement in 1945, was to maintain fixed, unitary and non-discriminatory exchange rates in accordance with common international monetary rules (Gold 1984: 1534, 1536).

As Barnett and Finnemore (2004: 31–4) have argued, the capacity to classify knowledge and to 'fix meanings' can constitute a key source of power for international organizations (IOs). At the same time, the power IOs may exercise through the classification and definition of social and economic phenomena is never absolute. How IOs define appropriate standards of policy conduct and the mechanisms they employ to prompt states to comply with these behavioural standards can stimulate intense political contestation or outright resistance (see Wiener 2007a: 6), even when new policy standards are enshrined from the start in their founding charters. This proved to be the case with the formal obligation for member states of the Fund to adopt common rules relating to current account convertibility.

Even in the most favourable macroeconomic conditions, allowing a national currency to be freely exchanged for foreign currencies is never a cost-free choice for policy-makers. The establishment of current account convertibility constrains the policy toolkit governments have at their disposal (including diminishing the effectiveness of capital controls), and may conflict with the economic interests and shared ideas of a range of influential domestic groups. But while governments may see the use of current account restrictions as beneficial to support particular developmental objectives, as a response to balance of payments shortfalls or as a means to channel foreign exchange to particular industries or social groups, the Fund's view has always been that such policies are 'dangerous substitutes for economic adjustment' that inhibit the proper functioning of foreign exchange markets (Simmons 2000a: 820).

Upon becoming a member of the Fund, a state's obligations with respect to current account convertibility are formally validated under Article VIII of its Articles of Agreement (or under the 'transitional' arrangements of Article XIV, discussed further below). Article VIII commits Fund member states to uphold two main rules. First, Article VIII section 2a stipulates that 'no member shall, without the approval of the Fund, impose restrictions on the making of payments and transfers for current international transactions'. Second, Article VIII section 3 stipulates that no member state is permitted to engage in 'any discriminatory currency arrangements or multiple currency practices … except as authorized under this Agreement or approved by the Fund' (IMF 2008). Under Article XXX (*d*) of the Fund's Articles of Agreement, current account transactions are defined as 'payments which are not for the purposes of transferring capital'. This includes (a) payments for trade in goods and services, and short-term banking and credit payments; (b) interest payments and net income from other investments; (c) moderate payments for amortization of loans or depreciation of direct investments; and (d) moderate remittances for family living expenses. This list is not exhaustive, and the Fund retains the formal right to determine – in consultation with a member state – whether specific transactions should be counted as capital account or current account transactions (IMF 2008). Repatriation and surrender requirements on exporters' foreign exchange earnings are not subject to the Fund's jurisdiction under Article VIII unless they involve multiple currency practices, while the Fund is formally charged with the right to approve 'temporary' exchange restrictions for members. When deciding whether to approve exchange restrictions the Fund takes into account a country's balance of payments position, whether exchange restrictions are discriminatory, how long exchange controls have been in place, as well as policy-makers' stated intentions and plans for phasing out controls (IMF 1984: 9; Quirk *et al.* 1995: 3, 8–9).

Although the Bretton Woods agreement succeeded in establishing a legal framework for international monetary relations and a functional definition of current account convertibility, the Fund's rules were deliberately ambiguous on the precise timetable for states to move to adopt their obligations under Article VIII. At the time this was a political necessity to allow the chief negotiators to reach a compromise agreement. On the US side, Harry Dexter-White's original proposal for a three-year time limit for states to shift from exchange restrictions to Article VIII compliance met with stiff resistance from British negotiators, especially John Maynard Keynes. As a compromise, negotiators agreed that after three years the Fund would conduct internal reports on states' exchange restrictions and after five years would commence bilateral policy consultations on exchange restrictions, which introduced the practice of Fund policy surveillance for non-borrowing states (Pauly 1997: 87). This exercise in norm ambiguity allowed states to maintain flexibility in the speed with which they moved to adopt current account convertibility, which might otherwise have involved unacceptable economic and political costs for governments, especially in the early post-war era when many countries faced severe economic circumstances such as a chronic shortage of US dollars to pay for imports (Eichengreen 1996: 109–10).

While framing the formal obligation to remove 'temporary' exchange restrictions in ambiguous language helped to achieve the immediate goal of securing broad state support for the overall commitment to the principle of universal current account convertibility, in the long term it left the Fund with few direct mechanisms to persuade recalcitrant member states to establish current account convertibility in practice. As a consequence, accepting 'Article VIII status' in the Fund has remained a voluntary choice for states, and policy-makers are able to continue to maintain existing restrictions and currency practices that are in place when a country joins the Fund for an unspecified transition period (Simmons 2000b: 581). This is formally permitted under Article XIV of the Articles of Agreement, which was included at the insistence of British negotiators at Bretton Woods (Eichengreen 1996: 98). Article XIV section 2 allows each state to 'maintain and adapt to changing circumstances the restrictions on payments and transfers for current international transactions that were in effect on the date on which it became a member'. The same section none the less commits states to 'withdraw restrictions ... as soon as they are satisfied that they will be able, in the absence of such restrictions, to settle their balance of payments' (IMF 2008). For member states that maintain exchange restrictions under Article XIV, the trade-off involves a requirement to hold regular policy consultations with the Fund staff on their movement towards current account convertibility, although the Fund's Articles of Agreement leave unspecified how long states can remain under the 'temporary' provisions of Article XIV (Pauly 1997: 87).

Despite the allowance for national discretion under Article XIV, the Fund actively seeks to persuade states to change their behaviour in order to shift them from maintaining restrictions under Article XIV towards accepting Article VIII status as quickly as possible (Simmons 2000b: 581). It is important to note, however, that a state's acceptance of Article VIII status does not necessarily mean that there are no current account restrictions in place. As discussed above, the Articles of Agreement explicitly give the Fund the power to approve temporary restrictions in certain circumstances, while some member states have occasionally introduced restrictions in violation of their Article VIII obligations without the Fund's approval. The Fund has sought to encourage states to accept their Article VIII obligations only when (a) they no longer have restrictions that would require the Fund's approval under Article VIII, and (b) they are satisfied that they are unlikely to need to adopt such restrictions in the future. According to Vicente Galbis (1996: 45–6), this reflects a desire within the Fund for the acceptance of Article VIII status to be seen as 'a public commitment on the part of the authorities to deal with balance of payments problems in future through appropriate adjustment policies (including exchange rate action) and financing rather than through recourse to restrictive exchange measures' (IMF 2008). Simmons's (2000b: 599) large-*n* research on when states choose to commit to the obligations of Article VIII also suggests that the ability of states to comply with the norms of current account liberalization in the future is an important factor in the decision to shift to Article VIII – states do not take the decision lightly. If the Fund encouraged states to accept their Article VIII obligations while they maintained policies that would require the Fund's approval, or when they were likely to reintroduce exchange restrictions, Article VIII status would carry less weight as a mechanism for the Fund to maintain compliance with the principle of current account convertibility or as a credibility signal to a state's wider international and domestic audiences.

The Fund has always had the formal right to push recalcitrant states to remove exchange restrictions if it judges that they are no longer warranted by a state's economic circumstances. Under Article XIV section 3 of the Fund's Articles of Agreement, the 'Fund may . . . make representations to any member that conditions are favourable for the withdrawal of any particular restriction, or for the general abandonment of restrictions, inconsistent with the provisions of any other articles of this Agreement' (IMF 2008). However, the Fund prefers to use intellectual persuasion and policy dialogue to nudge its members towards the removal of exchange restrictions and the acceptance of Article VIII status, rather than to make use of this provision to request explicitly that states abandon restrictions (Galbis 1996: 47). In addition, the Fund has promoted acceptance of current account convertibility through its technical assistance missions, and in some cases through including the establishment of current account convertibility as a policy condition in loan programmes (Quirk *et al.* 1995: 10).

In accordance with Article XIV section 3 of its Articles of Agreement, the Fund promotes transparency of the current account restrictions that governments maintain by releasing a summary of the exchange arrangements and the exchange/trade restrictions of each of its member states in its *Annual Report on Exchange Arrangements and Exchange Restrictions*, which has been published by the Fund since 1950. The entry for each member state of the Fund establishes the country's status under the Fund's Articles of Agreement (i.e. whether the state has accepted Article VIII obligations or whether it maintains restrictions under Article XIV), and presents an assessment of each country's exchange arrangements within a common classificatory matrix. Crucially, the report is a composite that is based on the Fund staff's analysis of a country's currency policies, rather than simply accepting what a government presents to the world as its official exchange arrangements. Because of the element of evaluation and interpretation by the Fund, the exercise constitutes a regular independent judgement by an external actor on the quality of a country's currency policies, measured against common policy standards.

These new 'rules of the game' for the international monetary system that were agreed at the Bretton Woods Conference have since been described as constituting 'a new formal global standard for market civilization' (Oliver 2006: 111). However, it took the Fund many years to transform the formal validity of current account convertibility into a *policy norm*, which now receives wide social recognition as an accepted policy standard around the world in both developed and developing economies. Allowing states to continue to operate 'temporary' exchange restrictions for an indefinite period under Article XIV before accepting their obligations to current account convertibility under Article VIII served to institutionalize the idea of convertibility as a universal obligation of Fund membership, while leaving the timetable for the full establishment of current account convertibility a subject of negotiation between individual governments and Fund staff during regular policy consultations (cf. Best 2005: 82). Owing to the flexibility of the policy implementation of current account convertibility the appropriateness of a shift to Article VIII status long remained contested by many of the Fund's member states, while others sometimes paid lip-service to their formal obligations under Article VIII without institutionalizing current account convertibility through changes in monetary behaviour.

Currency speculation and convertibility in Europe

The incidence of international policy diffusion is often expected to be highest among countries that share an ideological or cultural affinity (Underdal 1998: 21), and where states are members of – or profess a desire to join – an existing international social grouping. Moreover, existing research suggests that policy diffusion is likely to proceed in specific waves that are geographically clustered. As Weyland (2005: 294) suggests, '[b]old changes that happen next door are immediately available and thus grab the attention of decision-makers; there is no way *not* to consider such a reform'. Each of these factors shaped the international diffusion of current account convertibility in the post-Second World War era, with successive waves of policy diffusion often located within particular regions (first the Americas, followed by Western Europe) or within groups of states seeking to develop an investment-friendly reputation (such as post-communist economies). Building on these policy diffusion dynamics, the Fund has played an important role in promoting universal current account convertibility as a global policy norm. Within individual countries, this has involved the Fund variously acting as an *auditor* that monitors norm compliance, or as an *enforcer* that provides incentives for norm adoption or extends sanctions against 'norm rebels' (see Broome 2010). Most importantly, the Fund plays the role of an *intellectual actor* that seeks gradually to persuade decision-makers to change how they think about national economic management and the relationship between domestic economic activity and international markets. Yet achieving the social recognition of new economic ideas often entails a prolonged period of gestation. As the following two sections show, the diffusion of current account convertibility as a global policy norm was a painstakingly slow process, with the 'circle' from norm emergence to norm stabilization stretching over sixty years (see chapter 1).

In the industrialized world, many states initially continued to use multiple currency practices in the years following the establishment of the Fund, with thirty-six of the Fund's total membership of fifty-eight states using a form of multiple exchange rates in 1955 (Best 2005: 84). Among West European economies, acceptance of the current account convertibility policy norm proved much more difficult to achieve than policymakers had envisaged at Bretton Woods, when it was initially assumed that states would maintain exchange restrictions under the 'transitional' arrangements of Article XIV for only a limited period of time (Pauly 1997: 87–8). As Tables 6.1 and 6.2 show, the states that moved first to adopt Article VIII after the Fund was established were located in the Americas, with West European states only accepting Article VIII status in the Fund a decade and a half later. In part, this was because an early attempt to establish sterling–dollar convertibility ended in disaster when Britain lost US$1 billion of foreign exchange reserves during the six weeks that full current account convertibility was restored after 15 July 1947, with non-residents able to export capital through current account transactions owing to inadequate monitoring of capital transfers. The establishment of convertibility was a central condition in return for a US$3.75 billion loan to Britain by the USA, but from the signing of the loan agreement to the suspension of convertibility the cost of Britain's early attempt at establishing sterling–dollar convertibility amounted to US$3.6 billion (Best 2005:

Table 6.1 *Acceptance of Article VIII, 1946–60*

IMF member	Effective date of acceptance	IMF member	Effective date of acceptance
El Salvador	6 November 1946	Honduras	1 July 1950
Mexico	12 November 1946	Canada	15 March 1952
Panama	26 November 1946	Dominican Republic	1 August 1953
United States	10 December 1946	Haiti	22 December 1953
Guatemala	27 January 1947		

Source: IMF (2007a: 6–7)

Table 6.2 *Acceptance of Article VIII, 1961–4*

IMF member	Effective date of acceptance	IMF member	Effective date of acceptance
Belgium	15 February 1961	Sweden	15 February 1961
France	15 February 1961	United Kingdom	15 February 1961
Germany	15 February 1961	Saudi Arabia	22 March 1961
Ireland	15 February 1961	Austria	1 August 1962
Italy	15 February 1961	Jamaica	22 February 1963
Luxembourg	15 February 1961	Kuwait	5 April 1963
Netherlands	15 February 1961	Japan	1 April 1964
Peru	15 February 1961	Nicaragua	20 July 1964

Source: IMF (2007a: 6–7)

66–9). Two years later, following a recession in the USA in 1949 which depressed demand for European exports, pressure grew for Britain to devalue the pound as speculators found ways to circumvent UK exchange controls in order to convert their holdings of sterling into dollars. As with the failure of the 1947 attempt at establishing dollar–sterling convertibility, the Fund's authority was damaged when the UK informed the Fund management of its decision to devalue the pound by 30.5 per cent with only twenty-four hours notice, a decision which was followed within one week by currency devaluations in twenty-three other countries (Best 2005: 71; Eichengreen 1996: 105–6).

After more than a decade of preparation, European states eventually moved to accept current account convertibility between 1958 and 1961, with nine European states formally accepting Article VIII status in the Fund in February 1961 (see Table 6.2). This followed two developments that influenced the re-establishment of convertibility in Europe. First, under the European Payments Union member countries' currencies had effectively been convertible into other European currencies for current account transactions from 1954 (Eichengreen 1996: 114). Second, with the creation of the 'Euromarkets' in 1957 internationally active commercial banks could exploit 'off-shore' currency markets outside the jurisdiction of the Fund as a means to buy and sell US dollars in response to national exchange restrictions, thereby enlarging the international money supply (Burn 1999: 230; Helleiner 1994: 71–2, 84; H. James 1996: 151, 179–80). The emergence of the Euromarkets ensured that capital mobility came to play a much greater role in the international monetary system during the 1960s than had been envisaged at Bretton Woods, which further complicated the operation of the system. Coupled with the reluctance of national policy-makers to adjust their external payments position via further currency devaluations after the disastrous experiences of the late 1940s, the increase in capital mobility following the establishment of current account convertibility served to undermine the par value exchange rates system over the next decade, culminating in the Nixon administration's decision in 1971 to suspend the dollar's convertibility into gold at the official exchange rate of $35 per ounce (Best 2005: 110–11; Eichengreen 1996: 134–5).

Although the achievement of current account convertibility in Europe in the late 1950s finally brought the Bretton Woods system into full operation (at least among the industrialized countries), the Fund itself appeared to have played a marginal role in the process. According to the *Financial Times* in April 1956, the Fund was becoming a 'white elephant', and its 'attempt to encourage member countries to make wider use of its lending facilities seems to have failed' (cited in H. James 1996: 102). The Fund's direct influence seemed to be limited, in large part, because its own resources were inadequate successfully to underwrite a major economy's shift to current account convertibility, while the USA had opposed the UK's proposal for a substantial quota increase in the mid-1950s in order to enable the Fund to support sterling convertibility (H. James 1996: 101). Yet the Fund was closely involved – both formally and informally – with the restoration of current account convertibility in Europe. For instance, in return for a large US$738.5 million Fund standby arrangement in 1956, organized with the approval of the US Treasury, the view of British policy-makers shifted towards seeing the establishment of current account convertibility as a trade-off for the Fund's assistance with the country's balance of payments problems that resulted from the Suez crisis (H. James 1996: 102–3).

In the case of France, the Fund maintained pressure on the government in an attempt to persuade the country's policy-makers to adopt current account convertibility in return for assistance from the Fund in combination with additional sources of external finance, including the European Payments Union and the US Export-Import Bank (like Britain, this occurred in the context of political crises such as the war in Algeria). As part of the organization's efforts to persuade French policy-makers to shift towards convertibility, Fund staff devised detailed proposals and legislative changes to be included in the government's budget for 1958 and 1959, which were aimed at limiting the budget deficit and restricting the growth of domestic credit. The Fund's Managing Director, Per Jacobsson, quietly held policy negotiations with the French government over these proposals during a visit to Paris in December 1957 that was 'disguised as a private trip' (H. James 1996: 105), which helped to set the scene for the sweeping economic reform programme followed by General de Gaulle's new government after the founding of the Fifth Republic in 1958. Again, the move to convertibility in the case of France had to be supported by additional sources of finance, including credit lines from European central banks and a private US bank consortium, rather than relying on credit provided by the Fund alone (H. James 1996: 105–7).

The Fund therefore played an important role as a norm advocate that consistently sought to persuade European governments to adopt current account convertibility, and helped to co-ordinate financial assistance packages that could shore up governments' foreign exchange reserves and make the choice to restore convertibility more politically palatable. However, its own limited financial resources constrained the organization's ability to exercise a more direct influence over the timetable for re-establishing current account convertibility. While the Fund now has an arm's-length policy relationship with most Western economies that no longer draw on its resources (see Broome and Seabrooke 2007: 577–8), even during the Bretton Woods era – when European states did borrow from the Fund – the organization's resource limits constrained the influence the Fund could exercise over industrial economies. Rather than shaping national policy change through the control and distribution of sufficient financial resources on its own, the main roles the Fund performed in the shift to convertibility in Europe comprised (a) providing an important forum for international co-operation and the co-ordination of financial assistance (which depended on US support to be effective), and (b) acting as a diffuser of economic reform ideas, which could potentially exert an indirect influence over states' economic decisions through shaping the parameters of domestic policy debates and bureaucratic contests over policy change. By playing the role of a co-ordinating institution for assistance packages that were based largely on additional sources of external finance, the Fund was able to exercise an indirect influence over the path to current account convertibility in Europe (cf. Broome 2008). However, the organization's economic policy advice – and in particular its attempts to foster convertibility as a policy norm – had less of an impact than it would have had if governments had been offered sufficient loans from the Fund to cover the potential costs associated with the move to convertibility.

Currency convertibility and policy credibility in developing countries

Among scholars who have examined the evolution of the international monetary system after the Second World War, it is common to conclude a discussion of the shift towards current account convertibility with the establishment of convertibility in the industrialized European economies and Japan in the late 1950s and early 1960s (see Best 2005; Eichengreen 1996; Helleiner 1994; H. James 1996; Pauly 1997). While the restoration of convertibility in Europe in the late 1950s was clearly an event of great significance for the world economy, in terms of the Fund's campaign to diffuse the current account convertibility policy norm this was only the first chapter in a much longer story. For instance, although the Fund has always treated the currency restrictions that states are legally permitted to maintain under Article XIV as 'transitional', only 66 of the Fund's 152 member states had formally accepted Article VIII status at the beginning of 1990 (see Tables 6.1, 6.2 and 6.3). Moreover, among the majority of the Fund's member states that had not accepted their obligations under Article VIII were some thirty-six countries that had remained under Article XIV for more than three decades (Galbis 1996: 14–17, 54). At the same time, a number of states no longer maintained restrictions under Article XIV – or maintained only minor restrictions – but had not yet formally accepted Article VIII status (Galbis 1996: 38).

The Fund's systemic role was transformed in practice immediately following the breakdown of the Bretton Woods system in the early 1970s, and was formally altered with the ratification of the second amendment to the Fund's Articles of Agreement that became effective in 1978. This replaced the Fund's responsibility to oversee and approve adjustments in the par value of member states' exchange rates with a responsibility to exercise 'firm surveillance' over states' exchange rate policies (Best 2005: 121; Broome and Seabrooke 2007: 576–8). Nevertheless, while the balance of authority between the Fund and its member states over exchange rate policies shifted back towards exchange rate decisions becoming an internal decision for individual governments (Gold 1984: 1541), the Fund's authority to define what counts as a legitimate or an

Table 6.3 *Acceptance of Article VIII, 1965–89*

IMF member	Effective date of acceptance	IMF member	Effective date of acceptance
Costa Rica	1 February 1965	Solomon Islands	24 July 1979
Australia	1 July 1965	Finland	25 September 1979
Guyana	27 December 1966	Dominica	13 December 1979
Denmark	1 May 1967	Uruguay	2 May 1980
Norway	11 May 1967	St Lucia	30 May 1980
Bolivia	5 June 1967	Djibouti	19 September 1980
Singapore	9 November 1968	St Vincent and the Grenadines	24 August 1981
Malaysia	11 November 1968	Argentina	14 May 1968
Ecuador	31 August 1970	New Zealand	5 August 1982
Fiji	4 August 1972	Vanuatu	1 December 1982
Bahrain	20 March 1973	Belize	14 June 1983
Qatar	4 June 1973	Iceland	19 September 1983
South Africa	15 September 1973	Antigua and Barbuda	22 November 1983
The Bahamas	5 December 1973	Sri Lanka	15 March 1994
United Arab Emirates	13 February 1974	St Kitts and Nevis	3 December 1984
Oman	19 June 1974	Spain	15 July 1986
Papua New Guinea	4 December 1975	Kiribati	22 August 1986
Venezuela	1 July 1976	Indonesia	7 May 1988
Chile	27 July 1977	Portugal	12 September 1988
Seychelles	3 January 1978	Republic of Korea	1 November 1988
Suriname	29 June 1978	Swaziland	11 December 1989

Source: IMF (2007a: 6–7)

illegitimate exchange restriction, as well as its responsibility to encourage states to adopt current account convertibility and assume their obligations under Article VIII, remained firmly in place.

Despite retaining its systemic role to promote universal current account convertibility, by the end of the Cold War – nearly half a century after the Fund had opened its doors for business – the majority of the Fund's member states had still not accepted their obligations to current account convertibility under Article VIII. Among developing economies, in particular, progress towards the current account convertibility policy norm had proved to be a slow and uneven process. One study by a staff team from the Fund's Monetary and Exchange Affairs Department found that by the early 1990s only one-third of the Fund's developing member states had accepted their obligations under Article VIII, while one-sixth of those developing countries that had assumed 'Article VIII status' in the Fund subsequently reintroduced exchange restrictions (see Tables 6.1 and 6.4) (Quirk *et al.* 1995: 2).

Table 6.4 *IMF member states maintaining exchange restrictions under Article VIII or Article XIV, 31 December 1994*[a]

Africa	Central Asia	Europe	Former Soviet Union	Middle East	South-East Asia	Western Hemisphere
Angola	Bhutan	Albania	Armenia	Afghanistan	Maldives	Brazil
Botswana	Cambodia	Bulgaria	Azerbaijan	Algeria	Mongolia	Colombia
Burundi	China	Croatia	Belarus	Egypt	Philippines	
Cape Verde	Laos	Czech Republic	Georgia	Iran		
Eritrea	Myanmar	Hungary	Kazakhstan	Iraq		
Ethiopia	Vietnam	Macedonia	Kyrgyz Republic	Jordan		
Guinea		Poland	Moldova	Libya		
Guinea-Bissau		Romania	Russia	Mauritania		
Lesotho		Slovak Republic	Tajikistan	Somalia		
Liberia		Slovenia	Turkmenistan	Sudan		
Madagascar			Ukraine			
Malawi			Uzbekistan			
Mozambique						
Namibia						
Nigeria						
Rwanda						
Sao Tome and Principe						
Sierra Leone						
Tanzania						
Zaire						
Zambia						
Zimbabwe						

Note:
[a] Corresponds to IMF department groupings.
Source: Quirk *et al.* (1995: 4).

In January 1993, during the biennial review of the Fund's surveillance policies and following a recommendation by Fund staff, the Executive Board debated whether the Fund should make a further push to persuade member states to accept their formal obligations under Article VIII. This received majority support in the Board, with no Executive Directors explicitly arguing against the staff's proposal (IMF 1993b, 1993c). The US and UK representatives on the Board, in particular, were strongly in favour of encouraging wider compliance with Article VIII, with the US Executive Director stating that 'We fully agree [with the staff] that many members are overdue in accepting Article VIII status' (IMF 1993b: 21). The Board subsequently agreed that the Fund's renewed focus on advocating for the current account convertibility policy norm would continue to be pursued through its policy surveillance and loan negotiations, rather than using the provisions under Article XIV for the Fund to make an explicit request for a state to abandon exchange restrictions and accept Article VIII status. As the Russian representative stated to the Executive Board during the 1993 review of the Fund's surveillance policy, the Fund cannot directly exercise coercive power over its member states, but rather 'its influence depends on its moral and intellectual authority' (IMF 1993c: 16). The Board agreed that efforts to encourage the remaining member states that had not yet accepted Article VIII status to do so would take place within the existing surveillance framework of Article IV consultations, as well as negotiations over the use of Fund resources when member states sought approval for Fund-supported programmes (IMF 1993d: 18; Galbis 1996: 46).

The Fund's campaign to encourage member states to adopt Article VIII status produced immediate effects, with fifty-four countries formally adopting their Article VIII obligations from 1993 to 1996 (see Table 6.5). In many cases, member states that subsequently accepted

Table 6.5 *Acceptance of Article VIII, 1990–2007*

IMF member	Effective date of acceptance	IMF member	Effective date of acceptance
Turkey	22 March 1990	Central African Republic	1 June 1996
Thailand	4 May 1990	Chad	1 June 1996
Cyprus	9 January 1991	Comoros	1 June 1996
Tonga	22 March 1991	Republic of Congo	1 June 1996
Marshall Islands	21 May 1992	Côte d'Ivoire	1 June 1996
Switzerland	29 May 1992	Equatorial Guinea	1 June 1996
Greece	7 July 1992	Gabon	1 June 1996
San Marino	23 September 1992	Mali	1 June 1996

Table 6.5 (*cont.*)

IMF member	Effective date of acceptance	IMF member	Effective date of acceptance
Tunisia	6 January 1993	Niger	1 June 1996
Gambia	21 January 1993	Russian Federation	1 June 1996
Morocco	21 January 1993	Senegal	1 June 1996
Micronesia, Fed.	24 June 1993	Togo	1 June 1996
States of Lebanon	1 July 1993	Mongolia	1 February 1996
Israel	21 September 1993	Kazakhstan	16 July 1996
Mauritius	29 September 1993	Madagascar	18 September 1996
Barbados	3 November 1993	Namibia	20 September 1996
Trinidad and Tobago	13 December 1993	Ukraine	24 September 1996
Grenada	24 January 1994	China	1 December 1996
Ghana	21 February 1994	Yemen	10 December 1996
Uganda	5 April 1994	Georgia	20 December 1996
Bangladesh	11 April 1994	Guinea-Bissau	1 January 1997
Lithuania	3 May 1994	Lesotho	5 March 1997
Nepal	30 May 1994	Armenia	29 May 1997
Latvia	10 June 1994	Algeria	15 September 1997
Kenya	30 June 1994	Palau	16 December 1997
Pakistan	1 July 1994	Romania	25 March 1998
Estonia	15 August 1994	Macedonia, FYR	19 June 1998
India	20 August 1994	Bulgaria	24 September 1998
Paraguay	22 August 1994	Rwanda	10 December 1998
Samoa	6 October 1994	Mauritania	19 July 1999
Malta	30 November 1994	Brazil	30 November 1999
Zimbabwe	3 February 1995	Belarus	5 November 2001
Jordan	20 February 1995	Cambodia	1 January 2002
Kyrgyz Republic	29 March 1995	Zambia	19 April 2002
Croatia	29 May 1995	Serbia	15 May 2002
Poland	1 June 1995	Timor-Leste	23 July 2002
Moldova	30 June 1995	Democratic Rep. of Congo	10 February 2003
Slovenia	1 September 1995	Libya	21 June 2003
Philippines	8 September 1995	Uzbekistan	15 October 2003
Czech Republic	1 October 1995	Sudan	29 October 2003
Slovak Republic	1 October 1995	Cape Verde	1 July 2004
Brunei Darussalam	10 October 1995	Tanzania	15 July 1996
Botswana	17 November 1995	Colombia	1 August 2004
Guinea	17 November 1995	Iran	6 September 2004
Malawi	7 December 1995	Azerbaijan	30 November 2004
Sierra Leone	14 December 1995	Tajikistan	9 December 2004
Hungary	1 January 1996	Egypt	2 January 2005
Benin	1 June 1996	Vietnam	8 November 2005
Burkina Faso	1 June 1996	Montenegro	18 January 2007
Cameroon	1 June 1996		

Source: IMF (2007a: 6–7).

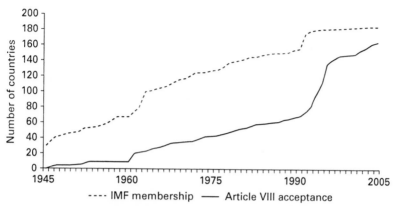

Figure 6.1 IMF membership and Article VIII acceptance
Source: IMF (2007a: 6–7).

Article VIII status were 'easy targets' that comprised a group of thirty-nine members identified by the Fund staff at the end of 1992 as no longer maintaining any exchange restrictions under Article XIV (IMF 1992: 46). In bilateral policy dialogue with this group of states, Fund staff could argue that there would be no policy autonomy cost for states that no longer maintained Article XIV restrictions to shift to Article VIII status, because any *new* exchange restrictions they might wish to impose would in any case require Fund approval under Article VIII. As Figure 6.1 demonstrates, however, over the course of the next decade the Fund had a high rate of success in persuading member states – both those that no longer maintained exchange restrictions and those that did – to accept their obligations under Article VIII. Following this renewed emphasis by the Fund, the proportion of its member states to accept Article VIII status increased from 43 per cent of members at the start of 1990 (66 of 152 states), to 55 per cent of members in February 1995 (100 of 179 states), to 90 per cent of members in November 2005 (165 of 184 states). By the end of 2005, therefore, the Fund's advocacy of the current account convertibility policy norm could legitimately be described as being accepted and complied with by an overwhelming majority of both developed and developing country Fund members.

In searching for an explanation for the Fund's high level of success during the 1990s and early 2000s in transforming current account convertibility – as defined under Article VIII of its Articles of Agreement – from a formally valid obligation on states into a socially recognized policy norm, the interface between the Fund's role as a norm advocate in the global political economy and the changing political and economic environment that states faced during this period is crucial. In particular, the breakdown of the Bretton Woods system in the early 1970s and the shift to a 'non-system' largely based on floating exchange rates both reflected and further reinforced a shift in the balance of authority between states and markets, where public power to determine national policy settings is commonly assumed to have weakened relative to private power (see Hall and Biersteker 1999). While the shifting balance of authority between states and markets has impacted upon the monetary policy autonomy of governments the world over – including the major industrialized economies (see Germain 1997: 162–5; Grimes 2003; Hassdorf 2005; McNamara 1999: 109–14; Sinclair 2005: chapter 6) – the change has perhaps been most keenly felt by developing, and especially low-income developing, economies.

A great deal of international political economy scholarship over the past twenty years has concentrated on examining the sweeping changes in economic ideas that have helped to set the scene for governments in many developing countries to switch their economic policy strategies in favour of economic liberalization and greater openness to international markets (see, for example, Simmons and Elkins 2004; Weyland 1998). For its part, the Fund has attempted to play an important advocacy role in diffusing ideas for economic liberalism among its member states in three main ways. First, the Fund has sought to exercise an intellectual influence over states' policy strategies by providing its members with a source of 'expert' knowledge on liberalization reforms implemented elsewhere (Barnett and Finnemore 2004: 68–9; Broome and Seabrooke 2007). Second, the Fund has attempted to reinforce the position of liberal reformers within national bureaucracies through lending credibility to their policy proposals and backing these up with its financial resources (Woods 2006: 72–3). Third, the Fund has sponsored economic liberalization programmes in an attempt to provide a credibility-enhancing 'commitment mechanism' for states to improve their reputations with both public and private international creditors (Broome 2008).

The Fund's efforts contributed to the diffusion of a range of policy ideas around the world during the 1990s that were previously seen as anathema to many governments, such as central bank independence and the general reduction of trade restrictions, which – combined with broader changes in the economic environment that states faced – helped to generate conditions that were more favourable for the stabilization of current account convertibility as a policy norm. As Table 6.5 shows, however, many of the states to adopt current account convertibility during the 1990s were post-communist economies that had only recently joined the Fund (see Broome 2010). The majority of post-communist economies made a rapid transition to currency convertibility (Stolze 1997), which may have increased the pressure on existing Fund members to recognize current account convertibility as an important signal of market openness in the post-Cold War era (Simmons 2000b: 583). Geography and regional linkages also appear to have played an important role in this process, with Table 6.5 suggesting that many states may have chosen to adopt current account convertibility in order to keep in line with policy reforms in neighbouring countries (see also Simmons 2000b: 584). With the Fund deliberately stressing the increased importance it attached to the acceptance of Article VIII status in its regular policy surveillance consultations with member states from the early 1990s (IMF 1992: 47), its efforts at intellectual persuasion – combined with the potential for borrowers to have current account convertibility included in loan agreement conditions and the increased risk for some states of suffering a reputational cost by being branded as a 'non-reformer' – were given an added impetus in an economic environment where many governments had begun to place greater importance on establishing 'policy credibility' with financial markets via liberal policy reforms (Grabel 2000; Rodrik 1989).

There will always be exceptions to any norm of state behaviour. As Figure 6.2 indicates, the Fund's campaign to promote current account convertibility as a policy norm remains unfinished business, with a number of Fund members continuing to maintain exchange restrictions under Article XIV or Article VIII (either with or without the Fund's approval).

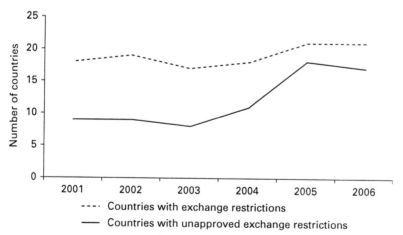

Figure 6.2 Article VIII countries maintaining exchange restrictions, 2001–6
Source: IMF (2007b: 22).

However, those Fund members that continue to either openly or informally contest the validity of the current account convertibility policy norm now constitute a small minority, most of which are authoritarian or semi-authoritarian states that tend to see the liberalization of exchange controls as a threat to regime stability. For instance, persistent 'norm rebels' such as Uzbekistan have accepted Article VIII status in the Fund and yet maintain a range of informal exchange controls, while formally enacting 'liberal' rules and denying the existence of any restrictions on convertibility (Gemayal and Grigorian 2006: 242). These exceptions notwithstanding, and in comparison with the Fund's more high profile and controversial campaign to establish *capital account* convertibility as a global policy norm in the 1990s (Leiteritz and Moschella, chapter 8 this volume), the Fund's recent attempts to persuade the bulk of its member states finally to accept their formal obligations to establish current account convertibility under Article VIII of its Articles of Agreement as socially legitimate can be judged a successful case of norm institutionalization. As a result, the Fund's advocacy of the current account convertibility policy norm is currently at the stage of norm stabilization – albeit with a low level of continuing contestation – within the broader 'norm circle' (see chapter 1).

Conclusion: convertibility as an IMF success story?

Although frequently discussed in the same breath, international agreements which lack social recognition are not policy *norms*. An international legal rule constitutes a formally valid obligation on states, yet it may often be honoured in the breach. In contrast, a policy norm that is recognized as both formally and socially valid implies a general acceptance by states that certain policy goals and the policy instruments employed to achieve those goals constitute a 'rightful' standard of behaviour. To be effective, international rules must become accepted by states as legitimate norms of appropriate behaviour which can then be reinforced by ideational sanctions such as shaming. The process through which international rules are transformed into global policy norms therefore implies a point at which states do more than voice rhetorical support for an international rule in principle, and back up this principled support with expressive actions by implementing concrete policy changes in practice. This should not be taken to imply that once this point is reached, and a global policy norm emerges, it is then internalized to the point that it subsequently directs actors' behaviour. Even when states shift from *principled support* for a global policy standard to *expressive actions* that indicate a more substantive process of legitimation, norm development remains an ongoing and contested political process (chapter 1).

As the case of the Fund's long campaign to promote universal current account convertibility demonstrates, there can be a significant time-lag between the emergence of a formally valid policy standard and the stabilization of that standard as a socially recognized policy norm. Moreover, flexibility can be crucial to the global diffusion of policy norms. With respect to currency convertibility, if Harry Dexter-White's original proposal for a strict three-year timetable for states to adopt current account convertibility had become a formal obligation of Fund membership it is unlikely that the Fund could have expanded as rapidly as it did during the post-war era. In particular, it is unlikely that the Fund could have incorporated new members so quickly during the two large waves of expansion that occurred during decolonization in the late 1950s and 1960s and later when post-communist states sought to join the organization in the 1990s. In these circumstances, an unexpected consequence of Britain's desire during the Bretton Woods negotiations to protect its own policy autonomy was to incorporate flexibility into the Fund's monetary norms for new members under the 'transitional' provisions of Article XIV. This helped to pave the way for the future expansion of the Fund's membership, which in turn set the scene for the Fund gradually to stabilize current account convertibility as a policy norm through providing material incentives for policy change, engaging in intellectual persuasion, and using informal sanctions such as public shaming and peer pressure as an increasing proportion of Fund members moved to adopt Article VIII status during the 1990s.

From this study of the Fund's efforts to advocate a formally valid standard of monetary behaviour as a socially recognized policy norm, it is clear that the influence an IO such as the Fund can exercise in the global political economy depends in large part on how successful the IO is at taking advantage of environmental changes to promote its aims. Although the Fund is sometimes described as one of the most powerful IOs in history (Stone 2002: 1), states remain sovereign actors and the Fund's influence depends on its intellectual authority and its capacity to persuade governments to enact policy changes through argument and material incentives rather than through more coercive means. Indeed, the Fund is clearly aware that it cannot force policy changes on unwilling governments, as evidenced by its reluctance to activate the formal provisions under Article XIV to make a direct request to states to remove exchange restrictions and its preference to seek changes through policy dialogue and persuasion. In this issue area, the Fund's capacity to exercise authority rests on its ability to fix the meaning of current account convertibility as a policy norm, as well as to advocate for social recognition of open current accounts when faced with a window of opportunity to facilitate a redefinition of actors' interests.

In its efforts to achieve norm stabilization through broadening the social acceptance of Article VIII status among developing countries during the 1990s, the Fund was able to draw upon two important factors to bolster its arguments. First, the fact that many states that remained under Article XIV no longer maintained significant exchange restrictions in practice, yet in some cases were unaware that new restrictions would require Fund approval under Article VIII, enabled Fund staff to persuade national officials that accepting Article VIII status would not come with a significant cost in terms of policy autonomy. Second, the changing political and economic environment states faced during the late 1980s and 1990s (and especially after the end of the Cold War), combined with the shift in economic ideas among many policy-makers in developing countries, made it possible for the Fund to link the formal acceptance of current account convertibility to the goal of improving a government's 'policy credibility' with international creditors and investors. In short, the Fund's importance for governments as a means to improve their standing with public and private providers of external finance can potentially afford the Fund an important source of indirect influence through shaping the parameters of 'appropriate' standards of policy conduct, thereby lending greater weight to the Fund's arguments in favour of the adoption of policy norms.

7   Bitter pills to swallow: legitimacy gaps and social recognition of the IMF tax policy norm in East Asia

Leonard Seabrooke

Introduction

As one of the world's premier institutions for global economic governance, the International Monetary Fund (IMF) is responsible for ensuring that its member states can pay their own way in the world economy. Accordingly, tax reform has been a key part of the IMF's mandate and the institution devotes substantial energy to advising its member states on how best to reform their fiscal revenue systems, particularly borrowing member states with loan programme conditions. Unsurprisingly, reforming a domestic taxation system raises a host of political issues, not the least who benefits from the redistribution of tax monies. As such, the IMF has a mixed record of success with tax reform within loan programmes, with 60 per cent of borrowing member states failing to meet their fiscal targets during the 1990s. In general, the IMF's failure rate in obtaining borrowing states' full compliance with reform programmes has *increased* in the past thirty years from 55 per cent in the early 1970s to 80 per cent in the late 1990s. At the same time, Miranda Stewart (2003) highlights that a 'remarkable consensus' or norm has emerged in recent years in the determination of tax policy design (see also Stewart and Jogarajan 2004).

In the past, reform programme failure has been explained by a lack of technical expertise in borrowing states, where the offering of technical expertise has been seen by the Fund as one of its key legitimating devices (Barnett and Finnemore 2004). Now, in addition to identifying the need for technical assistance, the Fund stresses how borrowing states often exhibit a lack of 'political will' to implement the Fund's recommended

This chapter was written while a visitor at the Norwegian Institute of International Affairs (NUPI), Oslo. My thanks go to the staff at NUPI for their hospitality. My thanks also go to André Broome, Ole Jacob Sending, Shogo Suzuki and the editors for their comments on an earlier draft. Special thanks go to the archivists in the International Monetary Fund Archives, Washington, DC, especially Madonna Gaudette, Premela Isaacs and Jean Marcoyeux.

reforms (Bird 2003: 94–5; Independent Evaluation Office 2003a: 30). In particular, staff from the IMF's Fiscal Affairs Department have argued that lack of success within tax reform programmes is often due not to insufficient technical information, or even financial assistance, but to lack of 'political will' to implement tough reforms within a programme cycle (Tanzi and Zee 2000). This view has also become commonplace in the policy-oriented literature, suggesting that 'political will' has normative force (Fjeldstad and Rakner 2003; Schick 2004). That political will constrains borrower action may be explained if social recognition from borrowing state officials is only *rhetorical and not practical*, so that it does not lead to actual policy implementation of the tax reform policy norm in accordance with mutually agreed programme targets. Norm adherence may then split into *rhetorical* acceptance through social recognition ('talk but not walk') and social acceptance combined with policy actions in line with IMF loan programme directives and targets ('talk and walk') (the exemplary study on rhetoric in the international political economy is Sharman 2006). Problems of cultural validation within borrower states (see chapter 1) will logically only make lip-service matters worse. Indeed, electoral pressures and borrowing governments' capacity to 'scapegoat' the IMF are obvious sources of frustration for the IMF's staff. In short, getting borrowing member states to swallow bitter pills within a three-year loan programme can be difficult.

In the terms favoured within this volume, while borrowing member states may have formally validated the IMF's Articles of Agreement and loan agreements on tax reform procedures, receiving only rhetorical social recognition from borrowing state governments that does not lead to policy implementation in line with loan programme procedures and principles can lead not only to performance failure, but to a weakening of the tax reform policy norm. Thus, while states and the IMF may formally agree and their officials signal social recognition, if it is but rhetoric then what may appear to be a strong norm may have a significant internal weakness. Such fragmentation of what is 'talk' and what is 'walk' will also permit norm contestation in subtler ways than open opposition. It may permit countries to provide a 'mimetic challenge' in that they may offer to reform in ways in which the IMF wishes (Hobson and Seabrooke 2007), but are then able to claim autonomy that prevents more extensive forms of norm internalization and socialization (Checkel 2005; Park 2010). At the same time, such autonomy must also be legitimated through domestic institutional change which, even if not within the IMF's standardized loan programme cycles (as is commonly the case), provides future constraints on the governments of borrowing member states. In short, cultural validity would lead to domestic policy change, whereas a lack of cultural validity could provide a source of norm contestation that challenges the Fund's policy norm in a multitude of ways that must be mapped and traced (on everyday practices and IMF policies, see Broome 2008).

This chapter attempts to do just that by making a conceptual twist in suggesting we might find some analytical clarity in understanding these dynamics through the notion of a 'legitimacy gap'. The legitimacy gap is understood as *the space between claims to the fairness and rightfulness of policy actions by those who seek to govern, and the conferral of legitimacy on these claims through policy implementation by those being governed*. Accordingly, I argue that the legitimacy of a system of power must be understood not only through the expression of *beliefs* that can be seen through formal validity demonstrated in policy documents, but also through the *expressions* of social recognition that leads to a change in borrowers' policy *practice*. The reform policy choice is taxation systems, specifically for revenue, since changes to taxation systems are intensely political and are critically important in determining how well states can weather financial crises. The emergence of the legitimacy gap may be seen as a problem tied to *rhetorical* social recognition over the policy norm and therefore operating procedures of the IMF, especially within the formal loan programme (cf. rhetoric and legitimacy problems with the anti-money laundering regime in Tsingou 2006). The gap may be closed in the long term as institutional changes made to support fiscal revenue systems that are more in accordance with the Fund's overall economic development approach take place. We therefore suggest that norm institutionalization, and socialization and internalization processes may be operating on different time horizons. This variance may be explained by merely rhetorical social recognition, and even deeper problems with cultural validation among borrowers, compared with Fund expectations of long-term norm socialization and internalization beyond its three-year programme loan cycles.

The analysis of legitimacy gaps in this chapter takes the form of a discourse analysis of Fund official documents on tax policy. The aim here is to separate the formal validity and social recognition, or 'talk', from the more substantive level of cultural validation that leads to policy change in line with programme targets, or 'walk'. Reform 'talk' and reform 'walk' have become increasingly distinct both within the Fund and in the relationship between the Fund and borrowers. Such a relationship may then encourage IMF staff to seek to persuade national officials culturally to validate the tax reform policy norm (discussed here as 'IMF friendly tax policies') and put it into practice to meet programme targets. Identifying a legitimacy gap is an important step in producing a fine-grained analysis of norm emergence and the informal and formal mechanisms for norm contestation. It may also suggest cases in which rhetorical social recognition is not tied to a lack of technical or financial capacity, but a fundamental problem with cultural validation of certain policy norms, a problem at the root of 'political will'.

To establish how a legitimacy gap has widened, a contrast between 'talk' and 'walk' is assessed for the period between 1965 and 2000. The analysis here is restricted to four states that were embroiled in the Asian financial crisis, namely Indonesia, the Philippines, South Korea and Thailand.[1] This follows the logic that the Asian financial crisis represents only a symptomatic 'turning point' rather than the cause itself. To clarify here, norm contestation may not only take place during periods of crisis and great uncertainty, but may be found in the separation of policy rhetoric and policy practices during a period of seeming normality (cf. Seabrooke 2007a).

An important source of change here may be internal dynamics within the Fund. I suggest that until the late 1980s the Fund used what André Broome and I have called 'associational templates' (Broome and Seabrooke 2007) to customize tax reforms for member states that could add an additional justification to legitimate reform policy advice. Within this sample, the Fund often told borrowing states that reforms were legitimate because they were appropriate for an 'Asian' state, with paired comparisons between states in the region often presented to the state in question. Associational templates may have performed an important function in harnessing social recognition for policy change rather than simply acknowledging the formal validity of Fund policies and proce-dures. Such templates, I suggest, may have weakened as more attention has been given to creating a single norm of 'world's best practice' policy. A weakening of the power of area desks to customize policies would help explain an increase in the 'gap' between the Fund's claims to the legiti-macy of its policies and what borrowers recognize as important for tax reform.

Through this lens, this chapter assesses the Fund's role as a tax reform policy norm advocate to four East Asian states through a discourse anal-ysis of primary documents related to loan arrangements. The three key findings are, first, that in formally and socially validating taxation reform

---

[1] This chapter is drawn from a broader study on how the IMF can customize policies so that the fiscal and financial reforms it advocates can receive domestic legitimacy within the member state and then lead to policy implementation. The project has studied these issues in three main areas of economic policy: fiscal governance, monetary policy and financial governance. A companion study on small open economies can be found in Broome and Seabrooke 2007. The chapter aims to reveal the disjuncture between formal validity and social recognition of the tax reform policy norm on the one hand, and cultural validation on the other. There is little room herein, however, to break down the analysis of the four cases into detailed domestic debates.

borrowers often 'talk the talk' without 'walking the walk'; second, that preliminary evidence suggests that templates have been replaced by a stress on adherence to a single tax reform norm that has converged on a world's best policy practice, through an ongoing engagement in long-term institutional reform and more mundane forms of change (such as technical assistance) and regulatory reform; and third, that this mix of aspirations for compliance with a single norm on tax reform through 'lip-service' and more micro-level attempts at persuasion does not tackle the IMF's legitimation problems head-on, leading the Fund to *violate* the formal validity of its Articles of Agreement in how it treats its member states.

The chapter proceeds as follows: first, a short discussion of potential sources of the Fund's international crisis of legitimacy; second, the proposition of a 'legitimacy gap' between claims and acceptance of Fund reforms is put forward, as well as the notion of associational templates that serve as legitimating devices for the Fund, and a lightning discussion of the Fund's policies on taxation and its relationship to broader work on discourse and conditionality; third, the presentation of empirical findings on the four East Asian cases; and finally, reflections on how the Fund's problem with rhetorical social recognition cannot be solved by a violation of its own formal validity, which will only exacerbate problems with cultural validation within borrowing member states.

Sources of the Fund's legitimacy crisis

Why does the Fund have a more general legitimacy problem? A host of scholars point out how the Fund's institutional structure predisposes it to the whims of the international political economy's most powerful states, especially the USA. A number of scholars have argued that a borrowing state's 'political proximity' to US national interest increases the likelihood of increased leniency on loan conditions (e.g. Dreher and Jensen 2007; Momani 2004; Thacker 1999). Others still have argued that the determination of voting rights within the Fund, according to subscription quotas, is a source of its declining legitimacy within the international political economy since the USA's 17 per cent share provides it with an immediate – and sometimes used – veto over 'special decisions' that require 85 per cent of votes to pass through (Leaver and Seabrooke 2000; Rapkin and Strand 2006). For critics, this basic voting structure has a disciplining effect on what range of policies are 'thinkable'. Lou Pauly, for example, argues that '[a]lthough most issues inside the Fund are decided through consensual procedures, everyone knows how votes would come out if they had to be taken' (1997: 113).

Furthermore, the fact that until recently no Western state needed a loan arrangement with the Fund since 1976 but the G7 states still comprise 45 per cent of the votes within the Fund suggests a great potential for Western bias in decision-making (for the current allocation of voting rights within the Fund, see www.imf.org). If we look at the top twenty-four industrial states in the world economy, then this figure increases to 60.3 per cent, while twenty-two emerging market states hold 20.4 per cent and the remaining 138 developing states garner 19.3 per cent of Fund votes (Truman 2006: 528). The under-representation of Asian states within the Fund's decision-making procedures, for example, was seen as great motivation for the creation of a regionally based international financial institution in the aftermath of the Asian financial crisis (Rapkin and Strand 2003). Such a response is suggestive of a weakened associational template in reform programmes propagated by the Fund – that policies had become 'one size fits all' rather than customized. More generally, the rights to membership within the Fund make it far less accountable than other international organizations (Woods 2001), an issue that has been noted by the Fund itself, primarily through former senior staff voicing dissatisfaction with the distance now between the Fund's expansive operations and their relationship to the Fund's original Articles of Agreement (Van Houtven 2002; cf. Feldstein 1999). Such dissent indicates that senior staff recognize a gap between the formal validity of Fund principles and procedures, and the potential for social recognition to become rhetorical.

In addition to the above formal politics, the Fund's treatment of its members has transformed dramatically in recent decades. The Fund's 'silent revolution' from the late 1970s to the late 1980s entailed a change from dealing primarily with system management for Western industrialized states to dealing with crisis management for developing states (Boughton 2001). Closely associated here were processes of financial disintermediation and securitization, especially in the USA, that led to a rapid expansion of global debt within the international financial order and a clear move away from traditional bank lending (Seabrooke 2001). Designed to deal with the management of national finances in a bank-driven credit system with a fixed exchange rate monetary system, this essentially left the Fund in an environment where developed states no longer needed its credit, because of the increased availability of private sources. Furthermore, developing states were increasingly operating in an environment with highly varied interest rates and currency rates, and with increased access to short-term debt trading rather than long-term bank loans.

Such a system provided Western states with more 'room to move' (Mosley 2002), and also allowed developing states some 'room to groove' within certain strictures (Seabrooke 2006a). However, it left the Fund dealing with currency and liquidity crises that were of a much bigger nature, and where its own financial resources were much smaller compared with private credit in the world economy (Bordo and James 2000). As a consequence, during the 1980s and 1990s the Fund's role became that of a crisis manager, especially in Latin America and Eastern Europe (Pauly 1997: 125–6). The 'Tequila Crisis' in Mexico during 1994–5 is a case in point, given that the Fund, following a US veto, broke its own rules to provide, with the USA and the Bank for International Settlements (BIS), a loan sufficient for Mexico to deal with its losses (Seabrooke 2001: 166). Given such changes, the Fund has also had to seek financial support from private 'supplementary financiers' who can provide capital for loans, but who require an increase in, and more uniform, loan conditions (Gould 2003).

Much of the work in development economics concentrates on how the Fund's problems, including its waning legitimacy, are a consequence of reform programme failures. Earlier work here pointed to how the Fund's structural adjustment packages of the 1980s created negative outcomes (Bienen and Gersovitz 1985; Haggard 1985; Nelson 1990; Siddell 1988), while more recent literature stresses how loan conditionality has become too homogeneous and insensitive to differences within borrowing states. Here the Fund is commonly seen as ignoring 'civil society' and pursuing 'neoliberal' economic reforms that ensure programme failure (Taylor 2004). The distortions of how these programmes are implemented have been directly related to the Fund's institutional arrangements and organizational culture (Babb 2005).

The evidence of the impact on Fund programmes is extensive. Development economists, in particular, have demonstrated that economic growth during a loan programme is more likely to drop rather than increase (Dreher 2006; Przeworski and Vreeland 2000), and that there are often even lower growth rates after the loan period (Barro and Lee 2004). Others argue that programmes can have positive economic growth effects (see Dicks-Mireaux et al. 2000), and that programmes do improve 'external fundamentals' (see Bird 2003: 101–2; Bordo et al. 2004). On compliance with the Fund's policy conditions, development economists have shown that this is often achieved during a loan period because of the Fund's threat to withhold credit if policy criteria are not met, but that the wheels fall off afterwards when policy implementation slows or is reversed (Evrensel 2002). Scholars have also pointed to the need to separate out the direct and indirect effects of IMF programmes and conditions, which raises the question of how we should evaluate their success, particularly given that even when Fund programmes do increase economic growth, they also often increase income inequality and political discontent (Garuda 2000).

In general, the overall assessment of the Fund's conduct is that its programme success has been weak, even according to the Fund's limited criteria for evaluating programme outcomes, and that it is increasingly relying on pressure to try and produce positive results. Here the Fund's new discourse on 'ownership', as well as 'transparency', is particularly important in demonstrating how it has changed its own conception of rightful conduct, even though its borrowing states may not have (Best 2005). The Fund's formation of the Independent Evaluation Office (IEO) in 2001 was an explicit recognition of the Fund's post-Asian financial crisis need to deal with rightful membership and rightful conduct problems by scrutinizing itself, or 'leading by example' on transparency and accountability (Independent Evaluation Office 2003b). The IEO's official purpose is to 'enhance the learning culture within the Fund, strengthen the Fund's external credibility, promote greater understanding of the work of the Fund throughout the membership, and support the Executive Board's institutional governance and oversight responsibilities'.[2] As such, the Fund's accompanying discourse that borrowing states must declare their 'ownership' of loan conditions is a demand for a public declaration from governments that loan programmes have practical social recognition, and that capacity also to receive cultural validation should be enhanced as well (Joyce 2002: 10).

Legitimacy gaps and taxation reform

To illustrate the difference between 'talk' and 'walk', I argue that we can trace a 'legitimacy gap'. This is the space between the legitimacy claimed by those who seek to govern, and the conferral of legitimacy on these claims through policy implementation by those being governed. In borrowing from Graham Bird's work on the Fund's 'conditionality Laffer curve' (2003: 122; see also Seabrooke 2007b), in Figure 7.1 I express this diagrammatically as a 'Reform programme feasibility curve with legitimacy gap'. In the diagram the line OX represents the optimal view often *ascribed* to the Fund – that as it increases the stringency of loan conditions, the likelihood of reform programme success will also increase. The line OX therefore represents claims, the 'talk', to the legitimacy of the tax reform policy norm. A number of conditions, marked on the diagram at B,

---

[2] IMF Executive Board Report to the IMFC on the Establishment of the Independent Evaluation Office and its Terms of Reference, www.imf.org/external/np/eval/2000/091200.htm, accessed 14 July 2008.

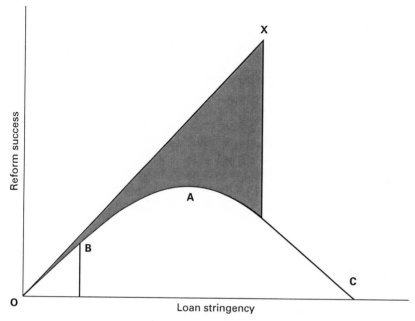

Figure 7.1 Reform programme feasibility curve with legitimacy gap

will be seen as standard and, as James Vreeland has discussed, are often desired by borrowing states because they are in line with their own economic policy objectives (2003: 56–7). But this holds true only up to a point, indicated by A, as when conditions are too stringent such that reform programme success diminishes. The curve OC represents the feasibility of *implementing* loan conditions, the 'walk' where cultural validation leads to the policy change requested by the Fund. The shaded area in Figure 7.1 represents this legitimacy gap between 'talk' and 'walk'. As this gap has widened over time, as I demonstrate below, it represents the real source of the Fund's international crisis of legitimacy. Narrowing the gap requires a resolution to the crisis (also discussed below), or, in the diagram, bending both the OX and OC lines to be more closely co-ordinated.

One means by which the Fund can try to reduce a legitimacy gap between 'talk' and 'walk' is by attempting to customize a policy programme for a borrowing state. In the past the Fund has done so through what I refer to as an associational 'template'. My reading of the Fund's archival documents (discussed in more depth below) suggests that while there is unquestionably an 'IMF friendly policy mix' (to increased Value Added Taxes, decrease tariffs and broaden income taxes) on the kinds of policies the Fund wishes for all member states, it also used 'templates' as comparisons within regions to legitimate policy advice. Borrowing states in Asia, for example, were given advice on the basis of what is appropriate for the region, or what is appropriate for an Asian country within a broader international organization like the Organization for Economic Co-operation and Development (OECD). Similarly, member states in Scandinavia were given advice on what is appropriate for a European Community, then European Union, member (see Broome and Seabrooke 2007). In this manner, the Fund could treat all members equally, as well as make a claim to customizing policy advice within a 'thick' domestic or culturally valid frame through a comparison of like economies.

Given the use of associational templates, we may think of how the Fund could encourage its 'IMF friendly' policies in borrowing states through the process depicted in Figure 7.2 (see also Broome 2008; Broome and Seabrooke 2008).

Here the 'IMF friendly' policy mix represents an independent variable, the use of an associational template the first conditional variable, with a second conditional variable in whether the borrowing state grants cultural validity to the IMF friendly policy by translating it into a domestic context, thus lending the reform programme domestic legitimacy. The first conditional variable is highly reliant on the presence of internal norm advocates within the IMF, which has a capacity to customize a norm for tax reform into a policy that is persuasive for a member state. Logically, the diminution of appropriate internal advocates within a formal policy programme may lead to a weakened compliance with a norm for tax reform. This may not be an outright rejection of the policy norm, but an opening gap between 'talk' and 'walk'. This will be determined by the power of external norm advocates in the second conditional variable, especially those located within the member state. If national officials can present arguments as to why reform in accordance with a policy norm is legitimate and persuasive, the chance of success in matching policy implementation to the policy norm is much greater. Here external norm advocates, such as external financiers, can rock the boat by pushing too hard and making translation of IMF policies into a domestic setting impossible. In a twist

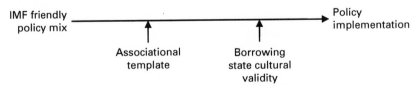

Figure 7.2 How the IMF influences member states

on the typical argument concerning norm advocates (see the review in chapter 1), norm advocates may push too hard and end up with their intended targets replying with 'lip-service' rather than implementing the policy norm.

In general, if both conditions in Figure 7.2 are achieved, policy implementation in accordance with the 'IMF friendly' tax reform policy norm may then be possible. As discussed below, this is increasingly less the case. Indeed, from my view the Fund in the past decade has placed less stress on trying to customize policies for member states and more on establishing a single 'world's best practice' norm or a 'standard of civilization' (Best 2005).

An analysis of Fund tax advice allows us to investigate the sources of crisis because it is precisely on this issue that the Fund has great difficulty in trying to reform borrowing states to place them in a better position to weather international financial crises, such as the Asian crisis of 1997–8. Moreover, in this policy area the Fund has a clear norm expressed as an 'IMF friendly' tax policy mix. Throughout the post-war period the Fund has encouraged its member states to integrate themselves into a free trading international political economy. It consistently advocates moving tax burdens away from international trade and import and export taxes, as well as taxes on capital income, and towards broad domestic sources, particularly consumption taxes. At the same time changes to tax systems are commonly regarded as unpopular economic policies to implement, even under loan conditions (Vreeland 2003: 51). In the contemporary period 60 per cent of borrowing states under Fund tax reform programmes fail to meet their fiscal targets, a problem the Fund now attributes to a lack of 'political will' (Independent Evaluation Office 2003a: 30; Bird 2003: 94–5). Tax reform therefore provides an especially significant test for analysing how the Fund can close legitimacy gaps between the 'talk' associated with its 'IMF friendly' policy norm and the 'walk' of policy understanding and cultural validation. The Fund has attempted to do this by increasing formal loan conditions that require borrowing states to implement tax reform programmes if they wish to continue to have access to Fund financial resources (Bulíř and Moon 2003: 5–6). Such a strategy, however, does not narrow but widens the legitimacy gap between the Fund and borrowing states by distancing the formal validity 'talk' from the 'walk' of borrower engagement. Similarly, it has been noted by those closely associated with the policy department responsible for the tax policy development within the Fund, the Fiscal Affairs Department (FAD), that 'political economy distortions' in borrowing states are responsible for the extent of programme failure on tax reform (Hemming 2003; Tanzi and Zee 2000). This recognition emerges also from the view that technical assistance alone is not sufficient to build

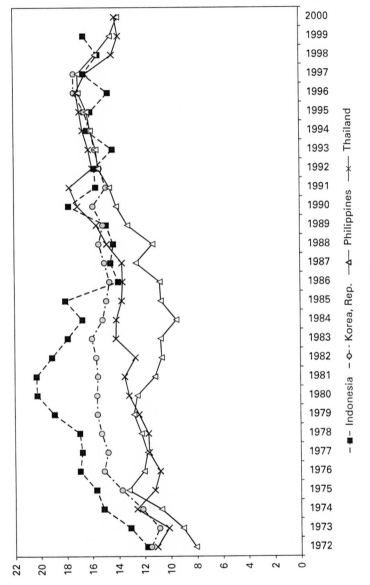

Figure 7.3 East Asian states' tax revenue as percentage of GDP

institutional capacities in borrowing states (see also Broome 2010). Indeed, technical assistance may provide necessary analytical tools for a state to succeed in the contemporary international political economy, but it may also provide a borrowing state with the right vocabulary to 'talk the talk' without necessarily 'walking the walk'.

Fund advice for tax reform in East Asia

The Fund's engagement with East Asian states on tax reform in the post-war period has been subtler than in other regions. While in Latin America during the 1960s the Fund proposed reforms that sought fundamentally to realign the distribution of property and income, in East Asia that emphasis was on removing a dependence on tariffs and export taxes, and on the generation of taxes upon personal income. Conditions on loans to Asian states were basic Fund-standards for most states, particularly the removal of multiple exchange rate practices and the imposition of domestic credit ceilings. In appealing for tax reforms the Fund commonly compared – and still compares – like economies, be they linked within a region or exhibiting close historical or cultural characteristics (such as Australia and New Zealand being considered European). Executive Board meeting minutes reveal that in the 1960s there was a discussion of how East Asia was 'taking off' (following W. W. Rostow) and that there was a burgeoning East Asian development model.

This is not to say that there was not significant variation in the relationship between the Fund and the states under examination here. Table 7.1 provides a quick summary of a qualitative assessment of the basic programme performance and loan conditionality relationships between the Fund and Indonesia, the Philippines, South Korea and Thailand. I stress here that these judgements are simply my qualitative assessment of the loan documents from 1965 onwards.

Figure 7.3 provides details on the tax revenue as a percentage of GDP for the period under investigation. It is important in providing further context for understanding the relationship between the Fund and how these four states differed in their fiscal positions. As can be seen, Indonesia

Table 7.1 *Programme performance and loan conditionality relationships*

	'Tough' conditionality	*'Soft' conditionality*
Programme success	Thailand	South Korea
Programme failure	Indonesia	Philippines

looks positive at first then drops (in line with the price of oil), South Korea has been a consistently strong performer, Thailand was also a reasonable performer (and received the least IMF assistance), while the Philippines spent most of the period in a state of relative disrepair (and received the most IMF assistance), before improving towards the end of the study.

South Korea represents the model student for most of the post-war period. South Korea frequently requested stand-by arrangements (SBAs) from the Fund for potential balance of payments disequilibria (with an agreement for every year between 1965 and 1977, see Vreeland 2003: 18). At least up to the late 1980s, Korea consistently underestimated its capacity to increase its fiscal revenue in comparison with Fund-direct fiscal targets. This occurred to the extent that by the mid-1980s the Executive Board openly questioned why Korea needed the SBAs at all and feared that their only purpose was to provide a 'seal of approval' to international financial markets (EBM/85/105: 21). The Fund also noted that the South Korean National Assembly was flexible in providing extraordinary approval of budgets in support of Fund reforms (SM/95/264). Of course this situation is somewhat different now following the Asian financial crisis, where the Fund felt it was 'scapegoated' when South Korea used loan conditions to push through unpopular economic reforms while blaming the Fund (cf. Mathews 1998: 752–3).

If South Korea represents the 'boy scout' in the story of the Fund and East Asian states as regards tax reform, then the Philippines may be considered a tad spoiled. Like Korea, the Philippines arranged a loan with the Fund for most of the period of study, and frequently drew upon the loan arrangement. From my assessment the loan conditionality for the Philippines, at least compared with its regional neighbours, is relatively soft and the Fund notes that the government commonly exaggerated its capacity to meet fiscal targets. Interestingly, the Fund is also critical of the Filipino Congress and its interference with Fund loan programmes.

If the Philippines is a case of frequent failure with little change in conditionality arrangements, then Thailand must feel like Wednesday's child, full of woe. Thailand has only arranged a handful of loans with the Fund during the period under investigation and received, relative to other states, tough conditionality considering its otherwise good economic performance. In the mid-1980s the IMF pushed heavily on Thailand to reform and the Thais withdrew from the loan altogether with strong public support. It is perhaps no surprise, then, that the Thais expected harsh treatment from the Fund once the Asian financial crisis emerged (and were, indeed, also treated harshly by the USA).

Finally, within this group Indonesia is the rebel. It went further than Thailand by withdrawing from the Fund altogether in 1965, only to rejoin in 1967. Indonesia for most of this period has had sporadic fiscal problems depending on the price of oil. When times are tough the Fund has proposed a raft of reforms for Indonesia, which were commonly accepted and not implemented. Once the price of oil rose, and fiscal revenues followed, Indonesia would then tell the Fund to go bunk. This relationship has been the case for the post-war period and provides some insight into why, during the Asian financial crisis, the Fund delayed the establishment of a loan (which permitted greater pressure for regime change from within) and why post-Suharto the Fund provides amazingly detailed and extensive reform programmes, including taxation.

Given this context, an analysis of how the Fund after the Asian financial crisis is embroiled in an international crisis of legitimacy should try to establish a history that can attempt to separate what is 'talk' as opposed to 'walk'. In this story the Asian financial crisis exemplified the disjunction between the formally valid policy norm and cultural validity, 'smoking out' governments and the Fund to speak plainly. None of this is to blame the states in question for the legitimacy gap, but to put forward the view that if achieving an 'IMF friendly' tax policy mix (described below) is the aim for the IMF it requires a couple of steps. The Fund may have social recognition and formal validity in Fund loan agreements, but if the policy norm does not translate domestically into changed policy practices from lacking cultural validity, policy change will not stick. Also, while changes to the tax system may be made during the programme cycle, this does not mean that the borrowing member states will meet its targets. Here we can distinguish short- and long-term games. While most of the attention given to studying how borrowers perform during a standardized loan programme focuses on the short term, we also need to consider the long term.

As stated above, the Fund has what could be considered an 'IMF friendly' mix of policies on taxation comprising the following: a preference for indirect taxation on consumption, a preference for the 'globalization' (broader application) of direct taxes (personal and corporate income, for example), and the reduction of taxes on trade. We can 'test' for 'IMF friendly' tax reforms by coding advice given in loan arrangements and then comparing this advice with policy action in our four East Asian states. To avoid talking about the Fund as a monolith, I have coded for advice from (a) the Executive Board ('EB') during its review of a loan agreement; (b) the advice from the Fund staff in preparing the loan agreement ('Staff'); and (c) the proposed changes from a borrowing member state when requesting a loan in their Letter of Intent ('State').[3] In doing so I

---

[3] The archival documents assessed here are all documents related to loan arrangements for the four East Asian states between 1965 and 2000, where available. These include the

have scored advice and proposals in the following way, giving a strong bias to the introduction of indirect taxes (such as VAT) and the reduction of tariffs, since these were clearly highlighted by the Fund as priorities:

- preference for increases in indirect taxes $(+2, -2)$
- reduction of trade and transaction taxes $(+2, -2)$
- 'globalization' of direct taxes $(+1, -1)$.

The data was collected from primary documents on fifty-one loan arrangements from the Fund archive in Washington, DC between 2004 and 2006 and supplemented with interviews with staff. Included here are Letters of Intent from borrowing member states (which are, of course, arranged between the IMF and the borrowing country in question), Executive Board Meetings minutes, and IMF staff reports on the loan arrangement. So, for example, if the Executive Board proposed in a loan agreement that the state should introduce a consumption tax, should reduce tariffs and globalize income taxes, then it would represent five points.

If the relevant staff department and the borrowing member state also advise and propose the same, this loan agreement would receive a total, and maximum, of fifteen points. As we can see from Figure 7.4, this is rare. What is noticeable is that most of the 'IMF friendly' policy push comes from the borrowing member state during the period in which a tax reform policy norm was in its stage of norm emergence (see chapter 1). This indicates an increased awareness among borrowing member states on what they think the IMF wants. We may also note the activity of the Fund staff in trying to reform states prior to the first debt crisis, but also that as we move into the 1990s the borrowing states know how to talk to the Fund and through 'Letters of Intent' are able to anticipate what they think the Fund will ask for. While this phenomenon is undoubtedly a consequence of power relations between the Fund and the borrowing state (as well as external influences), it is significant that states frequently offer to reform more than they are asked. If we break down who is asking for what, then there are more surprises. Figure 7.5 shows that while the movement towards indirect taxes is prominent on the agenda, the Fund staff and borrowing states are more vocal here. This is especially the case on tariffs, where states argued about the need to retain them until this became an explicit or implicit loan condition.

Figure 7.6 provides an initial cut on separating the 'talk' from the 'walk'. The assessment here is whether the borrowing states implemented the tax

Letter of Intent or Memorandum on Economic Policies from the intending borrowing member state to the IMF, the Staff Report on the loan arrangement, its likely success and conditions, and the Executive Board Minutes where the loan arrangement is discussed. For reasons of space I provide only the document codes when directly quoting an archived document. Any queries should be directed to me at l.seabrooke@warwick.ac.uk.

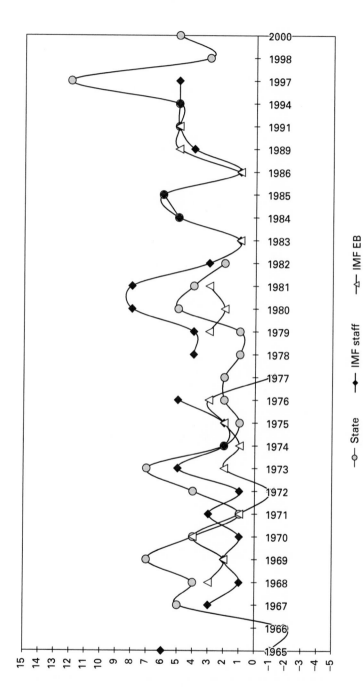

Figure 7.4 Who is asking for IMF friendly reforms?

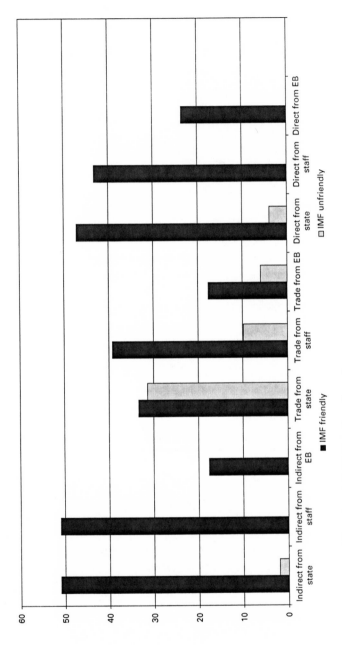

Figure 7.5 Who wants IMF friendly reforms?

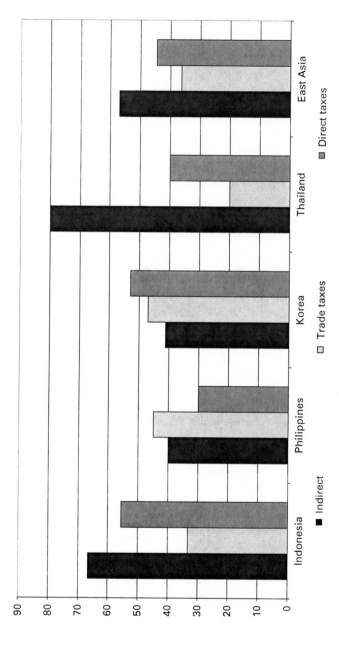

Figure 7.6 Who implements IMF friendly tax policies?

reform requested within the time expected by the Fund or offered by the borrowing state. The results suggest that the chief violator here is the Philippines, while South Korea and Thailand are both model students. Indonesia is notable here for being a star performer; however, it should be noted that most of the reforms it put in place were reversed once the first oil crisis emerged, providing it with a fiscal surplus. We can therefore state from the East Asia average, that while borrowing states are increasingly able to signal to the Fund that they want 'IMF friendly' policies, this is by no means a guarantee that the borrowers will implement them within a loan programme cycle. I have also examined whether there is a relationship between the size of the loan and a borrowing state's quota, on the logic that a larger loan would increase pressure upon the borrowing state to transform 'talk' into 'walk' by meeting fiscal targets established by the Fund staff. This is not the case. An increased loan size does not increase the likelihood that the borrowing state will meet agreed fiscal targets.

To avoid tarring all East Asian borrowing states with the same brush, some differentiation is required here from the Fund's archival sources, especially as this also provides some insight into how the Fund staff and/or Executive Board have identified why some borrowing states provided social recognition but not cultural validation.

In the Philippines, for example, the Fund has attributed failed tax reform and an incapacity to meet fiscal targets to 'political logjams', especially the power of the Philippines' Congress to veto tax reforms proposed by the Fund and agreed to in loans by the Philippines government. The Fund staff and the Executive Board both frequently pointed out to the Philippines that its tax/GNP ratio was far too low and that technical assistance was required (Executive Board Document/86/271). The introduction of a broad consumption tax failed for most of the 1980s (but was finally implemented in 1988), followed by the failure to expand it in 1994 when the Fund's advised reform was taken to the Supreme Court for 'unconstitutionality', and then again following its 1997 implementation through its Comprehensive Tax Reform Package (cf. Yoingco and Recente 2003). In the late 1990s the Executive Board commented, in its apolitical manner, that the role of veto power in the Philippines was an important determinant for reform (e.g. EBM/88/34–3/9/88). The Executive Board and IMF staff both discussed the presidential veto as too populist and a source of fiscal instability. The need for land reform and poverty alleviation in the Philippines, as well as the need to take high-income taxpayers in hand, was also discussed (EBM/88/34–3/9/88; SM/99/149).

In contrast to the Philippines, the Thais were treated with an iron fist. The Fund staff and Executive Board complained during the 1970s that Thailand was too reliant on tariffs and that political opposition was a source of ongoing impediments to tax reform. In the 1980s the Executive Board pointed out that as only 10 per cent of the population pay income tax the country should adopt a consumption tax like other states in the region 'at a similar stage of development'. Tax reform was included as a key element (but not a formal condition) of the 1985 loan and Thailand withdrew from it (EBM/87/165), in part as a result of popular opposition to a consumption tax. The introduction of a consumption tax was post-poned until 1992 and then introduced, against Fund advice, at a rate of 7 per cent, to 'gain public acceptance', according to Thai memorandums (the Fund recommended 10 per cent as a minimum). There was a strong perception that the lack of cultural validation or domestic legitimacy for reforms was the key obstacle to matching policy implementation with formal agreements to implement tax reforms. In short, the Thai case demonstrates the importance of cultural validity to affirm the legitimacy of the policy norm.

South Korea is the darling among this group for most of the post-war period. From 1965 onwards South Korea was considered by the Executive Board to be ripe for 'take off', and it was frequently noted that the National Assembly was willing to take on domestic costs to implement tax reforms, including the cutting of government expenditure and the early introduction of a consumption tax in 1977. At the same time, however, the domestic legitimacy of the tax system was tested through public opposition, leading the South Korean government to provide an income tax exemption for 95 per cent of the population in 1980, while not raising tariffs to compensate (SM/95/264). In the mid-1990s when South Korea joined the OECD, the Fund stopped using Asian states as South Korea's associational templates and began comparing the country with this new association.

For Indonesia, the Fund's key reform throughout the period was aimed at making the state less dependent on oil for fiscal revenue and at shifting the base to consumption taxes. Eventually a consumption tax was introduced in 1985 but there was no real change in the dependence upon oil, leading the Fund staff to start referring to oil as a fiscal and 'economic distortion'. As with South Korea and the Philippines, it is noteworthy that land reform was flagged by the Executive Board and by the IMF staff as a key concern for long-term fiscal sustainability. Also notable was the extent of fiscal reforms proposed by the Fund following the Asian financial crisis – proposals that were viewed domestically, and internationally, as a clear infringement of Indonesia's sovereignty. For example, Tommy Suharto's national car company was explicitly targeted as being in receipt of a corrupt subsidy (which it was) and there are meticulous lists of the individual items that should receive increases in excises, including the politically volatile issue of excise increases and subsidy cuts on basic foodstuffs. For these reasons the Indonesian 1998 loan package is often seen as an indicator of a return of a 'standard of civilization' being imposed, not only because of the extent of conditions but because the Fund sought to overpower, or at least force, cultural validation which ran directly against the need for legitimacy within the borrower state. Clearly such a strategy of 'legitimacy by proclamation' does not harness long-term social support (Seabrooke 2006b: chapter 2). Furthermore, the failures of the Indonesian government to implement many of the conditions led the Fund to hold up the 1998 Indonesian experience as an example of how a sense of 'ownership' of loan conditions must be held by the majority of a state's politicians and, in an interesting twist, by its bureaucracy (Ahluwalia 2003). This certainly stretches shared conceptions of both rightful membership and rightful conduct given that the implementation of Fund programmes is formally a matter for the domestic leadership to handle (Vreeland 2003: 163–4), without their bureaucrats swearing a de facto allegiance to Fund policies.

Resolutions?

This chapter suggests that in order to understand the sources of the crisis we cannot simply look at how the Fund misdiagnosed the Asian financial crisis and its behaviour since. Indeed, the Asian financial crisis represents only a very public 'turning point' in the longer development of what I have called here a legitimacy gap between the Fund's claims to the rightfulness of a policy norm and the conferral of these claims by borrowing states through cultural validation of the claims. As discussed above, tracing the development of this gap allows us to see not only how the Fund's policy advice has become more homogeneous as it has dropped the mediating tool of associational templates for a single norm of 'world's best practice', but also how borrowing states have exercised their capacity to 'talk' about their need for 'IMF friendly' policies to insulate themselves against financial crises without necessarily 'walking' through policy implementation. Indeed, a key lesson from the discourse analysis of Fund archival documents presented above is that borrowing states often ask to reform more than they are asked. This then requires us to analyse the empirical record to understand why a policy norm may appear to be stable and have social recognition but in practical terms is weaker than appearances would suggest. Legitimacy here is understood as a contest between claims from those who seek to govern, and conferrals or rejections from those who are governed, that are expressed in practices that follow from beliefs.

As seen above, there are significant legitimacy gaps between 'talk' and 'walk' in the relationship between the Fund and borrowing member states. Certainly, this is exacerbated by a perception that Fund-advised tax reforms are not appropriate and will not receive cultural validation by officials in borrowing member states. More research on internal dynamics within the Fund is needed to explore the process of how the Fund staff themselves design policies that are unlikely to be culturally validated. I have posited that, logically, if associational templates were replaced with increased stress on a norm of 'world's best practice', then rhetorical social recognition is more likely since it is difficult to legitimate such reforms while the borrowing government must also pay 'lip-service' to the IMF. Change may be occurring through institutional reforms that can lock in borrowing member states to a more IMF friendly tax system, but this is not occurring within the Fund's standardized programmes. Indeed, with regard to Fund programmes for improving fiscal revenue, FAD staff acknowledge that policy reforms within a loan programme cycle are more than likely to be unsuccessful, but that institutional changes are occurring if reform advice is seen through a longer-term policy horizon. While loan programmes typically last three years, institutional changes for fiscal revenue reform take a decade.[4] Recent research on the impact of Fund programmes also bears out the idea that the economic success of Fund programmes occurs after the formal arrangements have passed (Atoyan and Conway 2005), as well as the notion that the Fund is working towards a longer policy horizon than its formal institutional arrangements will permit. These changes stress the need for the Fund to realign its formal validity to improve the chance of obtaining cultural validation from borrowing member states and avoid what I have termed legitimacy gaps with cultural validity. Failing to do so will only prolong, and perhaps widen, the legitimacy gap between 'talk' and 'walk'.

---

[4] As commented to me in an interview with a staff member from the Fiscal Affairs Department, conducted August 2005.

Part Four

Norm subsiding

8 The IMF and capital account liberalization: a case of failed norm institutionalization

Ralf J. Leiteritz and Manuela Moschella

Introduction

While virtually all elements of the original agenda of the 'Washington Consensus' have become global policy norms over the course of the past twenty years, the case of free capital mobility stands out as an outlier. In his original formulation of the 'to-do-list' for economic reformers, John Williamson deliberately did not include capital account liberalization since he felt that no consensus could be reached in the late 1980s regarding its inclusion in the neoliberal reform package for developing countries (Williamson 1990).[1] Yet capital account liberalization did become associated with the original Washington Consensus and even without formal validity reached the stage of norm emergence.[2] A major driving force behind making capital mobility a policy norm was the International Monetary Fund (henceforth, the IMF or the Fund). However, despite strong support among the international financial institutions and the major powers in the global economic system, the unrestricted movement of international capital failed to leave the stage of norm emergence and to become a stabilized norm in the international financial system.

In order to account for this outcome, we trace the evolution of the IMF's thinking on capital account liberalization from the early 1990s to the present. Specifically, we review the Fund's initial position on the *benefits* of liberalization, defined in terms of economic growth and market

---

[1] In his well-known article from 1990 Williamson wrote that 'there is relatively little support for the notion that liberalization of international capital flows is a priority objective for a country that should be a capital importer and ought to be retaining its own savings for domestic investment' (Williamson 1990: 14).

[2] Capital account liberalization is a subset of financial liberalization referring to the reduction of policy barriers to the purchase and sale of financial assets across national borders (Williamson and Mahar 1998). Allowing domestic banks to take out loans from foreign banks, allowing foreigners to purchase domestic debt instruments and allowing foreigners to invest in the domestic stock market are three indicative examples of capital account liberalization. Capital account liberalization can be measured either qualitatively by looking at statutory changes in national regulations, or quantitatively by looking at changes in the values of economic variables (Edison *et al.* 2002).

discipline. In doing so, we argue that the IMF has progressively reinter-
preted the norm in terms of its allegedly welfare-enhancing effects, shifting from considering capital account liberalization as one of the essential
variables that explain economic growth, to questioning this logic, to then
highlight the positive alongside the negative effects of free capital mobility
for developing countries. The IMF still views capital account liberalization as a desirable economic policy choice for all countries in the long run.
However, primarily as a result of the impact of the Asian financial crisis,
the IMF has – in line with an emerging holistic development norm
complex – specified a range of necessary conditions before countries
should move to a completely open capital account.

Tracing the evolution in the Fund's thinking, we draw attention to
the reciprocal interaction of two sets of mechanisms – inside-out and
outside-in – that trigger policy norm change within the 'norm circle'
(see chapter 1). Specifically, we argue that both organizational culture
centred around the reigning neoliberal economic paradigm inside the
Fund and the level of acceptance of specific economic ideas outside the
Fund are crucial mechanisms in order to understand the rise of the capital
account liberalization policy norm and its failed institutionalization.[3]

The chapter proceeds as follows. In the first section, we outline a
theoretical framework that combines both inside-out and outside-in
mechanisms to explain the emergence and transformation of capital
account liberalization as a policy norm. The next section tells the story
of how the IMF came to view capital account liberalization as a desirable
policy for developing countries in line with the then predominant norm of
development, which specified a positive causal relationship between capital inflows and economic growth. In the following section, we highlight
the main changes in the Fund's discourse that occurred after the Asian
financial crisis in the late 1990s and we demonstrate how the unravelling
of the positive relationship between capital account liberalization and
economic growth changed the Fund's attitude on the issue of free capital
mobility. Finally, we conclude with some reflections on the current place
of capital account liberalization in the IMF's discourse and within an
emerging holistic approach to development.

Towards an explanation of the rise and fall of the capital mobility policy norm

The 'Washington Consensus' granted the liberalization of trade and
capital flows pride of place in the list of required policies to achieve

---

[3] On the intrinsic 'contestedness' of norms, see Wiener (2007a).

economic growth; the dominating discourse within the IMF led the organization to embrace a favourable view of capital account liberalization. At the beginning of the 1990s, the Fund endorsed the view that capital account liberalization is welfare-enhancing and that capital controls are both ineffective and harmful. By the end of the decade, the focus shifted from the benefits to the costs that financial liberalization entails, and from 'distaste' to 'qualified acceptance' of market-based capital controls. The circular form of the capital account liberalization policy norm – emergence, stabilization, contestation and finally transformation – raises some important questions. What are the actors and the mechanisms through which the idea of capital mobility became consensual within the organization? How was the idea institutionalized in the Fund's policies? Through which channels did it evolve? Two broad sets of explanations may be of help to answer these questions: the external imposition explanation, on the one hand, and the bureaucratic culture explanation, on the other.

The first explanation focuses on the economic interests of powerful Fund member states and the formal and informal channels through which their influence is exercised. Seen from this perspective, the IMF embraced capital account liberalization because it reflected the economic preferences of the so-called Wall Street–Treasury Complex (Bhagwati 1998; Wade and Veneroso 1998). According to this logic, the IMF willingly and enthusiastically forced the agenda of free capital mobility down the throats of recalcitrant developing country governments following the bidding of the US government. As Ngaire Woods argues, capital account liberalization became 'an article of faith' within the Fund because the policy was 'high on the agenda of the United States' (Woods 2006: 136). As a result, the Fund's discourse and subsequent policy towards the capital account were determined from *outside* the organization.

The second explanation emphasizes bureaucratic culture as the crucial variable to explain the trajectory of economic ideas within international organizations (Barnett and Finnemore 2004). In particular, the IMF's organizational culture is shaped by a shared belief among its staff in a macroeconomic paradigm, that is, an 'integrated set of theoretical and methodological propositions' (Evans and Finnemore 2001: 19) squarely rooted in neoclassical economic theory (Boughton 2004: 17). According to this explanation, starting in the late 1980s, IMF staff trained at neoliberal economics departments at US universities pushed their shared set of beliefs about the benefits of capital account liberalization on to the IMF (Chwieroth 2007b). In other words, the Fund's discourse and subsequent policy towards the capital account can be explained by factors and actors *inside* the organization.

While each of these explanations provides important insights into the trajectory of economic ideas within the Fund, they leave some important questions unresolved. If we accept the first explanation, we should expect to know which ideas will prevail within the Fund and when they will be endorsed in its operational practice by simply mapping the interests of its most powerful member states, that is, the group of industrialized countries, and the United States in particular. However, several empirical studies reveal that pressure from industrial countries is not always critical for the Fund's mission and operational practice. In moments of uncertainty, industrial countries do not always show a unified front and tend to rely on IMF staff expertise and advice. For example, as Michael Barnett and Martha Finnemore show, 'most ... forms of conditionality can be traced to the IMF staff and the intellectual equipment they use' rather than to the interests of member states (Barnett and Finnemore 2004: 47). While it is unlikely that the IMF undertakes policy initiatives against the explicit will of crucial member states, it is not simply the servant of member states' interests. The Fund, via its intellectual leadership, possesses the authority to advocate ideas without being expressly ordered to do so by its (powerful) member states. In addition, as several recent studies have shown (Abdelal 2007; Chwieroth 2008; IEO 2005; Leiteritz 2005), the IMF pursued capital account liberalization by proposing an amendment to its Articles in the absence of open support from the US government and the private sector.[4]

The second explanation, focusing on the Fund's organizational culture and expert authority, also offers a limited account of the rise and fall of the capital account liberalization discourse within the Fund. The support for capital account liberalization became consensual even in the absence of conclusive evidence of its benefits – a factor that the economics profession inside and outside the Fund highly values. While that may show the embeddedness of the neoliberal economic ideology among staff members, it conspicuously diverges from the usual practice of internal empirical validation for new policy ideas inside the Fund. Similarly, even in the absence of a general staff turnover and in the absence of straightforward evidence disconfirming prior beliefs, the IMF did none the less qualify its approach starting in the late 1990s.

The limitations of the existing explanations lead us to question the practice of opposing member countries' material interests to IMF staff

---

[4] For instance, one of the findings of Rawi Abdelal's work on the IMF's role in the promotion of global capital mobility is that 'none of the most influential bankers and investors in the United States were consulted when the amendment was first proposed, and, upon learning of the proposal, they opposed it altogether' (Abdelal 2007: 130).

ideas to explain the fate of the capital account liberalization policy norm. In an attempt to provide a more adequate explanation and in order to identify the mechanisms through which policy norms evolve within the Fund, we propose to combine both explanations by acknowledging that interests and ideas are not separate entities (Blyth 2002: 18). Rather, the interaction between staff ideas and countries' interests determines the success or failure of an economic idea in terms of its acceptance and resilience over time. Specifically, we argue that both bureaucratic culture centred around the reigning neoliberal economic paradigm inside the Fund and the level of acceptance of an economic idea outside the Fund are crucial factors in order to understand the fate of the capital account liberalization policy norm.

In particular, we argue that economic ideas held by IMF staff need to be socially recognized by member states as well as relevant external stakeholders in order to become institutionalized as policy norms and so endure over time. While organizational culture is the main filter through which an idea gains acceptance and subsequent dominance within the Fund, the main mechanism for the institutionalization of specific ideas as policy norms lies in their degree of acceptance and whether the external environment is favourable to normative change. It is the continuous interaction between inside-out knowledge production within international organizations and outside-in social recognition by external stakeholders that shapes the content and the legitimacy of economic ideas over time.

As a result, the consensus around capital mobility that developed inside the Fund in the late 1980s and early 1990s and which was endorsed by its membership cannot be adequately understood without embedding it into the historical context of the time.[5] Specifically, not only did the consensus reflect the theoretical assumptions that the IMF staff made in favour of capital account liberalization. It also reflected the choice of member countries to advance the cause of international financial integration, assigning priority to capital mobility in their economic policy. For industrial countries, that choice meant to consolidate and expand global economic integration. For developing countries, liberalizing the capital account held out the promise to them of being able to reach the income levels enjoyed by the advanced economies in less time. Given this consensus in favour of capital mobility, authorities in both industrial and developing countries started to open up their capital accounts and did not oppose the IMF's campaign for making capital account liberalization

---

[5] For the importance of 'historical embeddedness' for the understanding of politics, see Kratochwil (2006).

a global policy norm. In the remainder of the chapter, we show how our theoretical argument is supported by the empirical findings.

Transforming the idea of capital account liberalization into a policy norm

Capital account liberalization became an element of the Washington Consensus, even without being formally included in it (see Williamson 1990). That trend started in the developed countries in the 1960s and reached its formal conclusion in 1989 with the extension of the OECD's Code of Liberalization of Capital Movements to cover all international capital movements, including short-term financial transactions, which hit the developing world with full force in the late 1980s and early 1990s (Brune 2006). As had occurred in the industrial world, national policies in developing countries seemed to converge around full capital account openness, thereby transforming the idea into a global policy norm. In our analysis, we concentrate on one actor that several analysts consider crucial for this outcome: the IMF.[6]

Rewriting the Bretton Woods Consensus

According to the Fund's Articles of Agreement drawn up in 1944, each member state has the right to maintain controls on international capital movements, provided only that these controls do not restrict international trade (Article VI, section 3). This provision was directly related to the fact that capital controls constituted one important cornerstone of the 'embedded liberalism' compromise established after the Second World War. According to Keynesian thinking, capital controls were regarded as an important instrument of national policy-making in order to preserve the political independence of countries faced with the consequences of a liberalized international trade regime and within a system of fixed exchange rates (Kirshner 1999). In the presence of a strong need for full employment and growth and in the absence of a conventional adjustment mechanism for national economies following the war, such as expenditure-reducing policies, the retention of capital controls was a critical part of the emerging social

---

[6] We are, of course, cognizant of the fact that there is a substantial literature that privileges the role of domestic politics, pointing to political dynamics such as government partisanship, societal interest groups, voter preferences and rent-seeking politicians to explain financial internationalization. However, this line of reasoning neglects international actors behind the universal trend towards capital account liberalization. In our view, it is highly unlikely that only domestic-level explanations can account for this truly global phenomenon.

contract (Eichengreen 1996: 95). In fact, the IMF could even require the imposition of capital controls in order to prohibit the use of Fund resources to those countries that did not impose controls in the event of large or sustained capital outflows and declare the member state ineligible to use the Fund's resources if it failed to comply (Article VI section 1a).

In reality, however, the IMF has never invoked the provisions of Article VI enabling it to impose capital controls. Quite the contrary, the bailout of countries through the Fund occurred without imposing capital controls as early as the 1950s, and has been taken for granted ever since. The explanation given by the IMF for this policy choice contradicting its own statute has been to argue that an unchecked capital outflow will eventually cause problems for the current account and so indirectly affect the official remit of Fund authority (H. James 1996: 133–9, 161–5). As former IMF chief economist Jacques Polak put it: 'the Fund has wholeheartedly embraced capital account liberalization in its surveillance, financing, and technical-assistance activities without being hindered by a lack of mandate or by the dated provisions of Article VI' (Polak 1998: 50).

Justifying the need for a policy norm of capital mobility

The support for sweeping economic reforms in many parts of the developing world was at its height after the end of the debt crisis and the demise of the planned economies in the former socialist countries of Eastern Europe. Following the failed experiences with heterodox economic stabilization programmes in many countries in Latin America and Africa, new classical economics became the baseline in development thinking and led to what James Boughton has called the 'silent revolution in policy-making' (Boughton 2001). This normative framework includes a couple of principles such as a negative view on government intervention in the economy and the unqualified support for policy reforms that remove obstacles to the operation of free markets. In this framework, capital controls are regarded as a phenomenon that harks back to an earlier era in the history of the international financial system linked to extensive state interventionism. Based on its focus on economic efficiency rather than national autonomy, neoclassical economics espouses strong hostility to formal restrictions placed on the flow of private capital across national borders (Dornbusch 1998).

Despite a long-standing controversy in the academic literature,[7] the public stance of the IMF in the early 1990s leaves few doubts that capital

---

[7] On the one hand, defenders of capital account liberalization, based on neoclassical economic theory, have argued that it allows for an efficient allocation of capital and the diversification of risk boosting investment and economic growth (Obstfeld 1998). On the

account liberalization was given pride of place in the list of desirable economic policy reforms. Seen from 19th Street in Washington, the benefits of financial liberalization in terms of economic growth and market discipline were perceived as substantial: 'The globalization of financial markets is a very positive development,' former Managing Director Michel Camdessus (1995) forcefully and repeatedly argued, depicting capital flows as 'one of the driving forces of global growth in recent years'. The IMF's operational policies were also informed by the principle that capital mobility is a desirable policy choice for developed as well as developing countries (IEO 2005). Until the late 1990s, 'the Fund ... tended ... to welcome members' actions taken to liberalize capital account transactions' (IMF 1995a: 8, 9),[8] while it 'generally discouraged' the tightening of capital controls (IMF 1995a: 10).

In order to make the case for officially outlawing capital controls on a global scale, several lines of attack were mounted by IMF staff to demonstrate – at a minimum – the redundancy of and – at a maximum – the damage done by capital controls with regard to the success of economic policy and generally to portray restrictions on international capital movements as a hindrance for economic growth in developing countries.[9] First, their effectiveness was questioned, given the dramatic advances in information-processing technologies rendering existing government regulations putatively unenforceable. Following the establishment of current account convertibility in many developing countries at the end of the 1980s, market actors have been equipped with sophisticated tools to circumvent capital controls such as over- and under-invoicing of imports and exports, and otherwise to channel capital transactions through the current account.

Second, it was widely assumed that financial liberalization is somewhat of a latecomer compared with trade and current account liberalization, and that extending the economic logic from one arena to the other was only natural and unproblematic. For example, Manuel Guitián, the Director of the Monetary and Exchange Affairs Department at the IMF during the 1990s, saw no difference between liberalizing trade and financial flows, portraying them as equal in their fundamental opposition to closed economic systems (Guitián 1996b: 176). The well-known discourse about rent-seeking behaviour in national trade policies was

---

other hand, neo-Keynesian scholars have argued that capital flows are inherently volatile and that opening the capital account may thus lead to instability and does not promote economic growth (Stiglitz 2000).

[8] For more details on the Fund's treatment of capital account liberalization in its surveillance activity, see IMF (1997b).

[9] See, for example, Mathieson and Rojas-Suárez (1993) and Schadler *et al.* (1993).

transposed to the realm of monetary policy, where capital controls were seen as a protectionist instrument sheltering special interests in the domestic economy, thereby hampering the efficient allocation of resources in order to achieve economic growth, and encouraging the pursuit of 'inconsistent macroeconomic policies'. Chile-type controls on capital inflows were regarded as merely delaying 'adjustments to fundamental macroeconomic policies, such as fiscal policy and exchange rate policy' and contributing to 'distortions and inefficiency' (Quirk *et al.* 1995: 20). The Fund's preferred solution in the case of large capital inflows in the early 1990s was the opposite of imposing controls: the rapid transition to full capital account convertibility 'motivated by the openness of the economy in the context of limited administrative capacity' (Quirk *et al.* 1995: 24).

Making capital mobility an obligation: the capital account amendment

Pursuing capital account convertibility, in contrast to the current account, was not legally recognized as a task for the IMF – quite the opposite, in fact. As a consequence, the battle cry for staff and management, mostly located in the Monetary and Exchange Affairs Department as well as the Policy Development and Review Department, was to bring the lack of formal validity and the reality of organizational conduct in alignment by way of a change of the IMF statute. Similar to the goal of current account convertibility, the liberalization of international capital movements was to become an official mandate for the Fund along with an extended jurisdiction in what would have been the fifth amendment to its Articles of Agreement. Acknowledging that the IMF 'has in some cases encouraged developing countries to open their economies to foreign capital inflows and to liberalize restrictions on capital account transactions' (Quirk *et al.* 1995: 6) under the so-called Article IV surveillance consultations, financing arrangements and technical-assistance programmes to develop foreign exchange markets, the main goal of the proposed amendment was to provide formal validity and enforceability for lending decisions and policy advice, which had hitherto been given in a legal grey zone. The sympathy for capital account liberalization coming from the US Treasury and other major IMF shareholders reassured the proponents of the amendment within the IMF and enabled the management to launch a public campaign for the formal institutionalization of the emerging policy norm.

The context for tabling the capital account amendment occurred during the run-up to the Fund's Annual Meeting in 1997. The statement issued by the IMF's Interim Committee on 21 September 1997 regarding the liberalization of capital movements emphatically captures the prevailing sentiment during the first half of the 1990s:

It is time to add a new chapter to the Bretton Woods agreement. Private capital flows have become much more important to the international monetary system, and an increasingly open and liberal system has proved to be highly beneficial to the world economy ... Provided that it is introduced in an orderly manner, and backed both by adequate national policies and a solid multilateral system for surveillance and financial support, the liberalization of capital flows is an essential element of an efficient international monetary system in this age of globalization. The IMF's central role in the international monetary system, and its near universal membership, make it uniquely placed to help this process. (IMF 1997a)

The underlying goal of the amendment was clear: assuring the formal validity of the emerging policy norm of unrestricted global capital movements. Making capital account liberalization a central purpose of the IMF as well as extending its jurisdiction into this area represented a dramatic shift from what the founders of the organization had in mind some fifty years earlier. Following the example of current account convertibility (see Broome, chapter 6 this volume), the intention according to then IMF Deputy Managing Director Stanley Fischer was to establish 'a universally applied code of good behaviour in the application of capital controls, enabling the Fund to determine when macroeconomic, structural, and balance of payments considerations require adherence to – or permit exemptions from – obligations relating to capital account liberalization' (Fischer 1997: 13). Following the official green light at the 1997 Annual Meeting granted by the IMF Interim Committee, Managing Director Camdessus submitted a draft of the proposed amendment to the Executive Board in March 1998 (IMF Archives 1998d). The proposal did not include specific language for changes other than to include capital account liberalization in the mandate of the Fund (Article I).

Contrary to conventional wisdom there was strong support for the amendment among both industrial and developing countries: 'We can all agree', the Saudi Executive Director Abdulrahman Al-Tuwaijri stated in 1995, 'that capital account convertibility is both desirable and welfare enhancing for an individual country as well as for the world economy as a whole,' a principle shared by Simon N'Guiamba, Director of the African constituency, who went on to say that the liberalization of the capital account 'is an integral part of the reform of a country's financial system' (IMF 1995f: 21, 56). Even as late as April 1998, that is, in the midst of the Asian crisis, one of the multi-constituency Executive Directors concluded that '[c]hanging Article I of the Fund's charter ... is now more an issue of legislative technique than of political consensus building' (IMF 1998d: 14).

We can thus safely conclude that the norm of an open capital account policy did enjoy wide acceptance and legitimacy, among both industrial and developing country governments as well as among influential mainstream economists, all the way up to the outbreak of the Asian financial crisis. The benefits derived from the liberalization of international capital flows were widely acknowledged and the corresponding policy at the domestic level, helped or regulated by the IMF, was simply considered a matter of technicalities. In other words, the capital mobility policy norm was not challenged in terms of its social recognition and technical application. This consensus emboldened the IMF's management to propose the amendment in the first place and paved the way for its approval by the Fund's member states. It took a dramatic change in the 'outside world' which led prominent economists to change their views on capital controls and to a loss of member countries' confidence in the IMF to undermine this consensus and to derail the amendment.

The impact of the Asian financial crisis

'As a result of the criticism received during and after the crisis, the IMF is more vocal in pointing out the risks of rapid capital account liberalization. While such cautionary notes have always been present in IMF advice, today they are much more likely to be given greater prominence' (Dawson 2002). With these words, Thomas Dawson, former Director of the IMF's External Relations Department, captures the adjustment in the Fund's thinking on capital account liberalization that took place in the aftermath of the Asian financial crisis. Indeed, after 1998, the IMF's focus shifted from the benefits to the costs that financial liberalization entails and from 'distaste' for to 'qualified acceptance' of market-based capital controls. At the same time, the emphasis was much more explicitly placed on the sequence of the economic liberalization process. While this shift in thinking was by no means revolutionary, it was none the less substantial compared with the consensus that reigned in the first part of the 1990s.

Nowhere is this shift in thinking more evident than in the failure of the proposal to amend the Articles of Agreement. As a matter of fact, by the end of 1998, the amendment disappeared from the IMF's books – even though it had been high on the Fund's agenda during the previous three years. Interestingly, the amendment failed in the absence of a dramatic change in industrial countries' preferences for capital freedom and in the absence of IMF staff turnover. Rather, representatives of industrial countries continued advocating for the benefits of capital mobility (Summers 1998) and IMF management and senior staff kept battling to include capital account liberalization within the mandate of the IMF (IMF 2000).

Despite this distinguished support for capital mobility, the authorizing environment in which the IMF operates changed dramatically after the Asian crisis. The crisis, which was marked by a sharp reversal of capital flows and threatened the stability of the international economic system through financial contagion, vividly demonstrated the risks of rapid capital account liberalization, leading several member countries and the economics profession to question the arguments put forward by the IMF over the previous decade.

In light of the disruption caused by capital flight, numerous observers noted that the benefits of capital account liberalization needed recalculation, either for not having the costs of financial crises adequately factored in or because the gains in terms of economic growth had been exaggerated (Bhagwati 1998; Williamson and Mahar 1998). Furthermore, the crisis raised doubts about the alleged market discipline associated with financial liberalization. In this atmosphere, capital controls became (again) a plausible policy option (Krugman 1998). Even the Institute of International Finance (IIF), the global association of private financial institutions, became sensitive to arguments in favour of controls. While controls on capital outflows were still regarded as 'generally difficult to justify on efficiency or welfare grounds', controls on inflows appeared 'more acceptable than they had been before' (IIF 1999: ii). The support for capital controls coming from the academic and financial establishment added to the more radical advocacy articulated by non-governmental organizations and representatives of several developing countries.

In sum, when the economies of Thailand, Indonesia, South Korea and Malaysia, among others, suffered spectacular losses after years of outstanding economic growth, the authorizing environment that had allowed the institutionalization and diffusion of the Fund's ideas suddenly became a venue for contestation. In particular, the arguments that capital account liberalization is welfare-enhancing and that the IMF is a responsible manager of financial globalization were severely challenged (Sachs 1997; Stiglitz and Furman 1998).

These criticisms had an immediate impact on the Fund through two channels. First, they were influential from the *outside-in* through the pressure exercised by member countries on the IMF's Executive Board. The final stages of the debate on the amendment are illustrative here. From early 1998 onwards, Executive Directors became more vociferous in channelling their national authorities' concerns regarding pushing ahead with the capital account amendment against the background of global contestation. Several Directors articulated the preference of their countries for a thorough reconsideration of the merits of capital account

liberalization.[10] Against this background, they suggested the postpone-
ment of the discussion on the extension of the Fund's jurisdiction through
an amendment. This position was not confined to developing countries
only. Several representatives of industrial countries were now more cautious than before. For instance, substantially modifying his earlier position, the Japanese Director, Yukio Yoshimura, stated that in light of the
events in Asia 'the Fund could not say that no reversals of capital account
liberalization were appropriate' (IMF 1998e: 14).

Second, the criticisms affected the Fund's view on capital account
liberalization from the *inside-out*, that is, through the Fund's own bureaucracy. The Fund being an institution primarily staffed with PhD
economists, the criticisms levelled by the profession from which it recruits
could not easily be discarded. With a substantial part of the economics
profession forcefully making the argument that there is no clear connection between financial integration and economic growth and accusing
the organization of at least partially causing the economic downturn in
Asia, IMF staff started to reconsider the available evidence on capital
account liberalization. As a result, and meeting demands from the
Executive Board, the Fund staff submitted a number of research papers
to the Board beginning in early 1998, in which the consequences of
capital market integration were reassessed in an attempt to take stock of
the Asian crisis experience (IMF 1998a, 1998g).

Since 1998, the IMF has refined its view on capital account liberalization further, in an attempt to develop what Kenneth Rogoff (2002), the
Director of the Research Department between 2001 and 2003, called an
'eclectic approach' – an approach that contrary to the IMF's earlier policy
takes the specific conditions of countries with weak financial systems and
inadequate macroeconomic frameworks into account. Although some
authors argue that the IMF has not abandoned 'the neoclassical model'
that fails to recognize the imperfections in international capital markets
(Stiglitz 2004), recent IMF studies provide evidence of the evolution of
the Fund's thinking. We can appreciate the continuities and discontinu-
ities in the Fund's thinking by analysing how the new policy norm relates
to changes in the norm itself and to the Fund's operating procedures.

Today's capital account liberalization policy norm reflects important
continuities with the earlier neoclassical economic norm. Capital account
liberalization is still regarded as an inevitable and desirable economic
policy choice for IMF members. However, there has been a significant

---

[10] See, for instance, the remarks by Thomas Bernes, Executive Director for Canada (and a
host of smaller, mostly Caribbean countries), and Juan José Toribio, Executive Director
for Spain (and several Latin American countries); IMF 1998d: 8, 13.

reconsideration of *how* the benefits of liberalization can be realized. That is to say, the presumed positive and direct relationship between financial liberalization and economic growth has come under scrutiny. The benefits of liberalization are no longer considered to be direct and automatic. Capital inflows do not necessarily promote growth by providing finance for domestic investments and diversifying risks. Rather, the benefits of liberalization are supposed to be indirect or 'collateral'. For instance, in a recent study on the effects of financial globalization, a team from the IMF Research Department supports the view that 'far more important than the direct growth effects of access to more capital is how capital flows generate a number of . . . "potential collateral benefits"' (Kose *et al.* 2006: 8). These alleged benefits include strengthening domestic financial markets and institutional development, good governance and market discipline; these factors, in turn, are supposed indirectly to contribute to GDP growth.[11] In other words, in line with the shift away from the neoclassical economic model to an emerging holistic approach to economic growth and development outlined in this volume, the IMF has enlarged the range and scope of policies deemed necessary as preconditions for successful financial development.

In terms of operating procedures, the IMF's new policy norm entails a substantial revision of the accompanying practices that make capital account liberalization beneficial. In this context, the use of capital controls and the sequence of economic liberalization have received renewed theoretical and empirical attention. In particular, there seems to be a more accommodating attitude towards the use of capital controls. For instance, the Fund now displays qualified support for Chile-type controls on capital inflows, use of which was stigmatized in the first half of the 1990s (Eichengreen *et al.* 1999; IMF 1998c: 79, 150). Even though capital controls are still regarded as ineffective and distortionary in the long run (IMF 2007c: chapter 3), the recognition of the attendant risks of capital account liberalization demonstrated by the Asian crisis led the IMF to no longer regard market-based controls on capital inflows 'as incompatible with the still-desirable goal of capital account liberalization' (IMF 1998g: 49).[12]

In sum, the current IMF view on capital account liberalization builds on the realization that liberalization is not in and of itself a factor that contributes to economic growth and that its welfare-enhancing effects are

---

[11] See Rodrik and Subramanian (2009) for a critique of the most recent IMF approach to proving empirically the benefits of capital account liberalization for developing countries.

[12] Market-based controls 'include taxes and tax-like instruments that make their effect felt by altering relative prices, rather than through the use of administrative controls' (IMF 1998g: 49).

a function of other policies, including macroeconomic and regulatory policies. Acknowledging that the benefits of capital account liberalization are not direct but dependent upon other variables suggests that there are circumstances in which the costs of liberalization are substantial. Contrary to the early 1990s thinking that did not contemplate the possibility that financial liberalization could be welfare-reducing, today's view clearly acknowledges the possibility that capital account liberalization may not produce economic growth in the short and medium run. Drawing on extensive empirical research, a recent IMF study concludes that 'there is no strong, robust, and uniform support for the theoretical argument that financial globalization per se delivers a higher rate of economic growth' (Prasad *et al.* 2003: 3). As a result, a 'pragmatic approach to capital account liberalization' (Prasad and Rajan 2008) – as opposed to the previous ideological one, observers might presume – that takes into account the specific economic conditions in developing countries is now advocated.

Conclusion: the norm is dead, long live the idea

The fate of the capital account liberalization policy norm in the International Monetary Fund is an interesting case to consider in the context of this volume for several reasons. First, it is one of the few examples of an idea included in the initial Washington Consensus agenda that did not reach the stage of norm stabilization during the past fifteen years. Second, the fate of the capital account liberalization amendment sheds substantial light on the mechanisms of norm creation and policy change within the IMF. Specifically, our case study shows the interplay between inside/outside forces on the one hand, and ideational/strategic interests on the other. Third, it reveals the processes and mechanisms that can temporarily interrupt the 'norm life cycle' (Finnemore and Sikkink 1999), transforming it into a norm circle (see chapter 1). Finally, the prevalence – although in a modified fashion – of capital account liberalization as a policy norm of the international financial system relates to the existence or not of an emerging holistic approach to economic growth and development. In what follows, we elaborate on these four points.

In the middle of the 1990s, influential staff members and the management of the IMF felt encouraged to propose a change to one of the fundamental pillars of the organization. They were aided by external events favouring the removal of all remaining instruments of government intervention in the national economy and an ideological change in the economics profession towards the neoclassical orthodoxy. It is important to point out that they were acting strictly on ideational beliefs supporting the superiority of market-based solutions in economic policy rather than narrowly defined material interests.[13] The lobbying efforts of IMF staff members for the case of capital account liberalization started in the late 1980s with internal advocacy and tweaking the rules of the game in operational practice. Their hitherto limited fight to outlaw capital controls on a national level gained momentum in the early and mid-1990s, and turned into a cause at the global level. Going beyond advocacy and persuasion vis-à-vis developing country authorities on an individual level, the norm entrepreneurs aimed for the ultimate, irreversible stabilization of the norm. They considered amending the charter of the IMF as the adequate and most effective form of institutionalizing the norm of open capital accounts and thereby turning it into a strong global policy norm.

We have also highlighted that the norm advocates at the IMF did not act alone in their cause. We are aware that the IMF does not exist in a political vacuum and that its thinking and activities are connected to the wider social context outside the organization. Owing to the permeable borders between the Fund and its authorizing environment, mutually reinforcing interests and discourses focused on capital account liberalization did emerge. However, we do take issue with the claim that the idea of capital account liberalization was imposed on the IMF from the outside, in particular by powerful member states allied with private sector interests. This explanation cannot account for the emergence of the open capital account norm inside the Fund. Capital account liberalization was essentially a staff- and not a US- or Wall Street-driven turn at the IMF.

By early 1998, all seemed to be going well for the final transformation of the idea of free global capital mobility into a statutory element of the international financial system through an amendment to the IMF's Articles of Agreement (formal validity). The social recognition of capital account liberalization, among both industrial and developing countries, seemed so overwhelming that only 'a second great depression or a third world war' (Obstfeld 1998: 28) could stop the institutionalization of the new norm. However, as the old adage has it, 'something happened on the way to heaven', in this case the Asian financial crisis and its effects

---

[13] This was certainly the case for people like Guitián or Fischer who did not stand to benefit in material terms from open capital markets – at least while they were working at the Fund. On the other hand, it is an open question in the case of Camdessus. While certainly committed to liberal economic policy ideas (Abdelal 2007: 140), his interests in giving the IMF the mandate and the jurisdiction over the capital account policy of member states were not necessarily altruistic. It might well be explained in terms of strategic calculations having in mind the survival and self-aggrandizement of the organization according to a public choice perspective (Vaubel and Willett 1991).

on the open capital account discourse outside the IMF. Specifically, the reinterpretation of the effects of capital account liberalization in light of the Asian financial crisis, first outside the Fund and then inside, rapidly increased the level of acceptance of capital controls, making it virtually impossible for the Fund to pursue its amendment agenda.

As a result, capital account liberalization could not complete the 'norm life cycle' and become a formally valid policy norm. As the editors have put it in their introduction (chapter 1), institutionalization is not sufficient for a policy norm to emerge and stabilize. Indeed, the failed proposal to amend the Articles of Agreement did not allow the policy norm to stabilize in the international economic system. Absent social recognition among relevant stakeholders, the policy norm of capital mobility failed to reach the stabilization stage. Such acceptance is still lacking today. At least in the developing world, state practices in terms of capital account policy demonstrate significant variance, in some parts partially reversing the earlier trend towards placing fewer and fewer restrictions on international capital movements (Brooks 2004; Brune 2006).

In our view, capital account liberalization is not part of a revised or modified Post- or Anti-Washington Consensus on development policy. In particular, it seems that the Fund is still in the process of mapping the ground, trying empirically to disentangle the effects of capital account liberalization on economic growth. In this respect, the Fund has acknowledged that the empirical evidence for the unambiguously positive effect of capital account liberalization is still wanting (Prasad *et al.* 2003). As a consequence, although the IMF has recognized that the benefits of capital mobility are not automatic but dependent on policies and institutions, the Fund has not yet drawn any definitive conclusion on the relationship between capital mobility and economic growth. In fact, all empirical research dedicated to discovering the expected positive effects of capital account liberalization for economic growth based on cross-country growth regressions have ended in inconclusive findings at best or in outright failure at worst. However, the quest to find positive evidence continues unabated (Mishkin 2009; Obstfeld 2009), pointing to catalytic or indirect benefits of capital liberalization as the latest analytical innovation from the IMF (Kose *et al.* 2009).

In addition, capital account liberalization, as it is now interpreted within the Fund, hardly constitutes a modified or revised consensus because of several marked continuities with the past approach. Most importantly, the IMF has not moved away from the position that an open capital account does ultimately provide more benefits than costs and that capital controls are harmful and ineffective policy instruments in the long run (IMF 2007c: chapter 3, 9–12). Even in the midst of the current global financial crisis, the Fund has defended the ultimately positive effects that financial liberalization allegedly entails. For example, in a paper analysing the causes of the sub-prime crisis, Fund staff members argue that the crisis 'show[ed] the potential dangers of capital inflows [that] can lead to excessive risk taking and to exposure of domestic financial institutions, households, firms, to exchange rate risks'. However, this conclusion was predicated on the assumption that 'surely, the lesson [from the crisis] is not that capital flows should be sharply curtailed' (IMF 2009: 8).

As a result, and in conclusion, the global financial crisis demonstrates three points. First, although much more nuanced in its argumentation than at the beginning of the 1990s, the Fund has not completely given up its advocacy role for the capital mobility policy norm. For that to happen (yet) another ideational change, primarily in economic theory, has probably to take place first. Indeed, very few mainstream economists would contest the proposition that capital account liberalization is ultimately welfare-enhancing. What most economists and policy-makers argue about is the speed or (again) the sequence of economic liberalization and the required policies or domestic institutions for making capital account openness a successful policy norm.

Second, the fact that the current financial crisis has especially hit some of the most open economies among the group of emerging countries, such as in Eastern Europe, is likely to constitute a significant obstacle for the inclusion of the capital account liberalization norm within the emerging development consensus, at least in the short run. By now several distinguished economists have raised concerns about an excessive faith in the benefits of capital mobility, especially once a bubble bursts. After having analysed the mechanisms of contagion of the sub-prime crisis in emerging market countries, John Williamson and Arvind Subramanian (2009) concluded that 'the case for adopting capital controls as countercyclical macroeconomic policy, at least on some types of capital, has probably (in our view) been strengthened by the crisis'. Even from within the IMF, the potential use of 'constraints on the foreign exchange exposure of domestic institutions and other borrowers as a measure to reduce the risks deriving from the integration of the world's capital markets' (IMF 2009: 8) was suggested.

Third and related, in recent years IMF member states in the developing world have frequently resorted to limiting the inflow of international capital into their countries in order to assuage their negative effects for the national economy. As a result, at least the application of controls on capital inflows is now much more prevalent than during the 1990s. Outlawing such measures in order to allow for unfettered global capital mobility is thus far from sight. Capital account liberalization is still a choice, not a stable policy norm for developing countries in the Post-Washington Consensus era.

9 The World Bank's global safeguard policy norm?

Susan Park

> Bank management has identified ten key policies that are critical to ensuring that potentially adverse environmental and social consequences are identified, minimized, and mitigated. These ten are known as the 'Safeguard Policies' ...
> (World Bank 2008c)

> The dialectic between social science knowledge, practical experience, and policy guidelines shows how policy formulation must be approached as a set of evolving norms and not simply as diktats from above.
> (Cernea 1993)

Introduction

The World Bank established a set of stringent environmental policies for international development lending after environmentalists challenged its environmental impact in the 1980s (Gutner 2002; Park 2005b; Rich 1994; Wade 1997). Collectively these policies and the ideas underpinning them constitute a global *safeguard policy norm* that conveys legitimized, institutionalized practices for international development lenders. This chapter traces the arc of the Bank's safeguard policy norm through three stages: from its emergence in the 1980s, through to its stabilization in the 1990s, to possible decline in the 2000s. First, the chapter examines how and why the World Bank established the safeguard policy norm through internal innovation, policy sharing and, catalytically, from environmental non-governmental organizations' (NGOs) and industrialized member states' pressure. Second, the chapter details how the policy norm stabilized in the 1990s even as each individual policy was modified as a result of environmentalist, industry and member state engagement. Third, the decline of the safeguard policy norm is posited as a result of the Bank's 2005 Middle Income Strategy and shift towards a Country Systems Approach (CSA). Undertaken as a result of the lack of cultural validation of the safeguard policy norm among increasingly powerful middle income countries (MICs) in part because of Bank loans being undertaken by intermediaries, the CSA indicates a transition from a universal safeguard policy norm to a particularistic development approach for different borrowers. The chapter concludes by arguing that despite the Bank's safeguard policy norm being formally valid and socially recognized, the lack of cultural validation amongst its borrowers indicates a shallow form of norm diffusion by the World Bank.

Both rationalist principal–agent (PA) scholars and constructivists agree that IOs have some degree of autonomy in meeting their mandates (Barnett and Finnemore 2004; Hawkins *et al.* 2006; Park 2005b). Constructivists have examined how IOs, as autonomous agents, have diffused norms to other actors in the international system (Finnemore 1996). However, scholars continue to question whether ideas or material factors, either inside or outside IOs, principally determine their behaviour (Weaver 2007; Leiteritz and Moschella, chapter 8 this volume). In terms of the World Bank's environmental actions, it is well documented that external pressure has overwhelmingly, although not exclusively, influenced the Bank. As recapitulated below, both industrialized member states' material power (Bowles and Kormos 1999; Gutner 2002, 2005a; Nielson and Tierney 2003; Wade 1997) and socialization from environmentalists (Hunter 2008; Park 2005b, 2010; Rich 1994; Wade 1997) fundamentally shaped the Bank. While rationalists view the Bank's shift as materially induced, constructivists point to the role of norm advocates in socializing powerful member states and the Bank to prompt environmental behaviour (compare Nielson and Tierney 2003 and Park 2010).

This chapter extends the constructivist analysis of the Bank's environmental activities in two ways. First, it documents the Bank's changing practices through examining two important areas: the role of internal advocates in the Bank's environmental evolution (Fox 1998), and the safeguard policy norm's strength over time. It documents the role of internal advocates in providing blueprints and using persuasion practices for spreading environmental and social policies inside and outside the Bank. Internal norm advocates were given oxygen as a result of the external triggers for change, namely from environmentalist opposition to damaging Bank operations and increasing environmental degradation. As with the IMF's shift towards capital account liberalization (see Leiteritz and Moschella, chapter 8 this volume), both the outside-in and inside-out pressures were therefore crucial for the emergence of the safeguard policy norm. The chapter details the separate points of contestation between the Bank and external stakeholders for eight of the policies comprising the safeguard policy norm.[1]

---

[1] The safeguards OP7.60 on Projects in Disputed Areas (2001) and OP7.50 on Projects in International Waterways (2001) are not environmental and social safeguards per se and are

It also picks up where the environment/World Bank literature ends, by analysing how the Bank's policy norm was challenged in the 2000s. The possible decline of the safeguard policy norm in the 2000s brings us to the second point of the chapter: that the Bank backed off from diffusing the policy norm, revealing the extent to which the Bank's diffusion of the global safeguard policy norm to its borrowers was shallow, such that increasingly powerful 'middle-income countries' did not recognize the safeguard policy norm as culturally valid despite the policy norm's formal validity and social recognition.[2] The chapter therefore questions the Bank's power to shape borrowers' views on sustainable development despite articulations to the contrary (Goldman 2005).

An emerging global safeguard policy norm in the World Bank

All World Bank practices are governed by the organization's internal Operational Policies (OPs) which are derived, where relevant, from the Bank's Articles of Agreement.[3] The OPs cover activities including its business products, lending instruments and social and environmental protection measures. The World Bank's environmental and social safeguards constitute a *policy norm* because, as Benedict Kingsbury states, 'the internal policies and practices of international institutions' are an 'important body of normative practice' that remains under-examined (1999: 323). Norms are 'collective expectations about proper behaviour for a given identity' where, for example, adhering to a set of minimum environmental standards came to be an important part of development lending (Jepperson *et al.* 1996: 54). The Bank's safeguard policy norm is both constitutive and regulative, in creating new categories of actors and action (IOs and states that minimize development impacts on ecosystems) and safeguard policies to uphold them (where the latter determines the former). The idea of protecting the natural environment emerged within the

not discussed here. The 'top ten' policies were called 'the safeguards' and the name stuck within the Bank even though 'the suite of policies never did fit together'. Robert Goodland, personal communication, 13 March 2008.

[2] The World Bank categorizes its borrowers into high, middle and low income borrowers. Middle income countries (MICs) are calculated using the World Bank Atlas method. MICs are classified as ranging from US$976 to US$11,905 GNI per capita in 2008. See: http://web.worldbank.org/WBSITE/EXTERNAL/DATASTATISTICS/0,,
contentMDK:20420458~menuPK:64133156~pagePK:64133150~piPK:64133175~the-SitePK:239419,00.html, accessed 6 October 2009.

[3] Operational Manual Statements (OMS) and Operational Policy Notes (OPNs) are Bank guidelines. Most were upgraded to mandatory Operational Directives (ODs) and later converted into Operational Policies (OPs), which are essentially the same policies though less detailed.

World Bank in the 1980s with the 'do no harm' principle after environmentalists documented large-scale, high-profile, environmentally disastrous Bank projects (Gwin 1994; Rich 1994; Wade 1997). The principle was translated into specific policies designed to mitigate adverse environmental and social effects from development projects.

The Bank now has ten safeguard policies that include Environmental Assessment, Forests, Involuntary Resettlement, Indigenous Peoples, Natural Habitats, Pest Management, Physical Cultural Property, the Safety of Dams, International Waterways, and Disputed Areas (World Bank 2008b). The policies were framed as 'safeguards' by Bank management in 1997 in relation to external pressure over negative environmental and social project impacts (Davis 2004: 15–16, 24). The safeguards constitute a single policy norm because they incorporate a process of environmental assessment as well as issue-specific policies such as Forests. Environmental Assessment (EA) is, in fact, the 'umbrella policy' for the remaining policies because it assesses the extent to which a project requires oversight. Each project goes through a screening process to determine the type and depth of EA required, and which of the safeguards apply. The application of the EA depends on whether the project is classified as a high environmental and social risk (category A), less risky (B), no risk (C), or pertaining to a project undertaken by a financial intermediary (FI) (Park 2010: chapter 3).

The safeguards are formally valid as Operational Policies that are incorporated into borrowers' project loan agreements where required. The safeguard policy norm has been institutionalized within the World Bank through the project cycle (the main vehicle for project lending) and through its ongoing monitoring and evaluation procedures (Park 2010: chapter 3). The safeguards are internal yardsticks with which to assess the Bank's operations; indeed the Bank would be investigated for compliance by its own Inspection Panel from 1994. The safeguards are now socially recognized benchmarks for how to mitigate negative environmental and social impacts in the World Bank, in its borrowers and contractors, in other multilateral development banks (MDBs), and in some private sector lenders through the Equator Principles (Hunter 2008: 450). Through broad adherence and global use, the safeguard policy norm has been socially recognized by borrowers and other development actors. The idea of protecting the environment and society gained currency within the Bank to become 'actionable' or translated into specific Bank policies as a result of three factors: internal innovation (from inside the Bank), international norm emergence and policy sharing (outside the Bank), and pressure from environmentalists and industrialized member states (again from outside the World Bank).

First, guidelines on environmental issues emerged organically within the institution. President McNamara noted in a speech to the UN Conference on the Human Environment in 1972 that the World Bank established environmental guidelines in 1970 in order to 'devise appropriate safeguard measures which were then incorporated into project design and discussed with borrowers'.[4] In addition to issuing guidelines, the Bank's new Office of Environmental Affairs provided a comprehensive checklist of 'typical' environmental issues as well as 'several internal guidelines, handbooks, checklists and criteria ... to assist staff and borrowing countries in the preparation of projects' (Shihata 1991: 138–9). Stein and Johnson state that the Bank was the first lending institution to establish 'criteria for evaluating the environmental impact of its investment projects' (1979: 13, 14). Sector policies were published in rural development in 1975, in forestry in 1977, agriculture in 1978 and fisheries in 1982 (Shihata 1991: 139). In 1977, the Bank's ecologist Robert Goodland also prepared an Operational Manual Statement on the social and environmental aspects of dam and reservoir projects (OMS3.80).

Stein and Johnson argue that the preparation of policy papers on forests and rural water supply helped build 'new policy directions ... around sound environmental practice' which were then 'incorporated into the Bank's basic policy documents'. Further, 'the process of formulating these documents became an important means of expanding the Bank's environmentally oriented programmes and thinking' (1979: 12–13). The guidelines fit within the Bank's project cycle and exemplified the technical, apolitical and engineering culture of the World Bank (Miller-Adams 1999: 71).[5] In 1984 these guidelines were brought together under the 'Environmental Aspects of Bank Work' Operational Manual Statement (OMS2.36) policy for staff (Shihata 1991: 138–9; Wade 1997: 634).[6] Robert Wade's environmental history of the Bank states that OMS2.36 was silent on the shape, form and depth of EAs, which were left to the discretion of project officers (1997: 635).

Second, shared understandings on how to assess impacts on the environment began to emerge amongst member states and IOs (Mikesell and Williams 1992: 263). For example, the first environmental impact

---

[4] McNamara was influenced by wider debates on the environment in development (Park 2005b).
[5] The policies added to staff workloads without extra resource provision, thus making the safeguards an additional burden (interview with former environment staff, conducted 19 March 2008). Changing organizational structures within the Bank under President Wolfensohn compounded this with central environment staff trying to sell their services to operations staff working to a budget (Gutner 2005a: 20).
[6] All policies are in the Operational Manual for staff.

assessment (EIA) was established by the United States with the enactment of the 1969 National Environmental Policy Act (NEPA) requiring assessments for federal projects (Lee and George 2000: 3).[7] The NEPA 'has since provided a template for environmental assessment regimes the world over' (Holder 2004: 43). EAs became mandatory in disparate states such as Canada, France, Thailand and the Philippines in the mid- to late 1970s (Biswas 1997: 21). EIAs have now spread to more than a hundred developing countries while continuing to be rapidly adopted (Lee and George 2000: 3). By the mid-1980s, bilateral development agencies from the USA, Canada, Finland and Germany had established their own EIA frameworks and the European Economic Community established EA directives in 1985 while the OECD issued formal guidelines in 1986 (Civic 1997–8: 242, n 54; Holder 2004: 44–5). IOs would also establish their own guidelines: the United Nations Environment Programme (UNEP) in 1980, the World Health Organization in 1982, the World Bank in 1984 and the Asian Development Bank in 1985 (Holder 2004: 44; Wade 1997). In 1980, the European Economic Community, the World Bank, UNEP, the United Nations Development Programme (UNDP) and other multilateral development banks (MDBs) signed the New York declaration 'pledging the support of these institutions for the creation of systematic environmental assessment and evaluation procedures for all development activities' (Shihata 1991: 141; UNEP 1980). In 1980 information sharing between EA specialists also emerged in the form of a professional association.[8] Additional operational practices came from staff who brought their professional knowledge and outside experiences with them upon joining the Bank.[9] While the Bank now points to its leadership role on the use of EAs, in the mid-1980s it lagged behind bilateral development agencies (Wade 1997: 634). This would be rectified by the establishment of the Multilateral Financial Institutions Working Group on the Environment that comprises MDBs, bilateral and export credit agencies and is dominated by the World Bank.[10]

Finally and catalytically, the full suite of safeguards became institutionalized in the late 1980s and 1990s as a result of external opposition over the Bank's failure to prevent environmental disasters irrespective of its guidelines (Rich 1994). Elsewhere I have argued that the World Bank

---

[7] EAs here refer to all assessments tools for projects, policies, plans and programmes. EAs are broader than EIAs and until 1992 included social impact assessments (Goodland 2000: 19, 31).
[8] The International Association for Impact Assessment is a professional NGO to further the global use of impact assessments.
[9] Interview with Stephen Lintner, conducted 2001 and 2007.
[10] Interview with Stephen Lintner, conducted 2 February 2007.

internalized sustainable development norms, thus reconstituting its identity as a result of socialization by transnational environmental advocacy networks, which included the introduction of the safeguards (Park 2005b, 2010). To recap, in the late 1980s the Bank was increasingly challenged by environmentalists over its operational record after an internal review, the Wapenhans Report, identified more than a third of Bank projects completed in 1991 as complete failures (Wapenhans *et al.* 1992; Weaver 2007). Environmental opposition to the Bank gained momentum with mass campaigns against the Polonoroeste project in Brazil and the Narmada Sadar Sarovar dam in India among others, which led to the first independent investigation of a Bank project (Khagram 2004; Rich 1994). The final outcome, the 1992 Morse Report, documented that the Bank had failed to take a number of environmental and social considerations into account (Morse and Berger 1992).

Pressure from environmentalists and Bank member states including the USA and European donors led the Bank to agree to have Bank-wide procedures by 1988. Coercive pressure on the Bank came from the US Treasury, advocating for the US Executive Director to ascertain that sufficient guidelines were in place to ensure the systematic EA of all projects. This occurred when the US Congress, influenced by environmental advocates, was preparing to pass a law ensuring that all MDBs adopt EA principles and guidelines already used by UNEP, at the same time as considering requests for international development assistance contributions (Bowles and Kormos 1999: 217; Park 2005b). In 1987 the Bank underwent a restructure under President Conable, during which environmental NGOs and prominent member states pushed for the Bank to introduce mandatory EIAs and action plans (Gwin 1994: 49).

Under President Conable, the environment was elevated within the Bank through the creation of a strengthened Environmentally Sustainable Development (ESD) Department. Within ESD 'key figures such as Michael Cernea, Scott Guggenheim, Gloria Davis and Robert Goodland drove forward the introduction of environmental and social safeguard policies ...' (Hall 2007: 162).[11] According to Robert Goodland, 'identifying the need for a policy was relatively easy', as was drafting the policy and writing the technical paper outlining the reasoning for the environmental safeguard policy. Goodland stated that after drafting the policy, 'the draft was returned saying explain how you got there, explain how to implement, [provide the] background, [and] perspective'.

---

[11] Cernea's team included Scott Guggenheim, Dee Rubin and the newly appointed Robert Goodland; Gloria Davis would join the Bank later. Robert Goodland, personal correspondence, 8 March 2008.

The result was a 'how-to manual for the brief actual policy itself' which ended up being the three-volume EA sourcebook that remains the primary vehicle for explaining how to use the safeguards. This then had to be followed up with training and information seminars for Bank staff over a six- to twelve-month period, a process that would be required for each safeguard.[12]

The main obstacle Goodland notes was 'persuading the Bank to adopt the draft policy', which was 'always exceedingly difficult and time consuming'. Strategies for getting the Bank to adopt environmental safeguards included 'internal campaigns with distinguished outsiders', trying to 'generate outside NGO pressure on the Bank' and to 'get a VP [vice-president] or two to visit a horror story project in the field'. Having few internal environmental allies meant that Goodland 'tried any lever I could dream up'.[13] After trying vainly, Goodland failed to establish safeguard policies for the environmental impact of agricultural sub-sectors even though agriculture had been one of the earliest environmental guidelines within the Bank along with forestry and fisheries in the late 1970s, and was a major sector of concern for the Bank's economic development and poverty alleviation mandates. Member state and environmentalist pressure was therefore vital to the creation of *mandatory* Bank-wide Operational Directives (OD) on the environment, particularly OD4.00 in 1989, which upgraded the earlier 'Environmental Aspects of Bank Work' OMS2.36. Robert Goodland wrote this EA umbrella policy, which would include specific annexes for different environmental impact components.[14] For example, annex A detailed the project-screening system mentioned earlier and annex B was added for dams and reservoirs (which had previously been a stand-alone OMS).

The umbrella policy, OD4.00, was then revised in 1991 to accede to US pressure (which in turn was based on environmental NGO advice) to include public participation and broader EA disclosure (Goodland 2000; Wade 1997: 686–7). This became OD4.01 1991, a policy that remains in place today. Annex A on environmental screening and B on dams and reservoirs would remain, but throughout the 1990s other annexes, such as involuntary resettlement (OD4.30), and draft annexes for agricultural pest management (draft OD4.02), the protection and management of wildlands (OD4.04), principles to be applied to land settlement

---

12 Robert Goodland, personal correspondence, 8 March 2008. There are now source books for participation, involuntary resettlement and social assessment.
13 Robert Goodland, personal correspondence, 8 March 2008.
14 Robert Goodland, personal correspondence, 8 March 2008.

(draft OD4.31), indigenous peoples (OMS2.34) and cultural property (OD4.25) (Shihata 1991: 143–7), would subsequently be elevated to become independent mandatory Operational Directives. The next section details the contestation over the safeguards as a means of demonstrating how interactions between the Bank and external stakeholders had different trajectories for each policy, even as the safeguard policy norm began to stabilize inside the Bank and out.

Stabilizing the safeguard policy norm: institutionalization and contestation

Throughout the 1990s each policy was updated from the OMS/OPN standards, to the mandatory ODs, which would then be converted to a system of briefer Operational Policies (OPs) backed by more detailed Bank Procedures (BP) that are in place today (see Table 9.1). The updating and converting of the safeguards further institutionalized the safeguard policy norm in the World Bank. Internally the Bank reports high levels of compliance with the safeguards although such evaluations are not without problems (World Bank 2005a: 8, 12, 24, 2005i: annex 7, 37–9, 2006d: 67, 69). Externally the safeguards are socially recognized through their uptake by other MDBs, export credit agencies and private sector actors (Hunter 2008: 442; Miller-Adams 1999: 21; Park 2010; Wade 1997). The updating and conversion process was undertaken with external stakeholder engagement with NGOs and industry, creating a stable system of engagement. However, one can also point to varying trajectories of the different policies as they were contested throughout the consultation process. Eight of the ten safeguards are detailed here to demonstrate the importance of both inside-out and outside-in pressures for change.

The safeguard updates were driven by internal reviews of OMS/OPN standards and calls for comprehensive policy revision from internal specialists and external environmentalists as noted above.[15] Each of the safeguard policies would be modified depending on internal and external demand and endorsement from management and/or member states on the Board. During this period Bank lending in sectors known for their high environmental impact such as infrastructure, high dams and forestry declined, in some cases motivated by the fear of potential environmental opposition (Fox 2000; MacDonald 2001: 1018; World Bank 2000c,

---

[15] Some senior environment staff state that the various policy updates did not substantially change the content of the policies; Stephen Lintner, interview, conducted February 2007. Others disagree; Robert Goodland, personal correspondence, 13 March 2008.

Table 9.1 *World Bank environmental and social safeguard policies,*
1970s–2000s

Initial environmental and social policies and guidelines, 1970–1980s	Institutionalized safeguard policies, 1990s	Converted safeguard policies, 2000s[a]
OMS2.36 Environmental Aspects of Bank Work (1984)	OD4.01 Environmental Assessment (1991; OD4.00 1989)	OP/BP4.01 Environmental Assessment (1991) *OP/BP4.00 Piloting the Use of Borrower Systems to Address Environmental and Social Safeguard Issues in Bank Supported Projects (new, 2005)*
OPN 11.02 Wildlands: Their Protection and Management in Economic Development (1986)	OD4.04 Natural Habitats (1995)	OP/BP4.04 Natural Habitats (2001)
OPN11.01 Guidelines for the Selection and Use of Pesticides in Bank Financed Projects and their Procurement when Financed by the Bank (1985). Updated in 1987.	OD4.09 Pest Management (1996)	OP4.09 Pest Management (1998)
OMS2.33 Social Issues Associated with Involuntary Resettlement in Bank Financed Projects (1980). Updated in 1986 as OMS10.08 Operations Issues in the Treatment of Involuntary Resettlement in Bank Financed Projects.	OD4.30 Involuntary Resettlement (1990)	OP/BP4.12 Involuntary Resettlement (2001)
OMS2.34 Tribal People in Bank Financed Projects (1982)	OD4.20 Indigenous People (1991)	OP/BP4.10 Indigenous People (2005)
Forestry Sector Policy Chapter (1978)	OP4.36 Forests (1993) and Forestry Strategy (1991)	OP/BP4.36 Forests Policy and Strategy (2002)
OMS3.80 Safety of Dams (1977)	OP4.37 Safety of Dams (1996)	OP/BP4.37 Safety of Dams (2001)
OPN11.03 Management of Cultural Property in Bank Financed Projects (1986)	OD4.40/4.50 Draft Cultural Property (1991)	OP/BP4.11 Physical Cultural Property (2006)
OD7.50 Projects on International Waterways (1989)[b]	OP7.50 Projects on International Waterways (1994)	OP7.50 Projects on International Waterways (2001)

Table 9.1 (*cont.*)

Initial environmental and social policies and guidelines, 1970–1980s	Institutionalized safeguard policies, 1990s	Converted safeguard policies, 2000s[a]
Not a Bank issue pre-1990s	OP7.60 Projects in Disputed Areas (1994)[b]	OP7.60 Projects in Disputed Areas (2001)

Sources: Civic 1997–8; Goodland and Ledec 1989: 35, n 32; MacDonald 2001; Rich 1994: 154; Scudder 1997; Shihata 1991; Wade 1997; World Bank 1991a, 2008b.
[a] The safeguards were amended in 2004 to reflect the shift from adjustment lending to development lending (OP/BP8.60 Development Policy Lending) and in 2007 with the revision of the Emergency Recovery Assistance to OP/BP8.00 Rapid Response to Crises and Emergencies. The dates in the third column refer to the most recent update of the specific safeguard.
[b] Not discussed in this chapter.

2003a, 2003c: 6).[16] For example, infrastructure investment lending dropped by 50 per cent between 1993 and 2002 (World Bank 2003c: 2) while dam project loans fell by more than half between 1993 and 1997 (Khagram 2004: 198), and logging in moist tropical forests was halted.

First, the Bank's involuntary resettlement policy OMS2.33 was drafted in 1980 by Bank sociologist Michael Cernea (Cernea 1988; Miller-Adams 1999: 145; Rich 1994). This exemplifies *internal innovation*. It began as an informal sociological seminar series initiated in the mid-1970s. '[U]nder Cernea's leadership, and with the assistance of David Butcher, an effort was initiated within the Bank to take a more responsible position towards those relocated' (Scudder 1997: 675; Bebbington *et al.* 2006: 14; Vetterlein 2007: 526).[17] The World Bank 'pioneered the application of what was largely academic research to Bank-financed projects' (Scudder 1997: 668). A 1985 Operations Evaluation Department (OED) evaluation was undertaken soon after (World Bank 1985). OMS2.33 was both 'reaffirmed' and 'supplemented' in 1986 'with new elements and more precise norms' to become OMS10.08 'Operations Issues in the Treatment of Involuntary Resettlement in Bank Financed Projects' as a result (Cernea 1988: 2). Updated as OD4.30 in 1990, the Bank was the 'key agency pushing for

---

[16] This coincided with the Bank's move out of infrastructure to allow private sector growth (Miller-Adams 1999).
[17] David Butcher had devised the FAO's involuntary resettlement policy; personal correspondence, Robert Goodland, 8 March 2008. Both David Butcher and Thayer Scudder were leading social anthropologists on involuntary resettlement.

such guidelines with the result that ... similar guidelines ... [were] accepted by the OECD (1992)' (Scudder 1997: 674).

Thayer Scudder warned, however, that the 'current attempts within the Bank to establish guidelines dealing with environmental and cultural issues, including resettlement ... are worrisome' (1997: 668). Indeed, data on involuntary resettlement continued to suggest that it is 'virtually impossible to restore the living standards of the majority' and that 'there was little cause to believe that the overall record will improve' (Scudder 1997: 668). Ongoing battles over the viability of involuntary resettlement made this a highly contested policy. The Bank's resettlement practices were again reviewed by Cernea in 1993 in light of the mass forced resettlement resulting from the Narmada dam scheme, leading to the policy's revision (World Bank 1994c).

The Bank-wide review included field visits by the Environment Department staff as well as mission reports and reviews from the Legal, Environment and Operation Evaluation Departments (Scudder 1997: 676). The policy revisions were 'time consuming and costly ... The conversion of the resettlement policy, which involved hundreds of meetings, and five years of deliberation, created tensions with external stakeholders who felt that revisions did not go far enough ... and with staff and governments who felt that policies were becoming too cumbersome and prescriptive' (Davis 2004: 6, 25–6). The new policy was implemented in 2001. This lengthy process was repeated in relation to policies on Indigenous Peoples (Davis 2004: 26; Kingsbury 1999: 324), and Forestry (Flejzor 2007), while controversies over the Bank's dam policy led to the creation of the multi-stakeholder forum, the World Commission on Dams.

Second, the safeguard on indigenous peoples began with discussions in 1982 headed by Robert Goodland and environmental and indigenous rights groups such as Cultural Survival and Survival International, which were central to the establishment of OMS2.34 Tribal People in Bank Financed Projects. This took place during the preparation of the Polonoroeste project in Brazil (Gray 1998: 270; Khagram 2004: 192; Wade 1997: 630), where the policy came from inside the Bank as a result of engagement with external advocates (Bebbington *et al.* 2006: 21; Miller-Adams 1999: 145). This highlights the importance of *both internal and external advocates*. The updating of the OMS2.34 'Tribal Peoples' policy was then examined in a five-year implementation (desk) review, which was completed in 1987 by the then Office of Environmental and Scientific Affairs in the midst of massive external opposition to projects such as Polonoroeste, Narmada and Indonesia's Transmigration Plan (Gray 1998: 283). The updated OD4.20 Indigenous Peoples in 1991 incorporated the results of the review, Bank experience and 'current international thinking on indigenous peoples rights' (Davis 1994: 80). Kingsbury states that the World Bank was a leader amongst international institutions on adopting 'normative operational policies on issues affecting indigenous peoples', which were then emulated by the Asian and Inter-American Development Banks (1999: 323).

Third, on forestry the World Bank was an early innovator with the 1978 sector policy paper. This remained in place until concern over rapid deforestation and forest fires hit international headlines in the 1980s, including the Bank's involvement in the Polonoroeste project in the Amazon (Rich 1994). The controversy was fuelled by the creation of the intergovernmental Tropical Forest Action Plan (TFAP) which included Bank participation and aimed to ensure the sustainable use of tropical forests, but was seen by environmentalists as a means of protecting the logging industry (Mikesell and Williams 1992: 131). In 1990 the Bank presented a country paper on its 1978 forestry approach to its Board after industrialized Executive Directors requested a 'distinct World Bank position'. The approach paper noted the 'changes which had taken place in both the perception and understanding of forests after 1978', even though the 1978 policy paper incorporated environmental and social concerns in forestry projects (Kolk 1996: 222).

The first internal review of the Bank's forestry work was undertaken by the OED in 1991, covering forestry practices from 1949 to 1990 with emphasis on post-1978 lending (Mikesell and Williams 1992: 133; World Bank 1991b). This fed into the subsequent 1991 Forest strategy and the Bank's first new forestry policy since 1978. The 1993 OP4.36 Forests 'reflected the changing perceptions of forests and stressed the particular significance of forest ecosystems for the global climate' (Kolk 1996: 225). The 1993 policy was designed by a policy team that invited environmental NGOs such as Greenpeace, the Rainforest Alliance and the Natural Resource Defence Council for consultation. The debate would focus on the NGO demand to ban concessional logging in moist tropical forests. Some advocates within the Bank favoured limited concessional logging which created a public 'firestorm'. Although positions were divided in the Bank, the policy banned logging.[18] Soon after, Bank management argued that the ban resulted in a 'chilling effect' with Bank borrowers in forest management (Flejzor 2007: 92; Goodland 2000). A second team was therefore hired to redo the policy. Taking five years, the revised policy would emerge in 2002, dropping the 'no logging' part of the policy with

---

[18] Confidential interview with former World Bank forestry staff member, conducted 2 April 2008.

backing from management and the Executive Board.[19] The policy therefore weakened the Bank's protection of tropical forests but points to both
internal and external advocates in shaping the policy in the 1990s.

Fourth, the first terms of reference on dams within the Bank were
established in 1972 with the early operations of the Bank's Environment
Office (Dixon *et al.* 1989: 7). This was formalized in the late 1970s with
Goodland's OMS3.80 on Dams. With the shift to OPs the stand-alone
OMS was downgraded to an annex of the OD4.01 EA policy (1990).
Widespread criticism of the negative environmental impacts of dams in
borrowing countries grew throughout the 1980s and 1990s as dam
building triggered safeguards on natural habitats, dam safety, indigenous
peoples, involuntary resettlement and cultural property. Goodland and
Cernea recognized this from within the Bank but were unable to effect
change (Khagram 2004: 190). Critical internal evaluations of Bank practices were presented at a Bank seminar in 1987 entitled 'Dams and the
Environment: Considerations in Bank Projects' (Mikesell and Williams
1992: 80) as the Indian Narmada dam campaign intensified. The mass
campaign against Narmada led to the 'first comprehensive post-
evaluation of the big dams it had funded', the OED review on dams
beginning in 1994 (Khagram 2004: 190, 197, 203). The Bank devised an
independent safeguard, OD4.37 Safety of Dams, in 1996 when it also
released its evaluation outcomes for discussion in workshops with anti-
dam campaigners, academics and dam-building companies. Environmentalists rejected the OED's positive review of the Bank's dam
history and demanded an independent review. This led to the 1997
Gland Agreement amongst dam builders, anti-dam campaigners, the
International Union for Conservation of Nature (IUCN) and the
World Bank to establish the World Commission on Dams (WCD) in
1998 (Khagram 2004: 203–4; McCully 2001: xx). The WCD results
were released in 2000. While this fed into the updated OP4.37 Safety of
Dams in 2001, the Bank was not seen as taking key WCD recommendations into account (McCully 2001: liv). While the Bank was an early
innovator in dam safety, as with forests, it took mass *external* environmental opposition to pressure the Bank to further institutionalize a
safeguard on dams.

Fifth, the OPN11.01 was established on pesticide use in 1985, as a
result of *external pressure* from environmental NGOs. After NGOs sued
the United States Agency for International Development (USAID) for
funding pesticide use in the early 1980s, the Bank came under similar

---

[19] Confidential interview with former World Bank forestry staff member, conducted 2 April
2008.

criticism soon after. The Bank then hired a pest management specialist to write a policy for it. There was no internal opposition for the implementation of the pest management policy. The 1985 policy was a detailed technical policy which listed a range of pesticides that the Bank should not fund or should limit for use. This was then viewed as a blacklist by environmentalists, chemical companies and Bank staff, creating contestation between these actors over what was allowed to be financed and what was not.[20]

In the early 1990s the list of pesticides was dropped and a less-detailed pest management policy was introduced in 1998 together with a pest management handbook. The Bank also agreed to become part of an integrated pest management approach with the Food and Agriculture Organization in 1997. The umbrella NGO Pesticide Action Network increasingly challenged the World Bank's practices. Pest management specialists argued that the Bank's pest management policy existed on paper only. While the original policy brooked no overt opposition, the implementation of what became known as the integrated pest management approach was received through 'passive resistance'.[21] Pest management was considered the domain of the Bank's Agriculture and Rural Department although it had no pesticide specialist, had no pest management plans and did not review its own practices.

Further, operations staff were inadvertently swayed by the increasing connection with agri-business that was encouraged under President Wolfensohn's private sector development initiative (Miller-Adams 1999) to use pesticides rather than to limit their use.[22] This, former staff suggest, was because most staff are economists, not technical specialists. There are some safeguard specialists in each region but only three or four people in the Bank know pesticide management well.[23] The Agriculture and Rural Department viewed the safeguards as too dogmatic, in opposition to the central Environmentally and Socially Sustainable Development Network (ESSD), which want pesticide management to go much further. It was not until the new policy was created in 1998 that the Bank seconded a pesticide specialist to monitor the Bank's activities, and it would take until 2004 with the introduction of the multilateral environmental

[20] Confidential interview with World Bank Lead Ecologist, conducted 25 February 2009.
[21] Confidential interview with World Bank Lead Ecologist, conducted 25 February 2009.
[22] Confidential interview with former World Bank Agriculture and Rural Department staff member, conducted 19 March 2008. Pesticide Action Network, n.d. 'Pesticides and Biotech Companies: The Wrong Partners for the World Bank', World Bank Accountability Project, Newsletter accessed via www.panna.org.
[23] Confidential interview with former World Bank Agriculture and Rural Department staff member, conducted 19 March 2008.

agreement on Persistent Organic Pollutants (the Stockholm Convention) for the Agriculture and Rural Department to undertake a review of its pesticide management practices. At best, such practices demonstrate a lack of interest in the externally driven safeguard.

Sixth and seventh, Robert Goodland also wrote the technical paper and the policy for the 1986 Wildlands policy with George Ledec (OPN11.02) and the technical paper and later policy on Cultural Property in 1986 with Maryla Webb (OPN11.03), both of which would become ODs/OPs (see Table 9.1). Both safeguards were *internal innovations*. The technical paper for wildlands/natural habitats came from inside the World Bank. There was little in the way of external pressure for the policy, but there was internal opposition to it from the Board, management and staff. The updating of the policy was a less fraught process than was the experience for involuntary resettlement, indigenous peoples, forestry or dams. The process took months rather than years, which could be accounted for by the fact that the environmental NGOs with which the Bank engages on this issue are conservation practitioners rather than advocacy organizations. While there are some disagreements on whether natural habitats should be considered on a numerical basis in terms of calculating the cost of projects, natural habitats is the least contested of the safeguards. Perhaps the biggest obstacle for the use and implementation of the natural habitats policy within the Bank is whether staff are aware of its existence. Unlike involuntary resettlement, indigenous peoples and pest management, there is no mandatory plan to be implemented once the policy is triggered. Further, there is also the concern that borrowers may choose to involve the Bank for funding only once a habitat has already been substantially changed.[24]

From 1998 all of the safeguards were converted to Operational Policies (OPs). The shift aimed to 'provide clearer guidance on the Bank's policy to its staff' (Andrew Steer, head of the World Bank Environment Department, quoted in Civic 1997–8: 246). The conversion delineated the safeguards into mandatory OPs and Bank Procedures (BPs) with supplementary non-mandatory Good Practice (GP) notes. The Operational Policies are as formally valid as the directives were. They are approved by the Board of Executive Directors to 'establish the parameters for the conduct of the Bank operations' (Miller-Adams 1999: 22). Miller-Adams noted that the BPs are 'less binding' but 'spell out the processes and documentation needed to ensure that Bank policies are carried out in a consistent manner', compared with the Good Practice

---

[24] Interview with World Bank Lead Ecologist, conducted 24 February 2009.

notes that proffer advice and guidance on implementation (1999: 22).[25] The Bank invited comments from external stakeholders on the overall conversion process from ODs to OPs to ensure the conversion process kept the substance of the policies (Civic 1997–8: 247). Kingsbury for one argued that the OD4.20 Indigenous Peoples policy had improved (1999).

The entire policy conversion process was opposed by environmentalists (Lawrence 2005). Many saw this as a retreat of the Bank from the leadership it displayed in institutionalizing the safeguard policy norm. Civic argues that in the 1999 conversion of the OD4.01 EA umbrella policy to OP/BP4.01 statements were removed that could 'provide clarity of purpose and guidance to the borrower in preparing the EA and in observing sustainable development practices' (1997–8: 247).[26] She suggests that this may have resulted from the creation of the Inspection Panel such that the Bank tried to avoid being held accountable for borrower implementation of the safeguards, thus leading it to 'step aside from the role of policy standard-setter' (1997–8: 247). Indeed, there was a very real concern inside the Bank over environmental opposition to large infrastructure lending, with staff 'panel-proofing' to avoid environmentally damaging projects (Fox 2000). However, Benedict Kingsbury argues that the importance of the Inspection Panel should not be overstated, because the ODs/OPs are 'understood to be "binding" on Bank staff within the Bank management structure, but applied and enforced flexibly rather than "legalistically"' (1999: 329).

In sum, despite the conversion to OPs, the safeguards would form a normative structure for how development lenders such as the Bank incorporate environmental and social concerns into their operations. The safeguard policy norm stabilized in the 1990s when they became mandatory for borrowers through project loan agreements and for staff through the operational manual, with internal training sessions and sourcebooks detailing their application. However, this section also documented the various trajectories between the Bank and external stakeholders over each policy. It provides a more nuanced account of the safeguards, where, for example, internal norm advocates were innovators on involuntary resettlement, natural habitats and cultural physical property. Internal innovation also led to guidelines on environmental assessment, indigenous peoples, forests and dams, although all of these were given impetus in the 1990s and made mandatory as a result of external opposition from

---

[25] No bank procedure is issued where the World Bank's Environment Assessment Sourcebook (World Bank 1991a) applies (World Bank 2008b).

[26] Goodland (2000: 7) notes that some clauses were reinstated into the EA OD/OP4.01 safeguard by the Board.

Table 9.2 *Inside-out and outside-in factors triggering the introduction of the current safeguards*

Safeguard policy	Internal innovation	External demand	Both
OP/BP4.01 Environmental Assessment (1991)			X
OP/BP 4.00 Piloting the Use of Borrower Systems (2005)			X
OP/BP4.04 Natural Habitats (2001)	X		
OP4.09 Pest Management (1998)		X	
OP/BP4.12 Involuntary Resettlement (2001)	X		
OP/BP4.10 Indigenous People (2005)			X
OP/BP4.36 Forests Policy and Strategy (2002)			X
OP/BP4.37 Safety of Dams (2001)			X
OP/BP4.11 Physical Cultural Property (2006)	X		

environmentalists, where, for example, forest fires and anti-dam and indigenous peoples' rights campaigns demanded responses from the Bank's Board and management. In the case of dams this also led to a multi-stakeholder review process. In comparison, the trigger for a pest management policy is a clear example of an externally driven safeguard where the Bank wrote the policy in response to environmentalist demands. This section has detailed how internal advocates were able to establish blueprints for most of the safeguards, but where external pressure from environmentalists helped institutionalize the safeguard policy norm. Table 9.2 illustrates how some safeguards were driven by internal innovation, the pest safeguard from outside the institution, and how the strength of external opposition from environmentalists and member states strengthened individual policies in the 1990s, thus stabilizing the safeguard policy norm overall. The next section examines whether the rise of middle income countries is leading to the safeguard policy norm's decline and what this means in terms of the Bank's role as a norm diffuser in international development.

Decline of the global safeguard policy norm?

The global safeguard policy norm has been viewed as a 'compliance-driven approach' such that staff and borrowers have to meet formally valid policies and loan requirements, to which environmentalists hold the organization accountable (Wright 2007). Crucially however, the lack of cultural validation among increasingly powerful middle income country (MIC) borrowers would lead the Bank to curtail its use of the global safeguard policy norm in the mid-2000s, raising questions as to the depth of the World Bank's norm diffusion. An increasing sense of onerous obligation on behalf of borrowers, combined with concern over the costs of compliance and the need to enhance borrowers' development ownership, led the Bank's Board of Executive Directors to request management to introduce greater flexibility into the safeguard policy norm (World Bank 2002c: 1). The perceived lack of cultural validation of the policy norm by increasingly powerful MICs triggered the Bank's revision of the global safeguard policy norm, delimiting it to low income borrowers rather than for middle income countries. In this regard, norm renegotiation arises in new circumstances (Wiener 2007a: 13).

The Bank's 'bread and butter' business is MICs such as Brazil, China, Mexico, Turkey and South Africa (Weaver 2007: 502). Yet by the 1990s these countries were able to access (highly variable) private capital markets. By the early 2000s the Bank was concerned about its ongoing financial viability (Birdsall 2006; Mallaby 2005). Inside and outside the Bank many began to argue that the 'hassle factor' associated with the safeguard policy norm, along with the lengthy wait and cost of Bank loans, made the Bank increasingly unattractive (Birdsall 2006). This led the Bank to streamline its operations to make its policies more user-friendly, while MICs' continued interest in infrastructure and energy generation moved the Bank to re-engage in infrastructure, timber logging and large dams from the mid-2000s (Hunter 2008: 477; World Bank 2006a: 21). This drove President Wolfowitz to merge the ESSD Vice-Presidency with Finance Private Sector and Infrastructure (FPSI) in June 2006 to create the Sustainable Development Network (SDN). Safeguard compliance staff were also shifted into the Operations Policy and Country Service Network (OPCSN) to be integrated with operations staff.[27]

The Bank's revision of the global safeguard policy norm is part of its effort to become more 'client focused'. This was expressed through the pilot of a Country Systems Approach (CSA) to Operational Policies covering procurement, other fiduciary areas and the safeguards. In essence, this allows MICs to use their own national policies while 'streamlining policy conditionality in Bank lending operations' (World Bank 2005b: 1). A World Bank memorandum argued that the CSA would be open to countries that have policies 'equivalent to the Bank's policy

---

[27] Stephen Lintner, June 2007, Safeguard Policies Presentation to the World Bank Tokyo Office.

framework applicable to the operation, and where relevant country implementation practices, capacity, and track record are acceptable' (World
Bank 2005b: 2). This would further enhance borrowers' capacity and
ownership of their development while reducing Bank lending costs.

Draft proposals for a CSA were floated in 2002 although the desire for
greater borrower ownership had been discussed as early as 2000. The
Bank's Committee on Development Effectiveness (CODE) agreed to
incorporate environmental and social concerns into country systems if
they did not compromise 'the objectives and operational principles of its
safeguard policies'. CODE recommended testing the CSA's feasibility
through a 'programme of safeguard pilots' (World Bank 2005d: 5). Three
projects in MICs were approved by the Board in 2004 (Lawrence
2005: 11). The Board then demanded that a policy be in place to ensure
that the pilots were undertaken with due care for the safeguards.[28] As a
result, on 18 March 2005 the Bank approved a pilot of the CSA under the
new OP/BP 4.00 Piloting the Use of Borrower Systems to Address
Environmental and Social Safeguard Issues in Bank Supported Projects.
The CSA has been strongly opposed by environmentalists who see this
as a move by the Bank to weaken the global safeguard policy norm by
shifting responsibility to borrowers while undermining the scope of the
Inspection Panel, although the Bank states that its operations will be
unaffected.[29] The Bank envisaged creating fourteen pilot projects over a
two-year period (World Bank 2005d: 33).

Notably, the Bank defines any borrower from the International Bank for
Reconstruction and Development, but not its International Development
Association credit facility as a 'middle income country' (World Bank
2005b). This explains why, thus far, the Bank has undertaken CSA pilot
projects using national equivalent safeguards in Bhutan, Egypt, Ghana,
Jamaica, Romania (two projects) and Tunisia (World Bank 2008a).[30]
To date, the Bank's Independent Evaluation Group notes, using a
national equivalent safeguard policy norm in CSA pilot 'lending for
projects mapped to the Environment Sector Board [has] performed
poorly compared with projects in other sectors'. This has been as a result
of 'overly complex project design, a lack of institutional capacity for
implementation ... wavering political support, and weakness in ongoing

---

[28] Interview with Senior Environmental Specialist, conducted 24 February 2009.
[29] Letter to the Board of Executive Directors, 'World Bank's proposed middle income
country strategy threatens to weaken social and environmental standards', signed by
186 environmental organizations, dated 7 June 2004. Cited: www.bicusa.org, accessed
July 2006.
[30] The Bank's regions put forward these projects as pilots. Interview with Senior
Environmental Specialist, 24 February 2009.

co-ordination between implementing agencies and the Bank' (World Bank 2007: xv). Management's report to the Board has, however, noted that the CSA pilots have achieved borrower ownership over the EA and physical cultural resources safeguards, while the gap-filling measures for natural habitats, pest management, forests and the safety of dams have been adequate. Gaps between the Bank policy and national equivalent standards with involuntary resettlement are deemed too significant (World Bank 2008a: 2). In this regard, some policies may remain applicable for all borrowers, while the safeguard policy norm as a whole becomes limited and fragmented. The Bank intends to scale up its CSA approach from the project to the country level 'incrementally' in the future (World Bank 2008a).

Replacing the safeguard policy norm with the CSA for middle income countries exposes four issues. First, the MICs are a large and broad cohort of Bank lenders: eighty-six borrowers covering 63 per cent of Bank lending from 1995 to 2006. They are developmentally diverse, with the richest ten times wealthier than the poorest in this category (World Bank 2007: 3). With such a diverse new category of borrowers, this might open the door to further delimit the policy norm's applicability. The CSA undermines the *global* nature of the safeguard policy norm by creating particular norms for different categories of borrowers. Second, promoting a CSA for the MICs is based on the assumption that this diverse cohort of states is able to meet the equivalent standards. Arguably, evidence to date suggests that those chosen cannot (World Bank 2007: xv). Attendant to this is the recognition that the pilot projects have been for Category B projects rather than the high environmental risk Category A projects (World Bank 2007). While the Bank may be trying to further the ownership of sustainable development in MICs, it is as yet unclear that there is national equivalence between MIC environmental regulations and the global safeguard policy norm.

Third, undermining the safeguard policy norm by delimiting its application to low income countries may undermine the need for the World Bank in MICs. The safeguard policy norm 'adds value' to what the Bank offers borrowers compared with the private sector. This is the position being taken by the Bank's private sector financing affiliate, the International Finance Corporation (Park 2010: chapter 4). After all, the Bank cannot compete, nor according to its Articles of Agreement should it compete, with the private sector. Undermining the very policy norm that makes the Bank unique will not change the high levels of private sector capital currently available to middle income countries (although the global financial crisis may increase levels of project lending with safeguard implications). Further, introducing the CSA may have actually increased the Bank's costs through heightened monitoring and evaluation of national standards compared with their cost-saving objectives to retain MICs. It is unlikely that limiting the safeguard policy norm through the CSA will make Bank loans cheaper and therefore more attractive (Lerrick 2006). This undermines one of the reasons for introducing the CSA in the first place. What we are left with is a very strong signal, from the world's largest MDB, that the global safeguard policy norm is no longer appropriate for *all* international development projects. The CSA for middle income countries may have undermined the Bank's global safeguard policy norm without necessarily furthering sustainability within this new category of borrowers.

Finally, the process of delimiting the global safeguard policy norm by making it applicable only to low income countries raises concerns about the Bank's ability to diffuse norms. Much of the constructivist basis for arguing that IOs have authority and an independent effect in international politics is predicated on this fact (Finnemore 1996). Critical scholars go further to argue that the Bank fundamentally shapes the development discourse, ultimately influencing how borrower governments think and therefore act (Goldman 2005). That the Bank can spread sustainable development ideas, including the global safeguard policy norm, is demonstrated through its loan requirements and technical assistance, which inform borrowers' environmental regulations and procedures (for example, see Marschinski and Behrle 2007; Park 2010). What the shift towards the MICs is beginning to reveal, however, is just how shallow the Bank's norm diffusion actually is. Contra critical scholars like Michael Goldman, MICs are demonstrating their interest in moving away from the safeguard policy norm once they have the opportunity.[31] This indicates that the MICs recognize the safeguards' formal validity within the Bank and socially recognize them as necessary for Bank lending, but they do not see the safeguard policy norm as one they need to implement in their own domestic development operations. Now that the Bank has given them the opportunity to choose, they are choosing culturally valid, national, environmental standards.

Conclusion

This chapter examined the emergence, stabilization and possible decline of the World Bank's global safeguard policy norm. The World Bank established the safeguard policy norm through internal innovation, policy

---

[31] Both borrowers and donor member states favoured the shift to the CSA. Interview with Senior Environmental Specialist, conducted 24 February 2009.

sharing and, catalytically, from environmental NGOs and industrialized member state pressure. The safeguard policy norm was ascribed formal validity and institutionalized through the Bank's mandatory Operational Policies. The chapter then detailed the process of norm contestation throughout the 1990s with the updating and converting of each of the safeguards through interactions with environmentalists, industry, member states and the Bank. Each safeguard had a different trajectory even as the overall safeguard policy norm was socially recognized and stable in the 1990s. The chapter then documented how the safeguard policy norm was challenged by the Bank's 2005 Middle Income Strategy. The Middle Income Strategy revises the view of what is appropriate development assistance for different borrowers. The chapter suggests that the decline of the Bank's overall safeguard policy norm is determined by the lack of cultural validity among the Bank's increasingly powerful MIC borrowers. Far from making the Bank central to developing states' needs, the Bank has undermined its own relevance by delimiting the global safeguard policy norm. Future events may yet shed greater light on the safeguard policy norm's place within the norm circle.

10 The new public management policy norm on the ground: a comparative analysis of the World Bank's experience in Chile and Argentina

Martin Lardone

Introduction

Scholars have been dedicated to analysing the changes in the World Bank's discourse in general terms (Miller-Adams 1999; Paloni and Zanardi 2006; Vetterlein 2006) and in particular policy areas (Park 2007b; Stone and Wright 2007; Wade 1996).[1] Other works have focused on the conceptual and theoretical origins of the Bank's discourse (Anders 2005; Crawford 2006). Certainly the World Bank, and the multilateral development banks (MDBs) more broadly, play a key role in international policy networks. This is not just because of their capacity to financially condition states' domestic policies but also because of their role as diffusers of ideas and practices, and as producers of discourse and policy norms.

I analyse to what extent the policy norm that the World Bank has constructed for the modernization of public sector management has led to concrete measures in the programmes and projects of World Bank recipients. Comparing Chile and Argentina, this chapter examines how the World Bank spreads the new public management (NPM) policy norm, which is understood as results-based public management. This policy norm originated outside the World Bank but became an important set of policy recommendations used by the Bank to modernize the state in the context of the Post-Washington Consensus. Nevertheless, an important gap exists between the Bank's NPM policy norm and the reforms that the Bank manages to implement in recipient countries. This chapter

---

[1] A previous version of this chapter was discussed in the Graduate Conference 'Methodological Paradigms for a New Political Agenda' organized by the European University Institute, in Florence, in December 2007. I'd like to thank colleagues for comments received during that conference. The usual caveat applies.

addresses why the Bank's policy norm for public administration cannot be applied in the same way in two countries that have important relations with the World Bank.

Evidence outlined herein suggests that this is connected to the domestic conditions and the cultural validity of the policy norm within recipient states. For reasons that are related to the political economy of the public sector reform, borrowers socially recognize the NPM policy norm but they do not culturally validate it. Here, the capacity of the Bank to exert coercive pressure is limited. Indeed, the comparison between Chile and Argentina demonstrates that the type of reforms implemented in each case can be explained by domestic factors, which are also linked to each government's relationship with the Bank. Chile and Argentina have important but different relations with the Bank that can be explained by their economic and political conditions. Since the 1990s, Chile has become more economically stable than Argentina and has established relations with the World Bank based more on technical issues than on financial constraints. Therefore, the diffusion process seems to be less coercive in Chile than in Argentina. In short, the Bank has an important role to play in the diffusion of the NPM policy norm, but domestic conditions in the recipient countries are key factors to explain the adaptation or the poor implementation of this policy norm in each national case.

In this sense, I argue that to understand the process of adaptation and internalization of World Bank policy norms within a country-based approach it is necessary to focus the analytical lens on two levels or stages of the process: first, the internal operations of the Bank, and second, interactions between the Bank and its borrowers. The central questions of this work are: How do these policy norms become part of the Bank's operational procedures such as its central policy document, the Country Assistance Strategy (CAS), in each national case? Second, how does the process of adaptation and internalization of the NPM policy norm work? The argument made here is that the process of adapting the policy norm is a negotiation at two levels: first, a negotiation between Bank officials from different internal sectors of the Bank, and second, a negotiation with borrowers to socially recognize and culturally validate the policy norm. The chapter compares two dissimilar national cases, concerning the type of relations maintained with the World Bank, their financial evolution, and the type and sequence of the public sector reforms implemented.

Thus, this chapter is structured in the following way. In the first section, I analyse the origin and the nature of the NPM policy norm and its appropriation by the World Bank. Next, I explain the internal logic of the Bank for the production of this policy norm and how this affects the production of the CAS, including its sectoral components. In the third section, I compare how the policies for state modernization are developed by the Bank in both countries. I compare the Bank's NPM policy norm with its country programmes and with the modernization policies implemented by these recipient governments. Finally, I systematize some reflections on the strength of the Bank's NPM policy norm and the limits of its cultural validation in domestic settings.

The NPM and the World Bank

The NPM is a heterogeneous perspective on public management modernization that arose from the reform experiences of different industrialized countries, such as Australia, Great Britain, Japan, New Zealand and the United States, from the beginning of the 1980s. The idea of NPM was spread internationally by international organizations (IOs) like the OECD (Christensen and Lægreid 2001), the World Bank, and by regional MDBs including the Inter-American Development Bank (IADB). In particular, the World Bank and IADB have played a key role in the diffusion of the NPM policy norm to developing countries and especially to Latin America. Although these organizations have worked on the idea of the minimum state inspired by the Washington Consensus since the 1980s, a different policy norm was constructed during the 1990s. In effect, the World Bank engaged in a process of 'critical revision' of its policies in relation to state reform.

The most paradigmatic document of this critical revision of the Washington Consensus is the World Bank's 1997 annual *World Development Report* (World Bank 1997), where ideas of the NPM are already present. Indeed, the NPM norm was formally validated as part of the Bank's policy 'prescriptions' and recommendations by being incorporated as a loan condition for public sector reform from the beginning of the 1990s (World Bank 1995b). It is also important to consider that the subject of public management and administrative modernization is one of the central axes of the governance agenda adopted by the Bank from the beginning of the 1990s as a new way to approach the problems of development (Miller-Adams 1999). In this perspective the central preoccupation of the World Bank is the idea of state 'institutional capacity' to manage the process of development.

On the origins of the NPM, Hood (1991) emphasized the heterogeneity of this approach which he defined as an ensemble of more or less similar administrative ideas that have dominated the agenda of bureaucratic reforms in most of the OECD countries from the end of the 1970s. Concerning the conceptual and intellectual origins of this approach, Hood (1991) identified the confluence of two different thought traditions:

on the one hand, the 'new institutional economy', the developments of 'public choice' and the theories of transaction costs and 'principal–agent' models; on the other hand, the influence of the literature on private management on the analysis of the public sector, and the tradition of the international movement of scientific management. Certainly, the most important characteristic of the NPM *norm* has been the introduction of organizational models and techniques originating in the private sector as managerial models for the public sector (James 2001). Hood (1991) therefore defines seven main components of the NPM: the incorporation of professional managers into the public sector; standards to measure performance; an accent on control by results; the decentralization of organizational units; the incorporation of competition mechanisms within the administration; the 'import' of practices from the private sector; and a greater discipline in the management of resources. Peters (1997) classifies these reforms in three groups: 'market-oriented' reforms, 'participative' reforms and 'deregulation' reforms.[2] Thus far, the empirical evidence demonstrates that the components of NPM have spread unequally, and that they can be separated in the diffusion process (Peters 1997).

One important debate on NPM is on the effective impact of this approach on the administrative structures of the state (Dunleavy 1997). In other words, does the diffusion of this public management reform norm produce convergence in the way different public administrations are organized? Pollitt (2001) argues that there remains a persistent diversity of national administrative regimes and their practices. Although we can find convergence in the global discourse, organizational labels and some morphologic appearances, this does not necessarily translate into the core structures of public sectors around the world.

If we consider the mechanisms identified by DiMaggio and Powell (1991) to explain the diffusion of organizational models (coercive pressures, mimetic pressures and normative pressures),[3] the World Bank had been traditionally associated with the utilization of coercive mechanisms through the conditionality of its loans (Dolowitz and Marsh 1996), as has the IMF (Nooruddin and Simmons 2006). Nevertheless, several authors

---

[2] Other authors (Spink 1999) distinguish between the managerial ideas of two differentiated perspectives. One is the application of private management principles to the public sector, which is based on the widespread reform experiences of New Zealand and the United Kingdom and in the work of Osborne and Gaebler (1992) that inspired American administrative reform undertaken by the former US Vice-President Al Gore. The other is a political perspective that tries to rescue the political dimension of the state bureaucracy through the representation and accountability mechanisms of public administration.

[3] The limits of the rational model to explain diffusion processes are clearly identified by Weyland (2002), who proposes the utilization of the concept of 'heuristics' to analyse these phenomena.

have shown that the World Bank has been critically important in the diffusion of administrative reforms through normative pressures as well as coercive ones (Stone and Wright 2007; Teichman 2007; Woods 2006). Beyond conditionality, the Bank plays a prominent role concerning the diffusion of best practices, the packaging of ideas and the diffusion of standardized solutions to some identified problems (Sahlin-Andersson 2001). It also does a very important task in training national officials from client countries (Dimitrakopoulos and Passas 2003) and in the agenda-setting process (Weyland 2004), among other normative mechanisms. In brief, the argument here is that the World Bank plays an important role, both coercive and normative,[4] in the diffusion of the NPM policy norm in Latin America, but it is bounded by domestic conditions (Strang and Meyer 1993) in the recipient countries.

Thus, NPM has the 'advantage' of being a norm that includes a set of specific practices and measures that have been legitimized and institutionalized by governments and IOs, while offering a 'menu' of possible policy reforms in a general formulation.[5] This therefore allows the World Bank to adapt specific policy measures to its borrowers as well as giving leeway to national policy-makers and reformers to adapt their implementation to local conditions (Pollitt 2001). From the seven components of the NPM distinguished by Hood (1991) above, the standards to measure performance frequently mentioned in World Bank documents include the accent on control by results and discipline in resource management. As Hood (1991) explains, the policy prescriptions of the NPM norm do not appear in a single 'package', that is to say they do not appear at the same time and all together in the same country.[6] According to Hood (1991), the NPM norm is a frame of general application that he denominates as 'public management for all seasons'. This is because the NPM norm has appeared as a universal solution for different problems in any place and any area (such as health or education) and, because of its supposed 'political neutrality', the NPM norm has been presented as a set of policies in which different values can be translated (Hood 1991).

---

[4] I do not consider mimetic diffusion here because it is a more mechanic and bilateral process of diffusion (through peer-to-peer diffusion) where multilateral institutions do not play a role.

[5] Indeed, Christensen and Lægreid (2001) have analysed the diffusion process, focusing on the way ideas, solutions and methods originating at international level are modified when they are confronted with different political, administrative and historical contexts.

[6] On the debate about the NPM as a paradigm, see Massey (1997) and Gow and Dufour (2000). In this process of 'packaging' and diffusing the NPM policy norm, consultants (Saint-Martin 2000) and academics have been identified as other key actors (Pollitt 2001).

Therefore, the NPM norm seems to have the flexibility to close the gap between social recognition within the World Bank (staff and management) and cultural validation in domestic settings (borrower implementation). In this case, the instruments of adaptation and the reforms that are finally implemented are actually the result of a process of permanent interaction between Bank officials and borrowers. In terms of the norm circle I analyse the stabilization and contestation phases, or how the policy norm is contested and changed by the process of interaction between the Bank's organizational units and country officials inside the Bank, and between the Bank and its borrowers, in this case through comparing Chile and Argentina in the 1990s. First, however, the process of formal validation and social recognition of the NPM policy norm within the World Bank is examined.

The NPM policy norm and the World Bank

Certainly, the NPM appears as a sort of fashionable set of instruments that can be diffused through a direct (or bilateral) mimetic way from country to country (through peer-to-peer relations). In fact, this seems to be the story among OECD countries and other developed countries (Peters 1997; Sahlin-Andersson 2001).[7] Nevertheless, in Latin America the diffusion process is quite different (Nickson 2002), and the World Bank plays an important role, through both coercive and normative mechanisms as already explained. In this sense, to understand the process of adaptation of the NPM policy norm to the different countries it is first necessary to understand the mechanisms the World Bank utilizes to produce its country and sectoral strategies.

As the World Bank is organized as a matrix structure in which the regional areas are crossed with different policy networks,[8] the two main standardized procedures for Bank operations are the country assistance strategies and its sectoral strategies. This organization means that the country director co-ordinates the country strategy, for which s/he takes elements from the sectoral strategies and adapts them to country demands, to the policy agenda and to the loan portfolio that are then agreed upon by the Bank and the borrower.

The CAS sets out the Bank's diagnosis of the country's development and a selective programme of planned Bank support. This is tailored to

---

[7] For a further analysis of the international diffusion of public sector downsizing reforms in OECD countries, see Lee and Strang (2006).

[8] In fact, this is one of the structural reforms of the World Bank organization initiated in 1996 under President Wolfensohn.

the country's needs, against the background of the government's development objectives and strategy, the Bank's ongoing portfolio and the activities of other development partners. In the diagnosis stage, the CAS takes into account the performance of the Bank's portfolio in the country, the country's creditworthiness, its state of institutional development, its implementation capacity, the degree of governance, and other sectoral and crosscutting issues. Throughout preparation, the task team leader co-ordinates with relevant Bank units, development partners and other sources of expertise, in order to draw out informed views on the key issues to be highlighted in the CAS. The CAS is also developed in consultation with the government, usually through several ministries and agencies and at various levels. The final CAS review occurs after government and external stakeholder consultations have been held. The CAS ascribes formal validity to the policy norm because it is translated from the CAS into loan conditions. It also provides social recognition because each CAS is agreed upon by both Bank staff and borrowers.

Throughout the preparation of the CAS negotiation between different sectors of the Bank takes place. Each sector tries to include its policies and projects between the main axes of the CAS. Nevertheless, in this negotiation the Bank officials face a double restriction: they must negotiate with colleagues of other sectors for the resources destined to the country in the respective CAS, but also they must persuade the country officials concerning the projects of their policy area. Informally, the sectoral Bank officials maintain a more or less permanent dialogue with the national officials from the concerned ministry or agency. If both parts are interested in a specific project, soon they must follow the internal negotiations in the Bank and in the government so that this policy (or project) finally can be contemplated within the CAS. Regarding borrowers, this process is not always the same, and depends on the governing structure of the country. Here we can see the two dimensions of norm strength: social recognition within the Bank, and cultural validation within the domestic settings of borrowers (discussed in detail in the cases below).

The sectoral strategy, on the other hand, is defined in relatively broad terms and operates mainly as guidelines to be applied locally. In the case of the public sector the World Bank has a strategy for public sector modernization that is produced by the Poverty Reduction and Economic Management (PREM) unit, one of the sectoral networks of the Bank, within which is the Public Sector Group. In the last strategic document (World Bank 2000b) the World Bank introduced and adapted important policies that represent the NPM norm to the Governance Strategy, which became central within the World Bank during the

1990s.[9] This strategy clearly identifies three mechanisms of the NPM policy norm to promote public sector efficacy and good governance (World Bank 2000b):

- *internal rules and restraints* – for example, internal accounting and auditing systems, independence of the judiciary and the central bank, civil service and budgeting rules, and rules governing ombudsmen and other internal watchdog bodies that often report to parliaments;
- '*voice' and partnership* – for example, decentralization to empower communities, service delivery surveys to solicit client feedback, and 'notice and comment' regulatory rule-making; and
- *competition* – for example, competitive social service delivery, private participation in infrastructure, alternative dispute resolution mechanisms and privatization of certain market-driven activities.

These may involve a fundamental rethinking of the role of the state, often a key component of reform.

In sum, the CAS is the result of a very formalized process of internal negotiations within the Bank, in which each sector is constrained or empowered by the sectoral relations that it has in that country, and by the strategic importance of the country for achieving its own preferences, beyond the strategic importance of the Bank's preferences for implementing the country's policy agenda. Thus, the policy instruments of the NPM are channelled through a series of filters until they become concrete policy measures. First they are incorporated into the general discourse of the World Bank; then they are introduced in sectoral strategic documents. Formal validity of the NPM norm is formed through the Bank-wide strategy paper. As far as possible, they are incorporated into the Country Assistance Strategies. Social recognition inside the Bank is established in this process between thematic and country offices. Nevertheless, this last stage is the one that generates greater levels of disarticulation among the components of the NPM norm and applicable World Bank NPM policies, since it is here that the political priorities and policy preferences of each government enter the game. These governmental priorities are strongly connected with the margins of flexibility of the Bank to condition public sector reform. Thus, social recognition of the NPM norm (the agreement within the Bank) is linked with the cultural validity of the norm that refers to its application in different domestic settings. Diffusion goes both ways and is not merely coercive (from the Bank to the country) or normative in

---

[9] This strategy is detailed in other key documents of the Bank such as the *World Development Report (WDR) 2000/2001: Attacking Poverty* (World Bank 2001b), which contains a rich discussion of the importance of good governance and effective public sector institutions for poverty reduction. See also World Bank (1997).

the sense that the Bank establishes policy norms. But the policy norms are developed in negotiation with the countries, and these negotiations are composed by some degree of combination of coercive and normative mechanisms of diffusion.

The World Bank and state modernization in Chile and Argentina – what space for NPM?

Concerning Latin American states, the World Bank produced a series of documents that frequently used examples of the new public management policy reforms implemented in the OECD countries (Burki and Perry 1997, 1998). Nevertheless, for the case of Latin America, the NPM policy norm only enters the agenda in the second half of the 1990s, after structural adjustment policies had attempted to attack the region's fiscal crisis (Bresser Pereira and Spink 1999; Spink 1999). Notably, some authors (Cunill Grau 1997; Prats i Catalá 1998) argued that problematizing the size of the public sector and demanding downsizing did not modify the characteristics of the public administration of the developmental state in Latin America, mainly patrimonialism, clientelism and institutional weakness.

It is around these critics that a consensus arose in the region, including within the World Bank, with respect to the insufficiency and limitations of structural adjustment to construct a state with the institutional capacity to sustain economic reforms and to guarantee economic growth (Burki and Perry 1998). After two decades of investing mainly in public infrastructure, rural development and energy (Bresser Pereira 1995; Stone and Wright 2007) from the 1980s the World Bank had adopted a new model of financing: policy-based adjustment loans that were destined to foment structural reform in developing countries (Mosley *et al.* 1991). During the 1990s criticism of the 'low effectiveness' and imposition of MDB programmes made the World Bank and the International Monetary Fund (IMF) reconsider their mandates, responsibilities and policy instruments (Collier 2000). This diagnosis on programme effectiveness was important because conditionality had a low level of accomplishment (Wapenhans *et al.* 1992). In the 1980s, the Bank and the Fund took advantage of the financial crisis in Latin America to impose widespread and stringent prescriptions on borrowers. Certainly, Latin American states were willing to accept anything to obtain financial resources, but once they had reached economic stability, the conditions imposed by the Bank and Fund's programmes were pushed aside as they represented high political costs (Buira 2003a). In the 1990s, the World Bank would begin to incorporate the NPM policy norm into its lending procedures.

The capacity of the World Bank to diffuse the NPM policy norm is strongly conditioned by the domestic processes of each country, and by the type of relation that the Bank has established with that state. Here I will compare the strategies of the World Bank in Chile and Argentina. I will show that from a similar point of departure, in which financial crises opened the opportunity for the Bank to assist borrowers with structural adjustment programmes, the path that each country followed in its relations with the World Bank turned out to be very different.

State modernization agenda: what and when?

It appears that the state modernization agenda was much more related to the Bank's NPM policy norm in Chile than was the case in Argentina. Nevertheless, the origins of these agendas are explained by local variables rather than by the pressure or coercive diffusion capacity of the Bank. Irrespective, reforming the state was the basis for the World Bank to play a supporting role. A central difference between these cases is the sequence of those reforms. In the Chilean case state modernization arose once the process of structural adjustment had been accomplished, whereas in the Argentine case the agenda of state modernization was tied to the policy priorities imposed by recurrent fiscal crises.

In the Chilean case, the experience with loans and programmes of structural adjustment began prior to that in Argentina. Furthermore, in Chile the adjustment package was organized on the basis of a neoliberal programme that had already been in place since the 1970s. Under the advice of a group of technocrats known as the 'Chicago Boys', the military government implemented a package of structural adjustment (Fourcade-Gourinchas and Babb 2002; Murillo 2002). In this sense, the policies implemented by this economic team produced at that time, according to the World Bank, relative fiscal stability, an effective public management and a more flexible economy (World Bank 2002a). However, Chile did not escape the 'debt crisis' caused by the Mexican 'moratoria' in 1982, which affected almost all the countries of the region. It is in this context of crisis that the World Bank 'entered' Chile in order to finance the programmes of structural adjustment characteristic of the Washington Consensus era.[10] After the crisis, the Bank's programmes evolved to

---

[10] As the World Bank states, 'prior to 1983, the government's top economic team was not interested in having a meaningful policy dialogue with the Bank. While the Bank submitted important memoranda to the authorities showing that some of their policies were unsustainable, they ignored or rejected them. The result was little Bank activity, a loss of

support institutional reforms, investment in human resources and the management of public expenditure.

In Argentina the Bank's intervention was more contested and, to a large extent because of that, it occurred later than in the Chilean case. The World Bank began to recover its presence in Argentina after the advent of the democratic government of Raul Alfonsin. Towards the end of 1984 the first studies were conducted to identify the necessary reforms in Argentina and to plan the operations of the World Bank. Nevertheless, until the end of the 1980s this was not translated into a significant presence concerning the financial aid provided by this institution (Botzman and Tussie 1991; Lucioni and Dvoskin 2002). Towards the end of the 1980s the relations between the national government and the World Bank deteriorated and no new loans were granted. This can be explained, partially, as the result of the failure to achieve control of the fiscal deficit and to implement reforms that the World Bank had agreed with the Argentinian government (Machinea and Sommer 1990). The change of the Argentinian administration in 1989 took place in a context of a strong economic crisis, characterized by phenomenal inflation. After the inauguration of President Menem suspended negotiations with the World Bank were re-established (Rinne 2003). At the same time, the government began to implement policies of adjustment and fiscal reform that were in harmony with the ideas propagated by the Washington Consensus.

After the 1980s, the trajectories of each country with regard to their relations with the World Bank differ. The main divergence is that in the Chilean case financial assistance from the Bank was substantially reduced from the beginning of the 1990s, but the work of the World Bank within the country did not decrease qualitatively.[11] Furthermore, it engaged in narrow areas of technical assistance, sectoral studies and some programmes that focused on very specific areas selected by the Chilean government. In comparison, in the Argentinian case financial assistance grew substantially during the 1990s,[12] caused in part by the crises already

---

contact with Bank staff, and an empty loan pipeline. When the crisis exploded Chile was not considered creditworthy, and while the IMF was active the Bank was not' (World Bank 2002a: 13).

[11] From the beginning of the 1990s with the new democratic government, the Chilean strategy towards the Bank was very different. The government began implementing an economic policy that included *not* using credit (especially international lending) to finance their policies, while using some specific small World Bank resources for institutional strengthening. The government aimed to use the Bank's capacity in areas seen to be necessary for controlling, monitoring or creating more capacity.

[12] From 1990 to the end of 2001 the World Bank adjustment loans in Argentina were essential instruments for financing and technically shepparding the economic reforms (Lucioni and Dovskin 2002). This meant an important augmentation in operations with different levels of government, as much in number as in volume (Lucioni 2003).

mentioned, but also because of the political realignment in 1989, which generated a change of direction in economic policy and state reform.

From the 1990s, the first stage of state reforms implemented by Menem's government in Argentina was dominated by fiscal objectives: from measures of state downsizing to reduce the deficit held by public accounts, to decreasing the number of public employees, to reducing the number of national public sector agencies.[13] Shortly after, the government proceeded to reduce the state apparatus through two complementary efforts, that is, privatization and reducing the number of public employees. It also attempted to reconstruct the fiscal system to allow the reordering and the substantial growth of tax collection and better public expense planning and control (Ghio 2002). The second stage of reforms coincided with Menem's second term. One of the central mechanisms of this stage was the fusion of state agencies. The objective was to lessen the fiscal deficit through the reduction of the state apparatus. Nevertheless, this reform initiative gradually weakened as the central administration consolidated new structures that evaded the restrictions to prevent the creation of new national public sector agencies.[14] As soon as the urgency of the fiscal crisis abated, control over the public sector relaxed (Rinne 2003). In contradistinction to the Chilean situation, the Argentine government had to continue to resort to structural adjustment lending in order to face recurrent economic and fiscal crises during the 1990s. This

---

[13] In President Menem's first term his management style concentrated authority and resources in the figure of the president, and politically isolated the task force in charge of the reforms. The Executive Committee for the Control of Administrative Reform (CECRA) was created, a technical committee within the Ministry of Economy, to control reform implementation, and to work with the technical and financial assistance of the World Bank for these projects (Repetto 2001). Legislative approval of these reform packages was obtained through different strategies such as the use of presidential decrees, the economic emergency justification and agreements between the Union Civica Radical (UCR) and the Partido Justicialista (PJ) forced by the anticipated change of government, and strong PJ leadership PJ in Congress (Acuña and Smith 1996). But there was no medium-term political agreement that allowed the sustainability of the programme of reforms and its institutional consolidation as we saw in Chile.

[14] Furthermore, this stage coincided with the reform of the national constitution and the creation of the Chief of the Cabinet of Ministers (JGM) which became a competing agency with the Ministry of Economy, because of its budgetary competences, as well as the general direction of the public administration. In fact, the elaboration of the programme of state modernization in this second stage is attributed to the JGM in 1996, along with the responsibility of monitoring the programme in all areas of the national government. In this sense, the Ministry of Economy lost its centralized control of the state reform process and the fixing of budgetary priorities. Besides, we can observe in the Argentinian case a wider sectoral interaction between World Bank officials and government officials in different agencies and ministries, in short, a less centralized control of the strategy towards the World Bank.

resulted in the diminishing of government capacity to structure a policy agenda separate from its fiscal adjustment.

As Ghio and Etchemendi (1998) indicate, the administrative reform appeared to be a necessary and urgent policy in the context of Argentina's economic emergency, but this impulse lasted only a couple of years, and its implementation became politically difficult once the fiscal urgency passed. One of the main problems was that as the reforms were implemented to a large extent by presidential decrees to avoid legislative veto, the same ones could be easily reversed once the emergency was over (Oszlak 1999).

In the Chilean case, the 1980s policies of adjustment and privatization led to the deterioration of the capacity of public administration (Marcel 2005). The process of modernization of public management in Chile therefore acquired a strong impulse during the transition, becoming a specific agenda when the *Concertación*, a coalition of centre-left political parties that organized the opposition to Pinochet, took office (Armijo 2002; Marcel 2005). In the first period of democratic government, President Aylwin's administration from 1990 to 1994, state reform was not a priority given the importance of the issues related to the democratic transition. None the less, in this period isolated reforms did occur, although these were more a result of the actions of certain entrepreneurs within the state than from a structural agenda for state reform (Waissbluth 2005). During the 1990s, the Chilean government consolidated the state reform process, moving from prioritizing fiscal stability to being preoccupied with the quality of state functions. One of the 'alarms' the government perceived was that the budget allocation increase for key areas of the state's management did not visibly improve the quality and number of services offered. It was then under the leadership of the DIPRES (Budget Office – Ministry of Finances) that performance indicators for budget management began to be developed, as well as a pilot arrangement to promote the strategic planning of public services (Armijo 2002).

These advances were consolidated during President Frei's administration (1994–2000), when the subject of state modernization returned to the government agenda. This was spearheaded by the first project for the law of civil service reform. Finally, during the administration of President Lagos (2000–5) the state modernization policy was deepened, on the basis of extremely rigorous macroeconomic management. Nevertheless the cornerstone of the period was the agreement between the government and opposition for state reform. It was stimulated by a crisis produced by a corruption scandal in the Ministry of Public Works (MOP) that was known as 'MOP-GATE'. Certainly the scandals around the MOP opened a 'window of opportunity' for the agenda of state reform to be consolidated. Hence, within a few months, fundamental political initiatives for the reform had been approved by the legislative branch, including the law of civil service reform among others (Marcel 2005; Waissbluth 2005). This legislated for meritocratic selection for all positions of intermediate level in the public administration, and the designation of the directive positions through lists selected by an independent Council of High Public Direction.

It is very important to emphasize here that Chilean and Argentinian state capacity to fix their own agendas and policy strategies is related not just to the state administrative capacity but to the type of relations that it establishes with other political and social actors.[15] As we saw in Chile, relations between the government and opposition parties permitted a long-term policy reform for state bureaucracy professionalization.

Different World Bank strategies for different settings

It is fundamental to consider here that the World Bank's strategy of assistance for both countries was subsequently adapted to the domestic political agenda of its borrowers. In fact, with the first Chilean democratic government, the strategy of the Bank was concentrated in three pillars: (1) macroeconomic stability to support economic growth; (2) international opening of the economy to increase productivity; and (3) greater public expenditure on health, housing, education and social security (World Bank 1995d). The trends in Bank lending were consistent with those outlined in its strategy papers. The Country Strategy Paper[16] for 1986–8 identified structural adjustment as the main element of the strategy. The political and economic changes of the early 1990s coincided with a situation in which Chile needed less foreign lending. But the country still had large social gaps to bridge and it also needed to improve its infrastructure. The Bank's assistance strategies for 1993–5 and 1996–8 focused on developing human resources and transportation (World Bank 1995d).

The CAS for Chile in 2002 reflected the momentum that state reform and modernization had gained in the governmental agenda. This strategy fixed three ample objectives to support government programmes: (1) to

---

[15] One of the central features of the Chilean transition is the existence of a strong network of intellectual and technocratic groups embedded in the Chilean state structure. They play a key role in the progressive and gradual character, not just of the political transition, but also of the configuration of the policy agenda (Puryear 1994). These groups have been key players in the Chilean political debate since the 1970s, and particularly during the 1980s (Huneeus 2000; Santiso and Whitehead 2006; Silva 1991).

[16] The Country Strategy Paper is an antecedent of the CAS that existed in the 1980s, but did not include formalized dialogue and consultations with the government, civil society, different bank sectors and other counterparts.

maintain economic growth and social policy; (2) to increase social and economic inclusion, especially of the rural populations and vulnerable groups; and (3) the modernization of the state as the foundation of both previous objectives (World Bank 2002b). In this sense, an evaluation of the financial management performed in 2005 by the World Bank and the IADB stated that:

Chile is in the middle of the second generation reforms in the public sector. At the present, the objective is not just the fiscal discipline but the improvement of the quality of the public services, that is to say, in obtaining the effectiveness and efficiency of the Government. Such improvements are possible now, simply because they may be supported on the solid fiscal existing base of (i) stability, (ii) the financing assured, and (iii) a use of resources in agreement with the budgetary authorizations, with reliable information on the income, uses and financial positions. (World Bank and IADB 2005)

An important example of the way in which democratization instils new issues in the policy agenda of the government with the World Bank is the subject of decentralization. Before the restoration of Chile's municipal elections in 1991, the military junta had progressively decentralized some functions and services, assigning them to the municipalities. The central government, nevertheless, appointed mayors and maintained strict controls on policies and municipal expenses. Only with the return of democratic rule in 1990 did the Chilean government begin to implement the constitutional and legal reforms that would allow elections and political autonomy at municipal level (Serrano and Berner 2002; Valenzuela 1997). Starting with the democratic restoration, the Chilean government began to discuss reforms and modernization programmes at the subnational level with the World Bank. In the first place the government requested the preparation of the Pilot Project of Municipal Development (MDPP). Under the MDPP, the Bank financed a series of studies to direct the main political aspects and to apply some of the Bank's recommendations to the municipalities (World Bank 1998).

Thus, the Bank and the government decided to conduct a series of studies and technical assistance that allowed Chile to continue working with the World Bank in the evaluation of the public policies implemented by the government, including the professionalization of the civil service, the system of performance-based budgetary management,[17] and the

---

[17] The Chilean system of management controls and results-based budget consists of the following monitoring and evaluation tools: performance indicators, programme and agency evaluations (including comprehensive spending reviews), a bidding fund for public programmes, management improvement programmes linked to performance bonuses for central government employees, comprehensive management reports and focus on the programme evaluation tool.

system of programme evaluation. Furthermore, these economic and public sector works were very useful for the Bank to support lending operations and policy advice throughout. They emphasized elements that became the foundation of the Bank's strategy for Chile: stabilizing, adjusting and reforming the economy, consolidating growth, and consolidating other sector operations (World Bank 2002b).

Regarding the Argentinian case, after the frustrated attempts at reform from the 1980s, which ended in a serious economic crisis and a change of government, 'the Bank's assistance strategy, after some hesitation during 1989/90 at the very start of Argentina's structural reform process, gained momentum from 1991 onwards, pari passu with the introduction of the currency board arrangement, the core of Argentina's stabilization program' (World Bank 2000a: 1). From that moment on, the Bank's strategy towards Argentina during the 1990s did not experience substantial modifications, since the central problems identified did not change. What was modified was the focus on some of the points of the World Bank strategy as long as they registered advances in some of the reform processes. Thus, during the early 1990s the focus was public sector reform and privatization (as evidenced by public enterprise reform adjustment loans in 1991 and 1993, and a public sector reform loan in 1992), as well as financial sector adjustment (with a loan in 1993). In the Argentinian case, subnational issues were included in the World Bank agenda in this period, but with a series of incentives much more related to the solution of the fiscal problem compared with the Chilean case.[18] During these years, the Bank granted its first loans for local government projects, those that had been organized with the intermediation of the national government and then transferred to the provinces. The agreement of these loans responded to a strategy shared by the World Bank and the national government for programmes that had been implemented in the provinces for the reinforcement of their public sectors (Lucioni 2003; Vetter 1997).

The 1997 and 1998 CAS progress reports for Argentina were very explicit in proposing a Bank portfolio focusing on provincial reforms and social development. The FY97–00 CAS focused on (1) enhancing social development, including poverty alleviation and human resource development; (2) improving institutional performance and government capacity, particularly at the sub-national level; and (3) consolidating

---

[18] The question of tax and political relations with the provincial governments, in the context of a federal institutional structure like that of Argentina, was one of the government's central problems in controlling the macroeconomic and fiscal results of the reform programmes. Studies carried out at the time by the World Bank (World Bank 1990) indicated that provincial management accounted for a significant part of the consolidated deficit of the Argentinian public sector.

structural reforms, including public finance, the financial markets and the labour markets (World Bank 2001b). But one of the main risks of the portfolio continued to be the need to provide financial assistance in the case of external shocks, as occurred in 1998. This meant the necessity of modifying the lending programme to accommodate the urgent needs of the 1998–9 crises (World Bank 1997).[19]

As evaluated by the World Bank (World Bank 2000a: 7), 'the strong commitment by Argentina's top political leadership was clearly the key factor in the successful restoration of growth and stability during the 1990s as well as in the economy's ability to deal with external shocks'. But this was only true for the first generation reforms of the first part of that decade. The same Bank evaluation (World Bank 2000a) states that 'there is one important institutional weakness, however, that both the Bank and the government have ignored in the period of review: the administrative reform of the Federal Government'.[20]

The 1996 country assistance review for Argentina (World Bank 1996) had already found that the Bank's assistance outcome had been satisfactory starting in 1991, but that the institutional development impact had been modest and, above all, that the sustainability of the achievements remained in doubt. Even many of the reforms that had attained a significant degree of institutionalization like the Currency Board which established the country's foreign exchange regime and the relationships between the federal and provincial governments were clearly reversed after the 2001 crisis and the political changes that followed it. The new fiscal and economic context of the country has meant, from the devaluation and from the renegotiation of the external debt, a change in the situation of structural fiscal deficit, which significantly modified the government's priorities.

Conclusion

We have shown, in comparative perspective, that the Bank's capacity to spread the NPM policy norm is closely related to its capacity to adapt to

[19] In general, the largest volume of Bank commitments was for multi-sector lending: this consisted of two somewhat exceptional operations: a debt and debt service reduction loan in 1993, and the US$2.5 billion special structural adjustment loan in 1999 in response to the financial emergency (World Bank 2000a).

[20] 'The government took advantage of the recovery from the 1995 crisis to successfully consolidate, with Bank help, the reforms in the banking system. However, both the government and the Bank lost an opportunity to pursue more vigorously the reduction of the fiscal deficit, the introduction of flexibility in the labour markets and the improvement of the efficiency of the Federal Government during those good years, when the trauma of adjustment could have been substantially eased' (World Bank 2000a: 16).

different political and institutional contexts in the countries in which it operates. The comparison shows that domestic forces and processes have a critical role in conditioning states' engagement with the Bank's policy norms; moreover, they may become a serious obstacle to these kinds of policy reforms. The diffusion process in which the Bank became involved with recipient countries is a combination of coercive and normative mechanisms. In this sense, we have shown that the NPM policy norm originated outside the Bank, and went through a complex process of appropriation and adaptation that consisted of different institutional filters within the Bank and its borrowers. A first step is the more intellectual task of incorporating NPM components into the Bank through the creation of the Bank's NPM policy norm, which is ascribed formal validity through its procedures such as the CAS, as well as its main publications and in the sectoral strategy documents.

A second step is social recognition within the CAS formulation. As we have seen, this instrument allows the Bank to establish a more formal and active dialogue with the governments and other national actors, identifying at the same time high-priority lines of work in that country. In parallel, this means a process of negotiation and internal formulation within the Bank that is not separated from the process of persuasion and negotiation with country officials. As we can see from our country comparison, the mere emergence of a norm (formally validated in the strategy papers) is not enough for a norm to survive. Since norms are constantly contested when applied to domestic settings they have to be flexible.

Finally, this process leads to the third, and certainly most critical, step that is the bargaining process between the Bank's policy priorities and those of the governments. In this sense, one of the main differences between Chile and Argentina is the sequence and gradualism of the reforms. Whereas in the case of Chile the structural reforms of the Washington Consensus were already implemented with the support of the World Bank during the 1980s, Argentina delayed them until the beginning of the 1990s. In this case, the fiscal and financial instability of the 1990s implied that the agenda of state reforms was subordinated to the objective of reaching fiscal surplus. Furthermore, it created further complications for the planning of medium- and long-term actions with the Bank, since situations of financial emergency such as that of 1998 altered the programming of the government with the Bank and the management of the lending portfolio. Although it is certain that the different financial and fiscal conjunctures give governments different margins to manoeuvre in order to organize their policy options in relation to the World Bank, the cases here illustrate that other series of factors exist that affect one government's capacity to systematize a relatively stable policy agenda and to negotiate the support of the World Bank for such policies.

Certainly, the NPM norm is central to the governance discourse now propounded by the World Bank that argues that economic growth is not enough for development and that institutions matter. In this sense, state capacity is a critical condition to manage the development process and the NPM policy norm is strongly linked to enhancing state capacity. However, the analysis suggests that the limitations faced by the Bank in effectively solving the dilemma between the diffusion of the NPM policy norm and the means of operationalizing its policy norms on a country-case basis reflect a deeper need for cultural validation rather than formal validity.

Part Five

Conclusion

11 Do policy norms reconstitute global development?

Susan Park and Antje Vetterlein

Introduction

The IMF and the World Bank have taken up new ideas and retained old ones in ways which modify their policies and therefore actions, yet how and why they do so remains under-studied. In the introduction (chapter 1) we identified the need for in-depth empirical research investigating why the IMF and the World Bank behave the way they do. We outlined the constructivist parameters for examining how and why the Bretton Woods institutions came to own the policies they currently promote to developing countries. This conclusion draws together the results of the volume in response to the three key aims outlined in the introduction. First, the volume aimed to examine how ideas came to prominence within either the Fund or the Bank which were then translated into globally applicable approaches to economic growth and development, which we call policy norms. Second, the volume aimed to identify the strength of the policy norms currently advocated by the Fund and the Bank. This is important for examining the extent to which policy norms are emerging, stabilizing or declining, the last of which has not received much analytical attention to date. Finally, the volume aimed to identify the sources, triggers and mechanisms that lead to the formation and change of policy norms within these IOs. We analyse whether the processes inherent in the norm circle of policy norm development help us understand IO change and broader shifts within international economic growth and development.

Ideas versus power-based explanations of policy norm formation and change

First, IMF and World Bank operations are based on their policies, although there is little examination in scholarly studies on these two institutions as to how these policies are devised. We argue that the policies the IMF and the World Bank promote are based on ideas that may be generated from outside the Fund and the Bank or from within. We used

225

the concept of a policy norm, which we defined as shared expectations for all relevant actors within a community about what constitutes appropriate behaviour, which is encapsulated in (Fund or Bank) policy. In the case of the Fund and the Bank, these policy norms constitute both shared understandings of, and detailed policy prescriptions for, international economic development. As demonstrated throughout the chapters and summarized below, policy norms emerge as a result of a number of factors rather than from a single overarching influence. Each of the chapters traced the origin of the policy norm in question and mapped the policy-making process whereby the norm became actionable or translated into IMF and World Bank policy.

Rather than taking the power of member states, private interests or IO management as given, we aimed to identify the sources, triggers and mechanisms of change in these international organizations. For example, theoretical approaches recognize the relative autonomy of IOs in decision-making, but they tend not to examine how the IMF and the World Bank come to own the policies they promote to developing states. Power-based explanations devote their analysis to documenting how (powerful) states delegate to the Fund and the Bank in the case of the rationalist principal–agent (PA) model, or presume that private elites act in concert with these institutions to preserve their hegemony in the case of neo-Gramscians. In contrast, contemporary constructivists argue that the IMF and the World Bank have the power to diffuse norms throughout the international system, and make their own decisions based on their internal culture, norms and identity. In this volume we tried to advance knowledge about the IMF and the World Bank's motivations for action, and whether they fit these frameworks, by engaging in process tracing to document empirically how and why the IMF and the World Bank behave the way they do. We wanted to examine where the 'policy norms' they advanced came from and whether this demonstrated that these IOs are capable of change.

The results challenge assumptions of both state power and IO autonomy that are representative of current explanations of IO behaviour and change. We found evidence that norm advocates both within and outside the IMF and the World Bank do influence their behaviour, thus contributing to IO change. In some circumstances these norm advocates include member states but these 'principals' are often not the instigators of policy norms, nor do ideas for change necessarily always come from IO management and staff. Locating multiple sources of policy norm formation and change in this way breaks down the boundaries so assiduously constructed by rationalist PA model adherents, who focus on collective member states and IO interests as the central determinants of IO action. Moreover, the volume does not provide evidence to substantiate assumptions of either global hegemonic elites or complete IO autonomy in determining these IOs' motivation for behaviour. What we found instead is much more diverse interactions between state and non-state actors that engage in complex ways to shape policy norms that may be quite different from what norm advocates originally intended. Far from power shaping agendas in structurally determined ways, we discovered that the IMF and the World Bank were capable of change through the formation and modification of their policy norms, but that this did not necessarily accord with a systematic favouring of certain actors (powerful or non-powerful) over others. As discussed below, we also found that the IOs' internal norms, culture and identity do influence whether and how some ideas were picked up by the IMF or the World Bank to become policy norms.

From the nine cases analysed, we identify two axes delineating how policy norms emerge within the IMF and the World Bank, some of which, superficially at least, lend themselves to a rationalist PA model of analysis. However, if we were to hazard a guess on how policy norms such as capital account liberalization (CAL) or pension reform emerged within the IMF, we might assume that these came from powerful member states' adherence to neoliberal ideology and that this informed how they directed the Fund as their agent. While powerful member states in the Fund, such as the UK and the USA, did promote neoliberal ideology in the early 1980s, this does not actually explain how capital account liberalization or specific models for pension reform emerged in the Fund and the Bank as they did. Further evidence from other policy norms also does not fit the powerful states' interests argument propounded by rationalist PA model advocates. For example, current account convertibility (CAC) is formally valid within the IMF's Articles of Agreement (on the basis of powerful state negotiations at Bretton Woods in 1944), yet this does not explain why rapid action was undertaken to adhere to this policy norm fifty years later. Similarly, while many of these policy norms may favour private sector interests, there is no evidence to suggest that private sector actors were prominent in pushing for their formation. However, this does not mean that we cannot ascertain patterns of policy norm emergence within these IOs.

On the first axis, we identify that policy norms emerge either from inside the IO or from outside the organization. One of the basic theoretical premises of this volume was that norm advocates external to the Bretton Woods institutions could influence these IOs. This was confirmed in the empirical chapters. For the IMF and the World Bank, this includes the influence of member states as they determine the direction of these institutions but do not run them (this is left to senior management under the IMF's Managing Director or the Bank's President). Even if we discount the role of member states in shaping IOs 'from the outside' in order not to trivialize the proposition, the finding still holds. We discovered that other IOs such as the United Nations (UN) and non-state actors such as non-governmental organizations (NGOs) can and do influence the Fund and the Bank to take up policy norms such as poverty reduction, multilateral debt relief and environmental safeguards. If, however, one chooses to place member states as actors that operate inside IOs because of their privileged ownership status in determining the direction of these institutions, then this points to one avenue whereby internal mechanisms can trigger IO change. Again this is not the only means through which policy norms emerge inside IOs. We also identify policy norms that came from within the IMF and the Bank, such as capital account liberalization and gender and development (GAD) emerging from staff (management could also be norm advocates, although accounts herein do not provide any evidence of policy norms being generated by them[1]).

The discussion of staff actions versus member state influence brings us to the second axis: top-down versus bottom-up sites for policy norm emergence and IO change. If we look at externally generated norms we find evidence in some cases of top-down change from external normative influence on powerful member states that is then passed on to management and then to the staff (in the case of multilateral debt relief, for example). At this stage we did not find evidence of top-down internal influence from management to staff without member state deliberations at the level of the Board of Executive Directors in the Fund or the Bank. In other words, management did not introduce new ideas that became policy norms. In terms of bottom-up policy norm generation we can point to the infiltration of ideas from external actors such as other IOs and NGOs influencing the IO as well as internal accounts of change, where staff bring professional norms or ideas into the IO. Bottom-up processes blur the boundaries between inside and outside policy norm generation, again undermining rationalist PA model assumptions of member state power and IO autonomy. In some instances, such as gender and development and environmental safeguards, the norms were externally widespread. Yet in terms of the GAD policy norm, this was modified, changed and promoted through bottom-up internal processes. As a result both outside-in and inside-out, as well as top-down and bottom-up, sources of change are evident in how policy norms emerged and/or developed in the IMF

---

[1] Even the emergence of anti-corruption in the World Bank in the 1990s can be attributed to Bank staff rather than President Wolfensohn and Bank management (see Weaver 2008). Policy norms may, however, change as a result of ongoing IO operations which may be in part linked to management decisions; see, for example, tax reform in chapter 7.

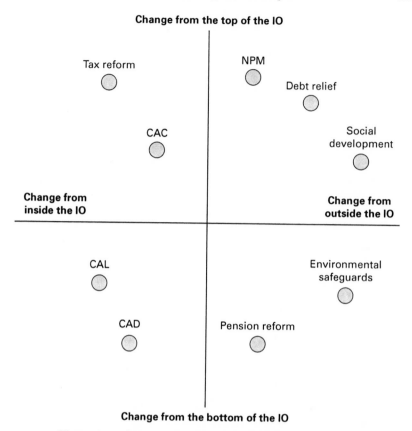

Figure 11.1 Sources of policy norm change in the World Bank and the IMF

and the World Bank. A classification of the nine cases along these two axes is shown in Figure 11.1.

Figure 11.1 demonstrates that the majority of IMF policy norms come from the top-down – from member states to management to staff. In the five cases examined, only capital account liberalization (CAL) came from staff and flowed upwards to management. In some ways this is linked to the research design of the volume: in examining policy norm stability we analysed already existing policy norms such as tax reform and current account convertibility (CAC). In other words, they were formally valid policy norms, although the social recognition and cultural validation of the policy norms respectively changed over time. They stabilized as a result of changes promoted by management and staff (on tax reform) or from management and staff responding to changing external conditions (regarding current account convertibility). In other respects, however, this also fits with the structure of the IMF as a hierarchical organization with a tight organizational culture which values authority and the apolitical nature of the economics profession. This emerged as a key determinant in each of the chapters discussing the IMF's take-up of ideas.

As a result, changing policy norms advocated by the Fund such as multilateral debt relief and social development were tackled at the external 'political' level between member states on the Board rather than from inside the organization at the staff level, where these ideas most likely would not have been socially recognized. The outlier in the IMF, capital account liberalization, succeeded as an internally generated policy norm where multilateral debt relief and social development perhaps could not, because it is based on foundations similar to those of the organizational culture of the Fund. This enabled the new norm to gain strength as it resembled both the apolitical nature and the economics propounded by the organization (leading it to become socially recognized). As a result, one can point to social recognition through the organization's culture, mandate and professional orientation determining whether policy norms emerge from within or from outside the organization.

In terms of the World Bank the results are more mixed. It is evident that ideas external to the organization are easier to take up for the Bank as was exemplified by the pension reform, environmental safeguard and new public management (NPM) policy norms. It is also evident that policy norms can emerge from inside the World Bank, as in the case of gender and development, even though gender equality is a widespread idea outside the organization. Yet it succeeded within the Bank because of the norm advocacy of staff, which was assisted by outside condemnation. In this regard the Bank may be more open to ideas generated outside the organization that it can 'make its own'. In terms of whether the Bank internalizes norms in a top-down or bottom-up fashion, the results are even. Of our four cases of policy norms within the World Bank two came from the bottom up, from staff (GAD) or from NGOs (environmental safeguards), while two came from the top down, from member states (pension reform and new public management).[2] As a result we can draw

---

[2] Of course the triggers may be different in relation to how a policy norm emerges from how a policy norm may stabilize or decline. For example, while environmental safeguards came from outside the World Bank as a result of bottom-up NGO activity with member state influence, the trigger for decline came from a change in borrower member states and is thus top-down and external. Figure 11.1 demonstrates where the policy norms emerged. At this stage we do not distinguish between borrower and donor member states, although this could be a further avenue for exploration.

some initial conclusions that as a larger, more professionally heterogeneous organization with a broader mandate, the Bank is more open to taking up ideas from a variety of sources. Applying these insights to other IOs necessarily means identifying the triggers of policy norm change in relation to the organizational culture and identity of the relevant organization.

The power of policy norms and triggers for change

The second aim of the volume was to question whether the policy norms that the IMF and the World Bank took up actually change throughout this process and over time. In other words, the authors challenge the stereotypical structural understanding of norms within the norm diffusion literature. This is characterized by assumptions that actors either take up norms or do not. The assumption that actors either do or do not respond to norms does not take into account the myriad ways in which norms themselves emerge, solidify, strengthen and even weaken and regenerate through interaction over time. Central to our understanding of norms is their reflexivity. Norms do not just exist out there; they are not immutable structures. Much of the norms literature has focused on documenting the structural impact of norms on international relations, particularly through shaping states' behaviour and identity (Kelley 2004; Linden 2002; Schimmelfennig 2005; see the special edition of *IO* 2005). Yet norms themselves change. The focus on 'norm entrepreneurs' such as IOs, transnational advocacy networks, NGOs and global civil society has aimed to show how a norm emerges to exert power over actors' (again usually states') behaviour (Keck and Sikkink 1998; O'Brien *et al.* 2000; Wapner 1996). For all the ink spilled on this issue, there is surprisingly little written on how norms transform over time (for exceptions see Sandholtz 2008; Wiener 2009). We argue that policy norms will demonstrate varying degrees of strength over time, which are determined by the degree to which it is contested either within collective actors like the Fund and the Bank or by actors external to them. Here we outline the three constituent components that characterize a policy norm's strength and identify the triggers for their emerging power or decline.

A policy norm may be strong or weak depending on whether it is formally valid, socially recognized or culturally valid. As sketched in chapter 1, policy norms are formally valid if they are institutionalized in international agreements or treaties, the IO's Articles of Agreement, loan agreements or policy documents including organizational strategy papers. Policy norms that have been formally validated are agreed upon by member states, the IO and often non-state actors. All of the policy norms discussed herein are formally valid in some way, generally through IO strategy papers and procedures. This includes multilateral debt relief, social development, pension reform, tax reform, gender and development, environmental safeguards and new public management. One very strong policy norm is current account convertibility which is institutionalized in the IMF's Articles of Agreement. Second, the social recognition of a policy norm indicates its informal strength because it demonstrates the degree of its acceptance amongst member states, management and staff through their interactions and practices. This is the crucial component in understanding the extent to which formal validity accords with current social understandings of the appropriateness of the policy norm within the IMF and the World Bank. We discovered divergent cases of strength across the constituent components. For example, the social recognition of capital account liberalization was strong enough for IMF staff to push for its formal validity by advocating its inclusion in the Fund's Articles of Agreement. In contrast, the social recognition of the tax reform policy norm was enacted through non-compliance with the formal valid understanding of tax reform (a situation that stabilized in the IMF).

Finally, cultural validation is important in addressing the link between formal validation and social recognition in cases where the policy norm is formally valid and socially recognized within the IO and is then applied in different borrowers' domestic settings. New public management is an example of a formally valid and socially recognized policy norm that does not show evidence of strong cultural validity in light of competing government pressures. It did not have the degree of cultural validity in borrowers that would demonstrate its strength in different realms from its origin. Invoking this conception of a policy norm's strength, each chapter classifies the strength of a particular policy norm and traces how it was produced, reproduced and transformed over time. As discussed in the introduction and detailed throughout the chapters, any one of these constituent components may become the focus of norm advocates pushing for change, or may weaken in light of changing circumstances. Assessing policy norms in this way provides us with the capacity to examine how policy norms vary in strength and power.

Three of the policy norms in this volume are gaining strength through social recognition leading to formal validity. These are classified as emerging policy norms: multilateral debt relief, pension reform, and gender and development. Three more policy norms are categorized as stabilizing: the social development policy norm is in the process of shifting from norm emergence to stabilization through gaining formal validity. Two others, current account convertibility and tax reform, are at the height of their taken for grantedness with strong formal validity and social recognition (though weak cultural validity in the tax reform case). Nevertheless, while these norms exist as stable, accepted and legitimate, they may over time become subject to contestation. To demonstrate how norms may then shift from being stable and exerting structural power to relative decline, we trace three policy norms that show signs of subsiding: capital account liberalization, environmental safeguards and new public management. At any given time, one can assume that a norm may become contested by either specific actors or groups of actors or as a result of events that challenge the strength of the policy norm (formally for CAL, socially for the environmental safeguard and culturally for the NPM policy norm). This therefore builds reflexivity into our understanding of norm change. In the chapters we found evidence of three triggers that may challenge the strength of the policy norm thus tipping it into a new phase: from emerging, stabilizing or declining (these phases constitute the circular process of norm change which we discuss below).

The triggers we identified are (1) the acknowledgement that certain policies do not work according to expectations, (2) external shocks, and (3) mass condemnation (the latter may be linked to policies not succeeding but also come from culturally disparate actors using different reference points for measuring that success). All of the chapters demonstrate one or more of these three triggers as playing a role in contributing to policy norm change. In some cases all three are evident, in others just one. As demonstrated these are both ideational and material triggers. As we discussed in chapter 1, what is important about material triggers is whether this revises actors' assumptions about what they consider socially appropriate, which may in turn change their conception of appropriate policy responses. These triggers are crucial factors because one can expect significant resistance to change. Change is slow in international bureaucracies such as the IMF and the World Bank because they have organizational cultures or identities through which new norms must penetrate. Change is also costly since habits and traditions must be adapted or reinvented. While the Fund is an economic institution, staffed almost exclusively by economists, the Bank is a large development agency with a more heterogeneous staff. Different levels of resistance can be expected according to the organizations' mandate and professional background of staff in relation to different policy fields.

The first trigger is the widespread acknowledgement that certain understandings of development problems and their attendant policy prescriptions do not work. This opens the policy norm space for alternative development practices. Widespread agreement on the need for change is a powerful propellant for discussing alternative means of understanding development problems. As Thomas Kuhn (1970) recognizes, normal science should be able to explain additional scientific evidence, but where pre-existing explanations cannot, a paradigm shift occurs. The acknowledgement of failure of previous approaches was evident in relation to triggering the emergence of multilateral debt relief and social development policy norms. Past policy norm failure also contributed to the emergence of the gender and development policy norm as internal norm advocates revised their means of addressing gender within the World Bank's work. New public management may yet be an example of the failure to impose, even through interaction between the Bank and its borrowers, a robust policy norm. In other words, the lack of cultural validation of new public management in borrowers such as Argentina and Chile may lead to the acknowledgement that this policy norm does not work as expected, although it may be too soon to tell.

Second, external shocks are also powerful triggers for change, where unforeseen circumstances radically revise taken for granted assumptions about how economics and development work and what policies are therefore most appropriate. External shocks include the Asian financial crisis or the collapse of the Soviet Union and the end of the Cold War, but are not limited to crises in the international system. The Asian financial crisis was evident in the emergence of the social development policy norm in conjunction with the acknowledgement of past failure and the third trigger, mass condemnation (discussed below). The conditions that produced the Asian financial crisis further enabled the stabilization of the current account convertibility policy norm where international political economy returned to the widespread acceptance of capital mobility. Moreover, the crisis further entrenched the tax reform policy norm within the IMF, although as Seabrooke discusses in chapter 7, the tax reform policy norm itself changed owing to the actions of IMF staff. The external shock of the Asian financial crisis triggered the decline of the capital account liberalization policy norm. Another shock, the end of the Cold War, led to the emergence of the pension reform policy norm as advocated by the World Bank for its new transition economy borrowers. In the case of environmental safeguards a dramatic rise in the economic wealth and development of World Bank borrowers over the past two decades created new circumstances requiring a new way of thinking about environmental standards and responsibilities for newly created categories of Bank borrowers (middle income countries). The changing fortunes of states may not be considered a shock but a rapid shift in states radically alters the structure of the international system in which IOs operate, and may therefore be considered an external trigger for change.

As can be seen, most of the policy norms were triggered either by acknowledged failure or by external shock. However, the third trigger, mass condemnation, occurs in conjunction with either the acknowledgement of past policy norm failure or an external shock (or both in the case of social development). This could be seen as the most important trigger, facilitating the acknowledgement of policy norm failure according to prior expectations or as the reaction reinforcing an external shock. Or it may be seen as the least important aspect of policy norm change, occurring as it does in relation to the other two triggers where it is not powerful enough to trigger policy norm change independent of the other triggers. Arguably it is difficult to disassociate the effects of mass condemnation from widespread acknowledgement of failure where, for example, this provides further impetus for change in the cases of multilateral debt relief, social development and revision to the pension reform policy norm. It also contributed to the internal efforts of gender and development norm advocates in the World Bank. Further effects of mass condemnation cannot be separated from external shocks where, for example, the IMF's position on capital account liberalization was widely condemned and this was seen to be the lesson drawn from the Asian financial crisis by the economic development community. As a result, mass condemnation can come either before or after other triggers.

Moreover mass condemnation appears as an attendant trigger in all three stages of the policy norm circle, demonstrating that the strength of the policy norm does not determine whether mass opposition is needed to trigger change. For example, mass criticism occurred in relation to policy norms that were emerging (multilateral debt relief, pension reform, gender and development), stabilizing (social development) and in decline (capital account liberalization). Notable also is the recognition that policy norms are triggered by *either* material events such as the Asian financial crisis and the end of the Cold War *or* ideational factors such as the agreement of widespread failure of a policy norm from expected outcomes. As a result, both normative and material triggers lead to policy norm change, and the individual chapters discuss in detail how changes in material circumstances influence shared understandings of economic development practices.

Policy norms within the norm circle: identifying mechanisms for change

Finally, the volume locates the policy norm formation and change process within a broader framework. In the introduction we established the concept of the norm circle, as a means of further identifying how ideas may change over time. In contrast to more linear or progressive understandings of normative change (Finnemore and Sikkink 1998; Risse and Sikkink 1999) we argue that norms change over time in a circular, ongoing, socially interactive process. Ideas do not disappear, they just change form. Evidence of the various policy norms suggests that there is an identifiable pattern in policy norm formation, stabilization and decline (which may regenerate in the future). This process is an ongoing one where a new norm emerges from a specific place in time and history. For example, an already existing norm might be increasingly contested or inflexible in a changing context. While there are numerous potential norms for particular economic and development issues only one will eventually resonate with relevant actors, leading it to become accepted and to stabilize, at which point it then begins to exert the structural power highlighted in the norms literature. Here we identify the various mechanisms of policy norm development evident in the norm circle.

In the *norm contestation* phase we highlight mechanisms of externalization and objectivation. Actors externalize themselves through a number of practices based on their specific dispositions. They therefore construct the world by projecting their meaning into 'reality'. As we have seen in the different policy norms, the triggers for such externalizations are manifold. These include the realization that specific policies yield negative outcomes, changing external conditions, or specifically well-targeted critiques by external actors that reveal new ways of looking at an issue. In that sense, there will be deviance from a particular norm at any given time. Indeed there have always been actors with different interests and ideas (or dispositions). For example, key IMF member states pushed the institution to adopt multilateral debt relief in direct contradistinction to the institution's position of not wiping off debt out of concern over moral hazard (see Momani, chapter 2). Not all instances of non-adherence to the Fund's core mandate and position on rejecting debt relief will be known and therefore opposed. However, by objectivation, a process through which the externalized products of human activity attain the character of objectivity, some of them enter the realm of shared knowledge. For all of the policy norms, and especially the ones in the norm emergence phase, the contributors examined what the common understanding of the policy problem was before the norm came into being and how it became prevalent enough to be understood as a norm that was translated into policy. Regarding multilateral debt relief, for instance, ongoing discussions by member states to wipe off the multilateral debt of highly indebted poor countries created an issue to be objectively analysed (which the Board subsequently voted the Fund staff to study), coalescing into a policy norm with specific policy prescriptions identified by IMF staff.

Not all 'deviant behaviours' turn into a new norm or change existing norms. Norm entrepreneurs or advocates actively foster particular ideas to become more common, forming norms (Finnemore and Sikkink 1998; Florini 1996). This leads to the first stage of *norm emergence*. Here the mechanisms of persuasion, arguing and negotiation kick in. Any stakeholder can be a norm advocate. What is of interest here is the conditions under which some are more successful than others, and are able to raise the awareness to a critical mass. NGOs for instance often play this role, but advocacy must reach a tipping point for the norm to stabilize and acquire structural power. Often, criticism and contestation or the promotion of alternative norms is supported by other crucial events that undermine the formal, social or cultural validity of entrenched normative understandings. This opens up the normative policy space for new norms to settle into the void. Norm advocates try to persuade and/or shame the IMF and the World Bank to adopt new policy norms. Regarding multilateral debt relief, the norm entrepreneurs included the UK and the USA, but they were increasingly backed by the World Bank, the Catholic Church and development NGOs. External actors persuaded the member states of the Fund to institute a multilateral debt relief programme. Member states, as norm advocates, negotiated with other recalcitrant member states over the issue. This allowed room for the IMF staff not only to be persuaded by arguments in favour of multilateral debt relief, but to do so in a way that would not threaten its organizational culture or the interests of its split Board. The case amply demonstrates these mechanisms at work.

The pension reform policy norm (Wodsak and Koch, chapter 3) also exemplifies strategies of persuasion, arguing and negotiation. In this case World Bank management and staff were the norm advocates, who aimed to persuade borrowers and the outside development community that its approach to pension reform was more appropriate and beneficial than pre-existing approaches. What makes these norm advocates successful is the ability to translate different ideas into the Fund's and the Bank's operations, where the Fund was convinced that there was an economic means of measuring debt relief and the Bank was able to combine its neoliberal economic perspective with its increasing social development agenda. These norms emerged to replace previous ways of viewing debt relief and pension reform. In the case of the gender and development (GAD) policy norm (Weaver, chapter 4) staff inside the World Bank aimed to persuade their superiors and colleagues through a number of strategies to consider women's roles in development through an economic lens. They therefore argued that improving gender equality could also contribute to poverty alleviation simultaneously. The externalization of Bank staff dispositions into advocating for the GAD policy norm came from the realization that furthering gender issues in the Bank through the women in development approach had not succeeded, even while gender equality is widespread outside the organization. Arguably, the GAD policy norm is entering the realm of shared knowledge inside the organization through employing economic data to speak for gender as well as economic development.

The second stage of the norm circle is *norm stabilization*. This is characterized by the growing legitimacy of the emergent norm. There are two consecutive mechanisms at work: habitualization and institutionalization. Through repeated externalized action certain behaviour turns into patterns that can be reproduced (such as policy creation and monitoring), which we refer to as habitualization. If these patterns are reciprocally reproduced through interaction they become institutionalized, where policies are acted upon by other development actors. Once a policy norm has been institutionalized they guide and constrain action. Further constructivist research has been undertaken on how this then leads to actors internalizing these norms, including how norms are re-projected into actors' consciousness during this process through learning and socialization (Checkel 2005; Park 2010), although this volume does not delve into actors' internal thought processes in this way (although some chapters do comment on the likelihood of IMF and World Bank staff internalizing policy norms). If the processes of institutionalization are successful the norm will be taken for granted and is no longer the subject of debate but stands for the dominant standard of appropriateness. The social development global policy norm is in the process of stabilizing while current account liberalization and tax reform have stabilized. As these cases show, stabilization did not come quickly. Only over time did the Fund and the Bank incorporate these policy norms, which in turn eventually led to changes in the IMF and the World Bank's procedures, including their organization-wide strategy papers, shifts in budgeting and resources, and organizational structures, indicating IO change.

Norms must resonate to gain acceptance among relevant actors. Institutionalization is not sufficient for a norm to stabilize. In other words, if policy norms do not have legitimacy through, for example, social and cultural validity, they will not be a standard for appropriate behaviour. Social and cultural validity provide cognitive explanations and justifications for the new norm, serving to integrate new meaning within already existing institutional processes. This enables conformity to the new norm where the appropriateness of attendant policies is not likely to be questioned. Therefore, as a specific norm emerges we can expect struggles of interpretation over how to understand the norm in the current context. In the case of social development in the IMF in chapter 5 we observed an ongoing struggle between those who believe economic growth is sufficient for poverty reduction and those who slowly understood that improved social conditions could actually enhance economic growth.

Both current account convertibility and tax reform policy norms have reached the stabilization phase, where these policy norms have been promoted by the IMF leading to social recognition by borrowers. For example, current account convertibility was given formal validity within the IMF's Articles of Agreement (Article VIII) at Bretton Woods in 1944. However, member states chose not to make membership conditional on states formally adhering to it. Instead they gave the Fund the ability to request that states remove exchange rate restrictions (Article XIV), which the IMF has been reluctant to use. While the formal validity of the policy norm has therefore existed as long as the organization has, states only began to follow the policy norm in large numbers in the 1990s. Member states thus began to habitualize the removal of exchange rate restrictions as a result of the changes in international political economy and attendant economic ideas. The process was further institutionalized by the IMF's use of persuasion, informal sanctions such as public shaming and peer pressure, and the provision of material incentives for states formally to shift their membership to Article VIII status. The process re-projected states' understanding of current account convertibility as socially acceptable and legitimate, which in turn led to its stabilization as a global policy norm.

In comparison the case of tax reform demonstrates how policy norms can emerge in diametric opposition to their formally valid policy. Tax reform within the IMF was based on 'IMF friendly tax reform' which took place within short-term standardized loan procedures. The Fund shifted its understanding of tax reform over time away from 'associational templates' towards a single world's best practice. Increasingly IMF borrowers tended socially to recognize the policy norm through their statements and loan agreements, regarding the need for IMF friendly tax reform, but tended not culturally to validate it. In this sense then, while the policy norm had both formal validity and social recognition, the policy norm did not have cultural validation. As a result, a process of habitualizing non-adherence to the Fund's policy norm stabilized over time. This process became institutionalized between the borrowers and the Fund whereby IMF staff recognize that tax reform cannot take place within the short loan cycles currently in operation. The tax reform case is unique in the volume for demonstrating how a process of non-compliance with a policy norm can be stabilized through interactions between borrowers and the IMF, even while there is strong formal validity and social recognition for tax reform by all.

The policy norms of capital account liberalization, environmental safeguards and new public management show signs of *subsiding*. Even if a norm has stabilized, become accepted as the global benchmark identifying appropriate action in international development for actors with a given identity, this does not mean that the norm becomes entrenched for eternity. It is always subject to contestation. As described in the norm contestation phase, based on their dispositions actors externalize actions that can be objectivated. This can lead to a new norm emerging. However,

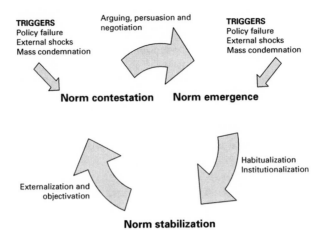

Figure 11.2 Stages of the norm circle and the triggers and mechanisms for change

this is not automatic. For a norm to change, something powerful must propel it, because norms are not merely external to actors (and therefore only a constraint on actions) but are constitutive of actors' identities, which determine their dispositions. As a result, changing norms also change actors' behaviour and identity, though again this is not the focus of the volume per se. As each of the chapters demonstrates, a policy norm may decline as a result of a lack of cultural validity, as is the case with the Bank's attempt to introduce the new public management policy norm into disparate borrowers' development agendas. The experiences of Argentina and Chile in implementing the new public management policy norm demonstrate how cultural validation determines how the policy norm may not easily translate into the domestic context of states according to the Bank's CAS, even with a high degree of social recognition and formal validity. In contrast, capital account liberalization was increasingly viewed within the IMF as vital for furthering international economic development. This was challenged by the outside economics profession and political economy community, but it was not until the financial crisis in Asia in 1997/8 that the policy norm was revealed to be inappropriate as a global benchmark and subsequently modified. In the case of environmental safeguards, the changing political economy of borrowers within the Bank caused a rethink of the use of the formerly institutionalized global safeguard policy norm. These cases demonstrate that there are different triggers for norm decline, although the norm contestation phase within the norm circle leads back to the norm emergence phase. These are represented in Figure 11.2.

Do policy norms reconstitute global development?

Thus far we have examined the various sources, triggers and mechanisms for policy norm emergence and change in the IMF and the World Bank. These were derived from the empirical research conducted in relation to these IOs, but the process of policy norm development could profitably be used to examine the relationship between norms, policy and change within other organizations. Yet the empirical data unearthed in this volume are also valuable in terms of their implications for the future of international development. In this regard, constructivism is important not only in identifying and analysing the construction of meaning (through the policy norm formation and change processes) but also for constructing reality (Guzzini 2000: 149). Regarding the former, the policy norms we examine construct specific understandings of development issues as socially appropriate. These are in different stages of the norm circle (emerging, stabilizing, declining) which indicate their strength in terms of their social acceptance. Regarding the construction of reality, policy norm changes in turn contribute to, and emerge from, broader socio-historical events. The collapse of communism and the untrammelled spread of capitalism at the end of the twentieth and beginning of the twenty-first century helped to trigger the emergence of some of the policy norms examined herein and aided the decline of others. Here we question the connection between the strength of the policy norms currently advocated by the Fund and Bank and what Steven Bernstein (2001) calls a 'norm complex'. Evidence of a norm complex, Bernstein argues, can be 'inferred from specific norms' (Bernstein 2001: 6; Wiener 2009). That is, if a number of similar policy norms promote similar goals, then a norm complex may exist. Hence we aim to analyse what linkages exist between the specific policy norms expounded by the Fund and the Bank at this point in time and the international system of economic development lending. In other words, we question whether we can make inferences about the broader international political economy from the combination of the nine policy norms the Fund and the Bank advocate.

In the introduction we used the Washington Consensus as an example of how the economic development order could change by taking up policy norms that diverge from narrow policy prescriptions for economic growth and development (using the norm circle, see chapter 1). To explain, the Washington Consensus is based on the neoclassical economic model that considers economic growth as *the* precondition for development. Specifically, economic growth will be achieved if inflation is kept low and savings high, or alternatively, by enhancing the capital stock through domestic savings or external transfers, and improving the allocation of resources. Developing countries are assumed to work like developed states, apart from resource allocation which is assumed to be much less efficient owing to market malfunctions. In this context, neoliberalism reiterates classical liberal economic theory to advocate a set of ideas based on the belief that the self-regulation of markets leads to an efficient allocation of resources. The only precondition for a market economy is free and well-functioning competition. Accordingly, development policy should focus on economic liberalization. Development is seen as a technical problem that can be resolved by applying the laws of economics. In other words, economic growth is a precondition for further 'progress' and development in societies, including poverty reduction, equality and sustainability. Development is measured through an increase in GDP per capita. Recognizably this understanding of economic development emerged in the 1980s and consolidated in the 1990s, with attendant policy norms promoted by the IMF and the World Bank.

Five of the policy norms examined here were initially developed with a clear emphasis on neoliberal economic policy prescriptions or were strengthened under the Washington Consensus: capital account liberalization, current account convertibility, tax reform, pension reform and new public management. The case of capital account liberalization is an example of a policy norm currently in decline. This demonstrates that the IMF was forced to add protective measures to the promotion of capital mobility while it failed in the staff bid to become institutionalized in the IMF's Articles of Agreement. The present stabilization of the current account convertibility policy norm, on the other hand, promotes economic openness and 'appropriate' macroeconomic policies. This policy norm could be considered neutral in terms of its contribution to a shift in development that takes other concerns such as social, cultural and environmental issues into account. It is neutral because it promotes economic development directly and poverty reduction indirectly. Both the tax and pension reform policy norms could be thought of as continuing the focus on purely economic development, except that the tax reform policy norm, while formally valid and socially recognized, was a policy norm that stabilized *non-compliance*.

The emergence of the pension reform policy norm by the Bank is also not a clear-cut case of enacting the Washington Consensus because it was motivated by the need to meet the social development requirements of transition economies. Further, changes to the policy norm through norm contestation modified its neoliberal prescriptions, indicating that it now attempts to reconcile social and economic objectives. Finally, the new public management norm did advocate the need to apply private sector solutions to state bureaucracies, but the case examined here demonstrated this policy norm is in decline owing to wavering cultural recognition in developing states like Argentina and Chile. Bar current account convertibility, all economic policy norms that contributed to the Washington Consensus have experienced refinements, adjustments or non-compliance which leave open the door for examining a broader understanding of economic growth and development as an economic *and* social process.[3]

In contradistinction, evidence from a number of policy norms does not fit the Washington Consensus. As a result, this may indicate the emergence of a new norm complex. After the 'lost decade' in the 1980s, when evidence surfaced that economic growth did not automatically lead to the modernization of societies and poverty reduction, the economic growth–poverty reduction nexus changed and so therefore did the definition of the policy problem. Since the late 1990s economic growth and poverty reduction are perceived as equal objectives for development. At times, poverty reduction is even depicted as a prerequisite of economic growth which reverses the causal relationship from the fundamental norm of the 1980s. If poverty reduction is a policy objective to start with rather than an effect of a trickle-down mechanism once economic growth has been achieved, different policies will replace the emphasis on economic development alone.

Some of the policy norms discussed in this volume go beyond narrow economic understandings of the purpose of economic growth and development. Both the multilateral debt relief and the gender and development policy norms focus on social issues. Similarly the shift towards stabilizing the social development policy norm in the Fund illustrates how the organization moved from a narrow focus on economic growth to poverty reduction as being a precondition for growth. In other words, these three policy norms contribute to a broader non-economic or holistic understanding of development. The decline of the environmental safeguard policy norm undermines the perception of a shift to a new broader norm complex. The addition of the environmental agenda to development practice which was initiated by immense protests in the 1980s was one of the first social issues that prompted the critique of the Washington Consensus (Vetterlein 2007). This is not to say that the environmental agenda has disappeared, yet relative to other non-economic issues it has lost some significance inside the World Bank (interview conducted in March 2004 in World Bank headquarters). Operationally, departments, staff and procedures are still in place even though, as chapter 9 details, the Bank's changing relationship with middle income countries is reconfiguring the appropriateness of applying the safeguard policy norm to these

---

[3] Moreover, all of these policy norms follow new transparency and participation procedures.

borrowers. As a result, while we can point to modifications of economic policy norms to incorporate new understandings of economic growth and development, both current account convertibility stabilization and environmental safeguard decline demonstrate a fluid and changing norm complex. As a result, while we cannot definitively say that the collection of policy norms here constitutes a new norm complex, we could argue that one is emerging.

If these nine policy norms are evidence that there has been a shift from the Washington Consensus towards a new norm complex, what might this constitute? Arguably we can point to a broader understanding of economic growth and development that takes economics and society into account. We could call such a norm complex holistic development. Holistic development is not exclusively about economic growth (Elson 2002; Kanbur 2001; Stiglitz 1998a, 1998b). Developing from a traditional to a modern society is therefore as much a cause of an increase in GDP as an effect (Stiglitz 1998a, 1998b). An increase in GDP per capita is therefore conceived as only one of the aims of the development agenda rather than the only one. This defines development as a transformative process that affects a society as a whole. Hence, while the advancement of the economy is still a crucial element of development, it is no longer considered as the only precondition to achieve other goals such as poverty and debt reduction, gender equality and sustainability.

To expand, the idea that the economy or the market is socially embedded, such that social conditions need to be fulfilled in order for the market to function, is nothing new. In *The Great Transformation*, Karl Polanyi (2002 [1944]) argued that markets can never be self-regulating, and that any attempt to turn them into self-regulating systems would fail, leading to large-scale institutional and social changes in societies. For Polanyi, the two world wars of the twentieth century provide evidence to support that thesis. His conception of the 'double movement' meant that those affected by the disembedding of markets would use the state to seek protection. The main lesson learned is that the 'economy is an instituted process' (Polanyi 1957) and cannot be perceived as something distinct from social relations. On the contrary, the market *is* a social practice. Following Polanyi one could argue that from the late 1970s onwards a period of disembedding set in, leading to the Washington Consensus at the policy level in the 1980s and 1990s. Polanyi argued that after a period of severe disembedding of the market from its social context, social forces mobilized to reverse these developments. Dani Rodrik (2000) detects five embedding market requirements for economies in developing countries to function properly: the protection of property rights, the regulation of markets, macroeconomic stabilization, social security and conflict management (Rodrik 2000: 3). Hence, the late 1990s signified a period of re-embeddedness which led to a shift in development thinking reflected in a number of specific policy norms which we argue constitute an emerging holistic development norm complex. Again this is not to attribute norm development as a shift towards a liberal progressive ideal end-point (Risse and Sikkink 1999). Rather we aim to capture the essence of the current mix of policy norms espoused by the IMF and the World Bank. That this may change in the same way that the individual policy norms may emerge, stabilize and decline was emphasized in the introduction.

That a new norm complex may be emerging is based on three shifts in understanding as regards the connections between economics and society. First, Washington Consensus policies were based on economic ideas that had short- to medium-term time horizons for their effectiveness. Based on the assumption of equilibria, the impact of policy reforms on developing states' distribution and growth would yield results within five to ten years. Yet broader understandings of development view such processes as long-term (Kanbur 2001). This is important on an operational level since it is reflected in establishing targets and monitoring indicators. Gore (2000: 794) refers to the Washington Consensus period as one of 'ahistorical performance assessment'. Second, the type of knowledge used in development practice has shifted. The most prominent example is the change from poverty as described merely in terms of income and GDP per capita to the understanding that poverty is a multidimensional problem (World Bank 2001). This has also often been labelled as a more people-centred approach that focuses on qualitative (in terms of experiences) rather than only quantitative (in terms of numbers and economic facts) information. The second dimension of this shift is linked to the new understanding of economic growth and development as a complex transformation process of a society which implies that it is country-specific and path-dependent and thus requires contextual knowledge rather than blueprint approaches. Finally, partnerships and country ownership are stressed in development practice which radically revises assumptions of developing state uniformity in their economic development trajectory and the apolitical nature of economic growth and development.[4] Overall, there is evidence to suggest, from the nine policy norms examined here, that the international development order is in flux, and that the policy norms of the IMF and the World Bank may be contributing to a new norm complex of international economic growth and development.

---

[4] Which procedures were implemented to reflect new policy norms within the Fund and the Bank are detailed throughout the chapters.

Conclusion

The role of the IMF and the World Bank will continue to be important as we move further into the twenty-first century, either through increased lending and policy advice, or through implementing the agenda of the G20. This volume has extended the scholarship on these international organizations in three ways. First, we provided comprehensive empirical analysis of the internal policy-making process of the IMF and the World Bank. Doing so enabled detailed examination of what drives powerful IOs in the international political economy. We unpacked the black box of these IOs to demonstrate the value of going beyond viewing IOs as merely agents that respond to member state demands as propounded by rationalist PA model accounts or beyond assumptions of transnational elites orchestrating IO actions. The volume demonstrates that IOs are as much shaped by their organizational culture and identity as they are by the material and strategic constraints in which they and their staff exist (indeed the former influences how the latter is understood). The book's nine policy areas across the IMF and the World Bank show the limits of conventional PA models and neo-Gramscian approaches with evidence of a variety of sources and triggers for Fund and Bank policy change (with attendant shifts in behaviour) that were rarely instigated by member states. Further, the case studies add to the relatively small number of analyses of IO change. Apart from some exceptions, few comparative IO studies exist (Barnett and Finnemore 2004; Hawkins *et al.* 2006; Miller-Adams 1999). The nine cases in this volume document how the same two organizations respond to different policy fields. Analysing the Fund and the Bank in this way again sheds greater light on the specific identities of these two institutions while also recognizing the potential universality of IO responses to internal and external sources, triggers and mechanisms for policy norm change and their attendant organizational effects.

Second, we identified the various sources, triggers and mechanisms that facilitate how the Fund and the Bank take up norms. This is important again for breaking down the barriers between internal and external, top-down and bottom-up accounts of policy norm change. Specifically, norms can and do emerge from a variety of sources inside and outside the organization (member states, staff, other IOs and NGOs).[5] The triggers of policy norm development are both material and ideational and they can substantially change IO behaviour through perceptions of policy failure,

---

[5] While none of the cases explicitly examined the influence of the private sector, no evidence emerged to suggest that private sector power was at work. This reinforces the argument that transnational elites are not the primary explanatory cause of IO behaviour across a range of issue areas.

external shock and mass condemnation – and often include more than one trigger. Examining the mechanisms of policy norm development provides insight into how norm advocates use a variety of strategies to enhance the take-up of ideas. This could also be applied to understanding not only the development of norms within and by IOs but how norm advocates elsewhere attempt to influence the world. By locating norms within a norm circle the snapshot of a norm's strength may be addressed while not discounting that it may exert structural power only at a certain point in time and may decline in power or regenerate.

Finally, we made the conceptual link between constructivist accounts of policy norm change, where meaning is constructed through a political process, and the meaning of reality – that connects policy norm creation and change to the broader international economic order. In doing so, we argue that the book demonstrates an increasing number of policy norms that bring a social and non-economic awareness to international political economy. On a more practical level, the contributions to this book offer a broad perspective on the policy norms that both organizations currently promote. Discussing them in the context of an emerging norm complex emphasized the extent to which these policy norms fit into an understanding of development that better captures the mix of current policy norms rather than framing international economic development as either the Washington Consensus or the Post-Washington Consensus. Tracing the development of these nine policy norms over time, and singling out the main forces behind their evolution, also serves as a means for future examination into how better to trigger change within these specific IOs, thus changing how we understand and therefore practise international political economy.

Bibliography

Abbot, Kenneth W. and Duncan Snidal 1998. 'Why States Act through Formal International Organizations', *Journal of Conflict Resolution* **42**(1): 3–32.

Abdelal, Rawi 2007. *Capital Rules: the Construction of Global Finance*. Cambridge, MA: Harvard University Press.

Acharya, Amitav 2004. 'How Ideas Spread: Whose Norms Matter? Norm Localization and Institutional Change in Asian Regionalism', *International Organization* **58**(2): 239–75.

Acuña, Carlos and William Smith 1996. 'La lógica política del ajuste estructural: la lógica de apoyo y oposición a las reformas neoliberales', *Desarrollo Económico* **36**(141): 355–89.

Ahluwalia, M. S. 2003. 'IMF Operations and Democratic Governance: Some Issues', Public Address to the General Assembly of the Club de Madrid, 1 November 2003, available at: www.clubmadrid.org, accessed 10 June 2008.

Anders, Gerhard 2005. 'Good Governance as Technology: Toward an Ethnography of the Bretton Woods Institutions', in David Mosse and David Lewis (eds.) *The Aid Effect: Giving and Governing in International Development*. London: Pluto Press: 37–60.

Armijo, Marianela 2002. 'Modernización administrativa y de la gestión publica en Chile', in Luciano Tomassini and Marianela Armijo (eds.) *Reforma y modernización del estado. Experiencias y desafio*. Santiago: LOM Ediciones, Instituto de Asuntos Publicos de la Universidad de Chile.

Atoyan, Ruben and Patrick Conway 2005. 'Evaluating the Impact of IMF Programs: a Comparison of Matching and Instrumental-Variable Estimators', unpublished paper, University of North Carolina at Chapel Hill.

Ayres, Robert L. 1983. *Banking on the Poor: the World Bank and World Poverty*. Cambridge, MA: MIT Press.

Babb, Sarah 2003. 'The IMF in Sociological Perspective: a Tale of Organizational Slippage', *Studies in Comparative International Development* **38**(2): 3–27.

2005. 'The Social Consequences of Structural Adjustment: Recent Evidence and Current Debates', *Annual Review of Sociology* **31**: 199–222.

Babb, Sarah and Ariel Buira 2005. 'Mission Creep, Mission Push and Discretion: the Case of IMF Conditionality', in Ariel Buira (ed.) *The IMF and the World Bank at Sixty*. London: Anthem: 59–84.

Baldwin, David A. 1993. *Neorealism and Neoliberalism*. New York: Columbia University Press.

Barnett, Michael 1999. 'Culture, Strategy and Foreign Policy Change: Israel's Road to Oslo', *European Journal of International Relations* 5(1): 5–36.

Barnett, Michael and Liv Coleman 2005. 'Designing Police: Interpol and the Study of Change in International Organizations', *International Studies Quarterly* 49(4): 593–619.

Barnett, Michael and Martha Finnemore 1999. 'The Politics, Power and Pathologies of International Organizations', *International Organization* 53 (4): 699–732.

2004. *Rules for the World: International Organizations in Global Politics.* Ithaca and London: Cornell University Press.

Barr, Nicholas 1994. *Labor Markets and Social Policy in Central and Eastern Europe: the Transition and Beyond.* New York: Oxford University Press.

2000. *Reforming Pensions: Myths, Truths and Policy Choices*, IMF Working Paper WP/00/139.

2006. 'Pensions: Overview of the Issues', *Oxford Review of Economic Policy* 22 (1): 1–14.

Barro, R. and J. W. Lee 2004. 'IMF Programs: Who is Chosen and What are the Effects?', *Journal of Monetary Economics* 52(7): 1245–69.

Bartkowski, Maciej 2006. 'The Unseen Power of the Professional Cultures Inside the UN Organizations', paper presented at the Annual Meeting of the Midwest Political Science Association, Chicago, April.

Beattie, Roger and Warren McGillivray 1995. 'A Risky Strategy – Reflections on the World Bank Report: Averting the Old Age Crisis', *International Social Security Review* 48(3–4): 5–22.

Bebbington, Anthony, Scott Guggenheim, Elizabeth Olsen and Michael Woolcock 2004. 'Exploring Social Capital Debates at the World Bank', *Journal of Development Studies* 40(5): 33–64.

Bebbington, Anthony, Michael Woolcock and Scott Guggenheim 2006. 'The Ideas–Practice Nexus in International Development Organizations: Social Capital at the World Bank', in Anthony Bebbington, Michael Woolcock, Scott Guggenheim and Elizabeth Olson (eds.) *The Search for Empowerment: Social Capital as Idea and Practice at the World Bank.* Bloomfield, CT: Kumarian Press: 1–21.

Bello, Walden F. 1994. *Dark Victory: the United States, Structural Adjustment, and Global Poverty.* London: Pluto Press.

Bernstein, Steven 2001. *The Compromise of Liberal Environmentalism.* New York: Columbia University Press.

Best, Jacqueline 2005. *The Limits of Transparency.* Ithaca: Cornell University Press.

Bhagwati, Jagdish 1998. 'The Capital Myth: the Difference between Trade in Widgets and Dollars', *Foreign Affairs* 77(3): 7–12.

Bienen, Henry S. and Mark Gerskovitz 1985. 'Economic Stabilization, Conditionality, and Political Stability', *International Organization* 39(4): 728–54.

Bird, Graham 1982. 'Conditionality and the Needs of Developing Countries', *Intereconomics* 17(1): 32–6.

2003. *The IMF and the Future.* London: Routledge.

Birdsall, Nancy (ed.) 2006. *Rescuing the World Bank: a Center for Global Development Working Report and Selected Essays*. Washington, DC: Center for Global Development.

Birdsall, Nancy and John Williamson 2002. *Delivering on Debt Relief: From IMF Gold to a New Aid Architecture*. Washington, DC: Center for Global Development and Institute for International Economics.

Biswas, Asit 1997. 'Water Development and Environment', in Asit Biswas (ed.) *Water Resources: Environment Planning, Management and Development*. New York: McGraw-Hill: 1–36.

Blackmon, Pamela 2008. 'Rethinking Poverty through the Eyes of the International Monetary Fund and the World Bank', *International Studies Review* 10(2): 179–202.

Blyth, Mark 2002. *Great Transformations: Economic Ideas and Institutional Change in the Twentieth Century*. Cambridge University Press.

Bøås, Morten and Desmond McNeill (eds.) 2004. *Global Institutions and Development: Framing the World?* London: Routledge.

Bokkerink, Sasja and Ted van Hees 1998. 'Eurodad's Campaign on Multilateral Debt: the 1996 HIPC Debt Initiative and Beyond', *Development in Practice* 8 (3): 323–34.

Boli, John and Georg M. Thomas 1999. *Constructing World Culture: International Non-Governmental Organizations since 1875*. Stanford University Press.

Bordo, Michael D. and Harold James 2000. *The International Monetary Fund: Its Present Role in Historical Perspective*, NBER Working Paper 7724. Cambridge, MA: National Bureau of Economic Research.

Bordo, Michael D., Ashoka Mody and Nienke Oomes 2004. *Keeping Capital Flowing: the Role of the IMF*, NBER Working Paper 10834. Cambridge, MA: National Bureau of Economic Research.

Borpujari, Jitendra G. 1980. *Toward a Basic Needs Approach to Economic Development with Financial Stability*, IMF Departmental Memorandum DM/80/16. Washington, DC: IMF.

Botchwey, Kwesi, P. Collier, J. W. Cunning and K. Hamada 1998. *Report of the Group of Independent Persons Appointed to Conduct an Evaluation of Certain Aspects of the Enhanced Structural Adjustment Facility*, Parts I and II. Washington, DC: IMF.

Botzman, Mirta and Diana Tussie 1991. 'Argentina y el ocaso del Plan Baker: las negociaciones con Banco Mundial', *Boletín Informativo Techint* (Buenos Aires) 265 (January/February).

Boughton, James M. 2001. *Silent Revolution: the International Monetary Fund, 1979–1989*. Washington, DC: IMF.

   2004. *The IMF and the Force of History: Ten Events and Ten Ideas that have Shaped the Institution*, IMF Working Paper WP/04/75. Washington, DC: IMF, available at: www.imf.org/external/pubs/ft/wp/2004/wp0475.pdf, accessed 30 January 2008.

Bowden, Brett and Leonard Seabrooke (eds.) 2007. *Global Standards of Market Civilization*. London: Routledge.

Bowles, Ian and Cyril Kormos 1999. 'The American Campaign for Environmental Reforms at the World Bank', *The Fletcher Forum of World Affairs* 23(1): 211–25.

Bresser Pereira, Luiz Carlos 1995. 'Development Economics and the World Bank's Identity Crisis', *Review of International Political Economy* **2**(2): 211–47.

Bresser Pereira, Luiz Carlos and Peter Spink (eds.) 1999. *Reforming the State: Managerial Public Administration in Latin America.* Boulder, CO: Lynne Rienner.

Broad, Robin 2006. 'Research, Knowledge and the Art of "Paradigm Maintenance": the World Bank's Development Economics Vice-Presidency (DEC)', *Review of International Political Economy* **13**(3): 387–419.

Brooks, Sarah M. 2004. 'Explaining Capital Account Liberalization in Latin America: a Transitional Cost Approach', *World Politics* **56**(3): 389–430.

2005. 'Interdependent and Domestic Foundations of Policy Change: the Diffusion of Pension Privatization around the World', *International Studies Quarterly* **49**(2): 273–94.

Broome, André 2008. 'The Importance of Being Earnest: the IMF as a Reputational Intermediary', *New Political Economy* **13**(2): 125–51.

2009. 'Money for Nothing: Everyday Actors and Monetary Crises', *Journal of International Relations and Development* **12**(1): 3–30.

2010. *The Currency of Power: the IMF and Monetary Reform in Central Asia.* Basingstoke: Palgrave Macmillan.

Broome, André and Leonard Seabrooke 2007. 'Seeing Like the IMF: Institutional Change in Small Open Economies', *Review of International Political Economy* **14**(4): 576–601.

2008. 'The IMF and Experimentalist Governance in Small Western States', *The Round Table: The Commonwealth Journal of International Affairs* **97**(395): 205–26.

Brune, Nancy 2006. 'Financial Liberalization and Governance in the Developing World', Ph.D. dissertation, Department of Political Science, Yale University.

Brym, Robert J., Stephanie Chung, Sarah Dulmage, Christian Farahat, Mark Greenberg, Manki Ho *et al.* 2005. 'In Faint Praise of the World Bank's Gender Development Policy', *The Canadian Journal of Sociology* **30** (1): 95–111.

Buira, Ariel 2003a. 'An Analysis of IMF Conditionality', paper prepared for the XVI Technical Group Meeting, G24, Port of Spain, Trinidad and Tobago, available at: http://www.unctad.org/en/docs/gdsmdpbg2420033.pdf, accessed 2 May 2010.

Buira, Ariel (ed.) 2003b. *Challenges to the World Bank and IMF: Developing Country Perspectives.* London: Anthem.

Bulíř, Ales and Soojin Moon 2003. *Do IMF-Supported Programs Help Make Fiscal Adjustment More Durable?*, IMF Working Paper WP/03/38. Washington, DC: IMF.

Bull, Hedley 1977. *The Anarchical Society.* London and Basingstoke: Macmillan.

Burki, Shahid Javed and Guillermo E. Perry 1997. *The Long March: a Reform Agenda for Latin America and the Caribbean in the Next Decade*, World Bank Latin America and Caribbean Studies, View Points. Washington, DC: World Bank.

1998. *Beyond the Washington Consensus: Institutions Matter.* Washington, DC: World Bank.

Burn, Gary 1999. 'The State, the City and the Euromarkets', *Review of International Political Economy* 6(2): 225–61.

Busby, Joshua William 2007. 'Bono Made Jesse Helms Cry: Jubilee 2000, Debt Relief, and Moral Action in International Politics', *International Studies Quarterly* 51(2): 247–75.

Callaghy, Thomas 2002. *Innovation in the Sovereign Debt Regime: From the Paris Club to Enhanced HIPC and Beyond*. Washington, DC: World Bank, Operations Evaluation Department.

Camdessus, Michel 1990. 'Aiming for "High Quality Growth"', *Finance & Development* 27(3): 10–11.

1995. 'The IMF and the Challenges of Globalization – the Fund's Evolving Approach to its Constant Mission: the Case of Mexico', address at the Zurich Economics Society, Zurich, Switzerland, 14 November.

Campbell, John L. 1998. 'Institutional Analysis and the Role of Ideas in Political Economy', *Theory and Society* 27(3): 377–409.

Cernea, Michael 1988. *Involuntary Resettlement in Development Projects: Policy Guidelines in World Bank Financed Projects*, World Bank Technical Chapter no. 80. Washington, DC: World Bank.

1993. *Sociologists in a Development Agency: Observations from the World Bank*, World Bank Reprint Series no. 463. Washington, DC: World Bank.

Checkel, Jeffrey 1999. *Why Comply? Constructivism, Social Norms and the Study of International Institutions*, ARENA Working Papers WP 99/24, available at: www.arena.uio.no/, accessed 3 May 2010.

2001. 'Why Comply? Social Learning and European Identity Change', *International Organization* 55(3): 553–88.

2005. 'International Institutions and Socialization in Europe: Introduction and Framework', *International Organization* 59(4): 801–26.

Christensen, Tom and Per Lægreid 2001. 'A Transformative Perspective on Administrative Reforms', in Tom Christensen and Per Lægreid (eds.) *New Public Management: the Transformation of Ideas and Practices*. Aldershot: Ashgate.

Chwieroth, Jeffrey M. 2007a. 'Neoliberal Economists and Capital Account Liberalization in Emerging Markets', *International Organization* 61(2): 443–63.

2007b. 'Testing and Measuring the Role of Ideas: the Case of Neoliberalism in the International Monetary Fund', *International Studies Quarterly* 51(1): 5–30.

2008. 'Norm Change from Within: the International Monetary Fund's Approach to Capital Account Liberalization', *International Studies Quarterly* 52(1): 129–58.

2010. *Capital Ideas: the IMF and the Rise of Financial Liberalization*. Princeton and Oxford: Princeton University Press.

Cichon, Michael 2004. 'Approaching a Common Denominator? An Interim Assessment of World Bank and ILO Position on Pensions', mimeo. Geneva: ILO.

Civic, Mélanne 1997–8. 'Prospects for the Respect and Promotion of Internationally Recognised Sustainable Development Practices: a Case Study of the World Bank Environmental Guidelines and Procedures', *Fordham Environmental Law Journal* 9: 231–60.

Clark, Ann Marie 2001. *Diplomacy of Conscience: Amnesty International and Changing Human Rights Norms.* Princeton University Press.

Collier, Paul 2000. *Consensus-Building, Knowledge and Conditionality.* Washington, DC: World Bank.

Comparative European Politics 2007. Special Issue: 'Contested Meanings of Norms – the Challenge of Democratic Governance Beyond the State', *Comparative European Politics* 5(1).

Cooper, Richard N. 1999. 'Should Capital Controls be Banished?', *Brookings Papers on Economic Activity* 1: 89–141.

Cortell, Andrew P. and Susan Peterson 1999. 'Altered States: Explaining Domestic Institutional Change', *British Journal of Political Science* 29(1): 277–303.

Cox, Robert W. and Harold K. Jacobson 1989. 'The Framework for Inquiry', in Paul F. Diehl (ed.) *The Politics of International Organizations: Patterns and Insights.* Pacific Grove, CA: Brooks/Cole: 101–16.

1999. 'Decision-Making', in Robert W. Cox and Timothy J. Sinclair (eds.) *Approaches to World Order.* Cambridge University Press: 349–75.

Crawford, Gordon 2006. 'The World Bank and Good Governance: Rethinking the State or Consolidating Neo-Liberalism?', in Alberto Paloni and M. Zanardi (eds.) *The IMF, World Bank and Policy Reform.* London: Routledge: 115–41.

Cunill Grau, Nuria 1997. 'Repensando lo público a través de la sociedad', Centro Latinoamencaro de Administracíon para el Desarrollo (CLAD). Caracas: Nueva Sociedad.

Cutler, Claire 2003. *Private Power and Global Authority: Transnational Merchant Law in the Global Political Economy.* Cambridge University Press.

Danaher, Kevin 1994. *50 Years is Enough: the Case against the World Bank and the International Monetary Fund.* Boston, MA: South End Press.

Davis, Gloria 2004. *A History of the Social Development Network in the World Bank, 1973–2002,* Social Development Chapters no. 56. Washington, DC: World Bank.

Davis, Shelton 1994. 'The World Bank and Indigenous Peoples', in Lydia van de Fliert (ed.) *Indigenous Peoples and International Organisations.* Nottingham: Spokesman: 75–83.

Dawson, Thomas C. 2002. 'The IMF's Role in Asia: Part of the Problem or Part of the Solution?', prepared text for remarks, Institute of Policy Studies and Singapore Management University Forum. Singapore, 10 July, available at: www.imf.org/external/np/speeches/2002/071002.htm, accessed 3 September 2007.

Deacon, Bob and Michelle Hulse with Paul Stubbs 1997. *Global Social Policy: International Organizations and the Future of Welfare.* London, Thousand Oaks and New Delhi: Sage.

Deaton, Angus 2006. *An Evaluation of World Bank Research, 1998–2005,* WB 18913. Washington, DC: World Bank, available at: http://econ.worldbank.org/ WBSITE/EXTERNAL/EXTDEC/EXTRESEARCH/0,,%20contentMDK: 21165468~menuPK:598503~pagePK:64165401~piPK:64165026~theSitePK: 469382,00.html, accessed 12 June 2007.

Dennis, Suzanne and Elaine Zuckerman 2006. *Gender Guide to World Bank and IMF Policy-Based Lending Action*, available at: www.genderaction.org, accessed 17 June 2008.

Development Committee 1990. *Development Issues, Presentations to the 39th Meeting of the Development Committee*, Development Committee Pamphlet no. 26. Washington, DC: IMF.

Dicks-Mireaux, Louis, Mauro Mecagni and Susan Schadler 2000. 'Evaluating the Effect of IMF Lending to Low-Income Countries', *Journal of Development Economics* **61**(2): 495–526.

DiMaggio, Paul and Walter Powell 1991. 'The Iron Cage Revisited: Institutional Isomorphism and Collective Rationality in Organizational Fields', in Walter Powell and Paul DiMaggio (eds.) *The New Institutionalism in Organizational Analysis*. Chicago University Press: 63–81.

Dimitrakopoulos, Dionyssis and Argyris Passas 2003. 'International Organizations and Domestic Administrative Reform', in B. Guy Peters and Jon Pierre (eds.) *Handbook of Public Administration*. London: Sage: 440–50.

Disney, Richard 1999. *Notional Accounts as a Pension Reform Strategy: an Evaluation*. Pension Reform Primer Discussion Paper 21302. Washington, DC: World Bank.

Dixon, John, Lee Talbot and Guy Le Moigne 1989. *Dams and the Environment: Considerations in World Bank Projects*, World Bank Technical Chapter no. 110. Washington, DC: World Bank.

Dixon, Nancy 1994. *Organizational Learning Cycle: How We Can Learn Collectively*. Maidenhead: McGraw-Hill.

Dolowitz, David and David Marsh 1996. 'Who Learns What from Whom: a Review of the Policy Transfer Literature', *Political Studies* **44**(2): 343–57.

Dornbusch, Rüdiger 1998. 'Capital Controls: an Idea Whose Time is Past', in *Should the IMF Pursue Capital Account Convertibility?*, Essays in International Finance, International Finance Section, Department of Economics, Princeton University, No. 207: 47–54.

Dreher, Axel 2006. 'IMF and Economic Growth: the Effects of Programs, Loans, and Compliance with Conditionality', *World Development* **34**(5): 769–88.

Dreher, Axel and Nathan M. Jensen 2007. 'Independent Actor or Agent? an Empirical Analysis of the Impact of US Interests on IMF Conditions', *The Journal of Law and Economics* **50**(1): 105–24.

Drori, Gili S., John W. Meyer and Hokyu Hwang (eds.) 2006a. *Globalization and Organization: World Society and Organizational Change*. Oxford: Oxford University Press.

Drori, Gili S., Yong Suk Jang and John W. Meyer 2006b. 'Sources of Rationalized Governance: Cross-National Longitudinal Analyses, 1985–2002', *Administrative Science Quarterly* **51**(2): 205–29.

Dunleavy, Patrick 1997. 'The Globalisation of Public Services Production: Can Government Be "Best in World"?', in Andrew Massey (ed.) *Globalization and Marketization of Government Services: Comparing Contemporary Public Sector Developments*. University of Portsmouth Press.

Edison, Hali J., Michael Klein, Luca Ricci and Torsten Sløk 2002. *Capital Account Liberalization and Economic Performance: Survey and Synthesis*, Working Paper No. 02/120. Washington, DC: IMF.

Eichengreen, Barry 1996. *Globalizing Capital: a History of the International Monetary System*. Princeton University Press.

Eichengreen, Barry, Michael Mussa, Giovanni Dell'Ariccia, Erinca Detragiache, Gian Maria Milesi-Ferretti and Andrew Tweedie 1999. *Liberalizing Capital Movements: Some Analytical Issues*, Economic Issues No. 17. Washington, DC: IMF.

Einhorn, Jessica 2001. 'The World Bank's Mission Creep', *Foreign Affairs* 80(5): 22–35.

Elson, Diane 2002. 'Gender Justice, Human Rights and Neoliberal Economic Policies', in Maxine Molyneux and Shahra Razavi (eds.) *Gender Justice, Development and Rights*. Oxford University Press: 78–114.

Emmerji, Louis, Richard Jolly and Thomas G. Weiss 2005. 'Economic and Social Thinking at the UN in Historical Perspective', *Development and Change* 36(2): 211–35.

Evans, Huw 1999. 'Debt Relief for the Poorest Countries: Why Did it Take so Long?', *Development Policy Review* 17: 267–79.

Evans, Peter and Martha Finnemore 2001. 'Organizational Reform and the Expansion of the South's Voice at the Fund', paper prepared for the G24 Technical Group Meeting, Washington, DC, 17–18 April.

Evrensel, Ayşe 2002. 'Effectiveness of IMF-Supported Stabilization Programs in Developing Countries', *Journal of International Money and Finance* 21(5): 565–87.

Falkner, Robert 2008. *Business Power and Conflict in International Environmental Politics*. Houndmills, Basingstoke: Palgrave Macmillan.

Feldstein, Martin 1999. 'Refocusing the IMF', *Foreign Affairs* 77: 20–33.

Fierke, Karin M., and Antje Wiener 1999. 'Constructing Institutional Interests: EU and NATO Enlargement', *Journal of European Public Policy* 6(5): 721–42.

Finnemore, Martha 1993. 'International Organizations as Teachers of Norms: the United Nations Educational, Scientific, and Cultural Organization and Science Policy', *International Organization* 47(4): 565–97.

1996. *National Interests in International Society*. Ithaca and London: Cornell University Press.

Finnemore, Martha and Kathryn Sikkink 1998. 'International Norm Dynamics and Political Change', *International Organization* 52(4): 887–917.

1999. 'International Norm Dynamics and Political Change', in Peter J. Katzenstein, Robert O. Keohane and Stephen D. Krasner (eds.) *Exploration and Contestation in the Study of World Politics*. Cambridge, MA: MIT Press: 247–77.

Finnemore, Martha and Stephen J. Toope 2001. 'Alternatives to "Legalization": Richer Views of Law and Politics', *International Organization* 55(3): 743–58.

Fischer, Stanley 1997. 'Capital Account Liberalization and the Role of the IMF', paper presented at the IMF's Seminar on Asia and the IMF, Hong Kong, 19 September, Washington, DC: IMF.

Fjeldstad, Odd-Helge and Lise Rakner 2003. *Taxation and Tax Reforms in Developing Countries: Illustrations from Sub-Saharan Africa*, CMI Report

2003(6). Bergen: Chr. Michelsen Institute Development Studies and Human Rights.

Flejzor, Lauren 2007. 'Explaining Change in the World Bank's Forest Strategy and Operational Policy', in Diane Stone and Christopher Wright (eds.) *World Bank and Governance: a Decade of Reform and Reaction*. London and New York: Routledge: 88–108.

Flockhart, Trine 2006. '"Complex Socialization": a Framework for the Study of State Socialization', *European Journal of International Relations* 12(1): 89–118.

Florini, Ann 1996. 'The Evolution of International Norms', *International Studies Quarterly* 40(3): 363–89.

Fourcade-Gourinchas, Marion and Sarah L. Babb 2002. 'The Rebirth of the Liberal Creed: Paths to Neoliberalism in Four Countries', *American Journal of Sociology* 108(3): 533–79.

Fox, Jonathan A. 1998. 'When Does Reform Policy Influence Practice? Lessons from the Bankwide Resettlement Review', in Jonathan A. Fox and L. David Brown (eds.) *The Struggle for Accountability: the World Bank, NGOs and Grassroots Movements*. Cambridge, MA, and London: MIT Press: 303–44.

2000. 'The World Bank Inspection Panel: Lessons from the First Five Years', *Global Governance* 6(3): 279–318.

Galbis, Vicente 1996. *Currency Convertibility and the Fund: Review and Prognosis*, IMF Working Paper WP/96/39. Washington, DC: IMF.

Garuda, Gopal 2000. 'The Distributional Effects of IMF Programs: a Cross-Country Analysis', *World Development* 28(6): 1031–51.

Gemayal, Edward R. and David A. Grigorian 2006. 'How Tight is Too Tight? A Look at Welfare Implications of Distortionary Policies in Uzbekistan', *The European Journal of Comparative Economics* 3(2): 239–61.

George, Susan and Fabrizio Sabelli 1994. *Faith and Credit: the World Bank's Secular Empire*. Boulder, CO: Westview Press.

Germain, Randall D. 1997. *The International Organization of Credit: States and Global Finance in the World-Economy*. Cambridge University Press.

Gerster, Richard 1982. 'The IMF and Basic Needs Conditionality', *Journal of World Trade Law* 16(November/December): 497–517.

Ghio, José María 2002. 'Modernización administrativa y de la gestión publica en Argentina', in Luciano Tomassini and Marianela Armijo (eds.) *Reforma y modernización del Estado. Experiencias y desafío*. Santiago: LOM Ediciones, Instituto de Asuntos Publicos de la Universidad de Chile.

Ghio, José María and Sebastián Etchemendi 1998. 'Fugindo do perigo: a política de reforma administrativa na Argentina de Menem', *Revista do Serviço Público* 49(2): 33–56.

Gold, Joseph 1984. 'Legal Models for the International Regulation of Exchange Rates', *Michigan Law Review* 82(5/6): 1533–54.

Goldman, Michael 2005. *Imperial Nature: the World Bank and Struggles for Social Justice in the Age of Globalization*. Yale University Press.

Goldstein, Judith and Robert O. Keohane 1993. 'Ideas and Foreign Policy: an Analytical Framework', in Judith Goldstein and Robert O. Keohane (eds.) *Ideas and Foreign Policy: Beliefs, Institutions, and Political Change*. Ithaca: Cornell University Press: 3–30.

Goodland, Robert 2000. *Social and Environmental Assessment to Promote Sustainability: An Informal View from the World Bank*, Environment Department Papers no. 74. Washington, DC: Environmentally and Socially Sustainable Development, World Bank.

Goodland, Robert and George Ledec 1989. 'Wildlands: Balancing Conversion with Conservation in World Bank Projects', *Environment* 31(9): 6–35.

Gore, Charles 2000. 'The Rise and Fall of the Washington Consensus as a Paradigm for Developing Countries', *World Development* 28(5): 789–804.

Gould, Erica R. 2003. 'Money Talks: Supplementary Financiers and International Monetary Fund Conditionality', *International Organization* 57 (3): 551–86.

Gow, James Ian and Caroline Dufour 2000. 'Le nouveau management public est-il un paradigme? Cela a-t-il de l'importance?', *Revue Internationale des Sciences Administratifs* 4: 679–707.

Grabel, Ilene 2000. 'The Political Economy of "Policy Credibility": The New-Classical Macroeconomics and the Remaking of Emerging Economies', *Cambridge Journal of Economics* 24(1): 1–19.

Graham, George and Stephanie Flanders 1995. 'Enthusiasm Cools for Debt Relief Proposal', *Financial Times*, 4 October: 4.

Gray, Andrew 1998. 'Development Policy – Development Protest: the World Bank, Indigenous Peoples and NGOs', in Jonathan Fox and L. Dave Brown (eds.) *The Struggle for Accountability: the World Bank, NGOs and Grassroots Movements*. Cambridge, MA: MIT Press: 267–302.

Grimes, William W. 2003. 'Internationalization of the Yen and the New Politics of Monetary Insulation', in Jonathan Kirshner (ed.) *Monetary Orders: Ambiguous Economics, Ubiquitous Politics*. Ithaca: Cornell University Press: 172–94.

Gstöhl, Sieglinde 2007. 'Governance through Government Networks: the G8 and International Organizations', *Review of International Organizations* 2(1): 1–37.

Guitián, Manuel 1996a. 'Concepts and Degrees of Currency Convertibility', in Manuel Guitián and Saleh M. Nsouli (eds.) *Currency Convertibility in the Middle East and North Africa*. Washington, DC: IMF: 21–33.

1996b. 'The Issue of Capital Account Convertibility: a Gap between Norms and Reality', in Manuel Guitián and Saleh M. Nsouli (eds.) *Currency Convertibility in the Middle East and North Africa*. Washington, DC: IMF: 169–88.

Gupta, Sanjeev and Karim Nashashibi 1990. 'Poverty Concerns in Fund-Supported Programs', *Finance & Development* 27 (September): 12–14.

Gupta, Sanjeev Louis Dicks-Mireaux, Ritha Khemani, Calvin Macdonald and Marijn Verhoeven 2000. *Social Issues in IMF-Supported Programs*, Occasional Paper no. 191. Washington, DC: IMF.

Gutner, Tamar L. 2002. *Banking on the Environment: Multilateral Development Banks and their Environmental Performance in Central and Eastern Europe*. Cambridge, MA: MIT Press.

2005a. 'Explaining the Gaps between Mandate and Performance: Agency Theory and World Bank Environmental Reform', *Global Environmental Politics* 5(2): 10–37.

2005b. 'World Bank Environmental Reform: Revisiting Lessons from Agency Theory', *International Organization* 59(3): 773–83.

Guzzini, Stefano 2000. 'A Reconstruction of Constructivism in International Relations', *European Journal for International Relations* **6**(2): 147–82.

Gwin, Catherine 1994. *US Relations with the World Bank 1945–92*, Brookings Occasional Chapters. Washington, DC: Brookings Institution.

Haas, Ernst B. 1990. *When Knowledge is Power: Three Models of Change in International Organizations.* Berkeley and Oxford: University of California Press.

Haas, Peter M. 1992. 'Introduction: Epistemic Communities and International Policy Co-ordination', *International Organization* **46**(1): 1–35

Haas, Peter M. and Ernst B. Haas 1995. 'Learning to Learn: Improving International Governance', *Global Governance* **1**(3): 255–85.

Hafner-Burton, Emilie and Mark Pollack 2002. 'Mainstreaming Gender in Global Governance', *European Journal of International Relations* **8**(3): 339–73.

Haggard, Stephan 1985. 'The Politics of Adjustment: Lessons from the IMF's Extended Fund Facility', *International Organization* **39**(3): 505–34.

Hall, Anthony 2007. 'Social Policies in the World Bank: Paradigms and Challenges', *Global Social Policy* **7**(2): 151–75.

Hall, Rodney Bruce 2003. 'The Discursive Demolition of the Asian Development Model', *International Studies Quarterly* **47**(1): 71–99.

Hall, Rodney Bruce and Thomas J. Biersteker (eds.) 1999. *The Emergence of Private Authority in Global Governance.* Cambridge University Press.

Hannan, Carolyn 2002. 'Gender Mainstreaming in the Work of the World Bank: Identifying the Potentials and the Challenges', presentation at a panel organized by the World Bank as a side-event to the 46th session of the Commission on the Status of Women, 4–15 March.

    2004. 'Gender Mainstreaming: a Key Strategy for Promoting Gender Equality at the National Level', UN-ESCP High-level Intergovernmental Meeting to Review Regional Implementation of the Beijing Platform for Action and its Regional and Global Outcomes. Bangkok, Thailand, 7–10 September.

Hassdorf, Wolf 2005. 'Emperor without Clothes: Financial Market Sentiment and the Limits of British Currency Machismo in the ERM Crisis', *Millennium: Journal of International Studies* **33**(3): 691–722.

Hawkins, Darren G., David A. Lake, Daniel L. Nielson and Michael J. Tierney (eds.) 2006. *Delegation and Agency in International Organizations.* Cambridge University Press.

Hedberg, Bo 1981. 'How Organizations Learn and Unlearn', in Paul C. Nystrom and William H. Starbuck (eds.) *Handbook of Organizational Design.* Oxford: Oxford University Press: 3–27.

Helleiner, Eric 1994. *States and the Reemergence of Global Finance: From Bretton Woods to the 1990s.* Ithaca: Cornell University Press.

Helleiner, Gerald K. 1987. 'Stabilization, Adjustment, and the Poor', *World Development* **15**(12): 1499–513.

Heller, Peter S., A. Lans Bovenberg, Thanos Catsambas, Ke-Young Chu and Parthasarathi Shame 1988. *The Implications of Fund-Supported Adjustment Programs for Poverty: Experiences in Selected Countries*, Occasional Paper No. 58. Washington, DC: IMF.

Hemming, Richard 2003. 'Policies to Promote Fiscal Discipline', paper presented to the Workshop on Internationalization and Policy Transfer, Tulane University, 11–12 April.

Hertz, Noreena 2004. *The Debt Threat: How Debt is Destroying the Developing World*. New York: Harper Business.

Hobson, John M. and Leonard Seabrooke (eds.) 2007. *Everyday Politics of the World Economy*. Cambridge University Press.

Holder, Jane 2004. *Environmental Assessment: the Regulation of Decision-Making*. Oxford University Press.

Holman, Michael 1995. 'IMF Cool to World Bank Debt Plan', *Financial Times*, 15 September: 6.

Holzmann, Robert and Joseph I. Stiglitz 2001. *New Ideas about Old Age Security – Toward Sustainable Pension Systems in the 21st Century*. Washington, DC: World Bank.

Hood, Christopher 1991. 'A Public Management for All Seasons?', *Public Administration* **69**(1): 3–19.

  1998. *The Art of the State: Culture, Rhetoric and Public Management*. Oxford University Press.

Huneeus, Carlos 2000. 'Technocrats and Politicians in an Authoritarian Regime: the "ODEPLAN Boys" and the "Gremialists" in Pinochet's Chile', *Journal of Latin American Studies* **23**(2): 461–501.

Hunter, David 2008. 'Civil Society Networks and the Development of Environmental Standards at the International Financial Institutions', *Chicago Journal of International Law* **8**(2): 437–77.

Hurrell, Andrew 2005. 'Power, Institutions and the Production of Inequality', in Michael Barnett and Raymond Duvall (eds.) *Power in Global Governance*. Cambridge University Press: 33–58.

Ikenberry, G. John 1993. 'Creating Yesterday's New World Order: Keynesian "New Thinking" and the Anglo-American Postwar Settlement', in Judith Goldstein and Robert O. Keohane (eds.) *Ideas and Foreign Policy: Beliefs, Institutions, and Political Change*. Ithaca: Cornell University Press: 57–86.

Independent Evaluation Office (IEO) 2003a. *Fiscal Adjustment in IMF-Supported Programs*. Washington, DC: IMF.

  2003b. *The IMF and Recent Capital Account Crises*. Washington, DC: IMF.

  2004. *Report on the Evaluation of Poverty Reduction Strategy Papers (PRSPs) and the Poverty Reduction and Growth Facility*. Washington, DC: IMF.

  2005. *The IMF's Approach to Capital Account Liberalization*. Washington, DC: IMF.

Institute of International Finance 1999. Executive Summary, unpublished memorandum, 20 January. Washington, DC: IIF Working Group on the Liberalization of Capital Movements, Institute of International Finance.

International Labour Organization (ILO) 2000. *Social Security Pensions – Development and Reform*. Geneva: ILO.

International Monetary Fund (IMF) 1984. *Review of Multiple Exchange Rate Regimes – Background Information*, SM/84/65, prepared by the Exchange and Trade Relations Department. Washington, DC: IMF.

  1986. *Fund-Supported Programs, Fiscal Policy, and Income Distribution*, IMF Occasional Paper no. 46. Washington, DC: IMF.

1990a. *The Fund and Poverty Issues – Report on Recent Experience*, Internal Document EBS/90/19. Washington, DC: IMF, The Secretary.

1990b. *Major Issues in the Evolving International Monetary System: Characteristics of a Successful Exchange Rate System*, EBS/90/15, prepared by the Research Department. Washington, DC: IMF.

1992. *Biennial Review of the Fund's Surveillance Policy*, SM/92/234, prepared by the Policy Development and Review and Research Departments. Washington, DC: IMF.

1993a. *Social Safety Net in Economic Reform*, Internal Document EBS/93/34. Washington, DC: IMF, The Secretary.

1993b. 'Surveillance over Exchange Rate Policies – Review', EBM/93/13, *Executive Board Meeting Minutes*. Washington, DC: IMF.

1993c. 'Surveillance over Exchange Rate Policies – Review', EBM/93/14, *Executive Board Meeting Minutes*. Washington, DC: IMF.

1993d. 'Surveillance over Exchange Rate Policies – Review', EBM/93/15, *Executive Board Meeting Minutes*. Washington, DC: IMF.

1995a. *Capital Account Convertibility: Review of Experience and Implications for Fund Policies*, SM/95/164 (7 July). Washington, DC: IMF Archives.

1995b. *Issues and Developments in Multilateral Debt and Financing of the Heavily Indebted Poor Countries (HIPCs)*, SM/95/29 (7 February). Washington, DC: IMF.

1995c. *Issues and Developments in Multilateral Debt and Financing for the Heavily Indebted Poor Countries – Further Consideration* (30 March). Washington, DC: IMF Archives.

1995d. *Minutes of Executive Board Meeting 95/19*, EBM 95/12 (24 February). Washington, DC: IMF Archives.

1995e. *Minutes of Executive Board Meeting 95/39*, EBM/95/39 (12 April). Washington, DC: IMF Archives.

1995f. *Minutes of Executive Board Meeting 95/73*, EBM/95/73 (28 July). Washington, DC: IMF Archives.

1995g. *Multilateral Debt of the Heavily Indebted Poor Countries*, SM/95/30 (9 February). Washington, DC: IMF Archives.

1995h. *Official Financing for Developing Countries and their Debt Situation*, SM/95/224 (1 September). Washington, DC: IMF Archives.

1995i. *Proceedings of the Headquarter's Conference on Income Distribution and Sustainable Growth*, Internal Document Sec/Circ/95/77. Washington, DC: IMF, The Secretary.

1996a. *Analytic Aspects of the Debt Problems of Heavily Indebted Poor Countries*, SM/96/23 (31 January). Washington, DC: IMF Archives.

1996b. *Debt Sustainability Analysis for the Heavily Indebted Poor Countries*, SM/96/22 (31 January). Washington, DC: IMF Archives.

1996c. 'Joint Press Conference by Philippe Maystadt, Chairman Interim Committee and Michel Camdessus', Managing Director, International Monetary Fund (29 September), available at: www.imf.org/external/np/tr/1996/tr960929.htm, accessed 2 May 2010.

1996d. *Minutes of Executive Board Meeting 96/12*, EBM/96/12 (12 February). Washington, DC: IMF Archives.

1996e. *Minutes of Executive Board Meeting 96/13*, EBM/96/13 (20 February). Washington, DC: IMF Archives.

1996f. *Minutes of Executive Board Meeting 96/24*, EBM/96/24 (20 March). Washington, DC: IMF Archives.

1996g. *Minutes of Executive Board Meeting 96/34*, EBM/96/34 (8 April). Washington, DC: IMF Archives.

1996h. *Proposed Action to Resolve the Debt Problems of the Heavily Indebted Poor Countries*, SM/96/57 (6 March). Washington, DC: IMF Archives.

1997a. *Interim Committee Statement on the Liberalization of Capital Movements under an Amendment of the IMF's Articles*, IMF Survey (6 October), available at: www.imf.org/external/np/sec/pr/1997/PR9744.HTM, accessed 2 May 2010.

1997b. *Review of Experience with Capital Account Liberalization and Strengthened Procedures Adopted by the Fund*, SM/97/32 Supplement 1 (6 February). Washington, DC: IMF Archives.

1998a. *Developments and Issues in the International Exchange and Payments System*, SM/98/172 (7 July). Washington, DC: IMF Archives.

1998b. *The IMF and the Poor*, Pamphlet Series no. 52. Washington, DC: IMF, Fiscal Affairs Department.

1998c. *International Capital Markets: Developments, Prospects, and Key Policy Issues*. Washington, DC: IMF.

1998d. *Minutes of Executive Board Meeting 98/38*, EBM/98/38 (2 April). Washington, DC: IMF Archives.

1998e. *Minutes of Executive Board Meeting 98/103*, EBM/98/103 (23 September). Washington, DC: IMF Archives.

1998f. 'Should Equity Be a Goal of Economic Policy?', *Economic Issues* no. 16. Washington, DC: IMF, Fiscal Affairs Department.

1998g. *Theoretical and Practical Aspects of Capital Account Liberalization*, SM/98/187 (17 July). Washington, DC: IMF Archives.

2000. 'IMF: a Virtually Universal Institution. Camdessus Years Marked by Progressive Process of Harnessing Globalization Benefits for all Members', *IMF Survey*, Special Supplement (February).

2007a. *Annual Report of the Executive Board for the Financial Year Ended 30 April 2007*. Washington, DC: IMF, available at: www.imf.org/external/pubs/ft/ar/2007/eng/pdf/file7.pdf, accessed 10 February 2008.

2007b. *Review of Exchange Arrangements, Restrictions, and Controls*. Washington, DC: IMF, available at: www.imf.org/external/np/pp/2007/eng/112707.pdf, accessed 12 February 2008.

2007c. *World Economic Outlook*, October edition. Washington, DC: IMF.

2008. *Articles of Agreement of the International Monetary Fund*. Washington, DC: IMF, available at: www.imf.org/external/pubs/ft/aa/index.htm, accessed 20 June 2008.

2009. *Initial Lessons of the Crisis*. Washington, DC: International Monetary Fund, available at: www.imf.org/external/np/pp/eng/2009/020609.pdf, accessed 2 May 2010.

International Monetary Fund (IMF) and World Bank 2001. *Macroeconomic Policy and Poverty Reduction*. Washington, DC: World Bank.

International Organization (IO) 2005. Special issue: 'International Institutions and Socialization in Europe', *International Organization* **59**(4).

Jachtenfuchs, Markus 1996. *International Policy-Making as a Learning Process? The European Union and the Greenhouse Effect*. Aldershot: Aveburg.

Jäger, Johannes, Gerhard Melinz and Susan Zimmermann 2001. *Sozialpolitik in der Peripherie. Entwicklungsmuster und Wandel in Lateinamerika, Afrika, Asien und Osteuropa*. Frankfurt: Brandes & Apsel.

James, Estelle 1996. *Protecting the Old and Promoting Growth – a Defense of Averting the Old Age Crisis*, Policy Research Working Paper 1570. Washington, DC: World Bank, Policy Research Department, Poverty and Human Resources Division.

1997a. *New Systems for Old Age Security: Theory, Practice, and Empirical Evidence*, Policy Research Working Paper 1766. Washington, DC: World Bank, Policy Research Department, Poverty and Human Resources Division.

1997b. *Pension Reform – Is There a Tradeoff between Efficiency and Equity?*, Policy Research Working Paper 1767. Washington, DC: World Bank, Policy Research Department, Poverty and Human Resources Division.

1998. 'New Models for Old-Age Security: Experiments, Evidence, and Unanswered Questions', *World Bank Research Observer* **13**(2): 271–301.

James, Estelle, James H. Smalhout and Dimitri Vittas 2001. *Administrative Costs and the Organization of Individual Retirement Systems: a Comparative Perspective*. Policy Research Working Paper no. 255. Washington, DC: World Bank, Development Research Group, Finance.

James, Harold 1996. *International Monetary Co-operation since Bretton Woods*. Washington, DC: IMF and Oxford University Press.

James, Oliver 2001. 'Business Models and the Transfer of Businesslike Central Government Agencies', *Governance: an International Journal of Policy and Administration* **14**(2): 233–52.

Jepperson, Ronald, Alexander Wendt and Peter J. Katzenstein 1996. 'Norms, Identity, and Culture in National Security', in Peter J. Katzenstein (ed.) *The Culture of National Security: Norms and Identity in World Politics*. New York: Columbia University Press: 33–75.

Jochnick, Chris and Fraser A. Preston (eds.) 2006. *Sovereign Debt at the Crossroads: Challenges and Proposals for Resolving the Third World Debt Crisis*. Oxford University Press.

Johnson, Omotunde and Joanne Salop 1980. 'Distributional Aspects of Stabilization Programs in Developing Countries', *IMF Staff Papers* **27** (March): 1–23.

Johnston, Alistair Ian 2001. 'Treating International Institutions as Social Environments', *International Studies Quarterly* **45**(4): 487–515.

Joyce, Joseph P. 2002. 'Through a Glass Darkly: New Questions (and Answers) about IMF Programs', *Wellesley College Working Paper 2002–04*. Wellesley, MA: Wellesley College.

Kakwani, Nanak and Kalanidhi Subbarao 2005. *Aging and Poverty in Africa and the Role of Social Pensions*, Social Protection Discussion Paper no. 0521. Washington, DC: World Bank.

Kanbur, Ravi 1987. 'Measurement and Alleviation of Poverty: With an Application to the Effects of Macroeconomic Adjustment', *IMF Staff Papers* 34(March): 60–85.

    2001. 'Economic Policy Distribution and Poverty: the Nature of Disagreements', *World Development* 29(6): 1083–94.

Kardam, Nuket 1991. *Bringing Women In: Women's Issues in International Development Programs*. Boulder, CO: Lynne Rienner.

    1993. 'Development Approaches and the Role of Policy Advocacy: the Case of the World Bank', *World Development* 2(11): 1773–86.

Katzenstein, Peter J. 1996. *Cultural Norms and National Security: Police and Military in Postwar Japan*. Ithaca: Cornell University Press.

Katzenstein Peter J., Robert O. Keohane and Stephen D. Krasner (eds.) 1999. *Exploration and Contestation in the Study of World Politics*. Cambridge, MA: MIT Press: 247–77.

Keck, Margaret and Kathryn Sikkink 1998. *Activists beyond Borders: Advocacy Networks in International Politics*. Ithaca: Cornell University Press.

Keeler, John T. S. 1993. 'Opening the Window for Reform: Mandates, Crises, and Extraordinary Policy-Making', *Comparative Political Studies* 25(4): 433–86.

Kelley, Judith 2004. 'International Actors on the Domestic Scene: Membership Conditionality and Socialization by International Institutions', *International Organisation* 58(3): 425–57.

Kende-Robb, Caroline 2003. *Poverty and Social Analysis – Linking Macroeconomic Policies to Poverty Outcomes: Summary of Early Experiences*, IMF Working Paper WP/03/43. Washington, DC: IMF.

Keohane, Robert 1988. 'International Institutions: Two Approaches', *International Studies Quarterly* 32(4): 379–96.

Khagram, Sanjeev 2004. *Dams and Development: Transnational Struggles for Water and Power*. Ithaca: Cornell University Press.

Khagram, Sanjeev, James V. Riker and Kathryn Sikkink (eds.) 2002. *Restructuring World Politics: Transnational Social Movements, Networks, and Norms*. Minneapolis: University of Minnesota Press.

Khundker, Nasreen 2004. 'A Gentle Touch? Gender and the World Bank: a Critical Assessment', paper prepared for 'Reforming the World Bank: Will the Gender Mainstreaming Strategy Make a Difference?' Washington, DC, January, available at: www.boell.org/docs/Khundker_GentleTouch.pdf, accessed 17 June 2008.

Killick, Tony 1982. *The Impact of the IMF Stabilisation Programmes in Developing Countries*, ODI Working Paper 7. London: ODI.

    (ed.) 1984. *The Quest for Economic Stabilization: the IMF and the Third World*. London: Heinemann Educational and ODI.

Kingsbury, Benedict 1999. 'Operational Policies of International Institutions as Part of the Law-Making Process: the World Bank and Indigenous Peoples', in Guy Goodwin-Gill and Stefan Talmon (eds.) *The Reality of International Law: Essays in Honour of Ian Brownlie*. Oxford: Clarendon Press: 323–42.

Kirshner, Jonathan 1999. 'Keynes, Capital Mobility, and the Crisis of Embedded Liberalism', *Review of International Political Economy* 6(3): 313–37.

Klotz, Audie 1995. *Norms in International Relations: the Struggle against Apartheid.* Ithaca: Cornell University Press.

Kolk, Ans 1996. *Forests in International Environmental Politics: International Organisations, NGOs and the Brazilian Amazon.* Netherlands: International Books.

Kopp-Malek, Tanja, Martin Koch and Alexandra Lindenthal 2009. *Die Europäische Kommission als lernende Organisation?* Wiesbaden: VS Verlag.

Kose, M. Ayhan, Eswar Prasad, Kenneth Rogoff and Shang-Jin Wei 2006. *Financial Globalization: a Reappraisal,* IMF Working Paper no. 06/189. Washington, DC: IMF.

Kose, M. Ayhan, Eswar Prasad, Kenneth Rogoff and Shang-Jin Wei 2009. 'Financial Globalization: a Reappraisal', *IMF Staff Papers* 56(1): 8–62.

Krasner, Stephen D. (ed.) 1983. *International Regimes.* Ithaca: Cornell University Press.

    1984. 'Approaches to the State: Alternative Conceptions and Historical Dynamics', *Comparative Politics* 16(2): 223–46.

Kratochwil, Friedrich V. 1989. *Rules, Norms and Decisions: On the Conditions of Practical and Legal Reasoning in International Relations and Domestic Affairs.* Cambridge University Press.

    2006. 'History, Action and Identity: Revisiting the "Second" Great Debate and Assessing its Importance for Social Theory', *European Journal of International Relations* 12(1): 5–29.

Kratochwil, Friedrich V. and John G. Ruggie 1986. 'International Organization: a State of the Art on an Art of the State', *International Organization* 40(4): 753–75.

Krugman, Paul 1998. 'Saving Asia: It's Time to Get Radical', *Fortune,* September 7: 27–32.

Kuczynski, Pedro-Pablo and John Williamson 2003. *After the Washington Consensus: Restarting Growth and Reform in Latin America.* Washington, DC: IIE.

Kuhn, Thomas S. 1970. *The Structure of Scientific Revolutions.* Chicago and London: University of Chicago Press.

Kuiper, Edith and Drucilla K. Barker (eds) 2006. *Feminist Economics and the World Bank: History, Theory and Policy.* London: Routledge.

Laffey, Mark and Jutta Weldes 2005. 'Policing and Global Governance', in Michael Barnett and Raymond Duvall (eds.) *Power in Global Governance.* Cambridge University Press: 59–79.

Lawrence, Shannon 2005. *Retreat from the Safeguard Policies: Recent Trends Undermining Social and Environmental Accountability at the World Bank.* Washington, DC: Environmental Defense.

Leaver, Richard and Leonard Seabrooke 2000. 'Can the IMF be Reformed?', in Walden Bello, Nicola Bullard and Kamal Malhotra (eds.) *Global Finance.* London: Zed Press: 25–35.

Lee, Chang Kil and David Strang 2006. 'The International Diffusion of Public-Sector Downsizing: Network Emulation and Theory-Driven Learning', *International Organization* 60(4): 883–909.

Lee, Kelly 1995. 'Neo-Gramscian Approach to International Organisation: an Expanded Analysis of Current Reforms to UN Development Activities', in

John Macmillan and Andrew Linklater (eds.) *Boundaries in Question: New Directions in International Relations*. London: Pinter: 144–62.

Lee, Norman and Clive George (eds.) 2000. *Environmental Assessment in Developing and Transitional Countries*. Chichester, NY: Wiley and Sons.

Leisering, Lutz 2007. 'Gibt es einen Weltwohlfahrtsstaat?', in Mathias Albert and Rudolf Stichweh (eds.) *Weltstaat und Weltstaatlichkeit: Beobachtungen globaler politischer Strukturbildung*. Wiesbaden: Verlag für Sozialwissenschaften: 187–209.

Leiteritz, Ralf J. 2005. 'Explaining Organizational Outcomes: the International Monetary Fund and Capital Account Liberalization', *Journal of International Relations and Development* 8(1): 1–26.

Lerrick, Adam 2006. 'Has the World Bank Lost Control?', in Nancy Birdsall (ed.) *Rescuing the World Bank: a Center for Global Development Working Report and Selected Essays*. Washington, DC: Center for Global Development.

Linden, Ronald 2002. *Norms and Nannies: the Impact of International Organizations on the Central and East European States*. Lanham, MD: Rowman and Littlefield.

Long, Carolyn M. 2006. 'An Assessment of Efforts to Promote Gender Equality at the World Bank', in Edith Kuiper and Drucilla K. Barker (eds.) *Feminist Economics and the World Bank*. London and New York: Routledge: 40–56.

Lucioni, Luis 2003. 'Orientación del financiamiento de organismos internacionales a provincias', *Serie Estudios y Perspectivas* no. 17 (December). Santiago de Chile: Oficina de la CEPAL en Buenos Aires.

Lucioni, Luis and Ariel Dvoskin 2002. *El financiamiento de la Banca Multilateral a la Argentina*. Buenos Aires: Centro de Estudios para el Cambio Estructural (CECE).

McCully, Patrick 2001. *Silenced Rivers: the Ecology and Politics of Large Dams*, 2nd edn. London and New York: Zed Books.

MacDonald, Erin K. 2001. 'Playing by the Rules: the World Bank's Failure to Adhere to Policy in the Funding of Large Scale Hydropower Projects', *Environmental Law* 31: 1011–49.

MacDonald, Mandy 2003. *Gender Inequality and Mainstreaming in the Policy and Practice of the UK Department for International Development*. London: Womankind.

Machinea, José L. and Juan Sommer 1990. 'El manejo de la deuda externa en condiciones de crisis de balanza de pagos: la moratoria 1988–89', Documento CEDES 59. Buenos Aires: CEDES.

McNamara, Kathleen R. 1999. *The Currency of Ideas: Monetary Politics in the European Union*. Ithaca: Cornell University Press.

Madrid, Raul L. 2005. 'Ideas, Economic Pressures, and Pension Privatization', *Latin American Politics and Society* 47(2): 23–50.

Mallaby, Sebastian 2004. *The World's Banker: a Story of Failed States, Financial Crises, and the Wealth and Poverty of Nations*. New York: Penguin.

2005 'Saving the World Bank', *Foreign Affairs* 84(3): 75–85.

Marcel, Mario 2005. 'Reflexiones acerca del proceso de modernización del Estado en Chile y desafios futuros', paper presented at the X Congreso Internacional del CLAD sobre la Reforma del Estado y de la Administración Publica, Santiago de Chile, October.

March, J. G. and Johan P. Olsen 1975. 'The Uncertainty of the Past: Organizational Learning under Ambiguity', *European Journal of Political Research* 3: 147–71.

Marschinski, R. and Steffen Behrle 2007. *The World Bank: Making the Business Case for the Environment*, Global Governance Working Paper no. 21, October, available at: www.glogov.org/images/doc/wp21.1.pdf, accessed 3 May 2010.

Martin, L. Lisa 2006. 'Distribution, Information, and Delegation to International Organizations: The Case of IMF Conditionality', in Darren G. Hawkins, David A. Lake, Daniel L. Nielson and Michael J. Tierney (eds.) *Delegation and Agency in International Organizations*. New York: Cambridge University Press: 140–64.

Massey, Andrew 1997. 'In Search of the State: Markets, Myths and Paradigms', in Andrew Massey (ed.) *Globalization and Marketization of Government Services: Comparing Contemporary Public Sector Development*. Basingstoke: Macmillan: 1–16.

Mathews, John A. 1998. 'Fashioning a New Korean Model out of the Crisis: the Rebuilding of Institutional Capabilities', *Cambridge Journal of Economics* 22 (6): 747–59.

Mathieson, Donald J., and Liliana Rojas-Suárez 1993. *Liberalization of the Capital Account: Experiences and Issues*, IMF Occasional Paper no. 103. Washington, DC: IMF.

Mearsheimer, John 1994/5. 'The False Promise of International Institutions', *International Security* 19(3): 5–49.

Mehra, Rekha and Geeta Rao Gupta 2006. *Gender Mainstreaming: Making It Happen*, International Center for Research on Women (ICRW), 30th Anniversary, available at: www.google.com/search?q=cache:9f6_uj0JuF8J: siteresources.worldbank.org/INTGENDER/Resources/ MehraGuptaGenderMainstreamingMakingItHappen.pdf+gender+main-nstreaming+making+it+happen&hl=en&ct=clnk&cd=1&gl=us&client=sa-afari, accessed 17 June 2008.

Melo, Marcus A. 2004. 'Institutional Choice and the Diffusion of Policy Paradigms: Brazil and the Second Wave of Pension Reform', *Dados: Revista de Ciências Sociais* 47(1): 169–206.

Meltzer, Allan H. (chair) *et al.* 2000. *Report of the International Financial Institutions Advisory Commission*. Washington, DC: US Government Printing Office.

Merrien, François X. 2001. 'The World Bank's New Social Policies: Pensions', *International Social Science Journal* 53(4): 537–50.

Meyer, John W. and Brian Rowan 1977. 'Institutionalized Organizations: Formal Structure as Myth and Ceremony', *American Journal of Sociology* 83(2): 340–63.

Meyer, J., Boli, J., Thomas, G. and Ramirez, F. 1997. 'World Society and the Nation-State', *The American Journal of Sociology* 103(1): 144–82.

Mikesell, Raymond and Larry Williams 1992. *International Banks and the Environment: From Growth to Sustainability: an Unfinished Agenda*. San Francisco, CA: Sierra Club Books.

Miller-Adams, Michelle 1999. *The World Bank: New Agendas in a Changing World*. London and New York: Routledge.

Mintzberg, Henry 1979. *The Structure of Organizations*. Englewood Cliffs, NJ: Prentice-Hall.

Mishkin, Frederic S. 2009. 'Why We Shouldn't Turn Our Backs on Financial Globalization', *IMF Staff Papers* 56(1): 139–70.

Momani, Bessma 2004. 'American Politicization of the International Monetary Fund', *Review of International Political Economy* 11(5): 880–904.

  2005. 'Recruiting and Diversifying IMF Technocrats', *Global Society* 19(2): 167–87.

Moore, David (ed.) 2007. *The World Bank: Development, Poverty, Hegemony*. Scottsville, South Africa: University of KwaZulu-Natal Press.

Morse, Bradford and Thomas Berger 1992. *The Independent Review of the Sardar Sarovar Projects*. Ottawa: Resource Futures International.

Moschella, Manuela 2008. 'Seeing Like the IMF on Capital Account Liberalization', paper presented at the Annual Conference of the International Studies Association, San Francisco, 26–29 March 2008.

Moser, Caroline and Annalise Moser 2005. 'Gender Mainstreaming since Beijing: a Review of Successes and Limitations in International Institutions', *Gender and Development* 13(2): 11–22.

Mosley, Layna 2000. 'Room to Move: International Financial Markets and National Welfare States', *International Organization* 54(4): 737–73.

  2002. *Global Capital and National Governments*. Cambridge University Press.

Mosley, Paul, Jane Harrigan and John Toye 1991. *Aid and Power: the World Bank and Policy-based Lending*. London: Routledge.

Murillo, M. Victoria 2002. 'Political Bias in Policy Convergence: Privatization Choices in Latin America', *World Politics* 54(4): 462–93.

Murphy, Josette 1995. *Gender Issues in World Bank Lending*. Washington, DC: World Bank, Operations Evaluation Department.

  1997. *Mainstreaming Gender in World Bank Lending: an Update*. Washington, DC: World Bank, Operations Evaluation Department.

Nelson, Joan M. (ed.) 1990. *Economic Crisis and Policy Choice: the Politics of Adjustment in the Third World*. Princeton University Press.

Ness, Gary D. and Steven R. Brechin 1988. 'Bridging the Gap: International Organizations as Organizations', *International Organization* 42(2): 245–73.

Nickson, Andrew 2002. 'Transferencia de políticas y reforma en la gestión del sector publico en América Latina: el caso del New Public Management', *Revista del CLAD Reforma y Democracia* 24: 113–42.

Nielson, Daniel and Mike Tierney 2003. 'Delegation to International Organizations: Agency Theory and World Bank Environmental Reform', *International Organization* 57(2): 241–76.

  2005. 'Theory, Data, and Hypothesis Testing: World Bank Environmental Reform Redux', *International Organization* 59(3): 785–800.

Nielson, Daniel, Mike Tierney and Catherine Weaver 2006. 'Bridging the Rationalist–Constructivist Divide: Re-engineering the Culture of the World Bank', *Journal of International Relations and Development* 9(2): 107–39.

Nooruddin, Irfan and Joel W. Simmons 2006. 'The Politics of Hard Choices: IMF Programs and Government Spending' *International Organization* 60 (4):1001–33.

Nye, Joseph S. 1987. 'Nuclear Learning and US–Soviet Security Regimes', *International Organization* **41**(3): 371–402.

O'Brien, Robert, Anne Marie Goetz, Jan Aart Scholte and Marc Williams 2000. *Contesting Global Governance: Multilateral Economic Institutions and Global Social Movements*. New York: Cambridge University Press.

Obstfeld, Maurice 1998. 'The Global Capital Market: Benefactor or Menace?', *Journal of Economic Perspectives* **12**(4): 9–30.

2009. 'International Finance and Growth in Developing Countries: What Have We Learned?', *IMF Staff Papers* **56**(1): 63–111.

Oliver, Michael J. 2006. 'Civilizing International Monetary Systems', in Brett Bowden and Leonard Seabrooke (eds.) *Global Standards of Market Civilization*. London: Routledge/RIPE Studies in Global Political Economy: 107–18.

Onuf, Nicholas Greenwood 1989. *World of Our Making: Rules and Rule in Social Theory and International Relations*. Columbia, SC: University of South Carolina Press.

Orenstein, Mitchell A. 2005. 'The New Pension Reform as Global Policy', *Global Social Policy* **5**(2): 175–202.

Orszag, Peter R. and Joseph Stiglitz 2001. 'Rethinking Pension Reform: 10 Myths about Social Security Systems', in Robert Holzmann and Joseph Stiglitz (eds.) *New Ideas about Old Age Security: Toward Sustainable Pension Systems in the 21st Century*. Washington, DC: The World Bank: 17–57.

Osborne, David and Ted Gaebler 1992. *Reinventing Government: How the Entrepreneurial Spirit is Transforming the Public Sector*. Reading, MA: Addison-Wesley.

Oszlak, Oscar 1999. 'Quemar las naves: o cómo lograr reformas estatales irreversibles', *Aportes para el Estado y la Administración Gubernamental* **14**(6): 73–99.

Palacios, Robert and Oleksiy Sluchynsky 2006. *Social Pensions Part I: Their Role in the Overall Pension System*, Social Protection Discussion Paper no. 0601. Washington, DC: The World Bank.

Paloni, Alberto and Maurizio Zanardi 2006. 'Introduction and Overview', in Alberto Paloni and Maurizio Zanardi (eds.) *The IMF, World Bank and Policy Reform*. London: Routledge: 1–26.

Park, Susan 2005a. 'How Transnational Environmental Advocacy Networks Socialize International Financial Institutions: a Case Study of the International Finance Corporations', *Global Environmental Politics* **5**(4): 95–119.

2005b. 'Norm Diffusion within International Organisations: a Case Study of the World Bank', *Journal for International Relations and Development* **8**(2): 114–41.

2006. 'Theorizing Norm Diffusion within International Organizations', *International Politics* **43**(3): 342–61.

2007a. 'Becoming Green: Diffusing Sustainable Development Norms throughout the World Bank Group', in Diane Stone and Christopher Wright (eds.) *The World Bank and Governance: a Decade of Reform and Reaction*. New York: Routledge: 168–88.

2007b. 'World Bank Group: Championing Sustainable Development?', *Global Governance* **13**(4): 535–56.

2010. *The World Bank Group and Environmentalists: Changing International Organisation Identities*. London: Manchester University Press.

Pauly, Louis W. 1995. 'Capital Mobility, State Autonomy and Political Legitimacy', *Journal of International Affairs* 48(2): 369–88.

1997. *Who Elected the Bankers? Surveillance and Control in the World Economy*. Ithaca: Cornell University Press.

Peters, B. Guy 1997. 'Policy Transfers between Governments: the Case of Administrative Reforms', *West European Politics* 20(4): 71–88.

Pettifor, Ann 2006. 'The Jubilee 2000 Campaign: a Brief Overview', in Chris Jochnick and Fraser Preston (eds.) *Sovereign Debt at the Crossroads: Challenges and Proposals for Resolving the Third World Debt Crisis*. Oxford University Press: 297–317.

Piercy, Jan 2001. 'Speech to the Opening of the Regional Gender Workshops, sponsored by the World Bank Operational Evaluation Department', July, available at: http://lnweb18.worldbank.org/oed/oeddoclib.nsf/a7a8a 58cc87a6e2885256f1900755ae2/e5e843d9d88b2a4685256c4b00740b6c/ $FILE/Jan_Piercy_foreword_to_gender_workshop.pdf, accessed 17 June 2008.

Pincus, Jonathan R. and Jeffrey A. Winters (eds.) 2002. *Reinventing the World Bank*. Ithaca and London: Cornell University Press.

Polak, Jacques J. 1998. 'The Articles of Agreement of the IMF and the Liberalization of Capital Movements', in Stanley Fischer, Richard N. Cooper, Rudiger Dornbusch *et al.*, *Should the IMF Pursue Capital-Account Convertibility?*, Essays in International Finance, International Finance Section, Department of Economics, Princeton University, no. 207.

Polanyi, Karl 1957. 'The Economy as Instituted Process', in Karl Polanyi, Conrad M. Arensberg and Harry W. Pearson (eds.) *Trade and Market in the Early Empires*. Chicago: Henry Regnery Company: 243–69.

2002 [1944]. *The Great Transformation: the Political and Economic Origins of our Time*. Boston: Beacon Press.

Pollack, Mark A. 1997. 'Delegation, Agency and Agenda Setting in the EC', *International Organization* 51(1): 99–134.

2003. *The Engines of European Integration: Delegation, Agency and Agenda Setting in the EU*. Oxford University Press.

Pollitt, Christopher 2001. 'Public Management Convergence: the Useful Myth?', *Public Administration* 79(4): 933–47.

Prasad, Eswar S. and Raghuram G. Rajan 2008. 'A Pragmatic Approach to Capital Account Liberalization', *Journal of Economic Perspectives* 22(3): 149–72.

Prasad, Eswar S., Kenneth Rogoff, Suang-Jin Wei and M. Ayhan Kose 2003. *Effects of Financial Globalization on Developing Countries: Some Empirical Evidence*, IMF Occasional Paper no. 220. Washington, DC: IMF.

Prats i Catalá, Joan 1998. 'Administración pública y desarrollo en América Latina. Un enfoque neoinstitucionalista', *Reforma y Democracia* 11: 7–49.

Princen, Thomas and Matthias Finger 1994. *Environmental NGOs in World Politics: Linking the Local and the Global*. London: Routledge.

Przeworski, Adam and James R. Vreeland 2000. 'The Effect of IMF Programs on Economic Growth', *Journal of Development Economics* 62(2): 385–421.

Puryear, Jeffrey 1994. *Thinking Politics: Intellectuals and Democracy in Chile, 1973–1988*. Baltimore, MD and London: The Johns Hopkins University Press.

Queisser, Monika 2000. 'Pension Reform and International Organizations: From Conflict to Convergence', *International Social Security Review* 53(2): 31–45.

Quirk, Peter J. and Owen Evans with Staff Team 1995. *Capital Account Convertibility: Review of Experience and Implications for IMF Policies*, Occasional Paper no. 131. Washington, DC: IMF.

Quirk, Peter (lead author) *et al.* 1995. *Issues in International Exchange and Payments Systems*. Washington, DC: IMF.

Rao, Vijayendra and Michael Woolcock 2007. 'The Disciplinary Monopoly in Development Research at the World Bank', *Global Governance* 13(4): 479–84.

Rapkin, David P. and Jonathan R. Strand 2003. 'Is East Asia Under-Represented in the International Monetary Fund?', *International Relations of the Asia Pacific* 3(1): 1–28.

2006. 'Reforming the IMF's Weighted Voting System', *The World Economy* 29 (3): 305–24.

Razavi, Shahra and Carol Miller 1995. *Gender Mainstreaming: a Study of Efforts by the UNDP, the World Bank, and the ILO to Institutionalize Gender Issues*, UNRISD Occasional Paper no. 4. Geneva: UNRISD.

Reinalda, Bob and Bertjan Verbeek 2001. 'Theorising Power Relations between NGOs, Inter-Governmental Organisations and States', in Bas Arts, Math Noortmann and Bob Reinalda (eds.) *Non-State Actors in International Relations*. Aldershot and Burlington: Ashgate: 145–58.

2004. 'The Issue of Decision-Making within International Organizations', in Bob Reinalda and Bertjan Verbeek (eds.) *Decision-Making within International Organizations*. London: Routledge: 9–41.

Repetto, Fabian 2001. *La política de las reformas administrativas en la Argentina'*, report presented to Congreso 2001 del LASA (Latin American Studies Association), Washington, DC.

Reus-Smit, Christian 1997. 'The Constitutional Structure of International Society and the Nature of Fundamental Institutions', *International Organization* 51(4): 555–89.

Rich, Bruce 1994. *Mortgaging the Earth: the World Bank, Environmental Impoverishment and the Crisis of Development*. Boston: Beacon Press.

Riggirozzi, Maria Pia 2007. 'The World Bank as Conveyer and Broker of Knowledge and Funds in Argentina's Governance Reforms', in Diane Stone and Christopher Wright (eds.) *The World Bank and Governance: a Decade of Reform and Reaction*. New York, Routledge: 207–27.

Rinne, Jeffrey 2003. 'The Politics of Administrative Reform in Menem's Argentina: the Illusion of Isolation', in Ben Ross Schneider and Blanca Heredia (eds.) *Reinventing Leviathan: the Politics of Administrative Reform in Developing Countries*. Miami: North-South Center Press, University of Miami.

Risse, Thomas and Kathryn Sikkink 1999. 'The Socialization of International Human Rights Norms into Domestic Practices', in Thomas Risse, Stephen Ropp and Kathryn Sikkink (eds.) *The Power of Human Rights: International Norms and Domestic Change*. Cambridge University Press: 1–38.

Risse, Thomas and Antje Wiener 1999. '"Something Rotten" and the Social Construction of Social Constructivism: a Comment on Comments', *Journal of European Public Policy* 6(5): 775–82.

Risse, T., S. C. Ropp and Kathryn Sikkink 1999. *The Power of Human Rights: International Norms and Domestic Change*. Cambridge University Press.

Rittberger, Volker and Bernhard Zangl 2006. *International Organization Polity, Politics and Policies*. Houndmills: Palgrave Macmillan.

Ritzen, Jozef 2005. *A Chance for the World Bank*. London: Anthem Press.

Rodrik, Dani 1989. 'Promises, Promises: Credible Policy Reform via Signalling', *The Economic Journal* 99(397): 756–72.

2000. 'Growth and Poverty Reduction: What Are the Real Questions?', available at: http://ksghome.harvard.edu/-drodrik/poverty.PDF, accessed 14 January 2008.

Rodrik, Dani and Arvind Subramanian 2009. 'Why Did Financial Globalization Disappoint?', *IMF Staff Papers* 56(1): 112–38.

Rogoff, Kenneth S. 2002. 'Straight Talk – Rethinking Capital Controls: When Should We Keep an Open Mind?', *Finance & Development* 39(4), available at: www.imf.org/external/pubs/ft/fandd/2002/12/rogoff.htm, accessed 3 May 2010.

Ruggie, John G. 1982. 'International Regimes, Transactions, and Change: Embedded Liberalism in the Postwar Economic Order', *International Organization* 36(2): 379–415.

1998. *Constructing the World Polity: Essays on International Institutionalization*. London and New York: Routledge.

2004. 'Reconstituting the Global Public Domain – Issues, Actors, and Practices', *European Journal of International Relations* 10(4): 499–531.

Sachs, Jeffrey 1997. 'The Wrong Medicine for Asia', *New York Times*, 3 November: A19.

Sahlin-Andersson, K. 2001. 'National, International and Transnational Constructions of New Public Management', in Tom Christensen and Per Lægreid (eds.) *New Public Management: the Transformation of Ideas and Practices*. Aldershot: Ashgate.

St Clair, Asunción Lera 2006. 'The World Bank as a Transnational Expertised Institution', *Global Governance* 12(1): 77–95.

Saint-Martin, Denis 2000. *Building the New Managerial State: Consultants and the Politics of Public Sector Reform in Comparative Perspective*. Oxford University Press.

Sandholtz, Wayne 2008. 'Dynamics of International Norm Change: Rules against Wartime Plunder', *European Journal of International Relations* 14(1): 101–31.

Santiso, Javier and Laurence Whitehead 2006. *Ulysses, the Sirens and the Art of Navigation: Political and Technical Rationality in Latin America*, Working Paper no. 256, OECD Development Centre. Paris: OECD.

Schadler, Susan, Maria Carkovic, Adam Bennett and Robert Kahn 1993. *Recent Experiences with Surges in Capital Inflows*, IMF Occasional Paper no. 108. Washington, DC: IMF.

Schick, Allen 2004. 'Fiscal Institutions Versus Political Will', in George F. Kopits (ed.) *Rules-Based Fiscal Policy in Emerging Markets: Background, Analysis and Prospects*. Basingstoke: Palgrave Macmillan: 81–94.

Schimmelfennig, Frank 2005. 'Strategic Calculation and International Socialization: Membership Incentives, Party Constellations, and Sustained Compliance in Central and Eastern Europe', *International Organization* **59** (4): 827–60.

2006. 'Competition and Community: Constitutional Courts, Rhetorical Action, and the Institutionalization of Human Rights in the European Union', *Journal of European Public Policy* 13(8): 1247–64.

Scholte, Jan Aart and Albrecht Schnabel 2002. *Civil Society and Global Finance*. London: Routledge.

Schweller, Randall and David Priess 1997. 'A Tale of Two Realisms: Expanding the Institutions Debate', *The International Studies Review* **41**(1): 1–32.

Scott, John F. 1971. *Internalization of Norms: a Sociological Theory of Moral Commitment*. Upper Saddle River, NJ: Prentice-Hall.

Scott, W. Richard 1992. *Organizations: Rational, Natural, and Open Systems*. Englewood Cliffs, NJ: Prentice-Hall.

Scudder, Thayer 1997. 'Resettlement', in Asit Biswas (ed.) *Water Resources: Environment Planning, Management and Development*. New York: McGraw-Hill: 667–711.

Seabrooke, Leonard 2001. *US Power in International Finance*. Basingstoke: Palgrave Macmillan.

2006a. 'Civilizing Global Capital Markets: Room to Groove?', in Brett Bowden and Leonard Seabrooke (eds.) *Global Standards of Market Civilization*. London: Routledge/RIPE Series in Global Political Economy: 146–60.

2006b. *The Social Sources of Financial Power: Domestic Legitimacy and International Financial Orders*. Ithaca: Cornell University Press.

2007a. 'The Everyday Social Sources of Economic Crises: From "Great Frustrations" to "Great Revelations" in Interwar Britain', *International Studies Quarterly* 51(4): 795–810.

2007b. 'Legitimacy Gaps in the World Economy: Explaining the Sources of the IMF's Legitimacy Crisis', *International Politics* 44(2–3): 250–68.

Seabrooke, Leonard and Ole Jacob Sending 2007. 'Norms as Doing Things: Reason and Strategic Action in World Politics', unpublished memo. Copenhagen Business School.

Sen, Amartya K. 2001. *Development as Freedom*. Oxford University Press.

Serrano, Claudia and Heidi Berner 2002. 'Chile: un caso poco frecuente de indisciplina fiscal (bailout) y endeudamiento encubierto en la educación municipal', Documento de Trabajo R-446, Red de Centros de Investigación, Banco Interamericano de Desarrollo.

Sharman, Jason C. 2006. *Havens in a Storm: the Struggle for Global Tax Regulation*. Ithaca: Cornell University Press.

2007. 'Rationalist and Constructivist Perspectives on Reputation', *Political Studies* 55(1): 20–37.

2008. 'Power, Discourse and Policy Diffusion: Anti-Money Laundering in Developing States', *International Studies Quarterly* 52(3): 635–56.

Shihata, Ibrahim 1991. *The World Bank in a Changing World: Selected Essays*. Dordrecht, Boston and London: Martinus Nijhoff.

Siddell, Scott R. 1988. *The IMF and Third World Instability*. London: Macmillan.

Silva, Patricio 1991. 'Technocrats in Politics in Chile: From the Chicago Boys to the CIEPLAN Monks', *Journal of Latin American Studies* **23**(2): 385–410.

Simmons, Beth A. 2000a. 'International Law and State Behavior: Commitment and Compliance in International Monetary Affairs', *American Political Science Review* **94**(4): 819–35.

2000b. 'The Legalization of International Monetary Affairs', *International Organization* **54**(3): 573–602.

2001. 'The International Politics of Harmonization: the Case of Capital Market Regulation', *International Organization* **55**(3): 589–620.

Simmons, Beth A. and Zachary Elkins 2004. 'The Globalization of Liberalization: Policy Diffusion in the International Political Economy', *American Political Science Review* **98**(1): 171–89.

Simmons, Beth A., Frank Dobbin and Geoffrey Garrett (eds.) 2008. *The Global Diffusion of Markets and Democracy*. Cambridge University Press.

Sinclair, Timothy J. 2005. *The New Masters of Capital: American Bond Rating Agencies and the Politics of Creditworthiness*. Ithaca: Cornell University Press.

Singer, David Andrew 2007. *Regulating Capital: Setting Standards for the International Financial System*. Ithaca: Cornell University Press.

Spink, Peter 1999. 'Possibilities and Political Imperatives: Seventy Years of Administrative Reform in Latin America', in Luiz Carlos Bresser Pereira and Peter Spink (eds.) *Reforming the State: Managerial Public Administration in Latin America*. Boulder, CO: Lynne Rienner.

Stein, Robert and Brian Johnson 1979. *Banking on the Biosphere? Environmental Procedures and Practices of Nine Multilateral Development Agencies*. Massachusetts and Toronto: Lexington Books.

Stewart, Miranda 2003. 'Global Trajectories of Tax Reform: the Discourse of Tax Reform in Developing and Transition Countries', *Harvard International Law Journal* **44**: 139–90.

Stewart, Miranda and Sunita Jogarajan 2004. 'The International Monetary Fund and Tax Reform', *British Tax Review* **2**: 146–75.

Stiglitz, Joseph E. 1998a. 'More Instruments and Broader Goals: Moving toward the Post-Washington Consensus', The 1998 WIDER Annual Lecture in Helsinki, 7 January, available at: www.globalpolicy.org/socecon/bwi-wto/stig.htm, accessed 11 February 2002.

1998b. 'Towards a New Paradigm for Development: Strategies, Policies, and Processes', 1998 Prebisch Lecture at UNCTAD in Geneva, Switzerland, available at: www.worldbank.org/html/extdr/extme/jssp101998.htm, accessed 11 February 2002.

2000. 'Capital Market Liberalization, Economic Growth, and Instability', *World Development* **28**(6): 1075–86.

2002. *Globalization and its Discontents*. New York: W. W. Norton.

2004. 'Capital-Market Liberalization, Globalization, and the IMF', *Oxford Review of Economic Policy* **20**(1): 57–71.

Stiglitz, Joseph E. and Jason Furman 1998. 'Economic Crises: Evidence and Insights from East Asia', *Brookings Papers on Economic Activity* **2**: 1–114.

Stiles, Kendall 1991. *Negotiating Debt: the IMF Lending Process*. Boulder, CO: Westview Press.

Stolze, Frank 1997. 'The Central and East European Currency Phenomenon Reconsidered', *Europe–Asia Studies* **49**(1): 23–41.

Stone, Diane 2003. 'The "Knowledge Bank" and the Global Development Network', *Global Governance* **9**(1): 43–61.

Stone, Diane and Christopher Wright (eds.) (2007). *The World Bank and Governance: a Decade of Reform and Reaction.* New York: Routledge.

Stone, Randall W. 2002. *Lending Credibility: the International Monetary Fund and the Post-Communist Transition.* Princeton University Press.

Strang, David and John Meyer 1993. 'Institutional Conditions for Diffusion', *Theory and Society* **22**: 487–511.

Streeck, Wolfgang and Kathleen Thelen (eds.) 2005. *Beyond Continuity: Institutional Change in Advanced Political Economies.* New York and Oxford: Oxford University Press.

Summers, Lawrence 1998. Remarks before the International Monetary Fund, US Treasury Press Release RR-2286, Washington, DC.

Tanzi, Vito and Howell Zee 2000. 'Tax Policy for Emerging Markets', *National Tax Journal* **53**: 299–328.

Tausch, Arno 2003. *The Three Pillars of Wisdom? A Reader on Globalization, World Bank Pension Models and Welfare Society.* New York: Nova.

Taylor, I. 2004. 'Hegemony, Neoliberal "Good Governance" and the International Monetary Fund: a Gramscian Perspective', in Morten Bøås and Desmond McNeill (eds.) *Global Institutions and Development: Framing the World?* London: Routledge: 124–36.

Teichman, Judith 2007. 'Multilateral Lending Institutions and Transnational Policy Networks in Mexico and Chile', *Global Governance* **13**(4): 557–73.

Teunissen, Jan Joost and Age Akkerman 2004. *HIPC Debt Relief Myths and Reality.* FONDAD: The Hague, available at: www.fondad.org/publications/hipc, accessed 2 May 2010.

Thacker, Strom 1999. 'The High Politics of IMF Lending', *World Politics* **52**(1): 38–75.

Toye, John and Richard Toye 2005. *The World Bank as a Knowledge Agency*, Overarching Concerns Programme Paper no. 11. Geneva: UNRISD.

Truman, Edwin M. 2006. 'An IMF Reform Package', in Edwin M. Truman (ed.) *Reforming the IMF for the 21st Century.* Washington, DC: Institute for International Economics: 537–40.

Tsingou, Eleni 2006. 'Building a Global Anti-Money Laundering Regime: the Many Faces of Legitimacy', paper presented at the International Studies Association Annual Convention, San Diego, 22–25 March.

Tzannatos, Zafiris 2006. 'The World Bank: Development, Adjustment, and Gender Equality', in Edith Kuiper and Drucilla K. Barker (eds.) *Feminist Economics and the World Bank.* London and New York: Routledge: 13–39.

Underdal, Arild 1998. 'Explaining Compliance and Defection: Three Models', *European Journal of International Relations* **4**(1): 5–30.

UNEP 1980. *Declaration of Environmental Policies and Procedures Relating to Economic Development.* New York: United Nations.

United States House of Representatives Financial Services Committee 2007. Oversight Hearing on 'The Role and Effectiveness of the World Bank in

Combating Global Poverty', 14 June, available at: www.house.gov/apps/list/ hearing/financialsvcs_dem/ht052207.shtml, accessed 2 May 2010.

Valenzuela, J. Samuel 1997. *Constitución de 1980 y el inicio de la redemocratización en Chile*, Kellogg Institute Working Paper no. 242. Notre Dame, IN: Kellogg Institute for International Studies, University of Notre Dame.

van Houtven, Leo 2002. *Governance of the IMF*, IMF Pamphlet Series. Washington, DC: IMF.

Vaubel, Roland and Thomas D. Willett (eds.) 1991. *The Political Economy of International Organizations: a Public Choice Approach*. Boulder, CO: Westview Press.

Vetter, David 1997. *Subnational Governments in a Stabilization Program: Lessons from the Argentine Provincial Projects*, Infrastructure Notes, The World Bank Urban no. FM-10. Washington, DC: World Bank.

Vetterlein, Antje 2006. 'Change in International Organizations: Innovation or Adaptation? A Comparison of the World Bank and the International Monetary Fund', in Diane Stone and Christopher Wright (eds.) *The World Bank and Governance: a Decade of Reform and Reaction*. New York: Routledge: 125–44.

2007. 'Economic Growth, Poverty Reduction and the Role of Social Policies: the Evolution of the World Bank's Social Development Approach', *Global Governance* 13(4): 513–33.

Vines, David and Christopher L. Gilbert 2004. *The IMF and its Critics: Reform of Global Financial Architecture*. Cambridge University Press.

Vreeland, James R. 2003. *The IMF and Economic Development*. Cambridge University Press.

Wade, Robert 1996. 'Japan, the World Bank, and the Art of Paradigm Maintenance: the East Asian Miracle in Perspective', *New Left Review* 217: 3–36.

1997. 'Greening the Bank: the Struggle over the Environment 1970–1995', in Devesh Kapur, John Lewis and Richard C. Webb (eds.) *The World Bank: Its First Half Century*. Washington, DC: Brookings Institution: 611–734.

2001. 'Showdown at the World Bank', *New Left Review* 7: 124–37.

Wade, Robert and Frank Veneroso 1998. 'The Asian Crisis: the High Debt Model Versus the Wall Street–Treasury–IMF Complex', *New Left Review* 228: 3–23.

Waissbluth, Mario 2005. 'Quince años de profesionalización en la gerencia pública de Chile', paper presented at X Congreso Internacional del CLAD sobre la Reforma del Estado y de la Administración Publica, Santiago de Chile, October.

Wapenhans, W. A. (chair) *et al.* 1992. *The Wapenhans Report, Portfolio Management Task Force*. Washington, DC: World Bank.

Wapner, Paul 1996. *Environmental Activism and World Civic Politics*. Albany: State University of New York Press.

Weaver, Catherine 2007. 'The World's Bank and the Bank's World', *Global Governance* 13(4): 493–512.

2008. *Hypocrisy Trap: the World Bank and the Poverty of Reform*. Princeton University Press.

Weber, Heloise 2002. 'The Imposition of a Global Development Architecture: the Example of Microcredit', *Review of International Studies* 28(3): 537–55.

Wendt, Alexander E. 1987. 'The Agent–Structure Problem in International Relations Theory', *International Organization* 41(3): 335–70.

Weyland, Kurt 1998. 'The Political Fate of Market Reform in Latin America, Africa, and Eastern Europe', *International Studies Quarterly* 42(4): 645–74.

2002. 'The Diffusion of Innovations: a Theoretical Analysis', paper presented to the 97th Annual Meeting of the American Political Science Association, Boston.

(ed.) 2004. *Learning from Foreign Models in Latin American Policy Reform.* Washington, DC: Woodrow Wilson Center Press.

2005. 'Theories of Policy Diffusion: Lessons from Latin American Pension Reform', *World Politics* 57(2): 262–95.

(ed.) 2006. *Bounded Rationality and Policy Diffusion: Social Sector Reform in Latin America.* Princeton University Press.

Wichterich, Christa 2007. 'The Re-discovery of Gender Inequality: EU–China Trade', *Development* (SID) 50(3): 83–9.

Widmaier, Wesley W. 2007. 'Where You Stand Depends on How You Think: Economic Ideas, the Decline of the Council of Economic Advisors and the Rise of the Federal Reserve', *New Political Economy* 12(1): 43–59.

Widmaier, Wesley W., Mark Blyth and Leonard Seabrooke 2007. 'Exogenous Shocks or Endogenous Constructions? The Meanings of Wars and Crises', *International Studies Quarterly* 51(4): 747–59.

Wiener, Antje 2004. 'Contested Compliance: Interventions on the Normative Structure of World Politics', *European Journal of International Politics* 10(2): 189–234.

2007a. 'Contested Meanings of Norms: a Research Framework', *Comparative European Politics* 5(1): 1–17.

2007b. 'The Dual Quality of Norms and Governance beyond the State: Sociological and Normative Approaches to Interaction', *Critical Review of International Social and Political Philosophy* 10(1): 47–69.

2008. *The Invisible Constitution of Politics: Contested Norms and International Encounters.* Cambridge University Press.

2009. 'Enacting Meaning-in-Use: Qualitative Research on Norms in International Relations', *Review of International Studies* 35(1): 175–93.

Williamson, John (ed.) 1990. *Latin American Adjustment: How Much Has Happened?* Washington, DC: Institute for International Economics.

1999. 'What Should the World Bank Think about the Washington Consensus?', paper prepared as a background to the World Bank's World Development Report 2000, available at: www.iie.com/publications/papers/paper.cfm?ResearchID=351, accessed 2 May 2010.

2000. 'What Should the World Bank Think about the Washington Consensus?', *The World Bank Research Observer* 15(2): 251–64.

2003. 'The Washington Consensus and Beyond', *Economic and Political Weekly* 38(15): 1475–81.

Williamson, John and Molly Mahar 1998. *A Survey of Financial Liberalization*, Essays in International Finance no. 211, Department of Economics, Princeton University.

Williamson, John and Arvind Subramanian 2009. 'The World Crisis: Reforming the International Financial System', essay prepared for publication in *Economic and Political Weekly* (Mumbai, India), 5 March 2009, available at: www.piie.com/publications/papers/subramanian-williamson0309.pdf, accessed 2 May 2010.

Wolfensohn, James D. 1996. 'People and Development', Annual Meetings Address. Washington, DC: World Bank.

Woods, Ngaire 2001. 'Making the IMF and the World Bank More Accountable', *International Affairs* 77: 83–100.

2004. 'Groupthink: the IMF, the World Bank and Decision-Making Regarding the 1994 Mexican Crisis', in Bob Reinalda and Bertjan Verbeek (eds.) *Decision-Making within International Organizations*. London: Routledge: 109–22.

2005. 'The Shifting Politics of Foreign Aid', *International Affairs* 81(2): 393–409.

2006. *The Globalizers: the IMF, the World Bank, and their Borrowers*. Ithaca and London: Cornell University Press.

World Bank 1985. *The Experience of the World Bank with Government-Sponsored Land Settlement*, Report no. 5625, Operations Evaluation Department. Washington, DC: World Bank.

1989. *World Development Report 1989: Financial Systems and Development*. Washington, DC: World Bank.

1990. *Argentina: Provincial Government Finances*. Washington, DC: World Bank.

1991a. *Environmental Assessment Sourcebook*, Vols. I and II. Washington, DC: World Bank.

1991b. *The Forest Sector: a World Bank Policy Paper*, Operations Evaluation Department. Washington, DC: World Bank.

1994a. *Averting the Old Age Crisis: Policies to Protect the Old and Promote Growth*. Washington, DC: World Bank.

1994b. *Enhancing Women's Participation in Economic Development*. Washington, DC: World Bank.

1994c. *Resettlement and Development: the Bankwide Review of Projects Involving Resettlement 1986–93*. Washington, DC: World Bank.

1995a. *Advancing Gender Equality: From Concept to Action*. Washington, DC: World Bank.

1995b. *Bureaucrats in Business: the Economics and Politics of Government Ownership*, World Bank Research Report. Oxford University Press.

1995c. *Enhancing the Participation of Women in Development*. Washington, DC: World Bank.

1995d. *Memorandum of the President of the International Bank for Reconstruction and Development to the Executive Directors on a Country Assistance Strategy of the World Bank Group for the Republic of Chile*, Report no. 14370-CH. Washington, DC: World Bank.

1995e. *Toward Gender Equality: the Role of Public Policy*, Vols. I and II. Washington, DC: World Bank.

1996. *Argentina Country Assistance Review*, Operations Evaluation Department, Report no. 15844. Washington, DC: World Bank.

1997. *World Development Report 1997: the State in a Changing World.* Washington, DC: World Bank.

1998. *Project Appraisal Document on a Proposed Loan in the Amount of USD 10 Million to the Republic of Chile for a Second Municipal Development Project,* Report no. 18563–CH. Washington, DC: World Bank.

2000a. *Argentina: Country Assistance Evaluation,* Report no. 20719, Operations Evaluation Department. Washington, DC: World Bank.

2000b. *Reforming Public Institutions and Strengthening Governance: A World Bank Strategy,* Public Sector Group, Poverty Reduction and Economic Management (PREM) Network. Washington, DC: World Bank.

2000c. 'Statistics on the World Bank's Dam Portfolio', available at: www.worldbank.org/html/extdr/pb/dams/factsheet.htm, accessed 25 February 2009.

2001a. *New Ideas about Old Age Security: Toward Sustainable Pension Systems in the 21st Century.* Washington, DC: World Bank.

2001b. *World Development Report 2000/1: Attacking Poverty.* New York: Oxford University Press.

2002a. *Chile: Country Assistance Evaluation,* Report no. 23627, Operations Evaluation Department. Washington, DC: World Bank.

2002b. *Memorandum of the President of the International Bank for Reconstruction and Development to the Executive Directors on a Country Assistance Strategy of the World Bank Group for the Republic of Chile,* Report no. 23329-CH. Washington, DC: World Bank.

2002c. 'Safeguard Policies: Framework for Improving Development Effectiveness, A Discussion Note', ESSD and OPCS (7 October). Washington, DC: World Bank.

2003a. *Forest Strategy Booklet 2003,* available at: www.worldbank.org/, accessed November 2006.

2003b. *Implementing the Bank's Gender Mainstreaming Strategy: Annual Monitoring Report for FY03.* Washington, DC: World Bank.

2003c. 'Infrastructure Action Plan', Report to the Executive Directors Informal Board Meeting, 8 July 2003, available at: www.worldbank.org/, accessed November 2006.

2003d. *Pension Reform – Issues and Prospect for Non-Financial Defined Contribution (NDC) Schemes.* Washington, DC: World Bank.

2005a. *2004 Annual Report on Operations Evaluation.* Washington, DC: World Bank.

2005b. 'Enhancing World Bank Support to Middle Income Countries: Management Actions Plan Progress Memorandum', 1 February 2005. Washington, DC: World Bank.

2005c. *Environment Matters 2005.* Washington, DC: World Bank, available at: www.worldbank.org/, accessed November 2006.

2005d. *Expanding the Use of Country Systems in Bank Supported Operations: Issues and Proposals,* Operations Policy and Country Services Report (4 March). Washington, DC: World Bank.

2005e. *Implementing the Bank's Gender Mainstreaming Strategy: Third Annual Monitoring Report, FY04 and FY05, Annexes.* Washington, DC: World Bank.

2005f. *Improving Women's Lives: World Bank Actions since Beijing.* Washington, DC: World Bank.

2005g. *Keeping the Promise of Social Security in Latin America.* Washington, DC: World Bank.

2005h. *Old Age Income Support in the 21st Century – An International Perspective on Pension Systems and Reform.* Washington, DC: World Bank.

2005i. *Quality of Supervision in FY03–04 (QSA6).* Washington, DC: World Bank.

2006a. *Annual Report.* Washington, DC: World Bank.

2006b. *Gender Equality as Smart Economics: a World Bank Group Gender Action Plan* (FY 2007–2010). Washington, DC: World Bank.

2006c. *Implementing the Bank's Gender Mainstreaming Strategy: Annual Monitoring Report for FY2004–2005.* Washington, DC: World Bank.

2006d. *Quality at Entry in FY04–05.* Washington, DC: World Bank.

2007. *Development Results in Middle Income Countries: an Evaluation of the World Bank's Support,* Independent Evaluation Group. Washington, DC: World Bank.

2008a. 'Evaluation of the Initial Phase of the Pilot Program for Use of Country Systems for Environmental and Social Safeguards: Lessons Learned and Management Proposal for an Incremental Scale Up of the Program', Memorandum and Recommendation of the President, available at: www.wds.worldbank.org/external/default/WDSContentServer/WDSP/IB/2008/01/09/000310607_20080109101841/Rendered/PDF/421050R200810005.pdf, accessed 2 May 2010.

2008b. 'Operational Manual – Safeguard Policies', Operations, Policy and Country Services, available at: www.wbln0018.worldbank.org/Institutional/Manuals/OpManual.nsf/, accessed February 19 2008.

2008c. 'Safeguard Policies', available at: www.web.worldbank.org/WBSITE/EXTERNAL/TOPICS/ENVIRONMENT/, accessed 10 February 2008.

World Bank and IADB 2005. *Republica de Chile. Evaluación de la responsabilidad financiera publica,* Informe No 32630-CL. Washington, DC: World Bank.

1994. *The Gender Dimension of the Bank's Assistance,* Operational Policy no. 4.20. Washington, DC: World Bank.

World Bank Operations Evaluation Department 2000. *Evaluating Gender and Development at the World Bank,* OED Precis Report, no. 200. Available at: http://Inweb18.worldbank.org/oed/oeddoclib.nsf/0/9d3efc4367300a7f852569df0071b6f7/$FILE/200precis.pdf, accessed 12 May 2010.

2001. *Integrating Gender into World Bank Assistance.* Washington, DC: World Bank.

2005. *Evaluating a Decade of World Bank Gender Policy, 1990–1999.* Washington, DC: World Bank.

Wotipka, Christine and Francisco Ramirez 2008. 'World Society and Human Rights: an Event History Analysis of the Convention on the Elimination of All Forms of Discrimination against Women', in Beth A. Simmons, Frank Dobbin and Geoffrey Garrett (eds.) *The Global Diffusion of Markets and Democracy.* Cambridge University Press: 303–43.

Wright, Christopher 2007. 'From "Safeguards" to "Sustainability": the Evolution of Environmental Discourse within the International Finance Corporation', in Diane Stone and Christopher Wright (eds.) *World Bank and Governance: a Decade of Reform and Reaction*. London and New York: Routledge: 67–87.

Yee, Albert S. 1996. 'The Causal Effect of Ideas on Policies', *International Organization* 50(1): 69–108.

Yoingco, Angel Q. and Lourdes B. Recente 2003. 'Is There Double Taxation in the Philippine Tax System?', *Asia-Pacific Tax Bulletin*, November/December: 398–402.

Index

CPSIA information can be obtained at www.ICGtesting.com
Printed in the USA
LVOW120301031012

301223LV00002B/85/P